CROSSROADS

Cynthia J. Arnson

CROSSROADS

CONGRESS, THE PRESIDENT, AND CENTRAL AMERICA 1976–1993

With a Foreword by John Felton

Second Edition

The Pennsylvania State University Press
University Park, Pennsylvania

Library of Congress Cataloging-in-Publication Data

Arnson, Cynthia J.
    Crossroads : Congress, the Reagan administration, and Central
America, 1976–1993 / Cynthia J. Arnson. — [2nd ed.]
        p.   cm.
    First ed. published: New York : Pantheon Books, © 1989.
    Includes bibliographical references and index.
    ISBN 0-271-01099-1 (cloth : alk. paper). —
    ISBN 0-271-01098-3 (pbk. : alk. paper)
    1. Central America—Foreign relations—United States. 2. United
States—Foreign relations—Central America. 3. United States—
Foreign relations—1981–1989. 4. United States—Foreign
relations—1989–1993. 5. Iran-Contra Affair, 1985–1990. I. Title.
F1436.8.U6A76   1993
327.730728—dc20   93-24810
                                                              CIP

Published by The Pennsylvania State University Press,
Barbara Building, Suite C, University Park, PA 16802-1003

It is the policy of The Pennsylvania State University Press to use acid-free paper for the
first printing of all clothbound books. Publications on uncoated stock satisfy the minimum requirements of American National Standard for Information Sciences—Permanence of Paper for Printed Library Materials, ANSI Z39.48–1984.

Contents

For Aileen and Arthur Arnson,
Gerry, and Zack

Foreword

For most of U.S. history, Central America was hardly a central concern of the leaders in Washington. It is true that the United States intervened militarily in the region whenever policymakers believed U.S. economic or strategic interests were threatened. Panama and Nicaragua drew particular attention and action from Washington beginning in the early 1900s, the former because of the U.S.-built canal, and the latter because it had a habit of producing political figures whom U.S. officials found distressingly independent.

But as a rule, Washington's diplomats and politicians kept Central America where they wanted it: on the back burner. Europe, the Middle East, the Soviet Union, and even Southeast Asia were judged to be of much greater significance to the United States, as long as the tiny "republics" of Central America remained stable and firmly under Washington's influence. Henry M. Kissinger, one of the most important U.S. foreign policy thinkers of the twentieth century, wrote two lengthy books covering the Nixon years without once mentioning any of the countries in Central America.

A combination of events in the late 1970s suddenly awoke U.S. interest in Central America: the political battles over the Panama Canal treaties from 1976 to 1978, the Sandinista revolution in Nicaragua in July 1979, and the overthrow of El Salvador's military dictatorship in October 1979. While important in and of themselves, those events took on special significance because they occurred in the context of divisions in the United States about America's role in the world.

The defeat in Vietnam had revived old isolationist tendencies among the American people, making them and many of their elected representatives wary of seeking military solutions to political and social problems overseas, especially in Third World countries where threats to U.S. interests were not immediately apparent. This attitude was most prominent among liberal Democrats, whose leaders had been responsible in the 1960s for the failed anticommunist crusade in Vietnam. Liberals in Congress gradually won enactment of a series of laws curtailing the president's ability to make unilateral foreign policy commitments, such as in the war in Vietnam. After Vietnam, those laws became the primary tools that congressional Democrats used to curb the actions of conservative Republican presidents.

American conservatives, fearing that the United States was about to surrender after one skirmish in the war against the communist advance, took up the liberals' fallen flag of U.S. internationalism. They argued that the United States lost in Vietnam only because it lost its will, and they demanded a more aggressive confrontation with the Soviet Union and its allies.

The emergence at the end of the 1970s of Cuban-aided leftist revolutionary movements in Central America, particularly in Nicaragua and El Salvador, provided an almost inevitable close-to-home forum for an extension of the American political battles over Vietnam. Ronald Reagan and other conservatives first raised the Panama Canal treaties as an issue, charging that the Ford and Carter administrations were willing to forsake U.S. strategic interests in hopes of pacifying unruly Latin neighbors. Panamanian logistical support for the Sandinista rebellion in Nicaragua gave the conservatives an opportunity to denounce what they saw as a broad threat to the U.S. interests in the region. With the Sandinista victory in 1979 and the rapid growth in 1980 of the leftist guerrilla movement in El Salvador, the United States suddenly faced direct challenges in two Central American countries.

Washington's debate about Nicaragua began immediately after the Sandinistas took power and continued with only minor variations for a decade afterward. The Carter administration first tried to co-opt the revolutionaries in Managua, offering them diplomatic recognition and economic aid. With conservatives opposing any U.S. backing for what they viewed as a communist government, Congress delayed approving the aid until well into 1980. By that time the Sandinistas were learning not to count on the United States and were becoming more and more dependent on Cuban and Soviet support. Just as Panama had supplied weapons to the Sandinista guerrilla movement, the Sandinistas, once in power, began shipping Soviet-bloc weapons to the leftist guerrillas in neighboring El Salvador—completing a revolutionary link that was to provide the Reagan administration's justification for direct intervention in Nicaragua.

Reagan took office in January 1981 determined to halt what he saw as the spread of communism around the world. The first test came in El Salvador, where the guerrillas had failed in their so-called final offensive against the government in the closing days of the Carter administration. Reagan acted quickly by committing the United States to bolstering the civilian-military junta there at whatever cost. As his confidence in U.S. power grew, Reagan began pursuing a greater ambition: not only halting but reversing Soviet advances in Afghanistan, Nicaragua, southern Africa, and elsewhere. Supporters called that policy the Reagan Doctrine, and the president's support for the contra rebels in Nicaragua quickly became the most controversial element of it.

Reagan's aggressive posture encountered the still-dominant reluctance in Congress to commit American resources—especially manpower—to Third World conflicts. That ideological clash was magnified by partisan politics and institutional considerations stemming from Vietnam.

A Republican president who had won a landslide election largely by portraying his Democratic opponent as weak, Reagan clearly sought to exploit Central America politically by applying the image of Jimmy Carter to the Democrats in Congress. By opposing his policies in the region, Reagan said, the Democrats were allowing the Soviet Union to gain a beachhead on the American mainland; the inevitable result would be expanded war and a tidal wave of refugees. Moreover, he charged that Congress was overstepping the bounds set by the Constitution for its role in foreign policy.

The Democrats, for their part, insisted that Reagan was ignoring the lessons of previous failed U.S. interventions in Latin America. To bolster their position politically, the Democrats played on public anxieties about another Vietnam and warned that Reagan's secret agenda was to send U.S. soldiers into the jungles of Central America. They also staunchly defended the constitutional right of Congress to influence foreign policy through its control of the purse strings.

For historical and political reasons, then, Central America policy became the most contentious foreign policy question of the Reagan years. El Salvador was the dominant issue at first, as Reagan and Congress battled over the direction of U.S. support for the war against the guerrillas. That dispute was settled, for all practical purposes, by the election in 1984 of Salvadoran President José Napoleón Duarte, who was widely admired on Capitol Hill as a genuine Latin democrat. Reagan's policy of backing the Nicaraguan contras gradually took the place of El Salvador on the agenda in Washington, developing into the single most divisive and bitterly fought foreign policy issue since the war in Vietnam. Reagan devoted more speeches to Nicaragua than to any other single topic. Congress debated contra aid more than a dozen times and took scores of votes on it between 1981 and 1988—so often that even the most avid partisans grew weary of the issue and hoped that somehow it would go away.

Changing historical and political factors led George Bush, when he took office as president, to alter many of the specific tactics—and in some cases even the overall strategy—of the U.S. approach to Central America. Bush had the good fortune to take office just as the Cold War was ending. The fall of communist regimes in Eastern Europe and the opening of the Berlin Wall in 1989 led the way to the subsequent collapse of the Soviet Union, giving politicians and policymakers in Washington an opportunity to rethink the fundamentals of America's role in the world. Central Americans of all political stripes also understood that the end of the Cold War would affect their lives. Leftist guerrillas and intellectuals were confused and disheartened by the events in the East, and many began looking for new options of compromise with their foes in the Latin oligarchies. In Managua, some Sandinista leaders realized that they could no longer depend on Moscow's aid pipeline. Military leaders and rightist politicians in countries such as El Salvador also began to see the fleeting nature of Washington's interest in, and support for, their battles with the left.

In Washington, Bush demonstrated an approach to political problems far different from Reagan's approach. Whereas Reagan was guided by a rigid set of ideological principles and bolstered by supreme confidence in the rightness of his beliefs, Bush's root philosophy was pragmatism. Bush and his chief aides, particularly Secretary of State James A. Baker III, were willing, even eager, to make whatever compromises were necessary to achieve a measure of political success on foreign as well as domestic issues.

These factors led Bush and Baker to make Nicaragua one of their highest priorities after taking office in 1989. But their goal was not Reagan's aim of ousting the Sandinistas from Managua; they sought to remove Nicaragua from the political agenda in Washington. Baker negotiated an agreement with Democrats in Congress that led to the ending of all U.S. military support for the contras and that set the stage for Nicaraguan elections in 1990. Officially, those elections achieved the end Reagan had long sought—the removal of the Sandinistas from office. But the unwieldy coalition led by President Violetta Chamorro soon fell apart, the Nicaraguan economy continued its freefall, and Washington rapidly lost interest in Nicaragua.

Similarly, events in El Salvador led to a reshaping of U.S. policy. Just two months after George Bush took office, the far-right ARENA party won elections in El Salvador. This result was not the disaster it once might have been, because a relative moderate, Alfredo Cristiani, now led the party and the country, and he seemed determined to gain at least some civilian control over the military. But one more upheaval followed a half-year later, when the guerrillas launched an intense military campaign against the capital. That offensive, though a failure militarily, provoked the Army's high command to strike against the people they saw as the intellectual patrons of the guerrillas: the Jesuit priests who ran the

Catholic university in a quiet San Salvador neighborhood. Early one November morning, a squad from the U.S.-trained Atlacatl Battalion entered the campus and murdered six priests (including the rector, Ignacio Ellacuría), their house-keeper, and her daughter. Although it took more than three years for a U.N.-sponsored Truth Commission to establish definitive proof that the high command ordered these murders, the atrocity immediately undermined flagging support in Washington for the Salvadoran military. Slowly, reluctantly, and under pressure from Congress, the Bush administration began to support U.N.-sponsored negotiations to end El Salvador's war. Those negotiations finally bore fruit with a peace agreement on the last day of 1991. A cease-fire went into effect in February 1992, and a year later the government slowly was making reforms enabling the left to become an integral part of Salvadoran society.

With clarity and insight, this book tells the story of how Central America took center stage in Washington during the Reagan years, only to fade from international attention during the Bush presidency. The book lays the groundwork of the post-Vietnam years of U.S. foreign policymaking and then describes in vivid detail the seemingly endless struggles between Reagan and his critics in Congress over Central American policy during the 1980s. This second edition also incorporates newly available information from the Iran-contra hearings and trials, documenting how the Reagan administration tried to use covert, illegal means to carry out a policy for which it had little public political support. Also, this edition was written after the collapse of the Soviet Union, lending it a new historical perspective.

During the late 1980s, when Central America was a fashionable topic in the United States, journalists, scholars, and direct participants wrote thousands of articles and numerous books on U.S. policy with respect to that region. The bulk of that material concentrated on the relationship between the Reagan administration and Nicaragua and El Salvador. Cynthia J. Arnson's book remains the only full-length examination of the confrontation over Central America between the presidency and Congress. While primarily a narrative of dramatic events, it provides a coherent analysis that puts the actions of Reagan, Bush, and their critics in historical and political context. The book also is unique in its clear explanation of how the opposing factions in Washington approached the issues of El Salvador and Nicaragua and sought to use those issues for their own benefit.

Cynthia Arnson was a direct participant in Washington's political battles during the Reagan years, serving first as a consultant for one of the human rights advocacy groups that raised concerns about El Salvador and later as a foreign policy aide to Representative George Miller (D-Calif.), a leading critic of

Reagan's policies in Central America. She offers strong criticisms of nearly all participants and demonstrates that politicians, on both sides of Washington's Central America wars, too often put partisan and institutional considerations ahead of sound policy and the best interests of the United States.

As her book concludes, Arnson notes that Washington has once again placed Central America on the foreign policy back burner. Obsessed by domestic concerns and the raging war in the former Yugoslavia, the Clinton administration has made minor shifts from Republican policy toward Central America but has demonstrated no intense interest in the region. Arnson raises the question of whether another cycle of war and tragedy in Central America is possible. During the 1980s, she notes, Washington poured billions of dollars into the region but made little progress in addressing the economic disparities that led to conflicts there in the first place. In the early 1990s, Americans north of the Rio Grande once again seem unconcerned about the problems of their neighbors to the south, and so there is little chance that reconstructing the war-ravaged countries of Central America will gain a high priority on Washington's political agenda.

John Felton
Senior Writer
Congressional Quarterly
1978–1990

Acknowledgments

The writing and rewriting of *Crossroads* has been, on and off, a fixture of my life for almost seven years. During that time, I have been extraordinarily blessed with the encouragement and advice of family, friends, and colleagues, without whom this book would not have been possible. In preparing the first edition, I owe a debt of gratitude:

to Congressman George Miller, for innumerable lessons about the ways of Washington, whose integrity, tenacity, and sense of humor are an ongoing source of inspiration;

to John Lawrence, Sylvia Arthur, Edie Wilkie, and Caleb Rossiter, who taught me through their example of hard work and dedication;

to Susan Benda and Holly Burkhalter, for unflagging friendship over the many months of writing and for keen insights into a process we shared;

to Jim Lobe, Michael Posner, Aryeh Neier, Joanne Omang, Alfonso Chardy, Ambassador Viron Vaky, Tony Lake, John Felton, Larry Garber, Gary Bland, Holly Burkhalter, and Susan Benda, who read all or parts of the manuscript, providing insights I greatly value; they bear no responsibility for any remaining errors of fact or judgment;

to Don Fisher, Gary Bombardier, and Janet Breslin, for allowing me to plow through their libraries of documents and hearings;

to Raymond Bonner, for sharing his vast collection of hearings on El Salvador and for introducing me to Gloria Loomis;

to Gloria Loomis, for her enthusiasm and for agreeing that the book was worth publishing;

to my teachers, Professors Riordan Roett, Robert Tucker, Frederick Holborn, and Bruce Bagley, for sharing their knowledge and experience during the years in which this project was a dissertation;

to the American Association of University Women, for financial support of the initial research;

to Gary Stern, Janet DiVincenzo, Peter Kornbluh, and Malcolm Byrne, for ably guiding my way through stacks of government documents;

to the Overseas Development Council, and particularly to Richard Feinberg, Cynthia Carlisle, and Bill Hellert, for the support and stimulation of interested colleagues and for generously providing me with space to work during the book revision;

to Susan Rabiner and Akiko Takano of Pantheon, for outstanding editorial assistance which improved and guided the manuscript to completion;

to Wendy Lustbader Grosskopf, author and friend, for reminding me that writing a book was like cutting the grass with a pair of scissors;

to my husband, Gerry Serotta, who kept me plied with animal crackers and sustained me through this process with unflagging friendship, encouragement, and love;

and finally to Zack, born with this book, for wonder, amusement, and joyous diversion.

Many have also recently provided invaluable support, without which I could not have attempted the second edition. My thanks go especially:

to Sandy Thatcher and Peggy Hoover of Penn State Press, for their confidence in the book and interest in seeing it take on a longer life;

to Carlos Sánchez and Taylor Reinhart, for providing much-needed and outstanding research assistance, and to Enrique Bossio and Brenda Baer, for providing assistance with the index;

to Kate Doyle and Malcolm Byrne of the National Security Archive, and to Gary Stern of the ACLU, for generously sharing collections of new documents and hearings;

to my colleagues at Americas Watch, for their passionate defense of the victims of Central America's wars and for indulging my desire to work on this project by granting extra leave time;

to Gary Bland, Allyson Collins, Larry Garber, David Holiday, Jim Morrell, and Bonnie Tenneriello, for lending their time and expertise to commenting on the manuscript;

to Teresa Whitfield, for sharing her brilliant work and insights on El Salvador;

to dear friends Madalyn Marcus, Lisa Newell, and Esther Siegel, for perspective and understanding;

to Jacob Marcus and Adina Siegel Tabor, for providing hours of precious work time;

to my husband, Gerry Serotta, for once again enveloping this project in love and encouragement;

and to Zack, who has accompanied me and developed a love for the computer during the writing, my infinite gratitude for once in a while going to bed early.

Chapter One

Central America and the Post-Vietnam Congress

On May 6, 1987, at 10:00 A.M., Senator Daniel Inouye of Hawaii pounded his gavel, calling to order the joint House-Senate committee to investigate the Iran-contra affair. It had been nearly six months since Attorney General Edwin Meese III had appeared before national television cameras to make a startling revelation: proceeds from the government sale of arms to Iran had been diverted to contra rebels fighting the government of Nicaragua.

The Reagan administration had traded arms to secure the release of U.S. hostages held in Iran, despite public pledges not to negotiate with terrorists. The administration then used the profits to purchase weapons for the contras, in violation of a congressional prohibition on such aid. "The story is both sad and sordid," Inouye intoned. "People of great character and ability holding positions of trust and authority . . . were drawn into a web of deception and despair."[1]

Thus began a four-month public investigation into what became the greatest catastrophe of the Reagan presidency. The American people felt betrayed by the selling of arms to Iran; only seven years before, extremists had seized and held hostage the staff of the U.S. Embassy in Teheran. And Reagan himself, elected in part to punish President Carter for his inability to resolve the hostage crisis, had pledged publicly never to deal with terrorists.

Policymakers in Washington, meanwhile, equally deplored the diversion of funds from the Iranian sales to rebels fighting the Nicaraguan government, after Congress had explicitly prohibited such aid. The Iran-contra committees convened, as Inouye put it, to "examine what happens when the trust which is the lubricant of our system is breached by high officials of our government" and "to find the facts lest we repeat the mistakes."[2]

For those who had witnessed the Watergate hearings of more than a decade before, the convening of the Iran-contra investigation elicited a sense of déjà vu.[3] Not only were the hearings held in the same Caucus Room of the Senate Russell Office Building. Many issues raised in the Watergate inquiry echoed in the spring of 1987: official involvement in illegal acts and cover-ups, the deception of Congress about the nature of administration activities, laws broken and circumvented, policies pursued without any reasonable hope of success. If Watergate had served as one of the launching points for a more aggressive congressional role in policymaking, the Iran-contra hearings now brought that effort full circle. The very fact of the hearings was testimony that a decade of efforts to curb executive branch powers had, in part, failed.

Despite the easy parallels to Watergate, the Iran-contra hearings differed in a fundamental way, involving the role of Congress itself. While Congress had been disengaged from the series of misdeeds that became the Watergate scandal, it had been deeply involved in the formulation of policy toward Central America. By providing funds for the administration to implement its policies, and by adopting or not adopting restrictions on the administration's approach, Congress was a participant in the conception, if not the actual implementation, of policy in Central America. Indeed, it would be impossible to understand U.S. policy in Central America without examining the interaction of Congress and the executive, the way congressional pressures altered executive branch policy, and the limitations of Congress's actual power to effect policy change. Policy outcomes were a product of the struggle between the two branches; those conflicts, in turn, took place within a historical and political context that defined the issues at stake as well as the institutional framework for addressing them.

The most important context that shaped policy debate over Central America was that of Vietnam. In the broadest sense, the struggle over Central America policy stemmed from the lack of a foreign policy consensus in the United States over the purposes of American power in the post-Vietnam world. The failure of the U.S. military effort in Indochina prompted a reexamination of the Cold War policy of containment of the Soviet Union, a policy that had provided for several decades of congressional-executive harmony.

Prior to Vietnam the United States, with congressional support, sent troops or unleashed the Central Intelligence Agency to counter radical social transformation in areas of the developing world. However, after Vietnam, leading up to and including the years of debate over Central America, no alternative principles surfaced to provide coherence and operative guidance to the makers of U.S. foreign policy.

In addition to calling into question the premises of U.S. foreign policy, Vietnam and Watergate served as catalysts for changes in the institutional relationships by which policy was made. The war ended several decades of congressional-executive cooperation over foreign policy and provided the backdrop for a reactivation of Congress's own foreign policy powers. In particular, Congress sought to redress the ways in which its own deference to the president had contributed to initial U.S. involvement in Vietnam and subsequent escalations of the war. Throughout the 1970s Congress reformed its own institutional structures and passed new laws to give the legislature greater oversight of and participation in foreign affairs. The Central American debate took place after, and largely as a product of, these changes. Congress not only possessed the power to participate in foreign policy, but, unlike in the decades after World War II, chose to exercise its capabilities.[4]

Central America became an area of interest to U.S. policymakers when political instability threatened social revolution. Poverty, military rule, and repression had characterized El Salvador, Nicaragua, Guatemala, and, to a lesser extent, Honduras, for many decades. These conditions attracted the attention of a handful of liberal reformers in the United States in the 1960s and 1970s, but it was not until revolutionary movements gained strength that the region as a whole moved to the forefront of U.S. policy concerns. The process began with the events leading up to the 1979 overthrow of Nicaraguan dictator Anastasio Somoza Debayle by guerrillas of the Sandinista National Liberation Front. It was the first armed overthrow of a government in Latin America since the 1959 Cuban revolution and signaled the end of a family dynasty that U.S. Marines had helped install in 1933.

The Carter administration attempted diplomatically throughout 1978 and 1979 to prevent Somoza's armed overthrow; failing that, they strove to befriend the new Sandinista regime. But the relationship soured as the Nicaraguan revolutionary coalition—a hybrid of Marxists, Christians, social reformers, and capitalists—fell apart. At issue were the pace and depth of socioeconomic transformation in Nicaragua, and changes in its foreign policy that drew the country closer to Cuba, the Soviet Union, and the Eastern bloc.

Meanwhile, conflict accelerated in nearby El Salvador. Young military officers feared a repetition of events in neighboring Nicaragua; only three months after Somoza's downfall in July 1979, they ousted the country's military leader and installed a coalition government with civilian participation. But the move came too late to halt rapid political polarization. Guerrillas of the left and mass-based "popular organizations" stepped up their demands for reform or replacement of the new government. Conservative military officers jockeyed to regain control of the situation and unleashed a wave of repression. By the time President Carter left office in January 1981, some 9,000 to 10,000 civilians had been killed, El Salvador's civilian-military junta had been reconstituted three times, and guerrillas, increasingly active since the late 1970s, had launched what they called their "final offensive" against the government.

The Carter administration attempted to channel the currents of change in a democratic direction. But Carter feared, as did President Reagan, that revolution provided new opportunities for enemies of the United States to extend their influence in an area of historical U.S. dominance. The Reagan administration differed from its predecessor by emphasizing the degree to which conflicts themselves were the product of Soviet and Cuban interference. It sought not only to prevent a left-wing takeover in El Salvador, but also to release Nicaragua from the hold of Sandinista revolutionaries who, in Reagan's view, were consolidating a communist beachhead on the mainland of North America.

In discussing Central America over the course of two administrations, policymakers pretended to agree over core values and desired outcomes: restoring stability, preserving democracy, excluding the radical left from power, and limiting Soviet inroads into the hemisphere. But there was profound disagreement over the particular policies to pursue and the consequences of failing to achieve U.S. goals. Deep divisions between political parties, between Congress and the executive, within Congress, and even within the executive branch itself characterized the Central America policy struggle, pitting against each other alternate conceptions of what was at stake for the United States and how best to protect U.S. interests.

The most persistent of these struggles was between Congress and the Reagan administration over the means and ends of Reagan's regional policy. President Reagan in the early days of his administration sought to make Central America a test case of U.S. resolve to draw the line against communism in the Western Hemisphere, attempting not only to assert U.S. military power but also to reaffirm the lead in a global struggle with the Soviet Union, seen as the "focus of evil" in the modern world.[5] The administration cast the conflict in East-West terms, deepened U.S. military involvement in the Salvadoran war, and helped organize and fund an army of *contrarevolucionarios,* or "contras," bent on toppling the Sandinista regime.

By adopting measures that appeared to militarize the Central American conflict, the administration triggered Vietnam-era fears of a direct U.S. intervention. By sponsoring an anticommunist insurgency for the purpose of reversing Soviet gains in the developing world, the administration rekindled a debate over the propriety of covert destabilization of foreign regimes. In short, the Reagan administration violated proscriptive injunctions about appropriate means and ends in U.S. foreign policy that had replaced the foreign policy consensus existing prior to Vietnam.

The Reagan administration linked policies in El Salvador and Nicaragua through its assertions—and conviction—that a revolutionary regime in Nicaragua was responsible for violence and upheaval in nearby El Salvador. Congress, however, responded to policies toward the two countries in ways that distinguished them from each other. Dissent over El Salvador policy stemmed not so much from a rejection of the administration's goal (defeat of a leftist-led guerrilla movement), as from policies that appeared to downgrade the social causes of the insurgency and promote a military solution to the conflict.

At first, congressional intelligence committees accepted the administration's rationale for arming the Nicaraguan contras—stopping an arms flow from Nicaragua to the Salvadoran guerrillas. Later, however, dissent in Congress represented a repudiation of the administration's goal (perceived over time as the overthrow of the Sandinista government) as well as the means to that end (covertly arming a paramilitary movement). Eventually Congress came to support the contra policy, accepting the rationale that U.S. objectives in Nicaragua could be attained through the application of military pressure. But a temporary agreement on means did not produce a consensus on ends; slim vote margins reflected underlying policy divisions that were left unsettled.

The Central America debate was thus a unique one in modern foreign policy. It occurred without a domestic consensus over appropriate foreign policy goals, particularly in dealing with the developing world's revolutions. It occurred close enough to the end of the Vietnam War that parallels between U.S. involvement in the two conflicts stirred domestic fears of military intervention and set limits on the U.S. approach. The debate occurred as Congress saw itself as an active participant, not just a passive bystander, in the formulation of foreign policy.

An administration committed to military assertiveness in a traditional U.S.

sphere of influence could expect to be challenged over the means and ends of its Central America policy. Yet as the contest demonstrated, a committed president could go a long way in stretching the parameters of debate and forcing Congress to deal with his agenda of policy concerns.

It would be a mistake, however, to view the entire congressional debate as an outgrowth of substantive differences over how to respond to events in the region. The nature of U.S. institutions and culture comprised a set of domestic political factors shaping and motivating debate.[6] The desire to preserve Congress's institutional prerogatives, for example, often generated conflict with the administration that had little to do with policy content. The Reagan administration heightened this institutional conflict by often failing to accept congressional debate and restrictions on policy as the legitimate outcomes of normal political processes. It attempted to circumvent Congress—the Iran-contra affair was only the most extreme example—when the legislature posed obstacles to the desired execution of policy. By viewing Congress as an adversarial institution to be overcome rather than accommodated, the Reagan administration heightened the procedural aspects of many disputes. In the words of former Senator Charles Mathias Jr. (R-Md.), "Nothing is so conducive to action as the sting of being ignored on your own territory."[7]

In addition, domestic political culture transformed aspects of the Central America debate into a referendum on who could lay claim to the best of U.S. traditions. Traditional values and shared history formed an important legacy of common, if unstated, beliefs. Positive concepts such as democracy and human rights, and negative ones such as anticommunism, suggested common frameworks for responding to the region's conflicts.[8] A successful policy, however, had simultaneously to emphasize both the positive and the negative. Initiatives pursued solely in the name of anticommunism, for example, invited critics to raise the banner of democracy and human rights.

One notion that served to unite the Congress and the administration was that U.S. power was a positive force in the world and that others would benefit by emulating the values, institutions, and political system of the United States. The promotion of pluralist democracy—if only as a symbol of U.S. intentions—was the stated goal of both the Reagan administration and its critics, even if policy approaches differed widely. Closely related to the preference for democracy was the belief that left-wing revolutions were oppressive to the people undergoing them and that governments emerging from them were hostile to U.S. interests.[9] Understanding the force of these core ideas helps to explain the difficulty of coming to terms with a revolutionary regime in Nicaragua and the enthusiasm for El Salvador's evolution toward an electoral system on the Western model.

A second notion, rooted less in ideology than in history, provided another common framework. With the articulation of the Monroe Doctrine in 1823, the United States had emulated European powers by declaring neighboring territory a "sphere of influence" from which foreign powers would be excluded in order to preserve security.[10] Two key concepts—that geographical proximity made Latin America of security interest to the United States, and that the presence of foreign powers represented a threat to that interest—shaped U.S. relations with the hemisphere for two centuries.[11] The Monroe Doctrine became a reference point for U.S. action long after European colonization of Latin America ceased to be a threat. In explaining why preserving stability in El Salvador was vital to U.S. interests, for example, John D. Waghelstein, commander of the U.S. Military Group in San Salvador in 1982 and 1983, stated simply, "El Salvador has been well within our traditional sphere of influence since the Monroe Doctrine, in 1823."[12]

With the advent of the Cold War following World War II, U.S. policy toward Latin America acquired the combined force of two traditions. One was based on historical hegemonic claims rooted in geography, the other on containment's principle of fighting communism and Soviet expansionism worldwide. Policy decisions throughout the postwar period acquired a particular urgency when social change or political instability threatened to bring "foreign ideologies"— communism associated with Soviet power—into the hemisphere.[13]

Because of this dual legacy, based on regional stakes and global postwar missions, Latin America took on special relevance for U.S. domestic politics. The charge that a politician was "soft on communism" in the Western Hemisphere or prepared to relinquish claims to geographic dominance stirred emotions that constrained the actions of elected officials in the White House or on Capitol Hill. President Reagan capitalized on U.S. preoccupations with preserving U.S. security in the Western Hemisphere, but he did not invent them.

As much as the history of U.S. relations with the Western Hemisphere provided a common legacy for Congress and the administration, congressional foreign policy activism in the wake of the Vietnam War divided the Congress from the president. Containment, after all, had not only represented a bipartisan foreign policy principle, but also had cemented a particular form of congressional-executive cooperation. Consider, for example, what had been Congress's deference to presidential authority in the heyday of the Cold War:

- In 1954, during the two-week period in which a CIA-backed force sought the overthrow of Jacobo Arbenz in Guatemala, Congress passed a resolution reaffirming U.S. determination to prevent communist interference in the Western Hemisphere.

- In 1962, during the Cuban missile crisis, Congress passed two resolutions: the first gave President Kennedy the power to call up 150,000 reservists for active duty, in order to demonstrate U.S. readiness to meet any contingency in Berlin or Cuba; the second authorized the president to take whatever actions were necessary to prevent the export of communism from Cuba to other nations in the Western Hemisphere and to prevent a buildup of Soviet offensive weapons in Cuba.

- In August 1964, President Johnson told Congress that a U.S. destroyer in the Gulf of Tonkin had been attacked by the North Vietnamese. Johnson asked for an expression of congressional support. Within days Congress passed the Gulf of Tonkin resolution stating that "the United States is . . . prepared, as the President determines, to take all necessary steps, including the use of armed force, to assist any member or protocol state of the Southeast Asia Collective Defense Treaty requesting assistance in defense of its freedom." The House approved the resolution unanimously; the Senate passed it with only two dissenting votes.[14]

This pattern began to change with the 1965 U.S. invasion of the Dominican Republic. In April and May 1965, President Lyndon Johnson sent more than 30,000 U.S. Marines to the Dominican Republic, ostensibly because "what began as a popular democratic revolution . . . very shortly moved and was taken over and really seized and placed into the hands of a band of Communist conspirators."[15] In September the House adopted a resolution endorsing the unilateral use of force by any Western Hemisphere country to prevent a communist takeover anywhere else in the hemisphere.

Chairman of the Senate Foreign Relations Committee J. William Fulbright (D-Ark.), however, suggested that such a characterization was flawed. In a lengthy floor speech in September 1965 he claimed that U.S. intervention had been "based on exaggerated estimates of Communist influence in the rebel movement." Johnson's explanation that U.S. military action was to protect American lives, Fulbright stated, "was more a pretext than a reason for the massive U.S. intervention that began on the evening of April 28."[16]

The perception that Congress had been misled was an important ingredient in the congressional challenge to foreign policy that spanned the next decade. Even more crucial was the growing conviction that U.S. policy was failing in Southeast Asia. A bipartisan majority in Congress deferred to the executive as long as U.S. actions abroad met with relative success in achieving foreign policy goals. That deference was lost in the quagmire of Vietnam.

The Decade of the 1970s:
Vietnam and the Congressional "Resurgence"

A brief overview of the 1960s and 1970s reveals important antecedents for the Central America debate. As in subsequent decades, a congressional challenge to presidential policy began with hearings. In early 1966, Fulbright chaired nationally televised hearings of the Senate Foreign Relations Committee on Vietnam, introducing new sources of expertise and providing a broad forum for organized, sustained dissent.[17] In a pattern repeated during the Central America debate, congressional doubts were reinforced by the assessments of former U.S. officials. By the late 1960s, prominent early supporters of the war, including former Defense Secretary Clark Clifford, publicly questioned the prospects for victory in Vietnam within a foreseeable period and with proportionate U.S. costs.[18] Events on the ground in Indochina and dissent back home led Congress to hold up a mirror: military escalation in Southeast Asia without a congressional declaration of war amounted, in the eyes of some, to a failure to exercise Congress's own constitutional authority.[19]

The clash between Congress and the executive over Vietnam took the form of a constitutional struggle, even though, as Fulbright reminded his colleagues, "it was not a lack of power which prevented the Congress from ending the war in Indochina, because Congress had the means, through its control of appropriations, to compel an early or immediate end" to the war.[20] Nevertheless, to restore congressional power in a system relying on executive-legislative checks and balances, Congress passed the War Powers Resolution in 1973. Its operative provisions were designed to prevent "future Vietnams" by mandating early congressional review of any decision to send troops abroad, and by giving Congress the power to compel a troop withdrawal once they had been committed.[21]

Watergate, with its revelations of presidential corruption and even criminality, served further to weaken the executive and undermine its prestige, paving the way for a congressional foreign policy challenge. In addition, Watergate hurt the electoral prospects of the Republican Party. In November 1974, three months after the Judiciary Committee recommended the impeachment of President Nixon, American voters elected an overwhelmingly Democratic Congress.

Seventy-five new Democrats comprised the largest freshman class since 1948; the class of 1974, dubbed the "Watergate babies," came to Washington with a certain amount of disdain for its institutions and elites.

"Because of the Watergate fallout," said former Representative Richard Ottinger (D-N.Y.), "everyone—whether they were liberal, moderate, or conservative—felt they were here to do congressional reform." "When we arrived," said Representative Matthew McHugh (D-N.Y.), "we had no stake in the status quo."[22] The "Watergate babies" pressed for internal changes in the Congress that opened up avenues of participation for junior members. The diffusion of power away from the party leadership made policymaking more chaotic, increasing discord within the Congress as well as between it and the executive.[23] During the Central America debates of the late 1970s and the 1980s, a multiplicity of actors with highly individual motivations, some of them without assignments to foreign policy committees, took an active role in raising issues and proposing alternatives.

Vietnam and Watergate thus contributed to changes in formal congressional capacities as well as attitudes. Congress wrote into law concrete prohibitions on certain forms of overseas involvement by the United States and approved numerous reporting requirements designed to enhance congressional oversight of the executive branch. From 1974 to 1976 the legislature voted to prohibit military aid to Turkey after its invasion of Cyprus, to end U.S. covert support to antigovernment rebels in Angola, to place statutory limits on foreign aid to South Korea, Vietnam, Cambodia, Chile, Indonesia, and foreign police forces, to require that proposals for major arms sales be reported to Congress and subject to congressional veto, and to require that trade with the Soviet Union be tied to its emigration policies. This ground swell of congressional activity was directed primarily at the developing world, where the failures of U.S. foreign policy had seemed most acute.

If Congress had leapt into the breach of a shattered foreign policy consensus, constructing a new set of principles for the conduct of foreign policy proved a more difficult task. It seemed clear that Congress knew what it was against: more sacrifice and expenditure in costly wars abroad.[24] But this negative consensus, however well it matched a national mood, did not substitute for a new set of overarching themes for the conduct of foreign policy.

Indeed, most of the major post-Vietnam foreign policy initiatives, from détente under President Nixon to global anti-Sovietism under Reagan, still emanated from the executive. When Congress acted, it was to revise, endorse, or prohibit foreign policy proposals initiated by the executive branch. The reactive mode of congressional foreign policymaking persisted. Central America was no exception to this pattern.

Two congressional initiatives of the 1970s, however, had a major impact on the way Congress addressed the crisis in Central America. The first was human rights. The U.S. failure in Vietnam appeared to demonstrate the dangers of propping up a repressive status quo in the name of fighting communism. A key foreign policy question thus became the internal nature of regimes receiving U.S. assistance. Human rights legislation passed by the Congress in the early and mid-1970s was an attempt to redress the postwar failure to consider the human rights records of U.S. allies, a failure which, it seemed, had contributed to the Vietnam fiasco.[25]

According to the emerging view, extreme repression was destabilizing to the regime practicing abuses. By breeding widespread discontent, human rights violations stripped legitimacy from a government, making it vulnerable to nationalist or revolutionary movements. Attention to human rights considerations, then, embodied more than simply humanitarian motivations; it was implicitly and explicitly a way of viewing the underlying causes of instability. Focusing on human rights violations was a way of warning U.S. allies in the developing world that they threatened their own future by continuing to practice abuses. It was also a reminder to the United States that governments that mistreated their own citizens were unstable and thus potentially unreliable allies. Human rights advocates suggested that U.S. benefits—particularly military aid— should be withheld from abusive regimes, and championed the vigorous use of diplomacy to ameliorate human rights conditions.

Given the prominence of human rights violations in Central America, it is small wonder that human rights issues figured so heavily in—indeed first prompted—the congressional debate over Central America. Major governmental and nongovernmental human rights organizations, including Amnesty International and the Organization of American States Inter-American Human Rights Commission, scored the human rights practices of the military governments in Nicaragua, El Salvador, and Guatemala.

Latin America provided the impetus for the second major congressional initiative relevant to the Central America debate—reform of the intelligence community. The revelations by the press in September 1974 of a covert U.S. role in destabilizing the regime of President Salvador Allende of Chile prompted the first congressional effort in the postwar period to oversee and restrict U.S. intelligence activities.[26] Disclosures in the *New York Times* in late 1974 that the CIA, in violation of its charter, had run a "massive" domestic intelligence operation further fueled the reform efforts. When Congress reconvened in

January 1975, both the House and Senate moved to set up committees to investigate alleged intelligence abuses.[27] In 1976 and 1977, the Senate and House, respectively, set up permanent committees to oversee the intelligence community and approve its budget.

Congress's early attempts to promote human rights and intelligence reform were limited, however, reflecting divisions among members about how far to go in restricting the executive branch. These divisions, in turn, set boundaries for the congressional discussion of Central America.

Congress and Human Rights: The Evolution of Policy

Two amendments to the Foreign Assistance Act of 1961 became the basis for tying human rights considerations to U.S. aid legislation. Section 116, sponsored by Representative Tom Harkin (D-Iowa), passed the Congress in 1975. The amendment stated that no economic aid could go to countries engaged in "gross violations" of human rights unless the aid would directly benefit needy people.[28] Section 502(b) of the Foreign Assistance Act prohibited military aid to countries engaged "in a consistent pattern of gross violations" of human rights, unless the president determined that such aid was vital to U.S. national security.

The wording of the prohibition regarding military assistance demonstrated that Congress was willing to give leeway to the administration in implementing the human rights requirements. The congressional mainstream, it appeared, viewed human rights legislation as a guide to more intelligent administration action rather than as an attempt to conduct a congressional foreign policy. In the words of Representative Donald Fraser (D-Minn.), chairman of the House subcommittee that conducted the most extensive human rights review, "both sections 502B and 116 provide the Executive with a general framework within which the Administration is expected to shape its security and development assistance programs. However, neither law dictates specific decisions; rather, each allows flexibility for action in individual circumstances."[29]

From the outset, however, Congress was divided over just how great that leeway should be. At the root of the controversy were two important, if unstated, divisions. The first was between those who feared instability in Latin America could threaten U.S. interests and those who believed it could not, regardless of the political outcome.[30] Liberals, including Harkin, feared that whenever the president had to choose between human rights and national security, the more cautious instincts of the bureaucracy would prevail. The tension between those who sought principally to guide administration policy and those who endeavored to obstruct it undergirded the early human rights debates over Nicaragua and El Salvador.

A second division, rooted in the very nature of the human rights coalition, meant that the human rights agenda envisioned by liberals would not always prevail. What enabled human rights legislation to pass the Congress was a coalition of reform-minded liberals interested in dissociating the United States from oppressive regimes and conservatives who viewed the laws as a way of reducing foreign aid spending or furthering ideological conflict with Marxist or communist regimes. Pressing human rights considerations when a U.S. ally was under attack by forces of the left split the liberal-conservative coalition. Mustering a congressional majority to support human rights sanctions under such conditions became extremely difficult.

Latin America and Reform of the Intelligence Community

Divisions within Congress also affected the way it approached reform of the intelligence community. In 1974 Congress had adopted the Hughes-Ryan amendment to the Foreign Assistance Act, named for its sponsors, Senator Harold Hughes (D-Iowa) and Representative Leo Ryan (D-Calif.). The amendment prohibited the CIA from engaging in actions other than intelligence gathering unless the president "finds that each such operation is important to the national security of the United States and reports, in a timely fashion, a description and scope of such operation to the appropriate committees of the Congress." *Finding*, used to describe the presidential directive initiating and authorizing covert activities, stems from this Hughes-Ryan language.

Hughes-Ryan was the first law ever passed by Congress specifically calling for congressional oversight of intelligence activities.[31] And to the dismay of the intelligence agencies, the law required the administration to report any new plans for covert operations to six congressional committees with access to intelligence information. The law reflected less a lack of faith in intelligence gathering than in those covert operations designed to influence the course of events in foreign nations. Like other initiatives resulting from the Vietnam War, the principal thrust of the legislation was anti-interventionist.

Several years after the Hughes-Ryan amendment was passed, an investigative committee led by Senator Frank Church called for new charters for the intelligence agencies as well as for a permanent Senate oversight committee to authorize yearly budgets for the intelligence community. The inquiry of the Church committee, formally called the Select Committee to Study Governmental Operations with Respect to Committee Activities, documented a string of CIA abuses, including plots to assassinate foreign leaders and overthrow foreign governments, and—in a violation of the CIA's charter—illegal surveillance of U.S. citizens.[32] The committee described its recommendations as designed to prevent "abuses that have occurred in the past from occurring again."

The principal leaders involved in the CIA review sought oversight of the intelligence community, not direct control of its activities. Senator Church himself led efforts to deny Congress a veto power over covert operations proposed by the administration. "We would usurp the role of the President as final arbiter of foreign policy," he said. The new committee "would have the remedy always available to Congress" should Congress disagree with the administration over a proposed operation. Congress "would control the purse strings, and could pull up on them if it saw fit."[33]

The bill to create a Permanent Select Committee on Intelligence passed the Senate in May 1976 without a provision allowing the committee to veto controversial covert operations. The House voted to establish its own oversight committee in July 1977. Control of the purse strings—deriving from Congress's control over the CIA budget—became, as Church predicted, Congress's way of terminating covert operations with which it disagreed.

The composition of the committees and tenure of their members shaped the way congressional oversight would be conducted. In the Senate, a fifteen-member committee included eight members of the majority party and seven members of the minority, a way of balancing representation so as to guarantee the greatest possible bipartisanship. In addition, senators could serve for a maximum of eight years, a way of preventing members from becoming too close to the agencies they were supposed to oversee. Senator Daniel Inouye (D-Hawaii) later the co-chair of the Iran-contra investigation, served as the first chairman of the Senate Select Committee on Intelligence.[34]

The House leadership, however, insisted that representation on the House Intelligence Committee reflect the overall party distribution of House seats, heavily favoring Democrats. Nine of the fourteen members of the House committee were drawn from the majority party, giving Democrats a decided advantage and heightening partisan conflict on questions of oversight. House Speaker Thomas P. O'Neill Jr. appointed Representative Edward Boland (D-Mass.) to chair the new committee. Boland was a close personal friend of the Speaker's, and a political moderate with long years of service on the Appropriations Committee. Former CIA Director Stansfield Turner called him an "impeccably fair man," an assessment later shared even by those on the Intelligence Committee opposed to Boland's efforts to curb covert operations in Nicaragua.[35]

In 1980 the process of refining committee oversight legislation culminated with the passage of the Intelligence Oversight Act establishing the obligations of the intelligence community to the Congress. In force when Congress began grappling with covert operations in Nicaragua, the act required the executive to keep Congress "fully and currently informed" of intelligence activities or "significant anticipated intelligence activity."[36]

Rather than require notification to Congress of covert activities under the Hughes-Ryan standard of "timely fashion," the Congress defined those occasions on which the president could dispense with "prior notice": in "extraordinary circumstances affecting vital interests of the United States," the president could limit notification to the chairman and ranking minority members of the intelligence committees, the Speaker and minority leader of the House, and the majority and minority leaders of the Senate. If the president did not comply with the prior-notice requirement, he had to report the operation "in a timely fashion" and "provide a statement of the reasons for not giving prior notice." The law thus introduced a new component of congressional oversight: Congress's desire to know of covert operations in advance, rather than within the vague period indicated by "in a timely fashion."[37] The Reagan administration's failure to comply with these notification provisions contributed to major difficulties with the Congress, not only over Nicaragua but also over the exchange of arms for hostages in Iran.

As subsequent events would show, however, effective oversight depended just as much on congressional vigilance as it did on executive compliance with the law. Some members of Congress seemed to prefer not to know about covert operations, recalling an earlier era when Congress left the conduct of foreign policy to the executive. In the words of Senator Barry Goldwater (R-Ariz.), chairman of the Senate Select Committee on Intelligence from 1981 to 1984, "I don't even like to have an intelligence committee. I don't think it's any of our business."[38]

Assessing the Changes:
Central America and the Post-Vietnam Congress

Congress's foreign policy activism during the 1970s thus took essentially three forms: (1) the cutoff of funds, to deny the executive branch the means to carry out various policies; (2) the passage of laws and amendments designed to influence administration policy and to guarantee Congress a role in making and overseeing critical decisions; and (3) the creation of new institutional structures through which new oversight was to be channeled.

These changes all had implications for the way Congress dealt with Central America policy. President Reagan did gain congressional backing for his policies in El Salvador and Nicaragua: in May 1984 a Democratic House approved for the first time the administration's full complement of military and economic aid for El Salvador, and in June 1986 approved military aid for contra rebels fighting the Sandinista government.

But the difficulties encountered by the president in achieving and maintaining congressional support were substantial. The tone and even the existence of debate set limits as to what was politically tolerable. And the persistence of controversy ruled out certain options, such as sending U.S. troops to the region, while making others, such as pursuing improvements in human rights, prerequisites for sustained congressional funding. Measuring whether the debate had any impact on the administration, by forcing it to do what it otherwise would not, is by nature a subjective judgment. The administration's own statements, however, suggested that congressional opposition to the course of policy was an important influence on its tone and substance.

A consensus was possible over El Salvador, for example, when the administration incorporated congressional concerns over human rights, social reform, and a political solution to the conflict into a revised policy. Ironically, some of the policy shifts—away from the harsh rhetoric of East-West conflict and toward curbing right-wing violence—occurred only after those administration officials most sensitive to concerns on Capitol Hill were removed in mid-1983, the height of an internal struggle for the soul of Reagan foreign policy.

Conversely, conflict over Nicaragua policy defied resolution because the driving force of the administration's ideological commitment to defeating the Sandinistas resisted the tempering influence of political realities in Congress. The administration's insistence on arming a contra rebel movement for purposes rejected by Congress led to a temporary cutoff of contra funds in October 1984. In convincing Congress to lift that ban, the administration was forced to agree to couple military pressure with diplomacy and to press for reforms in the contra leadership. The administration's failure to live up to those commitments, and the revelations that it had ignored the cutoff of funds even when in force, eroded congressional support for the contra program. By "wanting it all," a contra policy freed of congressional restraints, the Reagan administration risked "losing it all"—domestic backing for the contra war—demonstrating that fervor was no substitute for pragmatism in sustaining a policy over time.

Clues to determining how it is that the president achieved majority backing for his policies in Central America, only to watch those policies crumble in the waning days of his administration, lie in the environment in which congressional decisions were made. This environment was a product of congressional and public attitudes toward the presidency and toward the policies themselves, of institutional procedures and political alliances within the Congress, and of the external events that provided the context for congressional action. Appearing at different times and in different combinations, aspects of this environment accounted for congressional decisions.

Presidential Initiative

Despite the reassertion of certain congressional prerogatives in the 1970s, the executive branch—through the White House, the State Department, the Defense Department, intelligence agencies, and the National Security Council—still defined the broad outlines of a foreign policy approach. The executive begins a foreign policy program by introducing legislation, has wide powers to conduct negotiations, establishes broad foreign policy themes through speeches and unilateral policy declarations, and can avoid congressional involvement in foreign policy decisions through special legal provisions conveying such authority.[39]

On numerous occasions during the Central America debate, the executive branch used these powers of initiative to develop the climate in which Central America policy was discussed, at times creating incidents to which the United States ostensibly had to respond. As Alexander Hamilton wrote in the *Federalist Papers*, presidential power made it "easy . . . to fabricate pretences of approaching danger."[40]

Furthermore, the administration implemented foreign policy through its emissaries and embassies abroad. This monopoly on policy implementation made it difficult, if not impossible, for Congress to legislate an alternative foreign policy when the executive did not want to carry it out. In the words of Representative David Obey (D-Wisc.), "There isn't any way on God's green earth that we can instill in the Administration a will which is not there."[41]

However, because of what one former congressional aide called the post-Vietnam " 'demystification' of national security affairs," the president and members of his cabinet could no longer overwhelm the congressional rank and file with a sense of the "special character" of foreign policy.[42] Although the executive continued to possess both greater information and expertise about foreign policy matters than the Congress, the sense that the executive could and did make mistakes gave presidential critics more standing.

Presidential Legitimacy

Unlike in the 1970s, when Watergate and Vietnam weakened the institution of the presidency, the notion that the president ought to predominate in foreign policy persisted among key congressional leaders. In the words of the senior Democrat on and later chairman of the House Foreign Affairs Committee, Lee Hamilton: "As Commander in Chief of the armed forces and the principal governmental officer responsible for policy execution, the President is at the center of American foreign policy. People look to him for leadership and consider him their representative before the world."[43] Similarly, as the former chairman of the Senate Foreign Relations Committee, Charles Percy, put it, "Congress simply does not have the expertise, the capability, or the authority for dealing with the daily operations of government."[44]

During the Reagan years, the president's substantial personal popularity reinforced the standing of his office and made members of Congress more reluctant to challenge his policies, thus reducing Congress's potential power. In the words of former Representative Michael Barnes (D-Md.):

> By accepting the assertion of unlimited presidential power and discretion, we . . . effectively prevented ourselves from exercising the control that we should have exercised over our Central America policies. . . . Congress' constitutional powers of legislation and appropriation give us all the tools we need to say "no" to the President. But if we don't have the political will to use them . . . then the role of the Congress will continue to fall short of what, under our system, it should and must be.[45]

However, deference to presidential leadership was by no means automatic and was intimately linked to the legitimacy of the policies he carried out. When those policies were considered ill-advised, dangerous, or threatening to the constitutional system of checks and balances (all important components of the Central America debate), congressional activism increased. As Senator Christopher Dodd (D-Conn.) put it, "Congress only gets involved when it perceives the President is not following a wise policy."[46]

Partisanship

The notion that "politics stops at the water's edge"—that the United States must appear united in order successfully to pursue national interests abroad—mitigated interparty competition over foreign policy issues. Moreover, party loyalties usually ensured that the president enjoyed majority support within his own party.

However, strong ideological differences between Republicans and Democrats on foreign policy issues intensified with the election of Ronald Reagan as president in 1980. Central America policy in particular became an arena of intense partisan conflict, with the liberal wing of the Democratic Party driving the opposition to the president. The intense involvement in Central America policy of two consecutive House Speakers, Thomas P. O'Neill Jr. and Jim Wright, added to the partisan nature of the competition.

The 1980 election also resulted in six years of a House and a Senate led by different parties. Conflict over Central America policy became as much a struggle between the House and the Senate as it did between the Congress and the executive. The Republican-controlled Senate's tendency to support the president turned the House into the locus of opposition to the administration, forcing compromises that fell short of the position of either body.

What the cases of El Salvador and Nicaragua policy often illustrated, however, was the weakness of party identification in determining the outcomes of key votes. The president was rarely able to prevail when he lost more than a few votes from members of his own party, and he was never able to prevail without substantial crossover support from Democrats. Divisions within the Democratic Party played decisive roles in Reagan administration policy victories over aid to the contras and to El Salvador.

Most of the Democratic votes won by Reagan were from Southerners, members of what has been called a "conservative coalition" of Republicans and southern Democrats.[47] The rise of the Republican Party in the South somewhat diminished the importance of the "conservative coalition." Fifty years ago, for example, 117 out of 120 seats in thirteen southern states (the old Confederacy plus Kentucky and Oklahoma) were Democratic; in 1987, only 85 out of 124 were held by Democrats. The rise of Republican strength may have been a factor making southern Democrats more cautious on foreign policy and defense votes. The South continued to serve as a bastion of support for conservative causes, particularly when turmoil in Latin America raised the specter of unwanted waves of immigration.[48]

Regional Events and Perceptions of Them
Although it may seem self-evident, the course of regional events in Central America was important in motivating and shaping congressional action. The interpretation of events can be highly subjective, but what did occur was

important. The killing of U.S. nuns and of a Catholic archbishop in El Salvador, the censorship of opposition news media in Nicaragua, or U.S. mining of its harbors, provided the stuff of foreign policy debates. These events were the basis of congressional initiatives.

All developments were not viewed with equal objectivity, however, and the Central America crisis illustrated that ideological and political preferences played a role in determining which facts were relevant. American political values, such as individual freedom and respect for the law in international and national behavior, provided a filter through which policymakers determined the legitimacy of the actions of their own and foreign governments.

Players in Central America, however, often pursued courses of action determined by a regional or national logic, with little or no reference to the impact in Washington. Predictably, those who ignored American political values and sensitivities suffered the consequences, while those who learned to accommodate U.S. concerns reaped the rewards.

Congressional Procedure

As an institution Congress acted according to set procedures and debated foreign policy on a few selected vehicles. Legislation authorizing and appropriating funds for foreign activities—foreign aid, intelligence, military construction—became the means for influencing policy. These formal powers over money were augmented by informal means of influencing policy—sending letters, making speeches, passing nonbinding resolutions. While the former provided Congress with blunt, albeit binding, instruments for shaping foreign policy, the latter set the tone of policy debate, serving as a barometer of congressional sentiment.

As the Central America debate came to illustrate, moreover, the procedures under which measures were discussed on the floor—whether amendments were allowed, their order and structure, who got to offer them—often determined the outcome of policy discussions. The arcane details of these procedures can be confusing and may even obscure deeper policy issues. Nevertheless, an understanding of congressional process is key to understanding the outcomes of certain policy debates. An important example was the House's decision in June 1985 to provide nonlethal aid to the contras, a decision based in part on procedural issues.

Public Opinion

Opinion polls throughout the eight years of the Reagan administration showed consistent public opposition to a policy of backing contra rebels or providing military aid to the government of El Salvador. Congressional decisions to send aid to El Salvador and the contras thus occurred without the support of a majority of the public. Several days after Congress voted a major increase in aid to El Salvador, for example, a Harris poll found that 74 percent of Americans opposed increasing military aid.[49] Moreover, three months before the House voted in June 1986 to provide contra military aid, the American people opposed aid by nearly 2 to 1.[50]

However, polls also showed widespread public ignorance of Central American issues, with a majority of the public often unaware of whom the United States supported or opposed in the region. A poll found in June 1983, for example, that only 25 percent of Americans surveyed knew that the Reagan administration supported the government of El Salvador, only 13 percent knew that it sided with the contras in Nicaragua, and only 8 percent knew both. In April 1986, another poll showed that slightly more than a third of the public knew that the United States was supporting the contras and not the government of Nicaragua.[51]

The gap between public preferences and congressional votes, and overall public ignorance of Central America, suggested that members of Congress had substantial independence from their constituents in regard to foreign policy. At best, public opinion was one factor influencing congressional behavior, if not always a decisive one.[52]

To dismiss public pressures altogether, however, would be a mistake. Active lobbying by church and human rights groups and constituent letter-writing campaigns provided administration critics and skeptics a sense that they had a cushion of support to oppose the president. These domestic pressures reinforced members' willingness to oppose policy, often serving as a justification for such opposition. Conversely, domestic campaigns in favor of administration policy, particularly when they carried the charge that a member was "soft on communism," raised the costs of opposing the president. This was particularly true in Republican districts, or in Democratic ones with a strong conservative bias.

The Search for Consensus

If prerogatives, attitudes, and events framed the executive-congressional struggle over Central America, the national experience of Vietnam provided the gallery. The Reagan administration hoped that its sweep in the 1980 election had signaled the end of the "Vietnam syndrome"—a reluctance to defend U.S. interests with military force. But the administration quickly found that its zeal to confront communism in the hemisphere stirred up a hornet's nest of protest, not because members of Congress wanted to see communist victories in a region close to the United States, but because they feared that U.S. policies would lead to direct U.S. military involvement. Central America thus became not just a product of the Vietnam debate but a continuation of it,[53] an ongoing national search for the proper relationship between ends and means, and a definition of what interests would be worth fighting for.

Members of Congress and the administration attempted to apply the "lessons" of Vietnam to Central America and came to similar conclusions, but even these were inadequate guides for action. "The central lesson," said Senator William Cohen (R-Maine), for example, "was not that American power should never be used to defend the interests of those removed or remote from the United States. Rather, it was that we should never commit American sons to fight and die in distant lands unless we can persuade the country and the Congress that it is in our vital interest to do so."[54] Similarly, Secretary of Defense Caspar Weinberger stated: "Before the U.S. commits combat forces abroad, there must be some reasonable assurance we will have the support of the American people and their elected representatives in Congress. We cannot fight a battle with the Congress at home while asking our troops to win a war overseas."[55] Both policymakers seemed to agree that domestic consensus was important to the success of foreign policy, particularly if U.S. involvement could logically result in a commitment of troops.

But the Central America debate not only defied public and congressional consensus, it became a Reagan administration vehicle for trying to forge a new one. In that process the administration stretched Congress beyond the noninterventionist limits it had set after Vietnam, while the Congress denied Reagan the claim that he had freed the United States from its post-Vietnam shackles.

The eruption of a series of revolutions in a traditional U.S. sphere of influence during a period of post-Vietnam soul-searching in the United States produced a potent formula for foreign policy strife. Add to this already unstable mix an administration determined to step beyond an old consensus over containing communism in favor of a new global effort to reverse communist gains and one invited renewed struggle over the purposes of American power. Couple a post-Vietnam Congress jealous of its foreign policy prerogatives with an administration determined to pursue policy at any cost, and one ensured a legislative-executive struggle over process and procedure, not just policy content. Central America touched all of these nerves. It should appear as no surprise that the two tiny republics of Nicaragua and El Salvador so gripped and involved this nation.

Chapter Two

1976–1980:
Congress Discovers
Central America

Postwar congressional involvement with Central America began on June 8, 1976. At 2:05 P.M. in a small hearing room in the Rayburn House Office Building, Representative Donald Fraser, the chairman of the House Foreign Affairs Subcommittee on International Organizations, called to order the array of witnesses before him: a conservative Staten Island Democrat and personal friend of Nicaraguan President Anastasio Somoza, a Jesuit priest and professor at Nicaragua's National University, a 1972 vice-presidential candidate from El Salvador, and a Christian Democrat from Guatemala.

All three countries to be examined by the subcommittee were ruled by military dictatorships. All three had, by Latin American standards, received substantial assistance from the United States. All three appeared bastions of anticommunist stability. And all three, according to the Central American witnesses, were guilty of massive abuses of human rights, including murder and torture, disappearance, and prolonged detention.

Those who had lobbied Congress to hold the hearing hoped that establishing a record of human rights abuses would result in cutoffs or reductions in U.S. military aid, actions consistent with existing human rights legislation.[1] What is striking about the hearing in retrospect, however, is how little interest it generated. Beyond committed representatives on both sides of the human rights debate—those in favor of cutting aid and those defending the regimes in question—Congress as a whole remained indifferent to Central America policy. The seemingly monumental stakes that had developed by the early 1980s, and the overwhelming preoccupation with security aspects of the Central American crisis, were simply nonexistent in the mid-1970s.

The reason was simple. As the debate opened, no serious challenge—armed or otherwise—existed to threaten incumbent Central American regimes. The apparent lack of a security dimension, in turn, provided an opening for human rights activists in and outside Congress to press for the termination of U.S. assistance.

Once revolutionary movements began to threaten the survival of traditional U.S. allies, congressional interest in the region expanded. At the same time, congressional liberals and the Carter administration, which made human rights a central element of its foreign policy, were ambivalent about the degree to which human rights considerations should determine U.S. foreign policy when other interests were at stake. One lesson of Vietnam—that the United States should not prop up a regime that lacked popular support—exerted a heavy influence on policymaking during the course of the Nicaraguan revolution of 1977 to 1979, only to fade as turmoil in El Salvador threatened a repeat of the Nicaraguan revolutionary experience.

As prelude to the deeper policy clashes under the Reagan administration, moreover, congressional debates over Central America under Presidents Ford and Carter illustrated emerging patterns of congressional-executive competition. If indifference to congressional concerns regarding human rights during the Ford administration accelerated congressional activism, attention to those issues under Carter frustrated congressional initiatives. If liberals and conservatives in Congress used positions on powerful committees as leverage to gain concessions from the executive, the administration could still blunt congressional influence through its prerogatives of policy initiation and implementation. If Congress restricted administration actions by writing conditions into legislation, the administration could claim fulfillment of those conditions through its control of, and potential to manipulate, information. Members of Congress and the president shaped policy in response to regional events; neither could be indifferent to the domestic context in which those events were interpreted.

Central American issues first arose for the Congress and administration when the shattering of the Cold War consensus provided a historic opportunity to fashion a foreign policy based on standards other than anticommunism. President Carter attempted to do just that, promising in 1977 not to separate "the traditional issues of war and peace from the new global questions of justice, equity, and human rights."[2] By the end of his term in office, however, world events and domestic pressures combined to force Carter into retreat from principles—human rights, regionalism, the primacy of "North-South" economic issues over those of power politics—he had embraced early on.

Congress in particular was a force for conservatism, postponing an economic aid package to the new revolutionary government in Nicaragua for close to a year, thus stymieing the Carter administration's attempt to respond positively to change in the region. The 1980 presidential election brought the assault on Carter's foreign policy to a head. Facing an electoral challenge predicated on anti-Sovietism and a return to the Cold War, Carter renewed military aid to El Salvador, abandoning human rights concerns to the more traditional preoccupation with counterinsurgency.

Congress and Nicaragua: Early Stirrings

Because of the low level of congressional interest in Central America in 1976, individual members with a strong commitment to the issue had a disproportionate impact on policy. In the early stages of debate over Nicaragua, Representative John Murphy (D-N.Y.) and Representative Edward Koch (D-N.Y.) were the central protagonists. Murphy was a longtime friend of Somoza. The two had gone to military prep school together, and both had studied at West Point, although at different times. The Staten Island Democrat defended Somoza's human rights record at the Fraser hearings in June.

Koch, meanwhile, had developed an interest in Latin America as a member of the House Appropriations Subcommittee on Foreign Operations, which oversees foreign aid requests. Believing that efforts to promote human rights could best succeed in small countries where U.S. influence was great, Koch sponsored a successful amendment in 1976 to cut aid to the military government in Uruguay. "Once we won that," recalled Koch aide Charlie Flynn, "everybody and his brother trooped into our office and said, 'Hey, this guy can get something accomplished.' " Although Koch was not a member of the Fraser Subcommittee, he sat in on the hearings on Central America.*

Testimony during the June congressional hearings painted a stark picture of repression in Nicaragua. The information came principally from two sources with credibility in the Congress: the Catholic Church, and nonviolent opponents of the Somoza regime. Many of the individuals represented remained important figures in the Nicaraguan revolution and its aftermath. Jesuit priest Father Fernando Cardenal (later head of the Sandinista literacy campaign) accused Somoza of arbitrary detention, torture, and the mass executions of civilians. He submitted for the record a sworn statement by opposition newspaper editor Pedro Joaquín Chamorro, whose assassination helped trigger the Nicaraguan uprising; Chamorro graphically described the torture he had overheard and seen during a night in Somoza's prisons.† A letter from Monsignor Miguel Obando y Bravo, later a leading opponent of the Sandinistas, complained that censorship under Somoza constituted "an obstacle to the proper mission of the Church." Despite these testimonies, Koch wrote that he found the hearings "inconclusive" in establishing the record of human rights violations in Nicaragua.[3]

In a pattern that continued under the Reagan administration, the Ford administration's denials that there was compelling evidence of abuses set the stage for future confrontation with the Congress. "Guatemala, El Salvador, and Nicaragua are all recipients of U.S. economic and military assistance," said Hewson Ryan, acting Assistant Secretary of State for Inter-American Affairs. "In

---

*Representative Murphy tried to provide some counterpoint, setting up a meeting between Koch and General Somoza in New York. The two met over Memorial Day weekend 1977 in the general's penthouse suite of the Waldorf-Astoria hotel. "The purpose," recalled Koch's aide, "was to try to get him [Koch] off Somoza's case."

"You could tell [Somoza] knew how to bullshit very well," said Flynn. "He knew Americans." Somoza appealed to Koch's instincts as a lawyer, stressing that any anti-democratic measures taken in Nicaragua were to deal with the threat posed by Cuban-supported terrorists. Koch remained unimpressed, however, and, according to Flynn, emerged from the meeting in the lush New York hotel "even more determined to proceed."

Subsequently, U.S. Ambassador to Nicaragua James Theberge visited Koch in Washington to assure the congressman that systematic violations of human rights were not occurring in Nicaragua. Telephone interview, Charlie Flynn, December 4, 1986, and Edward Koch, "How a Foreign Government Won over the U.S. Congress," *Village Voice*, August 8, 1977, in *Congressional Record*, August 4, 1977, pp. 27124–26.

†Chamorro had been invited by the subcommittee to testify at the hearings, but Somoza refused him permission to leave Nicaragua, citing libel charges pending against him in Nicaraguan court.

each case, a review of all the hard evidence . . . did not yield the judgment that there had emerged a consistent pattern of gross violation of human rights. . . . We have been unable to establish that they have occurred . . . as a result of governmental decisions."[4] The administration also set out to discredit the testimony of witnesses with whom it disagreed, falsely maintaining that Pedro Joaquín Chamorro said Cardenal's testimony was based on "unfounded propaganda."[5] Both attempts stiffened congressional resolve to oppose aid: if the administration would not implement human rights legislation, Congress would have to take matters into its own hands.

When the Carter administration came into office with its stated commitment to human rights, new evidence of abuses in Nicaragua led Koch to sponsor an attempt to cut off military aid to its National Guard. The conservative Catholic hierarchy in Nicaragua issued a pastoral letter in January 1977 accusing the Somoza government of "the use of humiliating and unhuman methods: tortures, rapes, and even executions without previous civil or military trials."[6] Reports in the U.S. press further documented a pattern of Nicaraguan government brutality: in March 1977, *Time* magazine reported that government soldiers "shot, bayonetted, or strangled" men, women, and children; the *New York Times* reported that Nicaraguan priests had accused the National Guard of instituting "a reign of terror" in the countryside, "routinely killing and torturing peasant men, raping women, burning homes, and stealing crops and property."[7] A month later, the Foreign Operations Subcommittee on which Koch sat held two days of hearings on Nicaragua.*

The assessment of senior Carter administration officials of U.S. interests in Nicaragua contributed to the resolve to cut aid. Secretary of State Cyrus Vance agreed with members of the subcommittee that U.S. security interests in Nicaragua and in a country like South Korea were not at all comparable. Undersecretary of State for Security Assistance Lucy Benson was asked what would be lost if the United States suspended all aid to Nicaragua. She replied, "I cannot think of a single thing."[8]

On May 19, 1977, the subcommittee voted 5–4 to suspend $3.1 million in military credits. The full Appropriations Committee upheld the decision by one vote on June 14.

---

*El Salvador and Guatemala did not figure in the debates over military aid during the first year of the Carter administration because they had rejected U.S. aid following criticism of their human rights record. In the case of El Salvador, the gesture was largely symbolic, as aid had been suspended by the Ford administration following the conviction of Salvadoran Army Chief of Staff Manuel Alfonso Rodríguez for selling U.S.-supplied machine guns to the Mafia.

When the foreign aid bill came to the floor, however, Somoza's friends rallied to his side. Representative Charlie Wilson (D-Texas), who had become Somoza's main ally on the Foreign Operations Subcommittee, led a successful fight to restore the military aid. Wilson denigrated the testimony of "radical preachers" like Obando y Bravo and Cardenal and emphasized the long-standing ties of friendship between the U.S. and Nicaragua. He reminded his colleagues that Nicaragua had served as a stepping-off point for the 1961 CIA-backed invasion of Cuba at the Bay of Pigs. As a result, Wilson argued, "Nicaragua has been a continuous target for Castro." Somoza's military school chum Murphy went further, accusing newspaper editor Pedro Joaquín Chamorro of having "organized an armed invasion of Nicaragua" and of having "led public riots in the streets of Managua."

Others made less wild claims. The chairman of the House Foreign Affairs Committee, Clement Zablocki (D-Wisc.), said he opposed the aid cutoff as a matter of principle. It made no sense, he said, to "single out countries that are friendly to us in trying to get them to live up to our mores and our standards."[9]

Following a modest debate, the House voted 225–180 to restore aid to Nicaragua. The decision was the result of two principal factors.

First, in response to Koch's activism, General Somoza rallied his own lobbying operation in Washington. Former Florida Representative William Cramer was one of several paid Nicaraguan government agents who lobbied dozens of members, focusing particularly on conservatives who might have been inclined to vote against aid to Nicaragua as a way of reducing overall foreign aid spending. Several of those approached—including the ranking Republican on the House Appropriations Committee, Representative Elford A. Cederberg (R-Mich.), and Representative George O'Brien (R-Ill.) participated prominently in the floor debate. After the vote, Wilson and O'Brien dined with President Somoza.[10]

Second, despite the State Department's willingness to admit human rights abuses in Nicaragua, one top official worked against the cut. At first, said Koch's aide, "they [the State Department] weren't saying anything about the amendment, and we took that to mean they didn't oppose it." Then, however, Assistant Secretary of State for Inter-American Affairs Terence Todman sent a letter to the chairman of the Foreign Operations Subcommittee, with copies to Somoza supporters Cederberg, Murphy, and O'Brien. Todman promised that the administration would not sign a military aid agreement with Nicaragua until there had been an improvement in human rights, and that the State Department would consult with Congress prior to making such a decision.

Todman's promises tipped the balance in favor of restoring aid. Moderate

Democrats abandoned Koch and voted to give the administration flexibility in its conduct of foreign affairs. Paraphrasing President Carter, Representative Louis Stokes (D-Ohio) stated, "I would hope that the Congress would not tie my hands."[11]

The amendment lost. "We felt betrayed," said Flynn.[12]

The failure of Koch's effort to cut military aid to Somoza thus illustrates several important patterns of congressional action regarding human rights.

First, because human rights violations had not yet emerged as an obvious threat to the stability of the Somoza regime, the congressional debate reflected a remarkable lack of urgency. Human rights considerations remained the concern of a handful of liberals and even fewer moderates, who viewed the Nicaraguan abuses as a moral affront but could not muster enough support—or even interest—to take decisive action.

Second, an administration sensitive to the human rights concerns of liberals and moderates could divide the two groups by demonstrating a willingness to consult over future initiatives. Compromise, flexibility, and cooptation, reflected in Todman's letter, were important ingredients of administration success.

Third, even though Congress had passed a law withholding military aid from human rights violators, key moderates were reluctant to impinge on executive branch prerogatives to make aid decisions. The desire "not to tie the hands of the president" was particularly strong given the Carter administration's forceful public commitment to the furtherance of human rights.

Finally, conservatives who voted against foreign aid "giveaways" abandoned their opposition when an issue was cast in anticommunist terms. This was even more true when the target of an aid cut was an ally with a long history of "friendliness" to the United States.

The same lack of urgency characterized congressional attention to El Salvador, even though in the late 1970s there appeared to be no trade-off between promoting human rights and threatening the stability of the military government.[13] Only a handful of human rights activists—Representative Robert Drinan (D-Mass.), a Catholic priest; Senator Edward Kennedy (D-Mass.), whose foreign policy aide had been a Peace Corps volunteer in El Salvador; and Representative Tom Harkin (D-Iowa)—visited El Salvador or spoke out against abuses. Hearings on the fraudulent 1977 presidential elections attracted scant attention, even though witnesses issued prescient warnings about political polarization in El Salvador. Two figures who would later become key actors in Salvadoran politics—future president José Napoleón Duarte and future junta member José Antonio Morales Ehrlich—warned against branding as "Communist . . . any idea or activity, based on social justice." In contrast to the enthusiastic reception

Duarte would receive in Washington in the 1980s, however, only Harkin and Kennedy would meet with him in 1977.[14]

Attacks on the Catholic Church in El Salvador, including death threats against the entire Jesuit order in El Salvador, prompted another congressional inquiry;[15] and Father Drinan persisted in raising human rights issues with the Carter administration and the Congress, leading twenty-two members of the House in nominating Salvadoran Archbishop Oscar Arnulfo Romero for the Nobel Peace Prize. But because the Salvadoran government had protested human rights criticism by rejecting U.S. military aid, few mechanisms existed to translate human rights concerns into concrete influence over policy. The Salvador issue received scant attention in the Congress, an oversight many members would come to regret.

Congress and the Nicaraguan Insurrection

In 1978, events in Nicaragua aroused Congress and the Carter administration from their complacency. Following the assassination of *La Prensa* editor Pedro Joaquín Chamorro, widespread rioting broke out, followed by a general strike. Somoza's ensuing crackdown plunged Nicaragua deeper into political crisis, culminating in massive popular uprisings in September. During this period, Congress exerted a conservative influence on Carter administration policy, already constrained by the desire to preserve some elements of the status quo in Nicaragua.

Representative Wilson in particular continued to use his clout on the Appropriations Committee to press for aid to the Somoza government. In May, Wilson's lobbying led the State Department to release $160,000 in military credits for a Nicaraguan military hospital; that same month the State Department granted $12 million in economic aid that had been held up for human rights reasons. Wilson's lobbying was effective because he constituted a key "swing" vote on the Appropriations Committee, whose vote the administration wanted as it pressed for foreign aid increases. Wilson threatened to hold the entire 1979 foreign aid bill—not to mention increases in funding for international financial institutions— hostage to his demands for aid to Nicaragua. "Wilson was in all the time at the operational level," recalled a senior Carter administration official. Even if he was not solely responsible for administration actions, "he acted with very specific pressures."[16]

Lobbying by Somoza supporters in Congress produced results not only because the Carter administration took congressional pressures seriously and even overreacted to them, but also because the administration itself was deeply divided over how to treat a long-standing ally. In requesting a token military training program in mid-1978, for example, the Defense Department noted that the National Guard "is expected to continue to play a key role in the evolution of the country."[17] While agreeing on the desire to maintain influence in Nicaragua, administration officials were divided over whether to use the carrot or the stick in seeking human rights improvements. On June 30, President Carter wrote Somoza that "the steps toward respecting human rights that you are considering are important and heartening signs."[18] That letter became an embarrassment two months later when Nicaragua erupted into civil war, an uprising New York Times reporter Alan Riding called a "national mutiny" against the Somoza dynasty.[19]

The beginning of the uprising against Somoza and the Guard led to a frenzy of congressional activity on both sides of the political spectrum. These conflicting pressures served further to exacerbate divisions within the administration over how to cope with the Nicaraguan crisis.

Two congressional initiatives of September 22, 1978, illustrate the poles of congressional opinion. On the one hand, seventy-eight members of the House led by Democrats Murphy, Wilson, and McDonald urged President Carter to "do [your] utmost to demonstrate the support of the United States Government for the Government of Nicaragua and President Anastasio Somoza, a long and consistent ally of the United States."[20] The letter warned that "violence, urban terrorism and near civil war in Nicaragua [are] being carried out by a revolutionary group whose leaders have been trained in Havana and Moscow and whose goal is to make Nicaragua the new Cuba of the Western Hemisphere. . . . Should the lawful Government of Nicaragua fall, the Marxist terrorist forces would be the chief beneficiaries."[21]

On the other side of the Capitol, meanwhile, the Senate approved two amendments stripping aid to Somoza from the foreign aid bill. One, sponsored by Senator Mark Hatfield (R-Ore.), cut $150,000 in military training funds for the National Guard and passed with the support of the State Department. Frank Church, the chairman of the Senate Foreign Relations Committee, and Jacob Javits, the ranking minority member, persuaded their colleagues to cut another $8 million in economic aid. In an impassioned speech, Senator Church charged that Somoza faced "a national mutiny in which almost every sector of the country has united against a dynasty which has plundered the country for nearly half a century. . . . The longer Somoza . . . uses his armed guard to quell resistance, the more likely it is that another Castro-type revolutionary government will eventually emerge."[22] The House and Senate initiatives mirrored several dilemmas for Carter administration policymakers. Although few in the administration shared Representative Murphy's apocalyptic view that the choice in Nicaragua was Somoza or communism, there remained a deep distrust of the armed wing of the anti-Somoza movement and a desire to preserve some element of the National Guard as a bulwark against the guerrillas. A majority of the administration believed that Somoza was the core of the problem in Nicaragua, and that it would be best if he left, but the administration was hesitant about asking Somoza to leave.

At least one top official, however, was convinced that hopes for a "moderate" solution depended on convincing Somoza to step aside and give up power. Assistant Secretary of State for Inter-American Affairs Viron Vaky laid out this scenario in a September 1978 "executive session" with the Senate Foreign Relations Committee. The objective of U.S. policy, he said, was to promote change in order to ensure a moderate outcome in Nicaragua, given perceived opportunities to avoid "classical radicalization." Vaky came away assured of the committee's support for a multilateral mediation effort to attempt a transfer of power in Nicaragua via elections.[23]

A mediation effort by the United States, Guatemala, and the Dominican Republic collapsed in January 1979 when Somoza flatly refused to leave office. Senior Carter administration officials still remain convinced that Somoza's congressional supporters reinforced the dictator's intransigence. Wilson and Murphy visited Nicaragua at the height of the mediation in November 1978, holding a pro-Somoza press conference that left State Department officials "furious." Upon returning to Washington, Wilson charged that pressures on Somoza amounted to "encouraging communism in the Caribbean." Representative George Hansen (R-Idaho) also journeyed to Managua, demanding "an immediate end to our bullying" of the Somoza regime.[24]

"We had this sense," said a key U.S. policymaker at the time, "that Wilson and the others were telling Somoza, 'this is just the radicals in the State Department [telling you to leave] and they can't make it stick.' " Partly as a result of right-wing pressures in the United States, "the decision was never made: you, Somoza, have got to go."[25]

In the words of then–Secretary of State for Congressional Relations J. Brian Atwood, Carter "hesitated, he blinked, [when] confronted with the choice about whether or not Somoza had to go. Over the next several weeks, the resolution of the conflict became more military, less a compromise with the businessmen."[26]

"What the administration didn't do, and should have done," reflected former

Assistant Secretary of State Viron Vaky, "was rally our friends to offset that pressure" from congressional conservatives.[27]

Following the collapse of the mediation in January 1979, the Carter administration announced sanctions against Nicaragua, including the suspension, but not the cancellation, of aid projects. Wilson protested directly to the National Security Council, threatening as he had in the past to torpedo an entire year's foreign aid bill. Senators Kennedy, Cranston, Hatfield, Javits, and Sarbanes, on the other hand, wrote to Carter that they "welcome[d] and support[ed] your recent actions to disassociate the United States from the Somoza government" and urged the administration to consider "additional measures if the Somoza government persists in rejecting reasonable proposals for . . . future peace."[28]

In contrast to pressures from Somoza's allies in Congress, however, liberal pressures were vague and unfocused. Liberals called for additional economic sanctions against Somoza, but it was never clear that more pressure would achieve Somoza's resignation.[29] Wary of measures that would appear "interventionist," liberals avoided calling for the United States to force Somoza to leave office. Liberal silence on the matter of Somoza's resignation only added to the paralysis in the State Department.

Representative Murphy's chairmanship of the House Merchant Marines and Fisheries Committee, by contrast, gave conservatives another opportunity to influence U.S. policy toward Nicaragua. With oversight of the legislation to implement the Panama Canal treaties, the committee became the focus of conservative efforts to defeat the treaty legislation by linking the Nicaraguan and Panamanian issues.[30] Ranking Merchant Marine Committee Republican Robert Bauman (R-Md.) alleged that Panamanian General Omar Torrijos was engaged in arms trafficking to the Sandinista rebels. Murphy was not necessarily supportive of Bauman's perspective, but he was interested in enhancing his own influence with the administration over the Panama issue. As a result, Murphy scheduled June hearings on the gun-running charges.

Throughout the House debate over the Panama Canal treaties, Carter administration officials treated charges of Panamanian gun-running to the Sandinistas as a conservative diversionary tactic. This was despite evidence gathered by U.S. Customs agents that the head of Panama's intelligence service, General Manuel Noriega, faced potential indictment for the illegal export of arms.[31] Determined to pass the treaty legislation, administration officials apparently downplayed the evidence before members of Congress.

The Merchant Marines Panama Canal Subcommittee held two days of hearings on the gun-running charges in early June 1979, one week before the implementing legislation was scheduled for the House floor. Murphy attended the hearings briefly, saying that the smuggling issue raised "a serious question" about the future intentions of the Panamanian government in Central America.[32] According to a senior administration official, his appearance violated a January 1979 agreement between Murphy and President Carter not to link the Panamanian and Nicaraguan issues.

By acceding to efforts to link Panama and the Nicaraguan insurrection, Murphy leveraged a reluctant administration into endorsing his version of the Panama Canal implementing legislation. The bill that reached the House floor in June 1979 was Murphy's, and it passed the House by a comfortable 20-vote margin. Nicaragua had been a sideshow, but one that allowed a powerful committee chairman to put his stamp on a major policy initiative of the Carter administration.

Obtaining approval of the Canal legislation had absorbed the administration in its efforts with Congress for almost six full months. By June 1979, however, the fighting in Nicaragua had engulfed the entire country. According to one State Department official serving in the U.S. embassy in Managua at the time, "once the fighting spread to Managua in June, it was apparent there would be a total military defeat."[33]

In the middle of that crisis-ridden month, a few members of Congress called on the administration to recognize the inevitability of Somoza's downfall, in the hopes that a negotiated solution could still be achieved. Calling Somoza the "principal impediment to a political settlement," Senators Zorinsky, Lugar, McGovern, Kennedy, and Church asked Carter to "support those nations seeking his removal from power."[34] Three days later, in a speech before the Organization of American States, Secretary of State Cyrus Vance called for "the replacement of the present government [of Nicaragua] with a transitional government of national reconciliation."[35] The OAS subsequent adopted a resolution calling for the "immediate and definitive replacement" of the Somoza regime.[36] On the basis of the OAS resolution, U.S. envoy Lawrence Pezzullo headed for Managua to deliver an ultimatum to Somoza to leave office. The administration, reactively and forced by circumstance, had concluded that Somoza's prompt resignation was the only hope for staving off total military defeat.

Somoza's congressional backers, however, rallied behind him. When Pezzullo arrived for his first meeting with the Nicaraguan leader, Representative Murphy sat at Somoza's side. When Somoza left the room for consultations with his foreign minister, Murphy went with them. Several days after Murphy's return to Washington, Representatives Hansen and McDonald traveled to Managua to promise Somoza they would fight for a restoration of U.S. military aid.[37]

Neither congressional conservatives nor Somoza could stave off the National Guard's deteriorating military situation in July 1979. The initiative in Congress shifted back to the liberals, who sought to make the administration come to terms with a new government before Somoza's total overthrow. "Somoza will lose militarily because he has lost politically," said Senator Zorinsky. He urged the administration to "recognize the provisional government formed by the forces opposing the Somoza regime."[38]

On July 19, 1979, two days after Somoza finally left Nicaragua, Sandinista forces entered Managua. U.S. policy had tried and failed to prevent a Sandinista victory by force of arms. In retrospect, it appears that conservatives in Congress contributed to that failure by nourishing Somoza's illusion that he could stay in power long after he had lost the allegiance of his own people. Ultimately, some of the biggest losers were nonguerrilla forces, whose share of power diminished in the wake of a Sandinista military victory.

Congress and the Post-Somoza Order

Just as the Cuban revolution in 1959 had prompted sweeping changes in Kennedy administration policy toward Latin America, the Nicaraguan revolution triggered a deep caution within the Carter administration in dealing with turmoil elsewhere in Central America. In testimony that reflected the emerging regional perspective of the Carter administration, Assistant Secretary of State Viron Vaky told a House subcommittee in September: "Much of Central America, particularly the northern tier, is gripped by a polarizing, dynamic pressure for change, alienations and frustrations, violence, terrorism, and potential radicalization. . . . The central issue, in turn, is not whether change is to occur but whether that change is to be violent and radical, or peaceful and evolutionary, and preserving individual rights and democratic values."[39] The belief that the United States could control the velocity and direction of change in Central America underlay the Carter administration's two most important Central American initiatives after the Nicaraguan revolution: the decision to supply aid to the new Sandinista government, in an attempt to stave off its further radicalization, and a decision to provide military aid to the new Salvadoran government that emerged from an October 1979 military coup. Both initiatives depended on aid funds approved by Congress and provoked bitter struggles in the Congress over the U.S. response to revolution, and the means for fostering improvements in human rights. In 1980, El Salvador and Nicaragua became intimately entangled, not only in the minds of an administration confronting revolution, but also in the Congress, which threw obstacles in the administration's path at virtually every turn.

In the fall of 1979, the Carter administration moved quickly to befriend the new Sandinista government and immediately transfer small amounts of emergency aid. The attitude was, in the words of a senior policymaker, "The Sandinistas are in; the worst case has been realized; OK, now what do we do?"[40] The administration decided that the only viable option was to gamble on influencing the course of the Nicaraguan revolution, in the hope of preventing the consolidation of a Cuban-style regime with military and economic ties to the Soviet bloc. This meant bolstering non-Sandinista elements within the anti-Somoza coalition—the private sector, the Church, the independent press—in the hope that the reality of a war-devastated economy would force economic and political pragmatism on the Sandinistas. In the words of a senior U.S. diplomat in the region at the time, "The Sandinista movement does not represent a majority movement in Nicaragua. They had support because there was a consensus that Somoza should go. . . . Other elements deserve to be heard and survive."[41]

In the months after the Sandinista victory, Carter administration testimony before Congress was replete with the language of opportunity and risk-taking. "We recognize," Deputy Secretary of State Warren Christopher told a House subcommittee in September 1979, "that some elements of the present [Nicaraguan] Government might prefer a closed, Marxist society. . . . But the situation in Nicaragua remains fluid. The moderate outcome we seek will not come about if we walk away now. Precisely because others are assisting Nicaragua and may seek to exploit the situation there, we must not turn our backs."[42] Secretary of State Cyrus Vance summed up the "gamble" theme in a September speech: "We cannot guarantee that democracy will take hold there. But if we turn our backs on Nicaragua, we can almost guarantee that democracy will fail."[43]

President Carter sent a request for the Special Central American and Caribbean Security Assistance Act to Congress on November 9, 1979. The package included $75 million in economic aid for Nicaragua and small amounts of aid for other Central American and Caribbean countries. Of the $75 million for Nicaragua, 60 percent was to go to the private sector. The president urged "rapid congressional action" on the bill.[44]

But congressional action was anything but rapid. Over the next eleven months, conservatives mainly in the House waged a protracted battle to kill the Nicaragua funds. The tactics they used—amendments, delays, procedural skirmishes— were the standard measures available to Congress for opposing or modifying administration policy and were similar to those employed later by liberal opponents of the Reagan administration's Central America policy. The Carter administration resisted the interference, raising a key issue in congressional-executive foreign policy struggles that transcends individual administrations: Who controls? "The President needs the power to act," complained former U.S. Ambassador to Nicaragua Lawrence Pezzullo. "Once we made the decision in the fall of '79 to give the aid, we should have had the money in January."* In fact, the administration only had the money in September, long after its symbolic importance as a gesture of U.S. friendship had faded.

A majority of conservatives in the U.S. Congress viewed Nicaragua as already "lost" to communism and not worth a penny of taxpayers' assistance. Representative Robert Lagomarsino (R-Calif.) summed up the view when he said following a Foreign Affairs Committee trip to Managua, "If it looks like a Cuba, and walks like a Cuba, and quacks like a Cuba," "[then] like a duck, it is probably a Cuba."[45] Similarly, Senator Richard Stone (D-Fla.) said that assurances by Nicaraguan junta members that the government did not plan to ship weapons to Salvadoran guerrillas contradicted reports from intelligence sources. "I'm afraid I still have my doubts," Stone stated, "and I think we should check carefully on what happens down there before we commit ourselves too heavily."[46] In this climate of distrust, conservatives seized on actions of the Nicaraguan government that underscored their suspicions about its intentions and direction.

Reservations in the Congress about aiding the Sandinistas were reinforced by world events. The seizure of U.S. hostages in Teheran in November 1979 and the Soviet invasion of Afghanistan in December underscored apparent U.S. impotence in dealing with Third World revolutionary regimes and misjudgments of Soviet political and military intentions. President Carter seemed at best naive, at worst, weak and indecisive in dealing with forces hostile to the United States.

The hostage crisis and Soviet intervention in Afghanistan became deeply domestic U.S. events, as did the "discovery" of a Soviet "combat brigade" in Cuba.[47] Republicans turned the developments into an election-year slam, railing against a Democratic Party that was leading the U.S. into decline as a world

*Interview, New York, New York, November 7, 1986. Vice-President Walter Mondale expressed similar frustration. He complained on January 20, 1981: "I think one of the most grievous inadequacies of our present system is that the president of the United States, who has to conduct foreign policy, is left enfeebled in terms of . . . crucial foreign aid and military assistance. I could give you a hundred examples. It took us a year to get the little help we got in Nicaragua. . . . For crying out loud, let a president govern." Quoted in Murrey Marder, "Hill Fights Reagan for Soul of Foreign Policy," *Washington Post*, September 2, 1984.

power. Public rhetoric by both the administration and its opponents became tougher and more bellicose as national security issues became prominent in the campaign.

Such a climate shifted the debate over Nicaragua perceptibly to the right. Fears of a "second Cuba" and of Cuban and Soviet intervention in the region came to dominate public discourse on Central America. The determination to prevent "another Nicaragua" in El Salvador became not only national security obsession but domestic political necessity. "The domino theory lives," said Ambassador to Nicaragua Lawrence Pezzullo, "and Carter is using it to advantage. No President wants to lose something to communism during his watch."[48]

The House debate over aid to Nicaragua became, in fact, a referendum on whether or not members believed Nicaragua already was another Cuba. In the words of Representative Robert Bauman (R-Md.), a leading aid opponent, U.S. assistance "to keep [the Nicaraguan government] from turning communistic will fail because they already have a Communist government and they are dominated by Communists trained in Cuba. . . . This $75 million aid program . . . will brand the United States a 'patsy' in the eyes of the world."[49] Bauman and Edwin Derwinski (R-Ill.) persuaded the House on February 25 to go into a secret session—for only the second time in 150 years—to hear evidence of Cuban and Soviet-bloc involvement in Nicaragua.[50]

Only after four days of emotional debate did it begin to appear that the Carter administration had the votes to succeed in the House. In one of the most significant speeches of the moment, conservative Representative Henry Hyde, later a fierce proponent of contra aid, expressed his support for the aid package. "I want to try to put my foot in the door, if possible," Hyde said. "There is a Catholic church down there. There is a private sector, however beleaguered. There is a press, more or less free. I want to nurture those things, not extinguish them."[51]

In contrast to the wide 21-vote margin by which Nicaragua assistance passed in the Senate, the House passed the authorization bill 202–197, a narrow margin of only 5 votes. And this was only after House conservatives attached a series of amendments tying U.S. aid to the political evolution of the Sandinista government. The amendments required the executive branch to withhold assistance until the president issued a certification that the Sandinistas were not supporting terrorism in other countries nor violating human rights or free speech and labor union rights.[52] Senator Edward Zorinsky, a leading supporter of aid to Nicaragua, found the conditions so compromising of the administration's intent that he called the House bill a "legislative wreck."[53]

Given the depth of congressional suspicion of Nicaragua from the outset, and the precarious support for foreign aid in an election year, it may be remarkable that the assistance package survived votes in both houses at all. Equally noteworthy, moreover, is that the House vote was so close when the Nicaraguan junta exhibited its most pluralistic tendencies. By the time the aid bill passed Congress, no members of the government junta had resigned in protest over Sandinista policy, as occurred in later years. At least two delegations of prominent Nicaraguan businessmen had visited Washington, in October 1979 and February 1980, to lobby for the aid package.* "We are part of this revolution," insisted Enrique Dreyfus, a leading member of the Superior Council of Private Enterprise. "Our revolution has nothing to do with Cuba."[54]

The subsequent course of the Nicaraguan revolution led many congressional conservatives to feel vindicated for their reluctance to support the Sandinistas. At the time that the votes were taken, however, non-Sandinistas wanted the aid as badly as the government, in order to bolster their political position vis-à-vis the Sandinistas. Some conservatives in the Congress would even justify their later support for antigovernment rebels in Nicaragua on the basis of Sandinista "betrayal" of the original democratic commitments of the revolution; in fact, some of those most vociferous on the "betrayal" theme had never been willing to support non-Sandinista elements while there may still have been a reasonable chance of their survival.†

Following the House and Senate votes in early 1980, the $75 million aid proposal ran into an obstacle exogenous to the Central America policy debate.

---

*Of the seven members of the executive board of the Superior Council of Private Enterprise (COSEP) who arrived to lobby in Washington, three later became fierce opponents of the Sandinista government. One, Jorge Salazar, was killed by Sandinista security forces in November 1980. Another, Enrique Dreyfus, was jailed by the Sandinistas in October 1981 for signing a COSEP document denouncing government economic policies. A third, José Francisco Cardenal, became an organizer of the UDN-FARN (Nicaragua Democratic Union—Armed Forces of the Nicaraguan Revolution), one of the first armed groups fighting Sandinista rule.

†In voting to continue contra aid in mid-1983, for example, eight Foreign Affairs Committee Republicans claimed that "the Carter Administration and Congress tried very hard to develop a normal and mutually satisfactory relationship with Nicaragua. Not only did the United States immediately recognize the Sandinista Government, but it also followed that recognition with over $120 million in assistance."

Of the eight signers of the statement, four (Gilman, Lagomarsino, Roth, and Solomon) had voted against the $75 million aid package. Three (Winn, Hyde, and Bereuter) voted for it. An eighth (Siljander) had not been elected to Congress in 1980. U.S. Congress, House, Committee on Foreign Affairs, Report, *Amendment to the Intelligence Authorization Act for Fiscal Year 1983*, June 14, 1983, 98th Cong., 1st Sess., pp. 15–18.

In March, Senate Budget Committee Chairman Edmund Muskie (D-Maine) reported that Congress had already exceeded a spending ceiling established by the Fiscal Year 1980 budget. This eliminated the chance to include an aid appropriation for Nicaragua.[55] As the administration had feared, delaying the appropriation of the funds for Nicaraguan assistance allowed opponents greater opportunity to attempt to defeat the funding.

The reaction in Nicaragua to U.S. budgetary constraints was swift and even paranoid. Despite Ambassador Pezzullo's attempts to explain the budget technicalities to the Sandinista government, some Nicaraguan officials saw dire plots. "It is obvious that this imperialist attitude," said the government-controlled Radio Sandino, "is another maneuver by the most reactionary U.S. sectors which are trying to destabilize our revolutionary process." The secretary general of the Sandinista Farmworkers' Association charged the "beginning of an economic blockade."[56] As difficulties began to mount in Nicaragua, problems as diverse as capital flight and factory takeovers were viewed as a U.S. conspiracy. The uneasy friendship with the United States began to disintegrate into open hostility.

El Salvador

With the Nicaraguan revolution, interest in El Salvador grew beyond a small circle of liberals concerned with human rights. And with the growing interest, the nature of congressional concerns changed. What had been the one objective of congressional policy—the promotion of human rights—expanded to include the promotion of human rights within a context of maintaining internal stability. The rapid polarization and escalating violence in El Salvador following the coup on October 15, 1979, and the collapse of two governing coalitions within less than three months, raised fundamental questions about the government's ability to survive at all.

In the view of the Carter administration, "a takeover of El Salvador by the extreme left was unacceptable to the United States," even though U.S. Ambassador to El Salvador Robert White believed that the threat to the Salvadoran government "came much more from the extreme right with its killings and bombings than from the left."[57] Like the Carter administration, members of Congress feared a second revolutionary situation in Central America. Two overriding considerations, according to New York Democrat Mario Biaggi, were "our efforts to promote and protect basic human rights, and our efforts to prevent the threat of a Communist takeover in our own backyard."[58] As the two objectives became increasingly contradictory, Congress, like the Carter and subsequent Reagan administrations, would opt first for the preservation of order.

The $5.7 Million Reprogramming

Congressional attention to El Salvador in 1980 began, as it would end that year, with spectacular murders underscoring the problem of political violence.

On March 25, 1980, a line of hushed individuals snaked down the narrow corridors outside H-308 in the Capitol, where a key subcommittee was to begin hearings on a $5.7 million military aid request for El Salvador.[59] The mood was unusually somber, even stunned. Less than twenty-four hours before, the archbishop of San Salvador, Oscar Arnulfo Romero, had been gunned down in a hospital chapel while saying a funeral mass. The assassination represented a new peak in political violence that had already taken thousands of lives since October 1979, when a military coup deposed the regime of General Carlos Humberto Romero and installed a junta with civilian participation.

The archbishop had been an outspoken opponent of U.S. military aid to the new Salvadoran junta and had pleaded with President Carter not to send aid or advisers when reports of both surfaced in the U.S. press.[60] In a letter read during a Sunday homily in San Salvador's Metropolitan Cathedral, Romero stated that new aid would "without doubt sharpen the injustice and repression against the organizations of the people" and claimed that previous nonlethal aid had allowed the security forces to "repress the people even more violently, using lethal weapons."[61] Romero's death provoked an outpouring of indignation, with members from across the political spectrum denouncing the killing and calling for punishment of those responsible.

More than anything, however, the archbishop's death brought into sharp relief the relationship between U.S. military assistance and violence in El Salvador. On the one hand, the Carter administration argued that his death was an example of the kind of extremist violence U.S. aid was intended to stop. On the other hand, the U.S. church community saw Romero's martyrdom, and his opposition to military aid, as justification for not approving the reprogramming request. The churches mobilized to an unprecedented degree around the issue of military aid.

Underneath the raw emotion key policy questions remained. Who was responsible for the massive killing, and what should the proper U.S. relationship be with Salvadoran government forces? Even if Salvadoran government troops were involved in the repression, what, if anything, should be done to help them cope with right-wing attempts at destabilization and an acknowledged threat from the left? Were there elements in the army truly committed to reform and an end to past human rights abuses? The vote on the $5.7 million reprogramming thus shaped up as a fundamental test: of the Carter administration's credibility in promoting a Central America policy based on socioeconomic reform and human rights, and of the Congress's ability to make judgments independent of the administration, consistent with its prior emphasis on distancing the U.S. from regimes engaged in gross abuses of human rights.

The reprogramming of $5.7 million in nonlethal military aid for the Salvadoran army was a small sum of money, hardly decisive in any military sense but symbolic of U.S. support for the armed forces. Critics of the aid charged that "it would legitimate what has become dictatorial violence" and that political power in El Salvador lay "with old-line military leaders in government positions who practice a policy of 'reform with repression.'" A prominent Catholic spokesman insisted that "any military aid you send to El Salvador . . . ends up in the hands of the military and paramilitary rightist groups who are themselves at the root of the problems of the country."[62]

Protestant and Catholic church organizations overwhelmed congressional offices with letters, telegrams, and visits. They had one message: stop military aid.

Carter administration officials countered by arguing that the Salvadoran junta offered "the best chance for social change, political liberalization and respect for human rights in El Salvador." A Pentagon spokesman claimed that the aid would "help strengthen the army's key role in reforms," adding that the conflict was becoming regionalized as weapons reached the Salvadoran guerrillas through Honduras, with Cuban support.[63]

Given such starkly opposing viewpoints, how did the administration prevail over the predominantly liberal subcommittee? Several factors explain the decision to approve the reprogramming one week later.

First, the administration was able to demonstrate to subcommittee liberals that it shared their concern over repression. A summary of cables provided to the subcommittee from the U.S. embassy in San Salvador established that "the Ambassador is concerned over acts of repression caused by elements within the various El Salvador forces" and that "the embassy sees acts of violence from the right as more of a threat than those of the left."[64]

Adding to evidence in the cable traffic was the personal credibility of key administration policymakers. Ambassador White, who arrived in El Salvador only weeks before the subcommittee hearing, had gained a reputation as a tough human rights advocate during a previous stint in Paraguay. In a telegram read aloud on the day of the subcommittee vote, White assured undecided members that "there is no military solution to the problems of El Salvador" and that "as this government establishes its bona fides among the people, the human rights record of the armed forces will improve and incidents of excessive use of force to restore order will end."[65] Another Carter administration official, Deputy Assistant Secretary of State James Cheek, had served on the staff of subcommittee liberal Representative David Obey (D-Wisc.). Cheek converted Obey into one of the leading supporters of the aid on the subcommittee.

Second, the executive branch's superior access to intelligence gave them an advantage in manipulating policy statements to fit policy goals. Administration witnesses revealed information that supported their decision to grant military aid, while suppressing, or at least underplaying, facts that contradicted their position.

Central to the administration's argument, for example, was a characterization of the violence in El Salvador. According to Deputy Assistant Secretary of State for Inter-American Affairs John A. Bushnell, "Much of this violence is the result of attacks from the extreme right and the extreme left . . . some members of the military, individual officers, have been involved. . . . But it is not government-directed violence."[66]

A private assessment by Bushnell less than two weeks earlier, however, painted a different picture. A key U.S. policy objective, Bushnell wrote to the Secretary of State, was the "elimination of repression emanating from the armed forces, particularly the security forces (police and national guard) which are the greatest offenders."[67] According to a later study by a House intelligence subcommittee, moreover, little was known about violence by Salvadoran government and right-wing forces at the time: "relatively more is known," the report said, "about the organization and whereabouts of the insurgents . . . than about the circumstances or lines of authority resulting in abductions of alleged leftist sympathizers or in the depositing of bodies along Salvadoran highways during curfew hours."[68]

Third, while liberals on the Foreign Operations Subcommittee deplored the violence in El Salvador, they feared the alternative if the U.S. did nothing. "We have seen in other countries," said Representative William Lehman (D-Fla.), "that one form of violence, repression, tyranny, can too often be succeeded by even worse violence and repression and tyranny. . . . I dread the alternative that can come out of the left." Similarly, Representative Matthew McHugh (D-N.Y.) argued that "if this junta fails, the repressive elements of the government will be in control; that will be followed by a civil war, and I do not see how that benefits the El Salvadoran people." The lack of an attractive policy alternative in El Salvador paralyzed the Congress under the Carter as well as the Reagan administrations.

Finally, the administration's policy of support for the Nicaraguan government added to its credibility with liberals. "I do not see how we can, with a straight face, go to the floor," said Obey, "and suggest we ought to take a chance on affecting the conduct of a left-wing government in Nicaragua, if we are not willing to also take a chance on our policy in El Salvador."[69]

On a roll-call vote, which subcommittee member McHugh described as one of the most agonizing of his career, the panel approved the reprogramming, 6–3.

Aid to Nicaragua: The Deepening Struggle

Following the subcommittee vote to approve Salvador aid, Congress renewed its attention to Nicaraguan assistance. During the spring and early summer of 1980, the debate became deeply enmeshed with the evolution of Nicaraguan internal politics. Congressional opponents of aid capitalized on a series of Nicaraguan government crises—including the closing of *La Prensa* and changes in the composition of the Council of State that reinforced Sandinista power—to buttress their initial conclusion that Nicaragua was a communist government. That criticism was offset somewhat when a shake-up of the governing junta brought middle-of-the-road, non-Sandinista politicians into Washington's political scene. Arturo Cruz, a respected former international banker and Washington resident, made his debut with Congress in lobbying on Nicaragua's behalf for the aid package. When Cruz left the government and subsequently joined the contras, political allegiances he had developed eased the way for contra aid.

Doubts about the direction of the Nicaraguan revolution coalesced around a March 1980 trip by four high-ranking Sandinista leaders to the Soviet Union and Eastern bloc countries. In a joint communiqué published in *Pravda*, Nicaraguan leaders including Interior Minister Tomás Borge, junta member Moisés Hassan, and Defense Minister Humberto Ortega followed the Soviet lead on virtually every international issue, departing from a stated adherence to positions of the group of nonaligned nations. The condemnation of the U.S. "imperialist policy of interference" in Latin America did little to advance the Sandinistas' case in Washington.* Given deep-rooted suspicions of the Sandi-

---

*The communiqué, for example, "condemn[ed] the campaign of mounting international nista revolutionaries, any evidence of their "real" intentions reinforced inclinations to fear the worst. And the "worst case" scenario in Nicaragua involved any indication that, like Cuba, the government was aligning itself with the Soviet bloc and moving internally toward totalitarianism.

The mid-April resignations of Nicaraguan junta members Alfonso Robelo and Violeta Chamorro added to congressional fears about the revolution's course. Robelo signaled Congress that he continued to support the $75 million aid package, but considerable doubts about the government's direction remained. * Three members of Congress who had voted for aid to Nicaragua in February—Richard Cheney (R-Wyo.), Robin Beard (D-Tenn.), and Thomas Evans (R-Del.)—announced their decision to oppose funds for Nicaragua on subsequent votes, promising to vote against an upcoming, and normally routine, procedural motion to send the Nicaragua aid authorization bill to conference with the Senate.[70] Given the narrow 5-vote margin by which the aid had passed in February, the House leadership postponed the scheduled vote.

In an attempt to reassure undecided or skeptical members, Speaker O'Neill said that he wanted proof that Nicaragua was "worth trying to save." In angry reply, Sandinista leader Bayardo Arce wrote O'Neill rejecting "any pressures or interference" in Nicaragua's internal affairs.[71]

The substitution on the Nicaraguan junta of two moderates saved the prospects for aid in the United States. One, Rafael Córdova Rivas, was a member of Nicaragua's Conservative Party, the traditional opposition to Somoza and a cradle of the private sector. Another, Arturo Cruz, had been a member of the civic opposition's Group of Twelve during the fight against Somoza, and had first served in the new Sandinista government as director of the Central Bank.

---

tension in connection with the events in Afghanistan" and denounced the "threats, blackmail and provocations . . . against the Socialist Republic of Vietnam." "The USSR and Nicaragua," it said, "resolutely condemn the imperialist policy of interference in the internal affairs of the peoples of Latin America." The full text of the communiqué was inserted into the *Congressional Record* by Senator Jesse Helms, May 19, 1980, p. 11671. See also Terri Shaw, "Tour by Nicaraguans Strengthens Ties with Soviet Bloc," *Washington Post*, April 13, 1980.

*Following his April 21, 1980, resignation, Robelo told Americans for Democratic Action lobbyist Bruce Cameron that "in the political parlance of your country, Nicaragua is not a 'lost country.' . . . The aid package is still badly needed by my country and in the best interests of your country." In May Robelo sent a telegram to Representative Paul Simon (D-Ill.) and others stating, "Although I have political differences with the present government junta as a Nicaraguan politician fighting for democracy in my country I believe the approval of the aid package is essential for the future of a free Nicaragua and the relations between our countries."

Most important for the congressional debate, Cruz knew and understood Washington. He had lived in its suburbs for more than a decade while an economist for the Inter-American Development Bank. The appointment of Cruz and Córdova Rivas helped to calm fears in Washington that the government was sliding inexorably to the left and gave leading aid proponents the political capital with which to wage their fight.

In June 1980, Cruz came to Washington under the auspices of the Council of the Americas, a private-sector group representing U.S. firms with investments in Latin America. By then, in an action indicative of the political climate, the House had voted overwhelmingly to eliminate a small amount of military aid for Nicaragua from the foreign aid bill. Cruz arrived in Washington one day before another scheduled vote to strip economic aid to Nicaragua from the aid legislation. He met with dozens of members, including Majority Leader Jim Wright and Speaker O'Neill. "It all hung on this World Banker," recalled a top aide to House Speaker O'Neill.[72] Cruz's lobbying turned the House around.

Cruz's credibility was intimately linked to members' expectations about political evolution in Nicaragua and to their exaggerated faith that U.S. aid could produce a desired, moderate outcome. Informing his colleagues that President Carter had asked him to lead a delegation to Nicaragua that weekend, Wright pleaded with the House:

> Let me have the tools by which I can say to the people in Nicaragua: "the people of the United States have not deserted you. We haven't given you up for lost. We do want to work with you. We do expect you to establish free political institutions. We expect you to have regular, free, and orderly elections. We want you to respect private property and want you to respect human rights. . . ." I would have no credibility at all going to Nicaragua . . . if I were speaking for a Congress . . . which had just for the second time in 2 weeks publicly asserted its disdain for the Government and the people of Nicaragua. . . . Let me, I appeal to you, have the tools by which I can help salvage their friendship.

Speaker O'Neill gave the closing speech before the vote on aid for Nicaragua, the first time in close to twenty-eight years that he had spoken on a foreign aid amendment. Cruz had assured him, he said, "that Nicaragua desires a democracy and a productive economy" and that Nicaragua did not wish "to aline [sic] itself with the Soviet Union and with Cuba." Cruz's appointment to the junta, O'Neill concluded, "indicates a willingness by the leaders of Nicaragua to chart a course of political moderation and pluralism."[73]

In an overwhelming and surprising show of support, the House voted for the aid, 243–144. The 99-vote margin was the widest for any vote on aid to a Central American country during the Carter or upcoming Reagan administrations.[74]

Wright's and O'Neill's speeches highlighted what had become perhaps the central feature of the aid debate in Congress: the conditionality of U.S. support on a particular political outcome in Nicaragua. The Carter administration had wanted to reinforce the private sector in Nicaragua and to use its participation in the post-Somoza order as evidence that the revolution was worth supporting. The gamble to maintain pluralism in Nicaragua became the sole justification for providing aid, leading aid supporters to feel that they had a stake in the government's future direction. As the Sandinista government moved leftward, and key moderates resigned their government posts, congressional liberals and moderates felt betrayed. They had devised their own political imperative, as well as preference, to fight for a democratic outcome in Nicaragua.

As he had promised, Wright visited Nicaragua the weekend after the House vote.[75] At a farewell reception held for his delegation on the top floor of the Intercontinental Hotel in Managua, he addressed his hosts in perfect Spanish. He stated that he didn't know whether Nicaragua would be the country Pedro Joaquín Chamorro had envisioned. Then, referring to Chamorro's three sons, whose political views spanned the political spectrum, Wright expressed his hope for a Nicaragua "for all of the Chamorro brothers," a Nicaragua where there were "no winners and no losers" in the struggle for power.

Upon returning to Washington from Managua, Wright covered all fronts in what had become a personal crusade for the assistance. Attempts to defeat aid for Fiscal Year 1981 had been beaten back, but Carter's original request for $75 million had still not been appropriated. Wright reported to the president that the money had taken on "enormous symbolic importance" and that "everyone with whom we talked . . . considers it potentially decisive in shaping the future of U.S.-Nicaraguan relations." In a message to his Texas constituents, Wright played up the strategic importance of aiding Nicaragua, calling it "the focal point of a hemispheric struggle between Marxism and freedom." Wright assured his colleagues in the House that "the direction of the new Government in Nicaragua is still to be determined." The U.S., he said, had "done the right thing" in approving aid to Nicaragua.[76]

As the months stretched toward November, however, election year antipathy to foreign aid in an era of domestic fiscal restraint further saddled the Nicaragua request. Over the opposition of the chairman of the House Appropriations Committee, the Nicaragua package was incorporated into a supplemental funding bill for 1980. The Nicaragua appropriation ultimately survived, but this time by the narrowest of margins. Late in the evening of July 2, the House voted 199–197 to incorporate the foreign aid appropriation into the supplemental. The Nicaragua aid funds had weathered seven months of congressional combat, but the fight was far from over.

El Salvador and Nicaragua: The Crises Mesh

As finally approved by Congress, the Nicaragua assistance package required the president before disbursing aid to certify that Nicaragua was not "aiding, abetting, or supporting acts of violence or terrorism in other countries." Those in Congress who had sponsored the amendment assumed that Nicaragua, like Cuba in the early days of its revolution, would promote guerrilla activity in neighboring states. The amendment forced the administration to address an issue that conservatives thought Carter was ignoring.

Within the administration there did appear to be a struggle over the extent of Nicaraguan support for rebels in El Salvador. Indications of an internal debate over the certification emerged in early August, when conservative columnists Rowland Evans and Robert Novak reported that "two convoys of ships carrying Soviet arms from Cuba" had been unloaded in Nicaragua. The arms were part of a "growing arms cache" to be used "in the coming battle for El Salvador." The column cited "intelligence officials" as the source for the leak.[77] According to administration supporters of Carter's policy, the leak was an attempt by conservatives within the intelligence community and Defense Department to block the $75 million loan.[78] Senator Zorinsky, chairman of the Senate Western Hemisphere Subcommittee, wrote Carter asking him to resist the pressures based on "half truths, rumors, and unverified reports."[79]

Signature of the Nicaragua loan had been scheduled for early August. But amid the new political heat, Carter ordered a precertification review of available intelligence on Nicaraguan support for the Salvadoran guerrillas. The State Department submitted its assessment to Carter on August 23, finding that the evidence did not support the accusations against the Sandinistas.

In fact, according to a House intelligence subcommittee almost two years later, the intelligence community had "reached, and communicated quite clearly, a view that did not support the Administration's position." The CIA, according to the House subcommittee, found a "very high likelihood" that training and weapons support for the Salvadoran insurgents was occurring and "represent[ed] official FSLN policy."[80]

Not to certify would have prohibited the Carter administration from aiding the Nicaraguan government. After close to a year of work to gain congressional approval of the funds, the administration still believed the basis for its policy was sound. It therefore opted to comply with congressional restrictions by adopting its own standards of proof of Nicaraguan complicity in supporting the Salvadoran rebels. According to Carter's NSC Latin America aide Robert Pastor, the administration required conclusive *proof* of the reliability of reports received by the intelligence community, and evidence of Nicaraguan *government* involvement.[81] Finding neither, Carter certified on September 12, 1980.

Conservatives denounced the certification and demanded hearings, but congressional action could not change the certification. Once Congress had granted the administration authority to make its own determination about Nicaraguan arms shipments, there was little that opponents in Congress could do but yell. The objections raised by conservatives may have prompted the administration to be more forceful in conveying U.S. concerns to the Nicaraguans about support for Salvadoran guerrillas: two U.S. officials, including Ambassador Pezzullo, were instructed to meet with Nicaraguan leaders to stress that involvement with the Salvadoran insurgency meant the end of U.S. assistance.[82] The Nicaraguan government, as it would continue to do for the next several years, denied all such complicity.

During the final months of 1980, events in Central America and policy changes by the Carter administration spun out of the control of Congress. Moreover, political events in the United States—the landslide victory of Ronald Reagan as president on November 4, 1980, and the election of a Republican-controlled Senate for the first time since 1952—created a new context for future Central America debates.

Policy speeches by candidate Reagan illustrated how widely his approach to the problems of Central America differed from the Carter administration's. In March 1980 he had asked rhetorically, "Must we let Grenada, Nicaragua, El Salvador, all become additional 'Cubas,' new outposts for Soviet combat brigades? Will the next push of the Moscow-Havana axis be northward to Guatemala and thence to Mexico, and south to Costa Rica and Panama?"[83] Later in the year the Republican platform had "deplore[d] the Marxist Sandinista takeover of Nicaragua and the Marxist attempts to destabilize El Salvador, Guatemala, and Honduras." The platform opposed the Carter administration aid program for Nicaragua and foreshadowed subsequent efforts to overturn the Sandinista regime. "We will support the efforts of the Nicaraguan people," the Republicans said, "to establish a free and independent government."[84]

Reagan's tough rhetoric repudiated the Carter administration's attempt to work with or attempt to control the forces of change in the region. Reagan and his supporters also promised all-out efforts to combat Marxism in the hemisphere, without the encumbrance of soft-headed humanitarianism or illusions about the aims of the traditional adversaries of the United States. As a consequence, political actors in the region began to base their conduct within weeks of the U.S. elections on a reading of prospective U.S. policies; those actions, in turn, shaped future U.S. policy responses.

In El Salvador, for example, the actions of right-wing leaders and army officers seemed to indicate that they had revised their assessment of what the United States would tolerate in the name of fighting communism. On November 27, six leaders of the political opposition were abducted from a press conference and brutally murdered. Circumstances suggested the complicity of government security forces. Then, on December 2, Salvadoran security forces abducted four U.S. churchwomen living in El Salvador, whose work with the poor made them suspect as rebel sympathizers. The nuns' bodies were found in a shallow common grave two days later.

The killings brought home to the American public the brutality of Salvadoran government troops. No other event would dominate U.S. considerations of El Salvador policy over the next several years than what came to be called "the nuns' case." By mid-January, more Americans had been added to the roster of the dead. A free-lance journalist, John Sullivan, disappeared from a San Salvador hotel. Two U.S. labor advisers were riddled with bullets as they dined in the Sheraton Hotel with the head of the Salvadoran agrarian reform agency.

In Nicaragua, Reagan's election apparently helped to resolve a long-standing debate within the Sandinista directorate over aid to revolutionaries elsewhere in Central America, particularly El Salvador. According to published accounts of a *Washington Post* reporter and a former Sandinista foreign policy aide, the Sandinista leaders believed that the new administration would seek to undermine their revolution regardless of the conduct of the government. There was no reward for restraint.[85] In the view that prevailed, according to these accounts, the best—and perhaps only—defense of the Sandinista revolution involved creating diversions for the United States elsewhere in Central America. Weapons that had been stockpiled in Nicaragua over a period of several months were shipped out with a vengeance.

The Nicaraguan decision dovetailed with an assessment by the Salvadoran guerrillas that their country was ripe for insurrection. The blood-soaked history of 1980, culminating with the prominent murders of November and December, reinforced that conclusion. Guerrilla leaders surmised that they had one chance to seize power rapidly, before the incoming Reagan administration could consolidate and react. On January 10, 1981, in the waning days of Carter's presidency, the rebels launched what they called the "final offensive." They believed, erroneously, that a lame-duck president in Washington meant a vacuum of power in the nation's capital and an incapacity to mount a response.

The Carter administration moved swiftly to counter the Salvadoran guerrilla offensive as well as what was by now convincing evidence of Nicaraguan arms shipments. Military aid to El Salvador, suspended after the murder of the U.S. churchwomen, was reinstated on January 14, 1981, and then increased on January 17, with a pledge to "support the Salvadoran Government in its struggle against left-wing terrorism supported covertly . . . by Cuba and other Communist nations."[86] Carter used a special discretionary foreign aid account to transfer the funds without congressional review. For the first time since 1977, the aid included lethal weapons.

The Carter administration then cited evidence of Nicaraguan complicity in aiding the rebels and suspended outstanding portions of the $75 million aid package.[87] U.S. Ambassador to El Salvador Robert White dramatized the charges, stating that "approximately 100 men landed from Nicaragua" on Salvadoran shores.[88] White retracted the statement four months later, but he effectively silenced congressional critics. They could no longer oppose military aid on human rights grounds when there was evidence of external intervention in the Salvadoran war.

Thus, even before Ronald Reagan took office, essential threads of his policy were put in place by Carter: charges of foreign involvement in El Salvador's conflict, the suspension of economic assistance to Nicaragua, and the renewal of lethal military aid to a Salvadoran government facing an insurgent threat.

It would be a mistake, however, to exaggerate the continuity between two administrations. Reagan's abandonment of human rights issues in dealing with Central America, his determination to overthrow rather than shape the course of the Nicaraguan revolution, and his underplaying of the need to curb right-wing extremism and promote social reform were departures from the Carter policy. They formed integral components of a new approach aimed at combating perceived Soviet gains in the Third World and reasserting U.S. global power.

In many ways, the years 1976 through 1980 show that both Congress and two successive administrations failed to construct a new set of foreign policy principles to replace those buried with the U.S. defeat in Indochina. The result was a foreign policy of eclecticism, subject to competing pressures from different centers of power. The inconsistencies were especially keen in the emerging debate over Central America, which tested the depth of Congress's and the administration's human rights commitments against the longer-standing U.S. aversion to social upheaval in the Western Hemisphere.

Carter's attempts to accommodate the forces of change in Central America met stiff resistance in the Congress because they appeared to downplay the salience of a communist threat in the region. Although winning important victories on Capitol Hill, particularly regarding aid to Nicaragua, Carter lost the major battle to reshape the premises of U.S. policy toward the hemisphere. The incoming Reagan administration attempted to fill that void, believing the public would rally behind a show of strength in a historic U.S. "backyard." Like Carter, however, Reagan would find essential policy goals tempered by domestic political considerations. If there was no consensus behind the centrality of moralism and accommodation in an era of global change, neither was there support for a show of muscle devoid of humanitarian values or restraint.

Chapter Three

1981: The Reagan Offensive

The 1980 electoral landslide that brought Ronald Reagan to office appeared to signal a fundamental shift in public attitudes toward foreign policy, or so it was thought by Carter's conservative critics: America was tired of self-imposed post-Vietnam restraint, of being kicked around by a hostile Third World, while the Soviet Union exploited American weakness by expanding its military arsenal and intervening in local conflicts. Iran and Afghanistan, which seemed to have become household words, symbolized not only American impotence but also the inability of American leaders to respond to Soviet global challenges. Carter's talk of malaise and his apparent downgrading of the superpower status of the United States by considering it as one among many nations only deepened the sense of frustration over the decline of American power.

The Reagan camp rejected the implication that the United States had less ability to influence and control events abroad, and they interpreted the elections as a vindication of tough campaign rhetoric and the public's support for an activist foreign policy to reestablish American global primacy.[1] Central America provided the administration with its first opportunity to show resolve, for three principal reasons. First, because as the administration took office, its "worst dreams" were coming true, in the words of State Department official Luigi Einaudi. In El Salvador, "American weakness was being taken full advantage of by the enemy," while "an avalanche of intelligence information" demonstrated outside communist support for the insurgents.[2] Second, the guerrilla offensive in El Salvador fizzled after only a few days of fighting, making the country more attractive as a place to stem the tide of further left-wing advances. Third, the Soviet Union was unlikely to risk military confrontation with the United States in Central America. Reagan could stand up to communist powers and victory would not only be assured, it would be cheap.

In its first three months in office, the Reagan administration launched a concerted drive to convince the Congress, the public, American allies, and Latin American revolutionaries that the United States would not tolerate further communist gains in the region and would punish those who assisted the insurgent cause. From the beginning, then, it was apparent that U.S. policy toward Central America had two aspects, one a response to fast-breaking events in the region, the other aimed at proving something to the American people and the world about the enduring preeminence of U.S. power. Constraints on the Reagan policy, therefore, also arose from two sources: when events in the region proved unresponsive to Washington's remedies, and when the administration exceeded the limits of domestic tolerance for a reassertion of America's global role and a reorientation of underlying values.

This latter concern helps explain the difficulty the Reagan administration had in 1981 in convincing the Congress and the public that El Salvador was the place to "draw the line," in Secretary of State Alexander M. Haig's words, against Soviet expansionism. Both Congress and the public responded to Reagan's initiatives with skepticism and alarm. Harsh and bellicose rhetoric, intended to demonstrate the shedding of a post-Vietnam reluctance to use force, also aroused fears that U.S. force would eventually be used in El Salvador. Policy prescriptions—the sending of military aid and advisers, coupled with strident public campaigns about communist interference in El Salvador—also deepened qualms that the administration was fundamentally misreading the nature of the conflict and responding inappropriately as a result. The apparent discarding of human rights concerns miscalculated the depth of public acceptance of the U.S. role as a moral protector and promoter of human decency.

In many respects, the Reagan administration was its own worst enemy in

1981. Rhetorical overkill eroded the basis for cooperation with the Congress, which shared the administration's desire to prevent the radical left from coming to power in El Salvador. The Carter administration had understood the commonality of the administration's and the Congress's policy goals; the Reagan administration, however, shifted attention from the common ground to its own policies. This was done by denigrating or ignoring human rights concerns, raising the specter of military intervention in Central America, and suggesting that the roots of regional turmoil were principally, if not uniquely, external. As a result, by the end of the year, even a Republican-controlled Senate had adopted detailed conditions on U.S. aid to El Salvador, reflecting the fundamental lack of confidence in the direction of administration policy. The chastising lesson of Reagan's first year in office was that ideology was not necessarily a basis for a sound, consensus-building policy, even when the public appeared to thirst for boldness and self-assertion.

The Reagan Offensive

The very first foreign policy pronouncements by leading administration officials were meant to distinguish the Reagan administration from its predecessor: "International terrorism will take the place of human rights" as the underpinning of foreign relations, "because it is the ultimate of abuse of human rights," said newly confirmed Secretary of State Alexander M. Haig on January 28, 1981. Haig made it clear that the Soviets lay behind the upsurge in "rampant international terrorism" and decried the "unprecedented . . . risk-taking mode on the part of the Soviet Union."[3]

Focusing on the role of communist powers in fostering international terrorism led the administration to view the Salvadoran crisis in East-West terms. According to the administration's view, the key factor behind the Salvadoran upheaval was external support, manifested in an arms flow provided to the Salvadoran guerrillas by Soviet-bloc nations through their clients, Cuba and Nicaragua. Beginning in early February, the administration began to build a public offensive around the theme of the external origins of the Salvadoran crisis.

The offensive began with the leaking of portions of captured guerrilla documents detailing Soviet, Cuban, and Eastern-bloc support for the rebels. On February 17, according to the New York Times, Haig briefed NATO and other allied nations that "a well-orchestrated international Communist campaign designed to transform the Salvadoran crisis from the internal conflict to an increasingly internationalized confrontation is underway." Two days later the State Department provided European and Latin American embassies with a memorandum claiming that the Salvadoran conflict represented "a textbook case of indirect armed aggression by Communist powers." Haig accused Cuba, the Soviet Union, Vietnam, Ethiopia, and "radical Arabs" of "furnishing at least several hundred tons of military equipment" to the Salvadoran rebels. "Most," he said, "has entered via Nicaragua."[4]

The centerpiece of the administration's campaign was a white paper released on February 23, "Communist Interference in El Salvador," which claimed to present "definitive evidence" of foreign military support for the Salvadoran guerrillas. "Over the past year," the report stated, "the insurgency in El Salvador has been progressively transformed into another case of indirect armed aggression against a small Third World country by Communist powers acting through Cuba."[5] The view expressed in the white paper was straightforward: El Salvador's violence had external roots, and the conflict had strategic implications for the United States.

To underscore what the administration might do about the arms flow, officials issued a string of statements threatening military action against Cuba. "We do intend to go to the source with whatever means may become reasonably necessary," said Deputy Secretary of State William Clark on February 21. In response to a question as to whether the United States included as one option a naval blockade of Cuba, White House aide Edwin Meese stated with intended ambiguity that the United States "does not rule out anything" to stop the arms flow. In his memoirs Secretary Haig noted that, in his view, the administration should have contemplated "a full range of economic, political, and security measures" to curb Cuban and Soviet activities.[6]

By the end of President Reagan's first weeks in office, the administration had articulated an assessment of the nature of the problem in Central America and a strategy for dealing with it that included threats of military action.

At first, the administration's rhetorical initiative gained important support on Capitol Hill. This was particularly true in the Senate, returned in 1980 to Republican control for the first time in almost three decades. The new chairman of the Senate Foreign Relations Committee, Charles Percy (R-Ill.) stated after a briefing, "I think those outside forces should be on notice that this nation will do whatever is necessary to prevent a communist state takeover in El Salvador." The leadership in the House, moreover, where the Democratic majority had suffered a net loss of thirty-three seats, was initially willing to give the president the benefit of the doubt. Said Majority Leader Jim Wright, "Central America is probably more vitally important to us than any other part of the world. Our response . . . requires a bipartisan, unified approach."[7]

Reasons for backing the president varied. Some legislators genuinely welcomed Reagan's new "get tough" approach. According to Winslow Wheeler, a Senate Republican aide to Nancy Kassebaum, "the reaction was 'Thank god somebody is doing something.' The communists were going to take over [in the context of the final offensive] while Jimmy Carter was screwing around and wringing his hands."[8] Others, particularly Democrats, were simply cowed by the Reagan landslide: "The last election changed things," said Senator Paul Tsongas (D-Mass.). "Not only did we lose Democrats and liberals, but those who are left are so weary. Everyone is running for cover from Reagan and the conservative trend. Some people say, let the Administration go ahead and make its mistakes; that's the only way the public will understand."[9]

Almost immediately, however, signs of strain emerged. The administration's emphasis on international terrorism and East-West conflict represented a radical shift of the agenda away from the issues of human rights and reform; these issues, after all, had been the twin pillars of congressional concern regarding El Salvador even before the Carter years. Noticeably absent from administration statements was any reference to mass civilian killings or the murder of U.S. citizens at the hands of death squads or the security forces themselves, which figured prominently in press coverage of the region. Indeed, shortly after entering office, Reagan administration officials had removed Carter's outspoken ambassador to El Salvador Robert White, on the grounds that he and others on Carter's Central America team had functioned "in the capacity of social reformers and advocates of new theories of social change."[10]

At first the budding congressional concerns were expressed in private, or coupled with tentative expressions of support for the overall thrust of policy. "Haig is right, this is the place to draw the line," Senator Percy told a breakfast meeting of reporters on February 19. But, he added, "the repression is intolerable and the slaughter cannot continue." He then stated that the Salvadoran ruling junta was "as unpopular with their own people as was Vietnam," thus hinting at a link between popular legitimacy and the roots of revolt.[11]

Others, particularly members and staff who had served in Congress during the Vietnam War, drew the parallels between El Salvador and Vietnam by recalling intervention scenarios more starkly. Recalled Republican aide Wheeler, who attended an early briefing on Salvador policy:

> The sense was, these clowns are going to get us into big trouble again. The implication was that there was a huge international communist

> effort to take over little El Salvador and we had to show the world that we
> weren't going to get pushed around any more. . . . [The administration]
> kept promising us that if we gave them the required amount [of aid] that
> the war would end in a year. All that did was remind me of the "light at
> the end of the tunnel."[12]

Even before the Reagan administration had announced any concrete actions to
deal with the Salvadoran insurgency, then, members of Congress and their aides
rejected aspects of the administration's characterization of the Salvadoran conflict. They drew on their own institutional memory of the Vietnam War as well
as a decade of policy changes in its aftermath.

Congressional disquiet burst dramatically into the open on February 25,
1981, when Representative Clarence Long held the first public hearing on
Reagan policy in El Salvador. In a pattern that was to be repeated over and over
again in subsequent years, opposition to the policy was expressed most vehemently in the House, the only branch of government still controlled by the
Democrats in 1981, and in subcommittees, usually more liberal than the full
committee of which they were a part. The involvement of relatively few members
of a subcommittee allowed over time for the development of expertise far beyond
that of the entire House membership, even if actions taken by a subcommittee
were not always ratified by the larger body. Subcommittee hearings served,
however, as the most continuous forum for debate of Central America policy,
allowing for the questioning of administration witnesses and the presentation of
alternative points of view. This "informal power" over the tone and substance of
policy discussion was an important subcommittee prerogative.

As his star witness for the February 25 hearing Long called former Ambassador
Robert White, who less than one year earlier had been instrumental in
convincing Long's subcommittee (over the objections of the chairman) to
approve nonlethal military aid to the Salvadoran army. Removed from his post
by Reagan appointees, White lashed out at the policy and the Salvadoran
government. He drew a picture of the Salvadoran conflict that contrasted starkly
with Secretary Haig's portrayals.

"The security forces in El Salvador," he said in a tougher public assessment
than he had made as ambassador, "have been responsible for the deaths of
thousands and thousands of young people, and they have executed them on the
mere suspicion that they are leftists or sympathize with leftists. . . . The real
issue is how do you supply military assistance to a force that is going to use that
military assistance to assassinate, to kill, in a totally uncontrolled way?" Turning
to the Republicans on the subcommittee, White asked, "Do you want to

associate the United States with the type of killing that has been going on down there in El Salvador?"[13]

White's analysis of the source of the violence in El Salvador was reinforced by three congressmen, Representatives Bob Edgar (D-Pa.), Barbara Mikulski (D-Md.), and Gerry Studds (D-Mass.), who had visited Central America in January 1981. They stated that "by far the greatest responsibility for violence and terrorism rests with those forces now receiving U.S. guns, helicopters, grenades, and ammunition." Government troops, they concluded, had been "waging a systematic campaign of harassment, torture and murder against large segments of the Salvadoran population." Later that day, William Doherty, executive director of the American Institute for Free Labor Development, stated that "right wing security forces" had carried out 80 percent of the murders of peasants involved in El Salvador's agrarian reform program.[14]

What appeared to be near unanimity about the problem of political violence in El Salvador stood in sharp contrast to administration portrayals. Deputy Secretary of State John Bushnell insisted that the violent left was principally responsible for the slaughter in El Salvador. "I do not think the majority of those people [in El Salvador] have been killed by the security forces," he said. "The DRU [guerrilla directorate] itself has announced in its public announcements that it has killed 6,000."[15]

Bushnell's attitude toward who was responsible for the violence in El Salvador reflected a widespread sense of disbelief among high-ranking administration officials that reports of human rights abuses by government forces were true. In the words of Reagan's first ambassador to El Salvador, Deane Hinton, "a lot of people believed these incidents were manipulated, that they didn't take place." The reports were viewed as "disinformation," Hinton said, "by people inimical to the Administration" who were exploiting the human rights issue. "People thought *The Spike* was true," he said, referring to a 1980s novel depicting Soviet disinformation activities in the United States.[16]

By refusing to grant even minimum credibility to reports of brutality on the part of government forces, officials of the Reagan administration raised another fear: that an ideological commitment to defeating communism would eventually lead to the landing of U.S. troops in El Salvador. "The President has no intention of sending troops into El Salvador to get us involved in a Vietnam thing," observed Representative Long. "I don't think Johnson did either. . . . The point is, we get ourselves into a situation which makes action inevitable."[17]

Testimonies heard in Long's subcommittee were only a prelude to congressional debates over human rights and Vietnam analogies that would stretch over the next several months. Yet the hearing served as a kind of political barometer, signaling to the administration the limits of support for certain initiatives, as well as providing Congress with a body of evidence on which to challenge Reagan policymakers. Key witnesses in upcoming months—from Amnesty International and the Catholic Church, to a former Salvadoran military officer who linked the death squads with the security forces—reinforced claims about human rights abuses by the Salvadoran government.* Through the end of March, administration witnesses were subjected to a barrage of criticism from virtually every congressional committee and subcommittee with responsibility for foreign aid or foreign affairs. Bushnell claimed that such protest was the product of a "well-orchestrated effort" by a "worldwide communist network" and blamed the press for running the El Salvador story "five times as big as it is."[18] But the hearings put the administration on the defensive, forcing it ultimately to recast its policy in an attempt to regain congressional support.

Human Rights

At the core of the administration's unwillingness to acknowledge the full extent of right-wing and government-sponsored violence in El Salvador was a theoretical distinction between authoritarian and totalitarian regimes. As articulated most prominently by U.N. Ambassador Jeane Kirkpatrick, authoritarian regimes had the capacity to evolve in a democratic direction, while totalitarian regimes were impervious to change and more intrusive in cultural, political, economic, and religious life.

The Carter administration had erred, Kirkpatrick argued, by putting too much pressure on U.S. allies in Iran and Nicaragua, while ignoring the antidemocratic credentials of the forces opposing them. In practice, the distinction put forward by Kirkpatrick suggested a tolerance of the human rights abuses of anticommunist, pro-Western allies, while using human rights issues to further condemnation of communist states.[19]

---

*Salvadoran Captain Ricardo Alejandro Fiallos told Long's subcommittee in April, "Los Escuadrones de la Muerte [the death squads] are made up of members of the security forces, and acts of terrorism credited to these squads, such as political assassinations, kidnappings, and indiscriminate murder, are, in fact, planned by high-ranking military officers and carried out by members of the security forces." U.S. Congress, House, Committee on Appropriations Subcommittee on Foreign Operations, *Foreign Assistance and Related Programs Appropriations for Fiscal Year 1982*, Hearings, Part 1, 97th Cong., 1st Sess. (Washington, D.C.: U.S. Government Printing Office, 1981), p. 361.

When the Reagan administration in February nominated Ernest Lefever as Assistant Secretary of State for Human Rights and Humanitarian Affairs, it set off alarm bells on Capitol Hill. In 1974 Lefever had trivialized reports of torture in Chile by quoting a former State Department official who said that a "normal level of police abuse" was a "residual practice of the Iberian tradition."[20] In 1979 Lefever had recommended to a congressional subcommittee the removal of all legislation tying U.S. policy to a country's human rights practices. Lefever's nomination hinted not at human rights policy pursued by quieter means but at the abandonment of human rights considerations altogether. As if to underscore its disregard for the abuses of U.S. allies, the administration announced in early March that Argentine General Roberto Viola would soon visit Washington, following visits by a member of the Chilean junta and the Brazilian military. All three countries at the time were military dictatorships.

The administration's authoritarian-totalitarian distinction was largely rejected by the Congress, which had grappled with human rights in the 1970s as a universal issue and as a factor intimately linked to the stability, or instability, of U.S. allies in the Third World. "Savage murder is savage murder no matter who commits it," insisted Representative Mary Rose Oakar (D-Ohio), suggesting that the political orientation of an oppressor made little difference to the victim. Representative Mickey Edwards, a senior Republican on the House Foreign Operations Subcommittee likewise criticized the theory as counterproductive: "By supporting friendly but undemocratic regimes solely on the basis of their opposition to communism, the United States will perhaps gain a short term benefit at a very great long term cost," he said. "We run the risk of creating widespread and powerful anti-American feelings."[21] What members of Congress seemed to be saying—as they had in the 1970s—was that neglecting the human rights abuses of U.S. allies was not only inhumane but also contrary to U.S. interests.

Reflecting the lack of faith in the Reagan administration approach, the Senate Foreign Relations Committee voted 13–4 in June to reject Ernest Lefever as Assistant Secretary of State for Human Rights. His confirmation, said Chairman Percy, "would be an unfortunate symbol and signal to the rest of the world."[22]

The U.S. Churchwomen

Perhaps no issue more galvanized congressional and public opposition to the human rights policy of the Reagan administration as its treatment of the four

U.S. churchwomen murdered in December 1980. Reagan administration officials not only ignored the depth of sentiment around the killings but suggested—apparently without evidence—that the women were in some way responsible for their own deaths. The insensitivity on the part of the administration was later redressed, but not after causing a serious erosion of trust in the Congress.

To understand the congressional preoccupation with the murder of four American citizens amid a Salvadoran bloodbath, it is important to view the churchwomen as a symbol, readily understandable to Americans, of raw brutality in El Salvador. "Human rights abuses [in El Salvador] took on more concrete meaning for people when the women were killed," said a Senate Republican staffer who dealt with Central American issues. "It brought the killings home in a different kind of way than gross statistics" on the number of Salvadorans murdered. "These were Americans, not nameless, faceless campesinos and urban dwellers. It was very hard not to be very deeply affected by that, and a lot of Senators were. It created moral indignation."[23]

"Statistics on human rights didn't affect [members of Congress] as much as seeing and feeling that four North Americans and nuns were murdered in cold blood," explained Michael Posner, counsel to the churchwomen's families. "There are lots of statistics in Washington. [Salvadoran] deaths were one more set they couldn't absorb."[24]

The deaths of the four women also mobilized opinion in the U.S. church community against a U.S. policy that supported the government in El Salvador. An unprecedented and sometimes spontaneous lobbying effort flooded congressional offices with mail, telephone calls, and telegrams expressing outrage at the murders and demanding the punishment of those guilty and an end to U.S. support for the Salvadoran junta. The demands found resonance in the position of the Catholic Church of El Salvador and in the Catholic hierarchy in the United States. In early March Archbishop James Hickey, speaking on behalf of the U.S. Catholic Conference, called for an end to U.S. military aid to El Salvador. In April Acting Salvadoran Archbishop Arturo Rivera y Damas wrote Senator Kennedy asking for an end to U.S. military aid and support for a process of political dialogue in his country.[25]

Rather than indicate sympathy for the families of the churchwomen or respect for the depth of popular sentiment their deaths triggered, key administration officials responded to the murders with an indifference that bordered on derision. U.N. ambassador-designate Jeane Kirkpatrick committed a first gaffe even before President Reagan was sworn in, when she told the *Tampa Tribune* in December 1980 that "the nuns were not just nuns. The nuns were also political activists . . . on behalf of the [opposition] Frente and somebody who is using violence to oppose the Frente killed these nuns." The statement, which was repeated widely in congressional hearings and in the press, appeared to lay blame for the women's murders at their own feet. The families denounced it as part of a "smear campaign."*

Secretary of State Haig added to the controversy during testimony before the House Foreign Affairs Committee when he charged that "the vehicle that the nuns were riding in may have tried to run a roadblock or may have accidentally been perceived to have been doing so, and there may have been an exchange of fire."

Haig insisted the next day that his testimony had been misquoted by the press, but the transcript of the hearing established the press reports as accurate.[26] Even the Secretary's attempt to backtrack fueled the controversy. Pressed by Senator Claiborne Pell (D-R.I.) to clarify the suggestion that "the nuns may have run through a roadblock," Haig replied, "Oh, not at all. No, not at all. My heavens." Asked further whether he meant to infer by "exchange of fire" that the nuns had been firing at people, Haig quipped, "I have not met any pistol-packing nuns in my days, Senator."[27] Later, the State Department retreated from Haig's allegations. In a letter to Archbishop John Roach of the National Conference of Catholic Bishops, Undersecretary of State Walter Stoessel said that the department had "no evidence that the four American missionaries were engaged in political activity as we define it."[28]

The cavalier, if not disparaging, attitude displayed by top administration policymakers might have appeared less troubling if Salvadoran authorities could have pointed to any progress in investigating the murders or punishing the perpetrators. But press reports dovetailed with the sobering assessment provided by former Ambassador White: "No serious investigation was or is underway."[29]

What came to be known as the "nuns case," then, came to signify in a deeper sense the administration's overall lack of concern with the issue of right-wing violence in El Salvador. In fact, administration statements were replete with

---

*Lawyers Committee for International Human Rights, A Report on the Investigation into the Killing of Four American Churchwomen in El Salvador, New York, September 1981, Appendix 1–4. According to lawyer Michael Posner, Kirkpatrick denied to him and to a relative of one of the churchwomen ever having made the statement, insisting that the "comment was taken out of context" and that she had been "discussing the ubiquity of violence in a society in which some 13,000 Salvadorans and non-Salvadorans had died in the previous year." Interview, Michael Posner, New York, New York, November 9, 1986; and U.S. Congress, Senate, Committee on Foreign Relations, The Situation in El Salvador, Hearings, March 18 and April 9, 1981, 97th Cong., 1st Sess. (Washington, D.C.: U.S. Government Printing Office, 1981), p. 235.

condemnations of left-wing terrorism, but not once mentioned right-wing or government-sponsored violence during the heated months of February and March.* "We were just killing them [the administration] initially," said Vic Johnson, staff director of the House Western Hemisphere Affairs Subcommittee, "because they were on the wrong side of American values."[30]

"Your policy is in trouble," Senator David Durenberger (R-Minn.) wrote Haig in March, "unless there is clear evidence that rightist as well as leftist terror is being dealt with."[31]

The Ghosts of Vietnam

The downplaying of human rights concerns seemed to illustrate one lesson that the Reagan administration had failed to learn from the Vietnam experience: that backing a corrupt, brutal regime without popular support was a losing proposition, regardless of any intention to commit or not commit U.S. troops. What turned the Vietnam analogy into a major factor in a national debate, however, was the sending of military "trainers" and increased military aid to El Salvador in an atmosphere of strident rhetoric about Soviet involvement in the Salvadoran conflict.† As Representative Long had stated in late February, the issue was not so much the administration's oft-repeated determination not to send troops, but the degree to which U.S. intervention would become inevitable in face of a commitment not "to lose" El Salvador.

On March 2, 1981, the Reagan administration announced that it was sending $25 million in additional military assistance to the Salvadoran government and was dispatching four U.S. military teams, including Green Berets, to "train

---

*On February 18, for example, the State Department said that "violence is the enemy of all democratic change, of individual rights and of economic progress. *Those who are responsible for the violence and terrorism, with arms support from Cuba and other countries, are the real obstacle to negotiations.* We continue to impress on the GOES the importance of controlling violence, whatever its source" (emphasis added). On March 2, the State Department again emphasized in a press briefing that "the fundamental problem we face in El Salvador is to maintain the pace of economic and political progress in the face of deliberate efforts by the left-wing insurgents to disrupt that progress and to force the Government into a preoccupation with security concerns."

†The Department of Defense called U.S. military personnel in El Salvador "trainers" rather than "advisers," because, according to DOD, "advisers" accompanied troops into combat, an activity barred in El Salvador.

Salvadoran personnel in communications, intelligence, logistics, and in other professional skills."[32] The Carter administration had placed about twenty "trainers" in El Salvador in 1980, but had done so with little fanfare and without giving them a direct role in combat training. Sending advisers to train Salvadoran troops in counterinsurgency appeared to give the United States a more direct hand in the war. The central question in the minds of congressional policymakers was what would happen if U.S. training was not enough, or if U.S. personnel got killed in the course of their duties. Would the very placement of U.S. advisers in a situation as unstable as that of El Salvador's lead to deeper U.S. military involvement?

These questions arose from the collective memory of how the United States had become embroiled in combat in Southeast Asia, making Vietnam a metaphor for intervention by stages. According to a Senate Foreign Relations Committee report in the early 1970s, "The ever deepening ground combat involvement of the United States in South Vietnam began with the assignment of U.S. 'advisers' to accompany South Vietnamese units on combat patrols; and in Laos, secretly and without congressional authorization, U.S. 'advisers' were deeply engaged in the war in northern Laos."[33] Adding to the sense that the United States was standing on a slippery slope in El Salvador was the Pentagon's reported assessment of the Salvadoran army: that it was so ill-prepared to fight the insurgents that it had "no hope" of defeating them.[34] If the military situation appeared hopeless, and if the United States had as deep a stake in El Salvador as the administration claimed, then it appeared a reasonable deduction that advisers were only the first step in what could become burgeoning U.S. involvement.

A second reason the Vietnam theme resonated through the debate was the perception that the administration was seeking a military solution in El Salvador and lacked a policy for the resolution of deeper underlying problems. Said a liberal staff aide on the House Foreign Affairs Committee, "Military assistance was not the answer, because the problems were political and political problems were only made worse by the provision of military aid."[35] In the words of Senate Foreign Relations Committee Republican Nancy Kassebaum, "I am supportive of the thrust that the administration has taken in El Salvador, but I am equally concerned that we weigh out the need to balance every effort for political initiatives as well."[36]

If the Reagan administration had alarmed members of Congress by calling for increased U.S. military involvement, it also appears that they misinterpreted the mandate of the 1980 elections. Public opinion polls taken early in the Reagan administration indicated that the public shared—if not, in some cases, prompted—congressional fears about deepening U.S. military involvement.

According to a Gallup poll completed in mid-March 1981, two out of every three "informed Americans" feared that the situation in El Salvador would develop into "another Vietnam." And only 2 percent of the public thought that the United States should send troops to help the government of El Salvador.[37] Statements by members of Congress themselves indicate that public concerns translated directly into constituent pressure. According to Senator John Glenn (D-Ohio), "The contacts I have had, and the mail I have been receiving, . . . have indicated mostly a very, very great concern about what we're doing in that area."[38] Even the Reagan administration felt the potential for backlash. According to Haig in his memoirs, many of the president's top advisers feared that turmoil in Central America would sap public support for Reagan's domestic policy agenda.[39]

In addition to stirring general concerns about where U.S. policy might be heading, memories of Vietnam and the legislation inherited from those years prompted a congressional-executive skirmish over institutional prerogatives. Members of Congress claimed that the sending of advisers violated provisions of the War Powers Resolution and the Arms Export Control Act, which required reports to Congress when U.S. military personnel were sent into situations of hostilities or imminent hostilities.[40]

In fact, according to a report by the General Accounting Office, the Defense Department deliberately avoided issuing the report required by law by reversing a decision to designate El Salvador a "hostile fire area." In 1980 such a designation had been made following a series of violent incidents directed at U.S. personnel and embassy property during the year. According to the report of the comptroller general, the Reagan administration, however, "wished to preclude giving the impression that the United States had combat forces stationed in El Salvador" and wanted "to preclude . . . triggering the requirements" of the Arms Export Control Act.[41] Even after the administration revoked the designation, U.S. personnel in El Salvador continued to receive hostile-fire pay, an income supplement for serving in dangerous situations.

The GAO's report highlighted a central weakness in Congress's foreign policy role. With limited investigatory powers of its own, Congress was dependent on the administration for information on U.S. activities overseas. Although the administration was compelled to promise a limit on the number of U.S. advisers—a number fixed at fifty-five—it retained the power to direct their operations without explicit congressional interference.

Over the next several years the administration violated its assurances about the advisers to Congress several times, increasing their number, allowing them to carry M-16 rifles in combat zones, and permitting them to accompany

Salvadoran troops on field operations.[42] The debate over the advisers itself, however, seems to have had several concrete effects. First, it sent signals to the administration, and particularly to the professional military, that there was no mandate for deeper U.S. military involvement in El Salvador. Second, it compelled the administration to limit the number of U.S. advisers, thus putting the Salvadoran army on notice that it would have to fight its own war.

Bottom Lines:
The Nature of the Congressional Debate

As Congress formally grappled with the administration's actual proposals for aid to El Salvador in 1981, it did so within boundaries it shared with the administration. As articulated by Senator David Durenberger (R-Minn.):

> It is agreed that President Duarte represents the best chance for El Salvador to come to peace with itself. The debate separating critics and supporters of President Reagan's policy is over the kind and amount of support which we should provide to President Duarte, and not whether such support is merited at all.
>
> It is agreed that the armed leftist opposition in El Salvador represents neither the wishes nor the best interests of the Salvadoran people themselves. . . . The real debate separating critics and supporters of President Reagan's policies is over how best to isolate and deal with these terrorists, through military assistance or through reforms that eliminate the grievances upon which they depend for sustenance. In other words, there is both consensus and disconsensus.[43]

As the ensuing debates illustrated, Congress would not materially restrict the administration's ability to implement its policy by cutting off funds or setting absolute prohibitions on certain activities; that would compromise their shared goal of preventing a guerrilla victory. Rather, Congress set conditions on aid as a way to influence administration policy and force it to take into consideration certain elements of the Salvadoran situation, thereby placing policy on a sounder track for the achievement of U.S. objectives.

The first real test for the Reagan administration came, as it had for the Carter administration one year before, during a vote in the House Foreign Operations Subcommittee, chaired by Representative Long. When even a subcommittee with a majority of liberals could not muster the votes to cut U.S. aid, the beginnings of a pattern emerged. Cautious congressional attitudes and Congress's own rules and procedures combined to give the Reagan administration its first, telling victory in the battle over aid to El Salvador.

When the Reagan administration had announced on March 2 that it was increasing military assistance to El Salvador by $25 million, it had used special executive authority to transfer $20 million of the funds; the remaining $5 million were to be reprogrammed. The Republican-led Senate Foreign Operations Subcommittee approved the reprogramming on March 13 with little fanfare. Long's subcommittee followed suit on March 24, but only after considerable maneuvering.

What tipped the scales in the administration's favor in the House were the votes of two members of the full Appropriations Committee who were not members of its Foreign Operations Subcommittee. The chairman of the full Appropriations Committee, Representative Jamie Whitten (D-Miss.), and Representative Silvio Conte (R-Mass.), its ranking minority member, participated in the subcommittee debate by exercising special voting privileges pertaining to their rank on the full committee. Their decision to cast votes illustrated the priority the administration attached to the largely symbolic approval of the reprogramming, and its ability to put pressure on members of its own party and conservatives in the other. Secretary Haig personally phoned subcommittee members, including Conte, asking for their support.

The vote also reflected an attitude of deference to the president in the conduct of foreign affairs among congressional moderates. "We need to show the world that we too back up the President to this point," said Representative Whitten. "To fail on this small transfer of funds . . . would be misunderstood throughout the world."[44] Representative Conte echoed the chairman: "I will vote for approval of this reprogramming . . . because . . . the failure to support the President's policy to stand up to international terrorism and aggression will . . . send the wrong signal to Cuba and the Soviet Union." But, he added, principally in response to heavy constituent pressure and pressure from the Catholic Church, that his support was conditional: "I want to make it very clear, absolutely clear . . . that I will not support any further military assistance for the government of El Salvador unless and until the investigation of the killings of the Americans in El Salvador late last year has been completed."[45]

The 8–7 subcommittee vote in favor of the aid split largely along party lines. Only two Democrats, Whitten and Representative Charles Wilson, voted for the aid. For the first time in the Central America debate during the Reagan administration—albeit on a small scale—conservative southern Democrats joined with a block of Republicans to give the president a winning majority.

The Certification

Hard on the heels of the subcommittee vote, members of the House and Senate proposed legislation that would shape the congressional debate over El Salvador for the next several years. The approach was to condition aid to El Salvador on the fulfillment of specific requirements, rather than terminating aid outright. Legislation introduced by Representatives Stephen Solarz (D-N.Y.) and Jonathan Bingham (D-N.Y.) in the House and Senator Christopher Dodd (D-Conn.) in the Senate, required the United States to end U.S. aid to El Salvador and withdraw military advisers unless the president was able to "certify" that improvements or progress were under way in six areas: human rights, control of the security forces, economic reforms, the holding of elections, negotiations toward a political settlement, and investigations of the murder of the six U.S. citizens killed in late 1980 and early 1981.

The conditions reflected not a repudiation but a reorientation of the kind of support for the Salvadoran government. The certification's central thrust was that internal considerations in El Salvador, not issues of external subversion, had to be addressed. "Although I do not deny that there is an international dimension to the conflict," said Bingham, ". . . its roots are internal. Even without the flow of arms aid from Communist nations to the guerrilla insurgents, El Salvador would be undergoing a social revolution."[46]

From April until the end of 1981, the policy struggle in the Congress and between it and the executive centered on the toughness, wording, and desirability of the certification law. Despite the fact that the legislation granted the president the authority to decide whether the conditions had been met, the Reagan administration vigorously opposed its passage. Congress itself was divided over how far and how fast to push a U.S. ally combating an insurgency. The process of compromise resulted in a certification law that was far less draconian than that originally envisioned by its sponsors. Nonetheless, the adoption of the certification at all—particularly in a Senate controlled by President Reagan's own party—reflected the depth of congressional concern over the misplaced emphasis in the administration's approach.

The House Foreign Affairs Committee opened its session to consider the certification law amid reports of a grisly mass murder in El Salvador, carried out, according to news accounts, by "men in uniform and civilian clothes."[47] Against that backdrop, Representative Gerry Studds offered an amendment to terminate military aid to El Salvador. "The time has come . . . to stop the killing and start the talking," he said, expressing the view that the army would never reform as long as it felt confident that the United States would ensure its survival. Studds's amendment failed, 22–9, showing the limits of congressional opposition to the policy but allowing subsequent proposals to appear moderate by comparison.

Solarz and Bingham then offered their alternative approach: a "certification" by the president that conditions had improved in El Salvador, a determination that Congress had the power to veto. In order to gain a majority on the committee, however, the certification's sponsors needed the support of conservative southern Democrats as well as Republicans. Both groups wanted to be able to defend the administration's policy, and could not as long as it retained its more extreme aspects. Solarz and Bingham were forced to accept two key changes in the certification in order for it to gain enough support to pass.

First, Representative David Bowen (D-Miss.) proposed that Congress's veto power over the certification be dropped. Solarz accepted the change. Second, Representative Millicent Fenwick (R-N.J.) made a fundamental modification in the language of the proposed law: instead of requiring the president to certify that the government of El Salvador "has achieved" substantial control over its armed forces, the wording was modified to read "is achieving." The alteration thus changed the condition from an absolute one to one reflecting a process of improvement. With both alterations incorporated into the certification, it passed the Foreign Affairs Committee. Eight out of fifteen Republicans, including ranking minority member William Broomfield (R-Ind.), voted for the new conditions.*

The administration's El Salvador policy had confronted a major congressional test, emerging with both sides winning something. The administration lost its battle to prevent passage of the certification, but a major committee removed the teeth from an attempt to assert congressional control.

In May the Senate Foreign Relations Committee followed the House committee's lead, rejecting a concerted effort by the administration to have the

---

*A May 1, 1981, *Wall Street Journal* editorial called the certification "A Communist Victory." In response to the attack, Representative Fenwick justified her vote in a May 27 letter to the editor: "The establishment of conditions which must be certified by the President was intended to demonstrate to those members of the Hacienda [Treasury] Police and the National Guard who have been engaged in the killing and torture of civilians that the United States cannot continue to send arms if this continues."

certification dropped from proposed legislation. Secretary Haig wrote Senator Percy, claiming that extremists in El Salvador "will conclude from the legislation that they can force an end to U.S. assistance . . . by stepping up their violence to the point where it blocks further progress on the reforms." Deputy Assistant Secretary of State James Cheek argued in person that "once they're given a substantial incentive to achieve a suspension of American aid, we think they will do that." Conditions would tempt leftists, he said, to foster violence in hopes of getting Congress to end support.[48]

But Democrats and moderate Republicans on the committee were adamant. Aid would strengthen Duarte's hand, argued Senator Kassebaum when rightists realized that Congress could deny the aid necessary to fight left-wing violence. "We are really on the firing line," said Percy, referring to public fears about U.S. involvement in El Salvador. "We need to find some way to reassure them."[49]

The Foreign Relations Committee adopted the certification 11–1.[50] The law itself was an ideal political compromise: it allowed members of Congress to express their concerns about human rights without voting to cut off aid and thereby hamper the counterinsurgency effort. Members of Congress could tell their constituents and advocacy groups that they had not voted to give a "blank check" to the Duarte government or to the Reagan administration.

There was still a final hurdle: to secure floor passage of the draft bills proposing the certification. Mere committee adoption of Salvador legislation opposed by the Reagan administration, however, began to send loud signals to officials in Foggy Bottom. Some clearer articulation of policy would have to precede the garnering of bipartisan support for Salvador policy. That task fell to Assistant Secretary of State for Inter-American Affairs Thomas O. Enders.

Reequilibration: The Beginnings

"Congressional attitudes," explained State Department official Luigi Einaudi describing factions within the administration,

> were a source of major problems within the Administration. . . . I would draw the line between one school of people that believed that congressional restrictions, attitudes, and the values they reflected were serious and legitimate parts of the American political system, and any valid policy had to work within them; and opposed to that school of thought

were those who thought that those restrictions . . . were typical of what was leading to national failure and the decline in our foreign policy. And therefore instead of being lived with and agreed to, Congress had to be forced to accept its role as a "communist agent."[51]

Divisions within the administration over Congress's proper role in foreign policy closely paralleled ideological and practical divisions over how to execute Salvador policy. In the presence of such divisions, the debate in Congress was crucial in determining the administration's internal balance of power.

According to Einaudi, the choices were the following: "go the Argentine route," a reference to the Argentine junta's campaign of extermination in the late 1970s, "or bumble along and fight the war and build democracy at the same time. . . . The existence of Congress was crucial. It meant that the Argentine solution had to be ruled out."[52]

The effort to "build democracy" in El Salvador was far more, however, than a sop to congressional critics. It represented an assessment of some Reagan administration officials, similar to that of the Carter administration, that political reform and institution building were necessary complements of a military effort to contain or defeat the insurgency. The emphasis on democracy, and elections in particular, meant also that the administration could go on the ideological offensive by stressing positive American values. The administration could no longer be accused of seeking a "military solution" in El Salvador, even if elections were part of a counterinsurgency strategy, broadly defined, aimed at defeating the rebels.

In a speech to the World Affairs Council on July 16, 1981, Assistant Secretary of State Thomas Enders laid out the essentials of the new approach. He opened by lashing out at Cuban backing for the Salvadoran guerrillas and then largely dropped the East-West theme that had dominated administration policy pronouncements. Instead, Enders spoke of the need for "demonstrable progress in controlling and eliminating violence from all sources," and acknowledged "violent incidents recently attributed to the far right and to government forces." In marked contrast to previous denials of government-sponsored human rights abuses, Enders noted that "more Salvadoran Army leadership is needed, both to fight rightist death squads and to control security force violence." The remaining half of the assistant secretary's speech was devoted to the Salvadoran elections scheduled for 1982 and 1983; Enders invited "all parties that renounce violence . . . to participate in the design of new political institutions and the process of choosing representatives for them." He concluded by noting that "the search for a political solution will not succeed unless the United States sustains its assistance to El Salvador."[53]

The Enders speech was unable in the short term to undo the damage of the first several months of Reagan administration campaigning against external communist interference. Two months later, on September 23, 1981, the Senate opened debate on the certification, with Republicans and Democrats alike determined to include the conditions in the law.[54] Likening the Congress to a banker laying down conditions to a loan applicant, Foreign Relations Committee Chairman Percy said: "We have a responsibility to our own taxpayers and to our own conscience to state that there are certain goals on which we would like to see progress. . . . They are not absolutes; they ask for a sense of movement toward a goal or an objective. What we are looking for is progress."[55]

Senator Lugar, the administration's lone supporter during committee consideration of the certification, attempted to change the conditions into a nonbinding "sense of the Congress" resolution. He echoed Secretary Haig in arguing that right- and left-wing terrorists would step up their violence against the government if they thought that was a way of ending U.S. support. But most of the debate focused on whether or not the conditions strengthened or hurt President Duarte, who was himself in Washington. Before the Senate debate, Duarte had met with Foreign Relations Committee members. He pleaded for a repeal of the conditions and called them "an unacceptable imposition on a government friendly to the United States."[56]

Duarte's supplications fell on deaf ears, however. "If we continue to provide military aid, sales, and advisers to El Salvador on unconditional terms," said Senator Christopher Dodd (D-Conn.), "we will . . . have sealed the fate of President Duarte and of the moderate elements in his government." His comments mirrored the conclusion of the Foreign Relations Committee that "the amendment would strengthen President Duarte's ability to undertake the basic reforms necessary to bring peace to his nation."[57]

That view prevailed. On two votes, the Senate accepted the certification 54–42, and rejected, 47–51, the amendment to change the conditions into mere goals. Eight senators attempted to "have it both ways," voting first for the certification and then to dilute it into a nonbinding resolution.[58]

As finally approved by Congress in mid-December 1981, the two principal clauses of the certification required the president to end U.S. military aid unless he could report to Congress "that the Government of El Salvador is making a concerted and significant effort to comply with internationally recognized human rights" and that it "is achieving substantial control over all elements of its own armed forces, so as to bring to an end the indiscriminate torture and murder of Salvadoran citizens by these forces."[59]

By delegating to the president the authority to make the certification, Congress in essence guaranteed that it would be made: the president would have to certify in order to prevent the termination of U.S. assistance. By "throwing the monkey on the administration's back," in the words of a Senate Republican aide who requested anonymity, Congress absolved itself of any direct responsibility for ending U.S. assistance.

By requiring reports every six months, however, Congress ensured that the certification would serve as a forum "to force the Administration to pay more attention to this [the human rights] issue in a public way. It kept a low flame burning. It put them on the defensive."[60]

Nicaragua:
Overt Aid, Covert Beginnings

Reagan administration policies toward El Salvador and Nicaragua were deeply enmeshed from the outset of 1981, held together by the conviction that Managua nourished and sustained the Salvadoran guerrillas with equipment provided by the communist bloc. As in the case of El Salvador, those members of Congress responsible for overseeing Nicaragua policy shared the administration's stated policy goal—stopping a flow of arms from Nicaragua to the Salvadoran rebels. Unlike in the Salvadoran case, however, few policy initiatives required congressional ratification. The one major one—the beginning of covert activity—was reported only to the intelligence committees. Debate, therefore, was carried on in secret, or confined to a small number of members with a personal interest in following Nicaraguan developments.

The very procedures Congress had set up for overseeing intelligence operations guaranteed that its role in influencing the conduct of covert operations would be limited. Congress would be notified when the administration undertook covert operations, but the administration otherwise had wide discretion for putting into place an exile army to wage war against the Sandinista regime.

Early on in the Reagan administration, CIA Director William Casey brought the House and Senate Intelligence Committees a "finding" that covert operations in Central America were important to U.S. national security. Specific operations were outlined in only very general terms but centered on undercover political activity and propaganda, as well as the provision of "training, equipment and related assistance to cooperating governments throughout Central America in order to counter foreign-sponsored subversion and terrorism." Support for non-Sandinista political groups had reportedly begun during the Carter administration, so part of the proposal was not new. In view of substantial evidence of Nicaraguan help in supplying the Salvadoran guerrilla "final offensive," other aspects of the finding appeared reasonable, despite the heated rhetoric of the first months of the Reagan administration.*

The relative absence of controversy over the March finding appears to be rooted in its narrow scope as well as in convictions shared even by administration policy critics: that the Nicaraguan government had aided the Salvadoran guerrillas, despite occasional pauses and official denials, and that defeat of the Salvadoran insurgents was consistent with U.S. interests. Information about the arms flow that was available publicly—and from sources less ideologically committed than the Reagan administration—suggested that it did exist; shortly after leaving office, Carter's Secretary of State, Edmund Muskie, charged that Cuban arms and supplies being used in El Salvador were flowing through Nicaragua "certainly with the knowledge and to some extent the help" of Nicaraguan authorities.[61] And after all, it was the Carter administration that originally suspended disbursements of economic aid to Nicaragua during its final days in office.

Public actions toward Nicaragua taken by the Reagan administration therefore elicited little criticism. The 1980 law providing aid to the Sandinistas had, in fact, required an end to U.S. assistance if it engaged in the "export of terrorism." On February 10, 1981, U.S. officials announced the suspension of a $9.6 million sale of American wheat, and two months later formally suspended U.S. aid to Nicaragua. In making its announcement, the State Department even

---

*The quotation from the March 9, 1981, finding appears in a February 10, 1983, CIA memorandum, "Central America Guidelines," released during the 1992 trial of CIA Deputy Director of Operations Clair E. George. Before that time, the finding was mentioned in a National Security Council memorandum prepared in April 1982, "U.S. Policy in Central America and Cuba Through Fiscal Year 1984." A leaked copy of that document appeared in the New York Times, April 7, 1983. See also Don Oberdorfer and Patrick Tyler, "U.S.-Backed Nicaraguan Rebel Army Swells to 7,000 Men," Washington Post, May 8, 1983; and Christopher Dickey, With the Contras (New York: Simon and Schuster, 1985), p. 104. Deputy Assistant Secretary of State John Bushnell may have made an inadvertent reference to the March initiation of covert operations when he referred to the subsequent cutoff of U.S. economic assistance as resulting from a presidential "finding." Bushnell made his remarks on May 4, 1981, before the Senate Foreign Relations Committee. See Senate Committee on Foreign Relations, Foreign Assistance Authorization for Fiscal Year 1982, p. 453.

acknowledged that the United States had "no hard evidence of arms movements through Nicaragua during the past few weeks, and propaganda and some other support activities have been curtailed." Intelligence reports showed that the arms flow had slowed or stopped in response to U.S. representations, an assessment confirmed in Haig's memoirs. Wayne Smith, head of the U.S. Interests Section in Cuba at the time, later wrote that the suspension was evidence that the Reagan administration "had no wish to work with the Sandinistas."[62]

In a pattern that would continue into the early days of the covert war, opposition spokesmen inside Nicaragua who stood to lose from U.S. actions strongly condemned the move. Former junta member Alfonso Robelo "repudiated" the suspension of aid and called it an "aggression" against Nicaragua, using the same word as Sandinista leaders.[63]

As much as there was an early consensus around the arms flow issue, however, exaggeration of some of the available evidence served over time to undercut a broader base of support in Congress for a tough anti-Nicaragua policy. Secretary of State Haig repeatedly made declarations that overstepped the bounds of information available to the administration, charging within weeks of the administration's taking office that the Soviet Union had a "conscious policy" of providing concrete support to international terrorists; soon thereafter, officials at the CIA, the DIA, and the State Department stated that they had little evidence to substantiate the charges.[64]

Similarly, only six weeks after the State Department had announced that it had no evidence of ongoing Nicaraguan arms shipments to Salvadoran rebels, Haig told Republicans on the House Foreign Affairs Committee that the arms flow was "massive." State Department and intelligence community officials told the press that Haig's characterizations were incorrect and were based on reports of what the Salvadoran army believed to be true.[65]

Nowhere was the excess of ideology over information better demonstrated than in the case of the administration's white paper on communist support for El Salvador's insurgency. Beginning in March and continuing through June, a series of press articles highlighted serious inconsistencies between the documents released by the administration and the conclusions drawn from them. One of the first such examinations revealed that, in contrast to the administration's claim that the Soviet Union had masterminded the arms traffic, guerrilla representatives received a cool reception in Moscow and were concerned that other socialist-bloc help would be affected by the Soviets' reaction.[66] Most prominent was a report in the *Wall Street Journal* that stated that one of the officials responsible for the white paper described parts of it as "misleading" and "overembellished" and containing "mistakes."[67] Former Ambassador to El Salvador Robert White himself retracted his January 1981 claim that boats carrying guerrillas had come from Nicaragua and landed on Nicaraguan soil. White told the Senate Foreign Relations Committee, "I have become increasingly skeptical of the reality of that 'invasion.' "[68]

Such accounts did not have an immediate bearing on congressional considerations of Nicaragua in 1981. But they helped create a reserve of skepticism, even a radical sense of disbelief, that claims by the administration about Nicaragua's external activities were grounded in fact. The result was to give administration critics a psychological advantage in subsequent policy discussions, particularly those regarding Sandinista behavior.

If the initial covert elements of Reagan's Nicaragua policy were aimed principally at Nicaragua's external behavior, they were paralleled by overt attempts to maintain influence over Nicaragua's internal political evolution. Even after the suspension of U.S. aid in mid-1981, State Department officials continued to lobby actively in favor of economic aid to Nicaragua for the upcoming fiscal year. In the words of Deputy Assistant Secretary of State John Bushnell, "to terminate aid would be the sorts [sic] of events which would mean the game is over."[69]

While the aid requests were intended to support the private sector in Nicaragua, congressional liberals and moderates who had fought for aid to Nicaragua in 1980 had become increasingly disenchanted with any effort to influence the direction of Sandinista rule. Doubts about the Sandinistas' intentions, and particularly about their commitments to pluralism inside Nicaragua, increased dramatically throughout 1981. The Sandinistas, in turn, spurned congressional concerns as illegitimate and interventionist. Their attitude only contributed further to congressional disaffection.

One particularly illustrative exchange took place in late April, during a visit to Managua by Senators Dodd and Eagleton and Representative Barnes. The three arrived at what was expected to be a private meeting with the Nicaraguan junta, only to find a room full of television cameras and bright lights. Ortega used the occasion to give a long speech denouncing U.S. "imperialist" support for the Somoza regime, and the text of his lecture was subsequently printed in *Barricada*, the FSLN newspaper. Eagleton in particular was furious. At the airport he told reporters that the "political capital of Nicaragua is not Managua but Havana" and called private-sector figures "courageous oppositionists."[70]

Not all congressional concerns regarding Nicaragua, however, were focused on its internal political evolution. Representative David Bonior (D-Mich.), later a House leader in the fight against contra aid, denounced in March the use of Florida training camps by Nicaraguan exiles whose avowed purpose was the overthrow of the Nicaraguan government. Bonior called the exiles "Somocistas" and "terrorists" and called on the Reagan administration to enforce U.S. neutrality legislation prohibiting the use of U.S. territory for hostile actions against a country with which the United States was at peace.[71] As it would for years, the Reagan administration disavowed any connection with the camps and claimed that the neutrality laws did not apply to anti-Sandinista activity on U.S. soil.

The concerns about the direction of Reagan policy were deflected in proportion to Nicaragua's crackdown on non-Sandinista political forces. A low point came in late October 1981 when the government arrested four prominent private-sector leaders for publishing a communiqué critical of Sandinista economic policy. One of those jailed, businessman Enrique Dreyfus, had visited Washington as early as the week before to lobby in favor of economic aid to Nicaragua.*

A top official of the Sandinista Party's own foreign relations department, Julio López, arrived in Washington in the wake of the arrests. Part of his purpose was to explain them to Ambassador Arturo Cruz, who was on the verge of resigning in protest. At a lunch in the Capitol on October 27, which had originally been scheduled for members of Congress and Ambassador Cruz, López spent most of his time fending off questions about the Sandinistas' latest actions against internal critics.

House Majority Leader Jim Wright asked López a pointed question about cooperation agreements between the Sandinistas and the private sector, negotiated in 1980 while Wright was in Managua. According to a congressional aide, Wright had viewed the outcome of those negotiations almost as a personal commitment to him.[72] López evaded the question and launched into an attack on U.S. policy in El Salvador. Wright walked out of the dining room.

The sentiments were summed up by another participant in the session. "It is awfully difficult for the United States to contemplate developments in Nicaragua with much hope or confidence," said Representative Millicent Fenwick. "An emergency law that permits the jailing of people in this way is very discouraging. I voted for Nicaraguan aid before, but now I wouldn't vote to give them a dime."[73]

López's last-minute troubleshooting did not head off Cruz's resignation as

---

*On October 20, 1981, the Senate passed by voice vote a Zorinsky amendment for assistance "solely to the private sector." In a December conference with the House, the provision was changed to target aid to the private sector "to the maximum extent feasible."

ambassador on November 14, 1981. Cruz had served in the Sandinista government since it took power in 1979, and many members of Congress viewed his departure as a political omen: the Nicaraguan revolution's promises of pluralism were hollow in the face of determined radicalism on the part of Sandinista leaders. Following his resignation, Cruz criticized the Sandinistas but also chided the Reagan administration. "What the United States does not realize," he wrote, "is that its continuing mistrust of the revolution might be pushing the Sandinista Government to the left and forcing it, in spite of itself, to use just the kind of measures that the United States finds so troubling. . . . Washington's hard line continues to encourage the armed aggression of the counter-revolution."[74]

The Launching of the Covert War

Cruz's resignation coincided with the end of a three-month secret dialogue by Assistant Secretary of State Thomas Enders and the Sandinistas. According to press accounts and the recollections of those close to Enders's thinking, the talks were aimed at establishing a basis for bilateral toleration.[75] Enders sought an end to Nicaraguan support for insurgent movements in Central America and a curtailment, if not the elimination, of the Sandinistas' growing security ties to the Eastern bloc. In exchange, the United States would be prepared to tolerate Sandinista rule. By the end of October the talks broke down in a sea of mutual recriminations.[76] For the next several years, no serious diplomatic effort would attempt a modus vivendi with the Sandinistas.

Administration rhetoric grew harsher following the breakdown of the secret talks, abandoning all pretense of a search for accommodation. Asked during a November congressional hearing whether the United States would become involved in efforts to overthrow or destabilize the Nicaraguan government, Secretary Haig replied, "No, I would not give you such an assurance." Pressed further for an assurance that the United States did not contemplate covert or overt actions against Nicaragua, Haig retorted, "I'm not prepared to say anything of that kind."[77]

Four days later, on November 16, 1981, the National Security Council met to consider strategy for the entire Central American region. Although the NSC discussed a broad range of activities for carrying out U.S. policy in Central America and Cuba, the centerpiece was "support and conduct of political and paramilitary operations against the Cuban presence and Cuban-Sandinista support structure in Nicaragua and elsewhere in Central America." A CIA plan envisioned an initial spending of $19 million to build a 500-man force for such activity, noting that the Argentines were already training up to 1,000 men. The plan was to:

- Build popular support in Central America and Nicaragua for an opposition front that would be nationalistic, anti-Cuban, and anti-Somoza.
- Support the opposition front through formation and training of action teams to collect intelligence and engage in paramilitary and political operations in Nicaragua and elsewhere.
- Work primarily through non-Americans to achieve the foregoing, but in some circumstances the CIA might (possibly using U.S. personnel) take unilateral paramilitary action against special Cuban targets.[78]

On December 1, 1981, President Reagan signed the "finding," as required by law, indicating that such covert activity was in the national interest.*

CIA Director William Casey went to Capitol Hill later in December to inform members of the intelligence committees about U.S. plans. As he portrayed the program, "There would be a military arm and a separate, political arm which would attempt to secure support from other nations."[79] Casey's description immediately aroused serious concern, if not alarm: about the size and tactics of the proposed guerrilla force, about the ability of the United States to control them, and about the potential for sparking military confrontation between Nicaragua and Honduras, where the insurgents would be based. The chairman of the House committee, Edward Boland (D-Mass.), expressed these apprehensions in a letter to Casey within days of his appearance before the House committee, stating that the concerns were shared by both Democrats and Republicans. He asked for frequent briefings, given the many uncertainties surrounding the program.[80]

Although the Intelligence Oversight Act did not give the congressional committees authority to veto a proposed operation, it foresaw that the very process of oversight could give Congress a means of influencing the choice and conduct of covert operations: by submitting plans to the committee in secret, the CIA would expose proposed operations to a wider ratification procedure,

*The heavily censored finding was released through the Freedom of Information Act, confirming the date, Reagan's signature, and the approval of operations "to build popular support [deleted] that will be nationalistic, anti-Cuban and anti-Somoza" and to "support and protect the opposition [deleted] developing and training action teams that will [deleted] engage in paramilitary [deleted] operations."

thereby in principle contributing to wiser, and more politically sound policy. The experience of the next several years of covert operations against Nicaragua, however, demonstrated that congressional concerns were largely ignored, and that certain expansions of the program were not reported to Congress, precisely to avoid the limited debate facilitated by the reporting requirements.

The seeds of doubt planted in 1981 would grow into raging controversy as the Nicaragua program expanded and its original purpose was transformed. As in the case of El Salvador, shunting aside objections raised on Capitol Hill resulted in growing confrontation with Congress over the means and ends of Central America policy. The result was greater frustration for members of the Congress and the executive, and increasingly muddled policy as each branch of government struggled for advantage, if not decisive victory, over the other.

Chapter Four

1982:
Standoffs and Half Measures—
Congress Responds

Nineteen eighty-two was a year of half measures. Battles between the Congress and the executive were as emotional as those of 1981, but the outcome of the debates was less than definitive. Members of the Congress and the executive continued to treat each other principally as enemies to be overcome, rather than as partners to be accommodated. Yet neither branch of government had the power to force its will decisively on the other. The result was a certain standoff, contributing to a confusion of policy and a search, at least within the administration, for modes of coercing an uncooperative Congress to go along with Central America policy.

The administration traveled two principal avenues to divert the Congress from what was perceived as its excessive focus on human rights in El Salvador. The first was a renewed campaign to draw public attention to the Nicaraguan arms buildup and to that country's support for subversion in Central America, a way of forcing the Congress to deal with the administration's agenda of national security concerns. The second was the launching of the Caribbean Basin Initiative (CBI), a collection of aid, trade, and investment benefits to promote economic growth in the region, obtain more aid for El Salvador in the context of a regional initiative, and counter the perception that the administration was solely concerned with the security dimensions of area conflict.[1] Neither effort was entirely successful in overcoming resistance in Congress to administration policy in Central America, or recasting the debate on the administration's terms.

Regarding Nicaragua, for example, the administration succeeded in gaining important converts to the notion that the Sandinistas were deeply engaged in support for the Salvadoran insurgency. Early in the year, however, press leaks of U.S. covert operations against Nicaragua diverted attention from the Sandinistas' behavior to that of the Reagan administration. By December, Congress had become skeptical of an operation that appeared out of control and cast a symbolic vote to prohibit U.S. actions aimed at the overthrow of the Nicaraguan government.

Regarding El Salvador, Congress continued through the certification law to renew and control the debate over human rights. The administration twice certified that El Salvador had met the conditions necessary for a continuation of aid; debate over that certification illustrated that members of Congress felt betrayed by a violation of the spirit if not the letter of the law. The administration's effort to build democracy in El Salvador similarly showed mixed results. Although Salvadorans held a successful election in March, right-wing dominance of the new Constituent Assembly threatened the search for a moderate, reformist government. Congress reduced aid in response to Salvadoran government measures seen as inimical to socioeconomic reforms.

Even if Congress continued to deny the administration complete backing for its Central America policy, Congress was not successful in reordering the administration's priorities. It did not alter the overall East-West thrust of administration policy or compel an effort at a negotiated settlement in El Salvador.[2] The lack of congressional control over the implementation of policy, and, in the case of El Salvador, the sharing of common objectives with the administration, limited its ability to curb the administration's predilection for military solutions.

As in 1981, however, the debate in Congress continued to send political messages to the administration: the existence of controversy appeared to rule out certain options, such as sending U.S. troops to the region, while making others, such as pursuing some improvements in human rights, prerequisites for sustained congressional funding. By the end of the year these considerations visibly altered the tone if not the substance of policy.

Ironically, Congress's greatest impact on administration policy, particularly in El Salvador, was less a matter of conscious design than of institutional weakness and election-year politicking: a reluctance to approve increases in foreign aid at the same time that domestic programs were being cut. In the judgment of State Department officials, administration accomplishments in El Salvador—in containing leftist guerrillas and promoting electoral government— were sustainable only to the extent Congress proved willing to continue to appropriate the requested amounts of economic and military aid. When the year-end failure to enact a foreign aid bill resulted in dramatic reductions in aid, the administration was forced to adopt a new strategy to gain congressional backing for Salvador policy.

The El Salvador Certification:
Low Flame or Fraud?

As required by law, President Reagan issued in late January 1982 the administration's first certification on human rights in El Salvador. Immediately before the certification, a barrage of publicity charging the Salvadoran government with gross human rights abuses and backpedaling on reforms descended on the Congress. These reports—which starkly contrasted with subsequent administration portrayals of the situation—provided the grist for an emotional debate in congressional committees over the nature of the Salvadoran government and whether it warranted continued U.S. assistance.* Having structured the certification to require an end to U.S. aid unless the administration made a positive assessment of the Salvadoran situation, Congress, in effect, invited the administration to exaggerate, if not misrepresent, the extent of progress.

*A Pentagon assessment team had concluded in November 1981 that the Salvadoran armed forces "generally dismissed" the issues of "institutional violence" and "extreme rightist terrorism" and that there was no counterweight within the army "to oppose the propensity of the more conservative officers to tolerate the use of excessive force and violence." The report noted that "barbaric conduct ha[d] become the norm" for both sides in the conflict. Despite the Reagan administration's claim that it did not seek a military victory in El Salvador, the report recommended a "victory strategy" defined as "destroy[ing] the insurgents' will and capability to fight." Brigadier General Fred E. Woerner, "Report of the El Salvador Military Strategy Assistance Team," San Salvador, November 1981, pp. iv, 17, 24, 45, 47.

There was little question that Washington's political calendar—structured around certifications at six-month intervals—focused press and public attention on the human rights situation in El Salvador at the time of the first certification.

- Several days before the certification was due, the *Washington Post* reported that the Salvadoran peasant federation UCS claimed that "at least 90 officials" of peasant organizations and "a large number of beneficiaries" of the agrarian reform "have died in 1981 at the hands of ex-landlords and their allies, who are often members of the local security forces."[3]
- On January 25, William Ford, brother of slain Maryknoll Sister Ita Ford, asked President Reagan not to certify that progress had been made in the investigation of the murdered U.S. churchwomen. "Every indication seen by the families points to a cover-up by the Salvadoran government."[4]
- That same day, the Washington office of Amnesty International wrote members of Congress that "in the majority of the reported cases, official security forces have been implicated and that these human rights violations have occurred on such a massive scale that they constitute a gross and consistent pattern of human rights abuses."[5]
- On January 26, the American Civil Liberties Union and the Americas Watch, two U.S. rights organizations, released a thick report charging the Salvadoran government with "some 200 politically motivated murders a week, . . . the widespread use of torture by all branches of the nation's security forces," and "murder, mutilation, and torture" on the part of paramilitary forces.[6]
- On January 27, the *Washington Post* and the *New York Times* carried lengthy accounts of a large massacre in El Mozote, a town in northeastern El Salvador. The stories spelled out in grisly detail the discovery of charred skulls and bones, decomposed bodies and animal corpses, and smashed houses. According to the *Times*, relatives and friends of the hundreds of victims blamed the U.S.-trained Atlacatl Battalion of the Salvadoran army.[7]

Despite such an avalanche of bad news, few in Congress could have believed that the administration would fail to certify, thereby suspending U.S. military assistance. The Congress had asked the administration to supply the facts, had deprived itself of a veto over the certification, and had adopted the reporting requirement instead of voting itself to reduce or cut aid. The only issue, then, was whether and to what extent the administration would make an effort to defend the human rights record of the Salvadoran government as a justification for sending aid. It was the wide gap between what the U.S. government said and what private groups reported that provided the substance for the debate.

On January 28, President Reagan demonstrated the extent to which his administration would ignore or downplay Salvadoran human rights abuses. Reagan signed and forwarded to Congress Presidential Determination 82–4, ruling that "the Government of El Salvador is making a concerted and significant effort to comply with internationally recognized human rights." In a six-page, tersely worded justification accompanying the document, Reagan said that "statistics compiled by our Embassy in San Salvador indicate a declining level of violence over the past year and a decrease in alleged abuses by security forces. There has been a definite trend in this regard." The report further blamed the guerrillas for violence perpetrated by the Salvadoran armed forces. "Guerrilla bands routinely operate accompanied by family members and other non-combatants," the report said, "making it difficult to avoid non-combatant casualties when these groups are found and engaged by the military."[8]

Because Congress had no legislative power to reject the certification, it could only protest the very thing Congress as a body had given the administration: the unilateral power to determine that El Salvador qualified for continued aid.[9]

As could have been predicted, the ensuing hearings were raucous, angry, and rife with accusations that the administration was violating the letter and spirit of the law. In an opening statement on February 2, 1982, the chairman of the House Subcommittee on Human Rights, Don Bonker (D-Wash.), accused the administration of a breach of trust between the Congress and the executive: "Rather than outright prohibition of aid, the Congress has given the President discretion in providing assistance. If this is the Administration's response, then we should consider going back to amending the law and prohibiting all aid on a country-by-country basis. . . . Any such certification is an affront to this Committee and the Congress."[10] The reception in the Senate to the first certification was not much better. "Public confidence in the Administration's certification was shaken," said Senate Foreign Relations Committee Chairman Percy,

> by the recent report of extremely serious problems in the land reform program and of alleged massacres of from 200 to 950 people reported in the remote village of Mozote. We appreciate that evidence is difficult to come by and that frequently figures like this are exaggerated for political purposes, as appears to be the case here. But our confidence is not strengthened by subsequent reporting that Salvadoran Army units were involved in the violent murder and rape of civilians in a suburb of San Salvador.[11]

Part of the debate was engendered by a sense of affront. As Bonker had indicated, the Congress had given the administration the right to assess if sufficient progress was being made in the area of human rights, but it expected the administration to provide a realistic assessment of the situation as it existed and to admit shortcomings as they occurred. A central issue was assigning responsibility for the massive numbers of often gruesome civilian deaths.

Assistant Secretary of State Thomas O. Enders conceded to the Senate Foreign Relations Committee that "massive problems remain" with the human rights situation in El Salvador. But the State Department nonetheless maintained that determining who was doing the killing was next to impossible. That assertion clashed not only with the conclusions of private human rights groups, which assigned responsibility for the killings directly to Salvadoran government forces, but also with some of the administration's own private assessments. According to a secret CIA cable of October 1981, Salvadoran security and civil defense forces carried out "summary execution" of suspected rebel sympathizers and "many innocent people died falsely accused."[12]

The basis for the administration's public contention and its subsequent defense of the certification was a confidential cable of January 25, signed by U.S. Ambassador to El Salvador Deane Hinton:

> The killers of the majority are in fact the true phantoms of this struggle. Responsibility for the overwhelming number of deaths . . . cannot be fixed in the majority of cases. . . . It is generally believed in El Salvador that a large number of the unexplained killings are carried out by the security forces, officially or unofficially. . . . This [is] an impossible charge to sustain.[13]

For the members of Congress who believed outside human rights organizations rather than the State Department, the administration's characterization of the killings amounted to a cover-up of the practices of the Salvadoran military. Such a whitewash, it was argued, would weaken the efforts of civilian junta members to assert control over the armed forces.

"I am a political realist," said Representative Michael Barnes, chairman of the House Subcommittee on Inter-American Affairs. "I know the Administration is not going to stop aiding the Salvadoran military. But I am concerned about the signal being sent by this certification . . . that the United States condones these abuses."[14]

Moreover, members of Congress believed that focusing attention on human rights problems would exert pressure to end them. The certification, said

Representative Gerry Studds, "was designed to give you, the State Department, the executive branch, the leverage to compel the military junta in El Salvador to clean up its act. . . . You let them off the hook. . . . You have told them they can do virtually anything they choose to do and the United States will continue to support them." A number of more moderate and conservative members of the House Foreign Affairs Committee shared Studds's concern. "I'm sick of these choices," said Representative Dan Mica (D-Fla.). "To be told we either have to put up with the repression, or we have to let it go Communist. . . . I implore you to come back to us with some new alternatives. . . . [We] cannot tolerate what we have just certified."[15]

The problem, then, was less that a positive certification had been made to Congress than that it suggested that the administration was not delivering a strong rebuke to the Salvadoran army. The certification implicitly conveyed, said Vic Johnson, staff director of the House Subcommittee on Inter-American Affairs, that "all the concerns of Congress are irrelevant. You [the armed forces] have our support, as long as you want, to kill communists. We support you. You are an authoritarian and not a totalitarian regime."[16] The lack of public willingness to admit shortcomings detracted credibility from the administration's constant assurances that overtures were being made to the Salvadorans through "quiet diplomacy."*

Underlying the frustrations connected with the certification was a central ambiguity over what the law required. Was it "progress" in improving the human rights situation, or some absolute standard of conduct? Congressional compromises on the certification language in 1981 gave the administration substantial leeway in defining "progress" as sufficient for certification.† But what constituted progress? Salvadoran military expressions of intent? A decline in the numbers of

---

*In contrast to administration statements in Washington, U.S. Ambassador to El Salvador Deane Hinton used the congressional debate to send a signal to the Salvadoran army. On the eve of visits by several congressional delegations in February, Hinton spoke out against "serious excesses" by the government. "If there is one issue which could force our Congress to withdraw or seriously reduce its support for El Salvador," he told a business group, "it is the issue of human rights. . . . There is a limit, and at times this government has treaded dangerously close to that limit." Joanne Omang, "U.S. Envoy Warns El Salvador of Excesses," *Washington Post*, February 12, 1982.

†Note that the certification language proposed initially was changed from a requirement that the Salvadoran government "has achieved" control over the security forces to "is achieving" such control. This change allowed the administration to focus on a *process*, rather than an absolute *accomplishment* of an objective. Senator Percy's comments during the Senate floor debate on the certification refer explicitly to "progress" as justification for the certification.

people killed, tortured, and made to disappear, even if the numbers remained high? What can be said with certainty is that the administration construed these ambiguities as requiring minimal demonstrations of improvement, while some in Congress desired more substantial headway, if not the total elimination of abuses.

Another weakness with the certification was its inherently procedural nature: the administration made a certification, reported to Congress on its substance, and left Congress to debate the merits and drawbacks. Congress's role was similar to that exercised in any oversight process, and its control over policy was thus limited. First, the administration had a monopoly on policy implementation. Congress could *intend* for the administration to use the certification as leverage on the Salvadoran military, but it could not *force* the administration to exercise that influence. Second, although Congress could rely on outside witnesses and organizations for expertise, the administration possessed superior information about events on the ground and therefore a greater ability to manipulate information to its advantage. Congress's investigative possibilities, notwithstanding congressional and staff travel, were no match for the administration's.

A review of two aspects of the January 1982 certification illustrates the degree to which Congress was hostage to assertions made by the administration. In late 1982 the House Intelligence Committee's Subcommittee on Oversight and Evaluation examined the intelligence on which the first certification was based. In one instance the subcommittee found that the administration "supported policy claims with assertions based on little more than official statements of the Salvadoran military."[17] Had Congress known about the source of the information, administration claims would have been even less credible. In a second instance, the subcommittee examined embassy reporting regarding the alleged massacre in the town of El Mozote. Although the press had reported extensively on the incident, Assistant Secretary Enders insisted before several congressional committees that "no evidence could be found to confirm that government forces systematically massacred civilians . . . nor that the number of civilians killed even remotely approached the [number of] victims variously cited in press reports." Assistant Secretary of State for Human Rights and Humanitarian Affairs Elliott Abrams repeated the denials, insisting that the high number of victims reported in the press was implausible. To back up the administration's claim, Enders asserted that the U.S. Embassy had "sent two Embassy officers to investigate" the incident.[18]

According to the subcommittee report, however, the investigators "*never reached the towns where the alleged events occurred*," an admission included in the Embassy's own reporting from the field. In fact, the investigators had overflown El Mozote "in a helicopter." The administration's claim that civilians had died in a firefight rather than a massacre came from a "man from a town several miles away from El Mozote [who] *'intimated'* that he knew of violent fighting" (emphasis in the original).[19]

Over a decade later, exhumations of mass graves in El Mozote revealed that there had indeed been a massacre. Forensic anthropologists working with the United Nations Commission on the Truth for El Salvador uncovered 143 skeletons in one site alone, including 131 children whose average age was six. Ballistics experts concluded that many of those killed had been summarily shot with U.S.-made M-16 rifles.[20] Moreover, one of the U.S. Embassy officers who had been sent in 1982 to investigate what had happened at El Mozote stated publicly in 1993 for the first time that he believed "something bad had happened, . . . non-combatant casualties of a large number."[21] The Embassy officer said that he had informed Ambassador Deane Hinton of his impression; Hinton then discarded the possibility of a massacre in a January 31, 1982, cable to the State Department, which served as the basis for Enders's and Abrams's congressional testimony.[22]

The manipulation of information is significant only if one can argue that Congress would have acted differently if it had had access to the administration's internal working documents. Such an argument is difficult to make. Although a number of members of Congress believed that the certification was not taken seriously by the administration, there was little support for a toughening of its measures or a cutoff of military aid, as the law seemed to require. The reason was fairly simple: as in 1981, there was little support for ending aid to the Salvadoran government, an action that was seen as paving the way for a guerrilla victory.*

The administration played on these fears, arguing that the human rights situation would undoubtedly worsen if the Duarte government fell to the rebels and criticizing the certification's focus solely on government-sponsored violence. "It is no part of a human rights policy to allow the Duarte government to be replaced by a Communist dictatorship," said Assistant Secretary of State for Human Rights Elliott Abrams on February 8. "To acquiesce in this, to withdraw

---

*Several members of Congress did, in fact, mobilize to reject the certification. On February 2, 1982, Representative Studds introduced a resolution to declare the certification "null and void," and within a week he had picked up seventy-eight co-sponsors. Representative Richard Ottinger (D-N.Y.) led fifty-four members of Congress to write President Reagan asking him to withdraw the certification, charging that it was "contrary to documented facts." Congressman Richard L. Ottinger, "Lawmakers Challenge Reagan Assessment," Press Release, February 2, 1982, p. 1.

our support from the Government of El Salvador, would make a mockery of our concern for human rights." Similarly, declared Assistant Secretary Enders, "I wonder how it would promote human rights to repeat the [Nicaraguan] experiment in El Salvador."[23]

The administration was consciously emphasizing "bottom lines" and exploiting the congressional majority's own reluctance to do anything that could be portrayed as undermining the Duarte government. Thus, although most of the administration's congressional critics might have been frustrated and impatient, they lacked the votes to take tougher action. In amending the foreign assistance authorization for Fiscal Year 1983, the House Foreign Affairs Committee issued a mild warning emphasizing "its concern that the determination by the President [about human rights in El Salvador] . . . meet both the letter and the spirit of the law. The committee is interested in results, not just statements of intent or ineffective actions."[24] But results from the debate over the first certification were inconclusive. After circling each other like boxers in a ring, Congress and the administration withdrew to the corners; debate did not end, it was only postponed for another round.

Negotiations: Another Standoff

The drive by members of Congress to encourage if not require the administration to seek a political resolution of the Salvadoran conflict was at times motivated by one or more of four interrelated arguments: first, that the administration was, despite denials, considering the use of U.S. forces in Central America, a situation Congress and the American public greatly feared. On February 10, television crews added punch to the first concern when they filmed three U.S. advisers carrying M-16 rifles and other combat equipment in eastern El Salvador, where guerrillas had been most active. Second, even if such intervention was not being contemplated, it would become inevitable as the military situation continued to deteriorate for the Salvadoran government. Scarcely a month earlier, for example, the guerrillas staged a surprise raid on El Salvador's largest air base, destroying or damaging eighteen aircraft.*

Third, and to some extent underlying the first two arguments, was that the

---

*The Reagan administration cited the attack in providing an additional $55 million in military aid through emergency channels that bypassed congressional review. Even th administration justification was bogus: a decision to provide the aid had been made bef the guerrilla raid.

Salvadoran army was so repressive toward its own population and so riddled with corruption that it could never hope to gain the upper hand in the fight against the insurgents. In the short run, this argument proved the least defensible. And fourth, and perhaps more predictive, there could not be a strictly military solution to the Salvadoran conflict.

Administration officials did much to raise congressional alarm about the use of U.S. military force in El Salvador. In late 1981 the head of the U.S. Southern Command, Lieutenant General Wallace Nutting, declared that the military situation was a "stalemate" and that "in that kind of war, if you are not winning, you are losing."[25] In congressional testimony Secretary of State Haig threatened, for example, that the United States would "do whatever is necessary" to prevent the overthrow of the Salvadoran government.[26] A few days later Haig stated that "there are no current plans for the use of American forces" but added that "the sterility of drawing lines around America's potential options constitutes the promulgation of roadways for those who are seeking to move against America's vital interests." The administration was thus simultaneously denying it would intervene militarily and refusing to foreclose any options. Haig himself raised a Vietnam scenario. "We are going to succeed and not flounder as we did in Vietnam," he told the House Foreign Affairs Committee on March 2.[27]

In response to these kinds of statements, Senate Minority Leader Robert Byrd introduced legislation to amend the War Powers Resolution to prohibit the introduction of U.S. troops in El Salvador without the prior approval of Congress. Byrd's bill, which was never ratified by the Congress, represented an attempt to put a brake on any U.S. plans for intervention, on the theory that Congress, if consulted, would never acquiesce in such a politically unpopular move.

At the same time, asserting the relevance of the War Powers legislation to the Salvadoran situation exploited one of the Democrats' most potent anti-Reagan themes—that an administration disposed to military solutions was indeed going to involve the United States in a war opposed by the American people: a Newsweek poll published on March 1, 1982, showed that 74 percent of Americans familiar with Reagan policy believed that El Salvador could turn into the Vietnam of the 1980s. Eighty-nine percent of those familiar with U.S. policy said the United States should not provide troops.

The concerns reflected in Byrd's bill appear to have had an effect on the administration. On March 10, General David C. Jones, chairman of the Joint Chiefs of Staff, made an unusual disclaimer before the House Foreign Affairs Committee, stating that he did not "see any circumstances under which we would intervene with American forces" in El Salvador.[28] The congressional debate, it seems, had served to reinforce skepticism in the military that there was a political mandate for U.S. intervention in Central America. After Vietnam, the Pentagon was not about to commit U.S. troops abroad without a solid domestic consensus to back them.

Obliging the administration to pursue an alternative policy in El Salvador—one that would have preempted the decision ever to send troops—proved just as difficult to legislate, however, as did obliging the administration to show greater concern for human rights. Chief among those difficulties was the administration's monopoly on policy implementation. "It is very difficult for Congress to propose alternative policies that are not tied to specific programs," said George Ingram, a senior aide to the House Foreign Affairs Committee. "Negotiations are so dependent on the good will of the parties carrying them out. Congress cannot mandate that good will. We are hamstrung. We aren't the responsible entity to carry out policy."[29]

However, even when congressional committees did attempt to command an alternative policy by writing such provisions into law, the process of compromise within the Congress often left the provisions ambiguous. One example was a section of the certification law drafted in 1981, requiring a determination that "the Government of El Salvador . . . is committed to the holding of free elections at an early date and to that end has demonstrated its good faith efforts to begin discussions with all major political factions."[30] Did the language require the Salvadoran government to enter into negotiations with the opposition, or only, as the administration maintained in the certification, show that the government was encouraging the left to participate in upcoming elections?[31] The uncertainties about what constituted movement toward a political settlement allowed the administration to stick to its guns, rejecting direct talks between the warring parties that were aimed at anything more than securing the left's participation in the electoral process.

Even if a political settlement was read to require steps beyond the holding of elections, Congress was less than clear about what negotiations were intended to achieve. A Salvadoran government where rebels and Christian Democrats shared power? A restructured army? Senator Paul Tsongas (D-Mass.) promoted the idea of a "Zimbabwe settlement," where an insurgency was ended and a majority black government was brought to power through elections. But Enders rejected the Zimbabwe analogy as a false one, claiming that the Salvadoran guerrillas represented a minority of the population and had no claim on a share of power.

The lack of specificity about what talks were intended to produce, however, did not preclude a flurry of initiatives aimed at achieving a settlement in El Salvador through a diplomatic process, including one involving other Latin

American nations. These included several bills and resolutions, and a letter from 104 members of the House to Reagan asking him to accept a Mexican-Venezuelan offer to help negotiate an end to the Salvadoran war.

But the Congress as a whole was too divided to put teeth into any negotiations proposal. On March 2 the House voted 396–3 to press for "unconditional discussions among the major political factions in El Salvador in order to guarantee a safe and stable environment for free and open democratic elections." The debate itself showed that all sides claimed victory over a resolution open to several different interpretations.

"Support for the resolution is support for both President Reagan's ongoing policy and . . . the efforts of the Duarte government," said William Broomfield, ranking Republican on the House Foreign Affairs Committee. Countered Gerry Studds, "The President and his spokesmen have expressed opposition time and time again to precisely the sort of unconditional discussions called for in this resolution." The best summation was offered by Majority Leader Jim Wright: "I do not know how much good this resolution will do, but I support it because it puts us on the side of those who would settle their differences by ballots and not by bullets."[32]

Despite the inconclusive nature of struggles with the negotiations issue, however, the debate itself was causing consternation in the administration. A document drafted by Deputy Assistant Secretary of State Stephen Bosworth in mid-April 1982 noted that "we continue to face the threat of Congressional rejection of our Salvador policy through cutting off military aid or requiring negotiations as one condition of our semi-annual certifications."[33] Around the same time, a National Security Planning Group document noted "serious difficulties with U.S. public and Congressional opinion, which jeopardizes our ability to stay the course." The paper advocated "co-opting cut-and-run negotiation strategies by demonstrating a reasonable but firm approach to negotiations and compromise on our terms." The paper concluded with the need to "step up efforts to co-opt negotiations issues to avoid Congressionally-mandated negotiations, which would work against our interests."[34]

What the papers demonstrate is that, despite the inconsistencies surrounding congressional consideration of the negotiations issue, the administration viewed the congressional debates as a threat. The paper also illustrates the administration's mode of response to congressional concerns: to "co-opt" them while staying the course, rather than addressing or incorporating them in a revised policy. But as the upcoming policy showdown over the postelection Salvadoran government demonstrated, members of Congress, too, knew how to get what they wanted from the administration.

Elections and the Postelection Government

Congressional enthusiasm for the March 1982 elections in El Salvador had several sources. First, as Assistant Secretary Enders had recognized in July 1981, any attempt to defeat the insurgency had to involve an attempt at political reform, particularly given the Salvadoran electoral frauds of 1972 and 1977. Second, American political culture is imbued with the concept that the people rule and that those who rule them are freely chosen; it provided a congenial context for an electoral solution, particularly among members of Congress, themselves products of an electoral system. Third, in the presence of massive violence, the holding of an election provided a glimmer of hope that progress toward a peaceful resolution to the conflict was possible.

But there was caution as well as optimism. A leading candidate in the election was former Major Roberto D'Aubuisson, whose reputation in Congress preceded his entry into electoral politics. In February 1981, former Ambassador Robert White had called D'Aubuisson a "psychopathic killer"; in April of that year, White had given the Senate Foreign Relations Committee a set of captured documents that, according to White, provided "evidence that is compelling, if not 100 percent conclusive," of D'Aubuisson's responsibility for the assassination of Archbishop Romero.[35]

Even the Reagan administration had denounced the former major. Following a machine-gun attack on the U.S. Embassy in February 1981, Chargé d'Affaires Frederic Chapin had complained that it had "all the hallmarks of a D'Aubuisson operation"; in May, Assistant Secretary of State for Congressional Relations Richard Fairbanks wrote Representative Lee Hamilton (D-Ind.) that D'Aubuisson reportedly led "a right-wing terrorist group" called the Maximiliano Hernández Martínez Brigade. D'Aubuisson's reputation as a killer on the hard right and his campaign promises to "exterminate" the left and undo the 1980 socioeconomic reforms cast doubt on the election's capacity to bring about democratic results in El Salvador.[36]

The mood was perhaps best summed up by Representative John Murtha (D-Pa.), a hard-nosed conservative sent by Speaker Tip O'Neill in February 1982 to investigate conditions in El Salvador. Upon his return he said that the United States should support the elections if the voting was "free and open," if there was progress in human rights and agrarian reform, and if an acceptable "middle ground" won.[37] In other words, the outcome of the election would be just as important as the fact of an election itself.

Voting day proved favorable to both the electoral process and the administration. Newspapers carried ecstatic accounts of Salvadoran peasants walking for miles and standing in line for hours to cast their ballots.* Meanwhile, the guerrillas attempted to disrupt the election by attacking polling places and threatening Salvadorans if they voted. "The 1982 election was tremendously important," said Margaret Daly Hayes, senior Senate Foreign Relations Committee staff person for the Western Hemisphere, who accompanied the official delegation of U.S. observers. "The press was very much disposed to see El Salvador as a failure and the guerrillas as having the support of the people. The election proved to them that that was not the case."[38]

The U.S. observers announced that the elections were "fair and free" and concluded that "the tremendous turnout . . . underscores the sense of commitment of the people."[39] Overall reactions on Capitol Hill, however, were somewhat more cautious. "The masses down there appreciate the freedom of elections," said House Speaker Tip O'Neill. "I just hope they can bring a majority party to power that can bring all factions together." House Minority Leader Robert Michel gave a similarly mixed review: "No one can say what will happen next, but history will record that for one brief shining moment, amidst the darkness of war, the people at least voted in large numbers."[40]

Developments over the next weeks and months showed that congressional doubts were well placed: although Duarte's Christian Democratic Party won a plurality of Assembly seats, the Christian Democrats were outnumbered by a coalition of right-wing parties united by their opposition to a continued Duarte presidency and skeptical, at best, of the 1980 reforms. More important, the elections heightened the possibility that D'Aubuisson, whose ARENA party had captured almost 20 percent of the vote, could be appointed provisional president by the conservative Assembly majority.

Publicly the Reagan administration maintained that "what government is formed is basically an issue for the Salvadoran people."[41] But privately, top U.S. officials maneuvered behind the scenes to ensure that the postelection government would be palatable in Washington. That meant above all that D'Aubuisson

---

*See, for example, Richard J. Meislin's account in the March 29, 1982, *New York Times*: "There were people young and old—men with canes, women carrying babies and women expecting them. Their attire of vivid yellows and greens and reds and magentas gave the impression of a traveling rainbow as they surged on foot along the scorching highway toward voting places in eastern San Salvador." "I find words fail me," Deputy Assistant Secretary of State Everett Briggs told the Senate Foreign Relations Committee, "to express the depth of the emotional impact that this event made on me." U.S. Congress, Senate, Committee on Foreign Relations, *U.S. Policy in the Western Hemisphere*, Hearings, April 1, 20, 27, 28, May 4 and 26, 1982, 97th Cong., 2nd Sess. (Washington, D.C.: U.S. Government Printing Office, 1982), p. 11.

had to be denied the presidency. The administration chose to enlist members of Congress to deliver the message that future U.S. support would be contingent on a particular political outcome. This congressional-executive alliance worked because it was based on a mutuality of interests and a recognition of shared power. It was also testimony to the impact of prior congressional debates over human rights and social reform; by insisting on the internal roots of the Salvadoran conflict the Congress had set an agenda that the administration could no longer ignore.*

In a sense, the partnership between Congress and the administration in influencing the shape of the postelection Salvadoran government was what Congress had envisioned all along: giving the administration, which carried out foreign policy, the leverage to encourage or even impose policy changes on the Salvadorans. Ironically, the requirements of certification, which the administration had resisted as a way of exerting human rights pressure on the Salvadoran government, became one of the instruments of administration persuasion.

Ambassador Hinton circulated copies of the certification to Salvadoran leaders. When U.S. Ambassador-at-Large Vernon Walters arrived in El Salvador to mediate the postelection jockeying for power, the Embassy sent a letter inviting Salvadoran leaders to meet with Walters and reminding them that continuing U.S. aid was contingent on the emergence of a moderate government.[42]

The subtle and not so subtle messages were reinforced when a House delegation headed by Majority Leader Jim Wright arrived in San Salvador the first week of April. According to a U.S. Embassy account of a dinner with Salvadoran party leaders, "Members of CODEL [congressional delegation] Wright . . . drove home the importance to the U.S. Congress of a Salvadoran government of national unity which would include the PDC [Christian Democrat Party]. . . . All members of the CODEL hammered home the importance of demonstrating support for the reforms by action as well as by lip service. . . . If their listeners did not get the message, then they are not likely to receive the

---

*At the same time that the administration was pressing moderation in the postelection period, key officials were soft-pedaling D'Aubuisson, perhaps as a preemptive measure if he was appointed to a prominent role in the government. On April 1, 1982, Deputy Assistant Secretary of State Everett Briggs told the Senate Foreign Relations Committee that the Salvadoran right-wing parties "include some very liberal, . . . very moderate people." A May 1982 revised intelligence community profile of D'Aubuisson eliminated references in earlier profiles to charges that he was a leader of right-wing death squads and had participated in the murder of Archbishop Romero. See Senate Committee on Foreign Relations, U.S. Policy in the Western Hemisphere, Hearings, April 1, 20, 27, 28, and May 4 and 26, 1982, p. 14; and p. 14 of the House staff report cited in note 17 of this chapter.

word ever."[43] Wright's message in San Salvador was driven home in Washington by Senate Foreign Relations Committee Chairman Charles Percy, who said that "any government that does not include the Christian Democrats, which does not seek to bridge political differences in the interest of national unity and peace, will not be credible to Congress and cannot expect the support of Congress." Deputy Assistant Secretary of State Stephen Bosworth thanked him during the hearing for his statement.

In response to protests from the right wing that such pressures amounted to U.S. intervention in internal Salvadoran affairs, a diplomat replied, "That's not intervention. That's money" talking.[44]

While congressional representations were intended to influence the conservative Salvadoran parties, they may have had an even greater impact on the Salvadoran army. Perhaps as testimony to the military's dependence on U.S. assistance, the army assumed the role of broker between the political parties; it did not want the bickering of civilians to jeopardize military aid and therefore took the lead in hammering out an agreement that would be acceptable to the United States. According to accounts by Salvadoran politicians, leaders of each party were summoned to separate meetings with about two dozen army officers, representing the major services and field commands. They were told, "Here are three names [for provisional president]; pick one."[45] The military's preferred candidate for provisional president, Alvaro Magaña, was finally offered the post. Soon thereafter, the Assembly elected D'Aubuisson head of the legislature.

Postelection efforts by both the administration and the Congress were thus only partially successful in securing a centrist outcome in El Salvador: the Salvadoran election had been aimed at legitimizing the role of the Christian Democrats, but the opposite had been achieved. The Constituent Assembly, with a right-wing majority led by D'Aubuisson, held the power to rewrite the Salvadoran constitution and thus alter the juridical base for the socioeconomic reforms put into place by the Christian Democrats. Over the next several months the Assembly's attempt to rewrite Salvadoran agrarian law provoked a major clash with the Congress.

The army, conversely, emerged from the election seeing its immediate interests entwined with the fate of electoral politics. Congressional actions, however, had two contradictory effects. By linking U.S. aid to a particular political outcome in El Salvador, the Congress had heightened the army's political role in ensuring that outcome; by insisting on the development of democratic government, however, the Congress nurtured the army's tolerance for civilian, constitutional government. In both cases, the army expected to be rewarded. Perhaps the most telling remark of this period was an observation made by a House Foreign Affairs Committee aide who had accompanied Majority Leader Wright to San Salvador: "Defense Minister General García . . . stressed that the Armed Forces' conduct in the elections should be taken into account in U.S. Congressional deliberations."[46]

Congress and Agrarian Reform:
The Politics of Aid as a Weapon

Within weeks of its inauguration, the Salvadoran Constituent Assembly took action demonstrating the influence of its conservative majority. On May 18, 1982, the Assembly voted to cancel for one crop cycle the right of tenant farmers to claim title to the land they worked under the much hailed "land-to-the-tiller" program instituted during the Carter administration. Originally, the measure proposed by President Magaña covered cotton and sugar lands only. The Assembly included in its land-to-the-tiller exemption lands for cattle grazing and basic grains, thus affecting the vast majority of acreage potentially available to landless peasants. "If what they want is to kill the land reform," said Christian Democratic deputy Antonio Guevara, "they should call things by name and say so once and for all."[47] The cry of Christian Democrats found a ready ear in the U.S. Congress.

By circumstance, the actions by El Salvador's Constituent Assembly coincided with House and Senate consideration of various foreign aid bills. Congress, therefore, had an opportunity to use its control over aid to produce changes in Salvadoran behavior. In the most direct example yet of congressional influence over El Salvador policy, congressional committees threatened a cutoff of U.S. funds if the land-reform suspension remained in effect.

The chairman of the Senate Foreign Relations Committee, Charles Percy, set the stage for confrontation during committee consideration of the package of aid and trade benefits called the Caribbean Basin Initiative. He stated, "If the Salvadoran government is reneging on the land-reform program, then . . . not one cent of funds shall go to the government of El Salvador."[48] Ranking Democrat Claiborne Pell threatened to introduce an amendment prohibiting all aid to El Salvador if the agrarian suspension remained in effect.

Tough, concrete actions followed several days later. On May 26 the Foreign Relations Committee voted unanimously to reduce the administration's Fiscal Year 1983 aid request by $100 million, effectively freezing aid to El Salvador at the levels approved in late 1981.[49] Senator Christopher Dodd (D-Conn.), who had cosponsored the spending cut with Republican Senator Nancy Kassebaum, declared that "there should be no doubt in anyone's mind about where [the Salvadorans] are headed with land reform. They are out to destroy it." Senator Tsongas emotionally endorsed the reduction in aid: "If land reform is rolled back, the sense of betrayal among the campesinos . . . is going to be overwhelming. . . . D'Aubuisson is sticking it in our chest, time after time after time. . . . [It] comes down to this committee to finally say, enough is enough. . . . If we back down, the message to D'Aubuisson is very clear. Do what you want! We will be with you no matter what you do."[50]

U.S. Ambassador to El Salvador Deane Hinton hurried back to Washington to convince committee members that they had overreacted, saying that press reports had given the land reform alterations a "bum rap." He insisted that land-to-the-tiller had not been suspended, as reported in the press, but rather that El Salvador's Constituent Assembly had merely exempted from the law lands for four types of crops.[51] But his pleas fell largely on deaf ears. The Foreign Relations Committee action held. Meanwhile the House Foreign Operations Subcommittee voted on May 26 to reject the entire administration request for supplemental military aid, including $35 million for El Salvador. And Representative Zablocki, chairman of the House Foreign Affairs Committee, told Hinton in early June that he was postponing House consideration of the foreign aid bill in the wake of the Salvadoran Assembly actions. "If the situation is not more promising," Zablocki said, "we'll put it over until next year."[52] Events in El Salvador—symbolic and symptomatic of Assembly hostility to the reform program—had prompted decisive congressional action. In response, the Salvadoran Assembly moved within weeks to clarify—that is, exempt—the land-to-the-tiller program from alterations in agrarian reform. Congress had made good on a threat, and the Salvadorans had responded.

The Second Certification

In the inauspicious months of May and June, the Reagan administration prepared for the second certification required by law in July. It is not clear either from the public record or from private administration communications now available that the administration felt compelled to pressure the Salvadoran government for actual improvements in the human rights situation. What is clear, however, is that the necessity to certify caused the administration to approach the Salvadoran government in search of evidence it could use in making the certification. These overtures themselves, a kind of hammering away on the issues the Congress viewed as important, may have constituted a subtle message that over time sensitized the Salvadoran military, in particular, to steps that could be taken in their own self-interest.

The administration's distaste for the certification is reflected in a cable by Assistant Secretary of State for Human Rights Elliott Abrams, following a July visit to San Salvador. "The certification process is ridiculous," Abrams wrote, "a product of Congress's refusal to make decisions or to let the President make them. . . . The debate over El Salvador is conducted entirely in terms suggested and then defined by the Left. . . . We bear much of the blame for continuing to suffer this condition." Although Abrams stated that he "believe[d] we need to keep our human rights pressure on," he continued, "The congressional demand that we quantify and measure progress here every six months is absurd."[53]

The attitude of the Reagan administration's principal official responsible for human rights casts doubt on the extent to which the certification process had a concrete effect on administration human rights policy in El Salvador. More ambiguity over the extent of pressure exerted by the administration is revealed in a confidential cable signed by Secretary of State Haig to the U.S. Embassy in San Salvador in May 1982. The cable began:

> We consider it essential that progress be made in these three areas [development of democratic institutions, human rights, and land reform] if the government of El Salvador is to be successful in combatting the insurgency and if we are to sustain the support of the Congress for our economic and military assistance programs.

The cable then continued:

> You should engage [President] Magaña and appropriate cabinet members, as well as the Constituent Assembly leadership, in a discussion of our general policy concerns. You should indicate that we need by the end of June, a program of concrete *proposed* GOES actions which we could use in defending certification and maintenance of requested . . . assistance. . . . The upcoming July certification deadline should provide us the impetus to push through at least the highest priority steps now [emphasis added].[54]

Thus, it is not apparent from the text of the memo whether *actual* improvements were necessary or whether the administration sought from the Salvadoran government information which it could use to justify making the certification.[55]

Although neither of what Secretary Haig called in his cable the two "highest priority steps" had been taken by July, the administration certified on July 27, 1982, that "there are tangible signs of progress" by the Salvadoran government that warranted continued aid.* In contrast to the January certification, however, the one made in July admitted that "human rights violations and terrorism continued to be a major problem." The report cited "reports of human rights abuses on the part of various branches of the Salvadoran security forces . . . reports of torture and execution of prisoners and the participation of individual members of the security forces in right-wing terrorist activity continue, and in some cases are credible."[56] There was thus a notable shift in tone between the first and second certifications, and an even greater movement since 1981 in acknowledging the Salvadoran government as a source of violence against its citizens. The second certification—a fifty-page document with extensive appendices—made its January predecessor look skimpy indeed.

Although the second certification provided far more complete information than the first, it is not clear from the document, or from subsequent administration defense of it, that the administration's actual policy regarding human rights in El Salvador changed in 1982 as a result of successive certifications. The second certification, like the first, continued to substitute promises by the Salvadoran Ministry of Defense for concrete actions. The certification claimed, for example, that the "Minister of Defense has ordered that all violations of citizens' rights be stopped immediately and directed punishment of military offenders." As of early 1988 only one noncommissioned officer had been convicted for an abuse against a Salvadoran citizen.

Administration officials also made claims before Congress that their own cables did not support: the certification stated that "over the past six months 109 members of the Salvadoran Armed Forces were disciplined for various offenses" even though the Embassy warned that the information could not be confirmed and should therefore be used with the "proper caveats."[57]

Senior U.S. officials continued an effort to discredit the principal human rights monitoring group in San Salvador, stating erroneously that it had been repudiated by the Catholic Church.[58] And the State Department sought consciously to downplay the significance of a brutal torture case of a Salvadoran Green Cross volunteer known to U.S. Embassy officials, apparently, according to U.S. officials cited in the *Washington Post*, so as not to offend the head of the Salvadoran National Police.[59]

*These steps included transferring military and intelligence duties of the National Guard and Treasury Police to the army, and the formation of a civilian police force. This was not accomplished until 1992.

The congressional reaction to the second certification—it was a "close call," according to Assistant Secretary Abrams—showed that the administration's decision to admit certain shortcomings paid off with congressional moderates.[60] Foreign Relations Committee Chairman Charles Percy called the certification "accurate, appropriate, and right" and said that "it would be a tragedy to withdraw our support."[61] While liberals complained of the persistent gap between the administration's assessment and that of private observers, and one went so far as to call the certification a "dishonest document," the tone of questioning was more tired and frustrated than acrimonious.[62] On August 6, 1982, the Reagan administration seemed to be claiming victory in deflecting congressional attention from its sole preoccupation with human rights. "We've won," an official told the Wall Street Journal. "We've succeeded in making the issue of human rights in El Salvador boring."[63]

But human rights were less boring than nettlesome for officials responsible for carrying out U.S. policy from the U.S. Embassy in San Salvador. The need to issue certifications every six months began to magnify persistent failures to move ahead on human rights cases of symbolic importance in the United States. In late September a Salvadoran judge released from custody a National Guard lieutenant arrested for the assassination of the AIFLD advisers and head of the Salvadoran land-reform agency, on the grounds that there was insufficient evidence to hold him. AIFLD, which was deeply involved in the execution of U.S. policy in El Salvador, began to publicize evidence it had against the National Guard officer, Lieutenant Rodolfo Isidro López Sibrián. "We were being diddled by the Salvadorans," complained U.S. Ambassador Hinton. An official embassy statement said it was "dismayed and incredulous" at the judge's decision.[64]

The embassy comment came to underscore the differences between Washington and San Salvador, between those in the administration responsible for designing policy and those in the field designated to carry it out. Even if Congress could be mollified with tokens of progress in the AIFLD murder investigation, officials in the Embassy were confronted with the true obstacle to progress: López Sibrián, a former security aide to Assembly leader Roberto D'Aubuisson, was protected by connections to high-ranking Salvadoran officials and military officers. As a 1983 State Department report would later note, "The military exerts a pervasive influence over the nation and . . . has sought to shield from justice even those who commit the most atrocious crimes."[65]

Ambassador Hinton lashed out in frustration on October 29, 1982. In a speech to the American Chamber of Commerce that Ambassador Hinton insists had been sent to Washington for clearance, he declared:

In the first two weeks of this month at least 68 human beings were murdered in El Salvador under circumstances which are familiar to everyone here. Every day we receive new reports of disappearances under tragic circumstances. American citizens in El Salvador have been among the murdered, among the "disappeared." Is it any wonder that much of the world is predisposed to believe the worst of a system which almost never brings to justice either those who perpetrate these acts or those who order them? . . . If you are not convinced that I am talking about a fundamental and critical problem, consider these facts. Since 1979 perhaps as many as 30,000 Salvadorans have been MURDERED, not killed in battle, MURDERED [emphasis in the original].[66]

"The message is simple," Hinton said in an interview several days later. "El Salvador must make progress in bringing the murderers of our citizens, including those who ordered the murders, to justice. . . . If not, the United States, in spite of our interests, in spite of our commitment to the struggle against Communism, could be forced to deny assistance to El Salvador."[67]

Hinton's frank assessment was the harshest public criticism of the Salvadoran government that had been made by any Reagan administration official. But the comments did not reflect a new consensus within the administration on the importance of human rights considerations. On the contrary, Hinton's remarks were repudiated by National Security Council chief William Clark, who, in Hinton's words, viewed the speech as "leftist propaganda."[68] In anonymous comments to the New York Times, Clark, identified only as "an Administration official," stated that Hinton had been instructed to refrain from making public criticism of human rights abuses, and that his speech had not been cleared by the White House. It "took us a little by surprise," the "official" said. "The decibel level had risen higher than our policy has allowed in the past."[69]

Although the State Department closed ranks behind Hinton, they, too, softened his words. A text of Hinton's speech circulated in Washington deleted his reference to 30,000 Salvadorans murdered since 1979 and changed the phrase to: "Since 1979 perhaps as many as 30,000 Salvadorans have been killed illegally, that is, not in battle."[70]

In short, human rights policy remained confused. Although concerns expressed by Congress in Washington served as a backdrop for a growing embassy focus on the issue of right-wing violence, the administration as a whole was not prepared to embrace the problem as a central element of its El Salvador strategy. The indecision in the administration, meanwhile, was matched by institutional incapacity in the Congress: after failing to enact either a foreign aid authorization or appropriation for the upcoming fiscal year, Congress passed a December "continuing resolution" dramatically reducing the administration's request for military aid. Cuts proposed earlier in the year in angry response to the Salvadoran Assembly's suspension of the agrarian reform became the basis for a final appropriation of $26 million in military assistance, the same amount approved in 1981. Although the Salvadoran war was expanding, the money for it was not. What the administration came to view as a "funding crisis" had begun.[71]

Nicaragua:
A Policy Begins to Flounder

Early in 1982 the administration embarked on a concerted campaign to transform Nicaragua into a legitimate target of U.S. hostility. The verbal assaults—aimed at Nicaragua's support for neighboring insurgencies and at policies of internal repression—were consistent with the Reagan administration's view that the Sandinista government and its communist allies were principally responsible for regional turmoil. What is remarkable about the administration's effort is that the Congress largely accepted as valid the Reagan administration's characterizations of the Sandinista regime. Where Congress differed from the administration was over whether a policy of sponsoring covert operations against Nicaragua would produce desired results. The administration failed in providing a political rationale for the covert war. It could not convince Congress of the need to create a generalized opposition to the Sandinistas, as opposed to a force designed to stop Nicaragua's support for neighboring insurgencies.

The administration went on the offensive in early March, to pull Congress and the public away from their fixation on El Salvador. On March 1, U.N. Ambassador Jeane Kirkpatrick told a Senate subcommittee that a "dynamic of repression" was operating in Nicaragua and that the "process of eliminating and intimidating opponents was far advanced." Secretary of State Haig later denounced the Sandinistas' treatment of the Miskitos as "genocidal."[72] The message was that Sandinista behavior, ignored by human rights groups, the press, and the Congress, was as bad as or worse than El Salvador's.

The centerpiece of the offensive concerned arms shipments from Nicaragua to El Salvador. For months skeptics in the media and Congress had pressed the administration to substantiate the charges initiated in the 1981 white paper, later shown to be flawed. Haig had raised the ante when he told a House subcommittee that the administration had "unchallengeable" proof of "Nicaraguan involvement in El Salvador and Cuban involvement in the command and control of the operations in El Salvador today."[73] In response to persistent doubts, the Reagan administration organized closed-door briefings for members of Congress and influential members of the foreign policy community. Deputy Director of the CIA Bobby Inman and DIA Deputy Director for Intelligence and External Affairs John Hughes, meanwhile, held a public session featuring photographs taken by intelligence overflights of Nicaragua that showed extended Nicaraguan runways, burned Miskito villages, and military bases. *

Initially the briefings had the intended effect of generating support for the administration. On March 2, Senator Barry Goldwater, chairman of the Senate Intelligence Committee, stated that the intelligence review "left no doubt that there is active involvement by Sandinista government officials in support of the Salvadoran guerrilla movement." On March 4, Representative Edward Boland, chairman of the House Intelligence Committee, cited "persuasive evidence that the Sandinista Government of Nicaragua is helping train insurgents and is transferring arms and financial support from and through Nicaragua."[74] Boland refused to endorse the administration's claim that the Salvadoran insurgency was directed by non-Salvadorans. But the statements of the two chairmen together represented an important boost for the administration's case against Nicaragua.

While responsible entities in Congress embraced the administration's public rationale for U.S. policy toward Nicaragua, members of Congress not on the intelligence committees remained unaware that covert operations had begun. By March, however, details of the secret war initiated in 1981 began to seep onto the front pages of major newspapers, perhaps through deliberate leaks by high administration officials in order to scare governments in the region.[75] And within days of the press leaks, anti-Sandinista guerrillas destroyed two major bridges along the Nicaraguan-Honduran border, prompting the Sandinistas to declare a state of emergency. Almost immediately, congressional liberals—Barnes, Mc-

---

*The House Intelligence Subcommittee on Oversight and Evaluation later wrote that the briefing was "flawed by several instances of overstatement and overinterpretation" (see p. 8 of the staff report cited in note 17 of this chapter). The publicity offensive suffered an embarrassing setback on March 12 when the State Department presented to reporters a Nicaraguan purportedly sent by his government to fight with the Salvadoran rebels. The Nicaraguan, Orlando José Tardencillas, recanted and told an amused press corps that he had been tortured in El Salvador and threatened into collaborating with Salvadoran and U.S. officials. He said he had never been trained in Cuba and Ethiopia, as he had previously told his captors, and had gone to fight in El Salvador on his own initiative.

Hugh, Conte, Dodd, Tsongas—introduced a spate of bills to end military and paramilitary actions against the Sandinistas.

What skeptics rejected was the notion that the purpose of the covert operations was limited—that is, not aimed at the destabilization or overthrow of the Sandinistas. That goal—the overthrow of foreign governments—was deemed unacceptable as an aim of U.S. policy. Part of the objection was based on the lack of clarity in the administration's approach; Senators Dodd and Tsongas called the Nicaragua policy "as confused as it is dangerous."[76]

But the more important dispute was over values. In introducing a bill to prohibit the covert operation, Barnes called on the administration to adhere to the principles of "self-determination and non-interference."[77] McHugh and Conte stated that "activities designed to destabilize or overthrow the government of any nation . . . are inappropriate, and that outstanding grievances between different nations . . . should be resolved through peaceful negotiations."[78] The principles to which the United States subscribed as a nation, the norms of international law, and a faith in diplomacy over military action served as counterweights to the Reagan administration's preference for unconventional war. In the words of another House Democrat who requested anonymity, the overthrow of foreign governments was simply "none of our goddamn business."[79]

Behind the objections based on principle were those of practicality, but even these arguments were tinged by moral considerations left over from congressional investigations of covert operations in the 1970s. In a veiled reference to Chile, Barnes noted that "when we abandoned these principles [of self-determination and nonintervention] and contributed to the overthrow of leftist governments . . . the results have been disastrous. . . . Doing a Bay of Pigs number" on the Sandinistas, he said, would only push them further toward Cuba and the Soviet Union.[80]

The argument that U.S. policy was counterproductive became a major one in the arsenal of Reagan administration critics, in part because it found resonance among the Sandinistas' internal opposition. Those ostensibly supported by U.S. policy met with dismay the news of U.S.-sponsored covert activity against the Nicaraguan government. "When the moderates are all hanging in the streets of Managua," said former junta member Alfonso Robelo, "the United States says look what the Sandinistas did to the moderates and use it as a pretext for an invasion."[81] A member of Robelo's party concurred at a Capitol Hill conference in May:

> [Covert operations are] totally ANTI-DEMOCRATIC and condemn-
> able. They give more support to anti-revolutionary forces that are not

welcome to the Nicaraguan people. They give the FSLN Directorate the perfect excuse to justify Repression, Radicalization and to show unquestionably their leaning (preferred from the very beginning) toward the Soviet bloc . . . [and] neutralize the Moderate sectors that still have some influence in Nicaragua [emphasis in the original].[82]

The statements of anti-Sandinista Nicaraguans thus contained a heavy note of irony. The contra operation was designed in part to cause the Sandinistas to "make mistakes," by intensifying an internal crackdown that would cost the government important international support.[83] But by its earlier emphasis on internal repression in Nicaragua, the administration helped to establish a link: between deprivations of civil rights and civil liberties in Nicaragua and the administration's own sponsorship of armed opposition to the Sandinistas.

The administration's seeming indifference to the nonmilitary Sandinista opposition helped to deny congressional support for its policy. In April a House Foreign Affairs Committee aide noted that "most [Sandinista opponents] are convinced that the Sandinistas are determined to take the country down a totalitarian path," but added that "private sector leaders argued forcefully for continuation of U.S. economic assistance to the private sector."[84] In May, however, the administration lobbied the House Foreign Affairs Committee to drop a requirement in the foreign aid bill that $20 million in economic support funds go to non-Sandinista entities in Nicaragua.* Similarly, when former Sandinista hero Edén Pastora left Nicaragua and denounced the Sandinistas in April, U.S. officials attempted to stifle his activities, according to exiles close to Pastora, in favor of rightist National Guardsmen based in Honduras.[85] As the Reagan administration missed repeated opportunities to support political alternatives in Nicaragua, it lost the ability to capitalize on anti-Sandinista sentiments among even liberals in Congress.

Moving to Prohibit the Covert War

The misgivings expressed publicly in Congress following press leaks about the covert war began to reverberate through closed-door meetings of the House

---

*To counter the impression that it was abandoning the Nicaraguan opposition, the State Department in June reprogrammed $5.1 million in economic aid as a "symbol of political and moral support" for the Nicaraguan Catholic Church and private sector, according to AID official Otto Reich.

Intelligence Committee. Those with privileged access to information about the administration's operations in Nicaragua were also troubled by the disparity between the administration's stated goals and the chosen instruments of policy. Uneasiness grew as the intelligence committee could show little evidence that actual arms were being stopped on their way from Nicaragua to El Salvador. Information provided to the committee often appeared to be slighter than that served to the general public on the nightly television news; members were bound to secrecy about what they were told in committee even while the same issues were discussed openly in the press. CIA Director Casey mumbled so inaudibly in his appearances before the committee that speakers and a microphone were installed. The insurgent force continued to grow, albeit not by the leaps and bounds of subsequent months. Contra leaders openly expressed their central aim: the overthrow of the Sandinista government.

In that atmosphere, the Intelligence Committee fired a warning shot when Chairman Boland himself offered an amendment during consideration of the 1983 intelligence authorization. The amendment, which the committee adopted, was Boland's way of heading off a potentially broader assault on the intelligence legislation by liberals protesting the Nicaragua operation; before adopting Boland's amendment, the committee considered but rejected a motion to strike all funds for the program. Boland's counterproposal prohibited any U.S. actions for the purpose of overthrowing the Nicaraguan government or provoking a military exchange between Nicaragua and Honduras.

The idea was that by restricting the purpose of the contra operation the administration would be forced to keep its policy within limits. The provision—still secret—became law in September, when Congress approved the legislation authorizing intelligence activities for the coming year.

Despite pockets of opposition, the issue of the contras was still a minor one for Congress as a whole. Yet liberal Democrats opposed to the Reagan administration's Nicaragua policy attempted repeatedly to bring the issue before their colleagues. Through a series of amendments in the summer of 1982, liberals began to focus a light bulb, if not a spotlight, on what they saw as the growing danger of military confrontation in Central America.

One "vehicle" for opening debate was the military construction authorization for 1983. The administration had requested $21 million to improve airfields in the western Caribbean, most of which were located in Honduras. In a pattern that would continue for the next several years, the establishment of a U.S. military presence in Honduras through military exercises and military construction projects became a subcategory of the Nicaragua controversy. The apparent cooperation of Honduran military officers in harboring and supplying the contras, and the outbreak of border skirmishes between Nicaraguan and Honduran forces, aroused similar concerns.[86] Honduras set the stage for the first congressional debate over the covert war.

On June 30, 1982, Senator Claiborne Pell (D-R.I.), senior Democrat on the Senate Foreign Relations Committee, offered a floor amendment to prohibit the use of military construction funds to build or upgrade airfields in Honduras. In the short discussion, Pell charged that "the United States, by working closely with the Honduran military . . . could provoke the Nicaraguans into moves against Honduras."[87] Pell's amendment lost overwhelmingly, 65–29. The effort was repeated in the House in August by Representative Tom Harkin (D-Iowa), who claimed that "the danger is real of a war between Honduras and Nicaragua." Representative George Miller (D-Calif.) charged that the United States was staging a "provocation of the Nicaraguan government" by situating contra troops in Honduras and inviting a cross-border attack.[88] But Harkin's amendment also failed overwhelmingly, 280–109.

Although the amendments lost by large majorities, Congress within months would incorporate concerns expressed in the debate into the first legislative prohibition on the covert war. In the late summer and early fall of 1982 a flood of press reports from Central America brought Nicaragua before the public and Congress. These dispatches included a cover story in *Newsweek* on November 8, and lengthy on-the-ground reports in *Time* and the *New York Times*. One source who requested anonymity insisted that Casey himself was one source for the *Newsweek* story, a fact he admitted to members of Congress. The goal of the contra rebels—to overthrow the government of Nicaragua—the willingness of Honduran officers to lend sanctuary to the contras and their own troops if necessary to defeat the Sandinistas, and the deep involvement of the CIA in holding the operation together became plain for all to see.[89]

About this same time, in November and December 1982, the Reagan administration attempted the first of many secret reshufflings of the contra leadership. The goal was to reduce the participation of former National Guardsmen in the military force and incorporate opposition civilian politicians in a broader anti-Sandinista front. Ultimately, the administration hoped to present to the Congress and public a legitimate counterforce deserving of U.S. political and financial support. The effort involved intentional deception of the Congress for the purpose of continuing a controversial CIA operation.

CIA officials expressly assured contra leaders, for example, that they had U.S. backing to "march into Managua," while at the same time counseling the rebels not to say so publicly. "We were told to say only that the Sandinistas had betrayed their goals and purposes," said Edgar Chamorro, a contra leader from

1982 to 1984. "We were told to say that [we were] just denouncing repression and want democratization."[90] Accordingly, Chamorro denied during a press conference in December 1982 that the contras were former Somoza supporters "who want to restore a right-wing dictatorship" in Nicaragua. "We want a democratic process," he said, "that will lead to free elections."[91]

The attempt at repackaging came too late, however, to sidetrack liberal efforts to shut down the contra program altogether. Prompted by human rights activists opposed to U.S. Central America policy, Harkin prepared to go after the funding. A "Watergate baby," a liberal, an insurgent Democrat without an assignment to any of the committees overseeing foreign affairs or intelligence, Harkin had little but conviction to back his effort. He and his supporters pushed debate in the House far to the left of where the majority of its members were prepared to go. But án ensuing compromise resulted in at least some constraints on the covert operation. By forcing the issue onto the agenda, Harkin achieved one of his major goals.

The Adoption of the First Boland Amendment

During House consideration of the Department of Defense appropriations bill, which included the funds for U.S. covert activities, Harkin offered an amendment to prohibit funds for military operations "in or against Nicaragua." He hammered away at the twin themes of the covert war's immorality and counterproductivity: "If you do not like the Nicaraguan government," Harkin said, "there probably would be nothing you could do to strengthen their hand better than supporting the very hated Somocista Guards along the Honduran border." The United States "would appear hypocritical" if it charged the Nicaraguan government with the export of subversion and terrorism, he said, if "the United States is engaged in much the same type of activity."[92]

Boland let the debate proceed before taking the floor to oppose Harkin's amendment and propose a compromise. "Your Intelligence Committee," he said, "is as concerned about the substances of the allegations concerning paramilitary activities in Nicaragua and Central America as all of you." Those same concerns, he explained, led to committee adoption of classified language prohibiting the use of U.S. funds to overthrow the government of Nicaragua or to provoke a military exchange between Nicaragua and Honduras. Boland noted that the language had been adopted by the House and Senate and was "agreeable to the executive branch." He asked Harkin to withdraw his amendment and accept the Intelligence Committee's substitute. Harkin agreed, and the Boland substitute was adopted unanimously, 411–0.[93]

Like other measures adopted in Congress by large bipartisan majorities, however, the Boland amendment could have initially appeared meaningless, "blue smoke and mirrors," in the words of Senator Dodd.* Opponents of the covert war could claim that they had voted to limit it, while supporters could note that since the stated purpose of the operation did not envision overthrow of the Sandinista government, administration actions would not be affected. Both interpretations are correct, and no doubt account for the Boland amendment's wide appeal. Many liberals, in fact, felt embarrassed that the Boland amendment was all they could get.

But the measure had two other important consequences. First, it established as a legal norm that U.S. policy was not to oust the Sandinistas from power. Senator Moynihan wrote Casey in late December stating that Congress expected the CIA to conform its activities to both the letter and the spirit of the law.[94] Second, the amendment put Boland in the position of vouching publicly for the purposes of the covert operation. In the words of one House Democrat, it was now "Boland's ass in the sling." As the covert war widened, and as contra leaders grew bolder in announcing their determination to overthrow the Sandinista government, it was ultimately Boland whose prestige was on the line with his colleagues. The amendment set the stage for a clash with the administration, which refused to live even within its modest provisions.

*Congressional Record, December 21, 1982, p. S 15899. On December 18, Senator Dodd attempted an amendment along the lines of Harkin's, but the measure was tabled, 56–38. A Boland-type substitute offered by Senators Moynihan and Chafee was not voted on. The House-passed Boland amendment was incorporated into the Fiscal Year 1983 resolution for continuing appropriations, signed into law on December 21, 1982. Because the Boland amendment was on an appropriations bill, it lasted only for the life of the appropriation—that is, one year.

Chapter Five

1983:
The President Steps In

In 1983, battles between the Congress and the executive over Central America policy expanded to a new level of intensity. Although other foreign policy crises, such as those in Lebanon or Grenada, caused Central America to slip occasionally from the top of the congressional agenda, the issues in Central America—human rights violations in El Salvador, the possibility of a Vietnam-type intervention in El Salvador the question of U.S. intentions in funding the contra war against Nicaragua—remained constant. But solutions, even signs of progress in achieving U.S. goals, remained elusive. The administration deepened U.S. military involvement in the region by increasing aid, conducting military maneuvers, and providing greater support for covert operations. These actions, however, intensified congressional fears that U.S. policy was dangerously on the wrong path. As the Reagan administration became more determined to exercise its will in Central America and Congress increasingly balked at administration designs, President Reagan himself took the lead in efforts to gain public support for administration policy.

The president's personal involvement and public leadership on Central American issues began with a trip to the region in November and December 1982; in 1983 it was reflected most prominently in a March speech devoted to El Salvador and an April address to a special joint session of Congress. Reagan's involvement had several important consequences. First, by putting a domestically popular president in the forefront of efforts to win over Congress, the White House raised the political costs of opposing the president's program and made the differences more partisan. This was particularly true in the House, where midterm elections produced a net gain of twenty-six Democratic seats. Second, the creation of a crisis atmosphere, intended in part to rouse the public and political leaders to the dangers of the communist threat, had the effect within the administration of causing less ideological officials to step back from expressing reservations about the direction of policy. "Your loyalty to the President was questioned if you suggested there were two ways to skin a cat," in the words of a White House official. "No one wanted to get in front of a moving train."[1]

By dwelling on the themes of security and anticommunism in the Western Hemisphere, the president provided a rallying point for his supporters. He transformed much of the Central America debate into a domestic one, substituting broad appeals to standing up to communism and rallying around the flag for detailed arguments about what was happening in the region and how we might influence events there. In so doing, Reagan helped to undermine a system of checks and balances within his own administration; urgency led to recklessness, even if a crisis atmosphere strengthened executive dominance in the conduct of foreign affairs.

The first attempts to inject an aura of crisis into the Central America issue produced greater polarization over policy in the short run. Rather than capitalize on elements of a consensus over defeating the guerrillas and promoting reform in El Salvador, the president's new strategy prolonged confrontation, making the administration's motives and actions the subject of intense scrutiny. Key moderates in both parties—the same coalition of Democrats and Republicans that had agreed on a certification strategy—began to campaign vocally against U.S. policy toward El Salvador. The debate over military intervention heated up as the administration insisted that vital national interests were at stake, even while the Salvadoran army appeared to be faltering in its war with the guerrillas. To protest policy, Congress made recourse to its most powerful lever: control over aid. In defiance of the administration, committees and subcommittees slashed proposals for increased Salvador funding by up to half.

Nicaragua policy suffered most as a result of the increased freneticism within the White House, where policymakers adopted a cavalier approach to limits and restraints imposed by Congress. Early in the year, House Democrats frequently alleged that the administration was violating the 1982 Boland amendment by supporting Nicaraguan insurgents whose stated goal was the overthrow of the Sandinista government. Members of the House frustrated with the administration's apparent indifference to the Boland amendment searched for more drastic measures to control or influence policy. In July the House voted to prohibit entirely covert operations against Nicaragua, making the most definitive congressional statement yet against Reagan administration policy in Central America. In both the Salvadoran and Nicaraguan cases, vague legislative injunctions of previous years were replaced by tougher restrictions or flat-out bans on funding. The president had raised the stakes. Congress was fighting back in kind. In a pattern reminiscent of the earliest days of the Reagan presidency, the administration appeared to be its own worst enemy.

Viewed in a longer-term perspective, however, 1983 marks the beginning of an ultimately successful administration attempt to force the Congress to deal with its agenda of Central America concerns. The president's ability to dominate and set the tone for foreign policy debate—a function not only of the office but of Reagan's substantial personal appeal—began to influence outcomes in Congress in the administration's favor. The president's renewed emphasis on the danger of falling dominoes and the Marxist threat in the Western Hemisphere, coupled with attacks on the patriotism of those who disagreed, forced Reagan's opponents to address his agenda as a condition of dissent. Over and over again, administration critics in Congress were put on the defensive, feeling compelled to demonstrate that they were just as resolute about standing up to communism in Central America, just as convinced of the threat, and just as opposed to the establishment of communist regimes in the hemisphere as were Reagan administration supporters.

The feelings of defensiveness came to a head in October, when some 4,600 U.S. troops invaded the Caribbean island of Grenada. Undertaking what President Reagan called a "rescue mission" of U.S. citizens, U.S. forces removed the left-wing government and defeated Cuban workers who resisted the invasion. The U.S. action had been approved by the Organization of Eastern Caribbean States and quickly commanded public support across the United States. Congressional liberals opposed to the show of gunboat diplomacy were silenced when a bipartisan House delegation returned from Grenada concluding that the U.S. military action was justified.[2]

The Administration Shift in Tactics

Backdrop

To understand why the administration decided to raise the prominence of Central America in a national context and involve the president directly, it is important to view what the administration had hoped to accomplish by the end of 1982. According to a relatively optimistic confidential State Department briefing paper of June 26, 1982:

> The trend of events in Central America is now running in our favor. . . . Assuming that Cuba and Nicaragua do not substantially increase the stakes in Central America, the secret to success will be a steady and sustained effort. . . . *Our principal difficulty in pursuing this policy will be to obtain the required Congressional support. Human rights concerns, diminished but still present fears of a Vietnam-style escalation, and other competing concerns are all obstacles.* . . . If we are unsuccessful in these [upcoming aid] votes we will face increased chances of a political/military debacle in Central America with grave national security consequences [emphasis added].[3]

By the end of 1982, however, Congress had denied the administration the financial and political support it said it required. The failure of all but the economic assistance portions of the Caribbean Basin Initiative, and the year-end freezing of military aid to El Salvador at 1981 levels, produced what one State Department official called "a major hindrance to the prosecution of the war" in El Salvador.[4] The December adoption of a partial legislative ban on covert activities against Nicaragua showed growing resistance to administration policy, even if the Boland amendment allowed covert operations to continue. And late in the year, political momentum around a proposal for a regional peace initiative was growing in the House. The specter of congressionally mandated negotiations, raised in an April 1982 National Security Council document, again lifted its head.

The difficulties with Congress mirrored—the administration said produced—an impasse in the Salvadoran war. As 1983 opened, FMLN guerrillas capped a fall offensive by seizing a large town in an economically important eastern province. In January a top Salvadoran army commander staged a mutiny in order to force the resignation of the Salvadoran defense minister, whom he viewed as incompetent. The insubordination of Lieutenant Colonel Sigifredo Ochoa threatened the unity of the Salvadoran armed forces.

In the wake of these events, U.N. Ambassador Jeane Kirkpatrick traveled to Central America between February 3 and 12, 1983. She returned with the distressing assessment that Soviet influence in the region was growing, worsening the prospects for U.S. policy in the region, particularly if funding levels remained constant. Kirkpatrick, trusted by the president and sharing his ideological commitment to combating communism, met with him in the Oval Office upon her return. She, more than any other official in the administration, was responsible for creating the crisis atmosphere of the next several months.[5]

The set of adverse circumstances generated by events both on Capitol Hill and in the region served to divide the administration into two camps. According to 1987 interviews with past and then-current State Department officials, one line of thinking, personified by Assistant Secretary of State Enders, viewed the late-1982 congressional actions as a warning signal that policy might not be sustainable over the long term. As in Vietnam, domestic divisions over policy in Central America threatened the ability of the United States to "stay the course." Therefore U.S. policy had to pursue, or at least appear to pursue, a resolution of the conflict in Central America. Supporting negotiations as a political stratagem was not to be ruled out, particularly in light of the Hill's insistence on a political settlement.

In late December, Enders drafted a "two-track" proposal emphasizing negotiations as a tactic to obtain political support while aid levels were sustained or increased. Embodied in the Enders approach was the assumption that Congress could only be convinced to go along with administration policy, particularly in Nicaragua, if there appeared to be a political purpose to U.S. pressures. The two-track proposal was the logical successor to Enders's July 1981 speech emphasizing elections in El Salvador, which had succeeded in taking the edge off congressional-executive confrontation by substituting a political strategy for heated references to East-West conflict. Nonetheless, Enders's rivals in the administration opposed to any suggestion of negotiations with communists leaked the existence of the two-track paper to the press in February, presumably as a way of killing it.[6] News coverage focused on El Salvador, even though State Department officials involved in policy at the time indicated in interviews that it was more predominantly concerned with Nicaragua: given the perceived inability of the contras to overthrow the Sandinista regime, there was a need to capitalize on contra pressures by pursuing negotiations with the Sandinistas.

Opposed to Enders's strategy was an impressive array of senior administration officials who shared President Reagan's ideological concerns about hemispheric security: in addition to Kirkpatrick, Undersecretary of Defense Fred Ikle, Deputy Assistant Secretary of Defense Nestor Sanchez, National Security Adviser William Clark, and CIA Director William Casey. What appeared to unite these policymakers was not only the conviction that little had been accomplished in Central America, but also an assumption that communist powers only negotiated to gain a temporary tactical advantage, while they amassed the power to pursue their objectives by force. Negotiations, therefore, disarmed democratic states while allowing communist ones to buy time.

According to this group around the president, the problem was not with a failing policy but with a failure to pursue that policy with enough vigor and resources. Members of this inner circle wanted the administration to be more aggressive in taking its case before the American people. They also shared a dislike for the "fancy-pants diplomats" at the State Department, always so concerned about diplomacy. Tom Enders, the towering bureaucrat whose arrogance, in their view, was matched only by his control over policy, was a particular target of contempt.[7]

Ultimately, the proponents of a more aggressive posture, domestically and in the region, won the internal policy battle. President Reagan's personal involvement in the issue was the most tangible evidence of the triumph of Kirkpatrick and her ideological allies. Although the president offered some limited concessions to domestic opponents—appointing a bipartisan policy commission on Central America and naming a special negotiator for the region—the thrust of his efforts was toward greater confrontation and deeper military involvement; a quadrupling of military aid to El Salvador in March, the holding of large-scale military maneuvers off the cost of Honduras in July, rapid expansions of the contra forces throughout the year. The White House gained control over an Office of Public Diplomacy to sell Central America policy to the American public, a measure initially welcomed by moderates in the administration as a way of "sending the nutsos out to drum up support in Kiwanis clubs."[8]

The State Department, which had reluctantly learned to consult with the Congress (if only to coopt its concerns), declined in influence, only to gain it back temporarily at year's end to salvage El Salvador policy. By May, Enders had lost enough power in the administration's internal councils that he resigned. In his place rose a group of administration hard-liners less frustrated by congressional meddling in policy than contemptuous of the role Congress claimed for itself in foreign policy matters. This group was determined to produce a legislative lineup behind the president by asserting the president's right as the nation's chief executive to carry out foreign policy free of congressional restraint. This expansive view of the president's powers spawned contempt for the prerogatives of Congress and, ultimately, the law.

El Salvador

As in 1982, the presentation of the third presidential certification on human rights in El Salvador in January provided a procedural imperative to focus attention on El Salvador. But this time oversight committees used the event of a certification to structure an overall evaluation of U.S. policy toward El Salvador. On virtually all fronts—the execution of the war, the investigation of the murders of U.S. citizens, the consolidation of civilian rule, the initiation of a political dialogue—progress by the Salvadoran government seemed limited or nonexistent. And in spite of or because of this limited progress, the administration was proposing an expansion of U.S. involvement in El Salvador.

The certification itself was unusually blunt in characterizing the Salvadoran human rights situation, reflecting a State Department decision to be "totally frank" with Congress where "elements of the case are weak."[9] In contrast to the first certification, the third certification noted that "human rights abuses continue and . . . the further development of democracy and the protection of human rights are not to be taken for granted." The document scored the "systematic ineffectiveness" of the Salvadoran judicial system and asserted the need for "further improvement in military discipline."[10] In defending the certification before the Senate Foreign Relations Committee on February 2, 1983, Assistant Secretary Enders stressed the need to end "political violence, including that of government forces" and later implicated security forces personnel in torture carried out in clandestine detention cells. Deputy Assistant Secretary of Defense for Inter-American Affairs Nestor Sanchez noted that "the Salvadorans are at least now taking prisoners," a retroactive admission that the Salvadoran army had a practice of executing rather than jailing captured guerrillas.[11]

Administration officials were careful to couple these criticisms with reservations about the certification process and its linkage to military aid. But they acknowledged that aspects of the certification had been helpful in securing improvements in Salvadoran performance. Nonetheless, the administration maintained, as it had in the past, that despite shortcomings improvements were sufficient to warrant continued U.S. assistance.

In ensuing weeks both Enders and the new Secretary of State, George Shultz, employed combinations of confrontation and conciliation in dealing with congressional committees. They sought to underscore the consensus between the Congress and the administration over the desirability of defeating the Salvadoran guerrilla movement by reminding legislators that they had authorized military assistance to El Salvador because "the survival of that country is important to American security."[12] The efforts to dwell on common ground seemed a reminder that Congress was a co-participant in the Salvadoran drama; by approving or denying aid, Congress was sharing in the responsibility for the success or failure of U.S. policy.

At the same time, top administration officials suggested policy approaches that raised renewed questions about how to achieve shared objectives. Both Enders and Sanchez revived Vietnam-era domino theories in attempting to stress the importance of El Salvador to U.S. security interests, recalling the rhetoric of early 1981.* And confronted with congressional insistence on political negotiations in El Salvador, Shultz testily rejected any approach allowing the guerrillas to "shoot their way into power."[13] Still later, Shultz went on the attack against church-led opposition to U.S. policy, denouncing "churchmen who want to see Soviet influence in El Salvador improved." (Shultz's remark, which was widely reported at the time, was deleted from the published record of the hearing.)[14] The "get tough with Congress" tactics coincided with policy struggles within the administration in the wake of Kirkpatrick's trip.

The result of these tactics was even deeper skepticism among previous administration supporters. Calling the attacks on the Catholic Church "outrageous," Senator David Durenberger (R-Minn.) wrote President Reagan that "if the government of El Salvador faces imminent collapse, as some have suggested, the ultimate cause is its political ineptitude and not its military weakness."†

---

*According to Enders, "In El Salvador, if we allow a government that is reforming itself . . . to be knocked off by guerrillas who don't have the people with them, then no Government in the isthmus will be safe." According to Sanchez, "There are plans . . . that we have found out about and that have been reported that they [unspecified] are not only aiming at establishing a Communist government in El Salvador and consolidating their position in Nicaragua, but also in the rest of Central America." And Studds asked: "Sort of a domino kind of thing?" Sanchez responded: "Yes, if you want to call it the domino theory." U.S. Congress, House, Committee on Foreign Affairs, Subcommittee on Western Hemisphere Affairs, *Foreign Assistance Legislation for Fiscal Years 1984–85*, Part 7, Hearings and Markup, March 1, 16; April 12, 13, 1983, 98th Cong., 1st Sess. (Washington, D.C.: U.S. Government Printing Office, 1983), pp. 7, 31.

†Text, Letter of Senator Dave Durenberger to President Reagan, March 3, 1983, pp. 1– 4. In February, for example, the *Washington Post* reported that recent guerrilla advances "have led Salvadoran officers and their U.S. advisers to the grudging conclusion that the

The perception—to a certain extent shared privately by administration offi-cials—that U.S. policy was not working in El Salvador conflicted with the practical, problem-solving orientation of American politics, the desire to see results. "Who is winning?" demanded Senator Mark Hatfield (R-Ore.), chair-man of the powerful Senate Appropriations Committee. Senator Nancy Kasse-baum (R-Kans.) called El Salvador policy "a little bit like the game of 'Pin the Tail on the Donkey.' We are blindfolded and sort of just hoping that we hit the right spot." The guerrillas, she said, "have seemed to gain in strength . . . despite the military assistance in the last two years that we have given."

These concerns were echoed by other Republicans, still troubled by the Salvadoran failure to control political violence against Salvadoran and U.S. citizens. Said Senator Arlen Specter (R-Pa.), a member of the Foreign Opera-tions Subcommittee, "It doesn't look like progress to me. . . . The conclusion [of the certification] is very, very troublesome."[15]

The substantive differences over what to do in El Salvador mounted when the administration suggested that it might use emergency drawdown authority to boost aid to El Salvador without congressional approval. Defense Secretary Caspar Weinberger told the House Foreign Affairs Committee in February that "one way or another" the United States was going to send an additional $60 million in military aid, a comment that was made before any administration decision on how much aid to request. Weinberger's announcement angered members of Congress across the political spectrum that congressional powers over foreign aid were being usurped by the administration.[16] Contradictory statements by the administration regarding the extent of the emergency so complicated the situation that the administration abandoned its plans to use executive drawdown procedures. *

Army, as it now stands, does not have the manpower, training or planning capability to defeat the insurgents." In March, the New York Times, citing American and Salvadoran officials, concluded that "El Salvador needs better battle leadership, personal motivation and field training as much as it needs ammunition, helicopters and guns." See Christopher Dickey and Edward Cody, "Rebel Victories Spur Calls for More Aid to El Salvador," Washington Post, February 13, 1983; and Drew Middleton, "Salvadoran Army's Troubles," New York Times, March 5, 1983.

*On March 1, Deputy Assistant Defense Secretary Sanchez said that the Salvadoran army "could be down to less than 30 days supply" and Enders maintained that "there are no bullets left available" in El Salvador. This assertion was undercut two days later by Assistant Secretary of State for Security Assistance William Schneider, who told a House subcommittee that the prediction that the Salvadoran army would run out of ammunition was based on the presumption of far heavier combat, "for example, . . . if Nicaragua decided to invade with its 40,000-man army." House Committee on Foreign Affairs,

In the midst of all these controversies, President Reagan unveiled the administration's formal request for additional military aid. The speech to the National Association of Manufacturers on March 10 was his first devoted entirely to a Central American country. "The problem," the president said in an echo of the early themes of his administration, "is that an aggressive minority has thrown in its lot with the Communists, looking to the Soviets and their own Cuban henchmen to help them pursue political change through violence."[17] The proposal for an emergency package of $298 million for the region included $110 million in military aid for El Salvador. It was almost twice what Secretary Weinberger had earlier said was needed, partially in recognition of the fact that Congress would cut back the funding to make its mark on policy. The request for a doubling of aid, however, magnified the alarm felt on Capitol Hill.

Senator Daniel Inouye (D-Hawaii), ranking Democrat on the Senate Foreign Operations Subcommittee, was one of the first to speak out, delivering a blistering attack on administration policy in a speech on the Senate floor. Inouye had a reputation as a quiet "inside player," a man known for his patriotism who had lost an arm in World War II. Inouye had supported early U.S. policy in Vietnam and had come to regret that stance. Now the parallel between Vietnam and El Salvador—the steady escalations of estimates of what was needed to achieve success—was too striking for him to remain silent.

Policymakers in the State Department and White House "are mistaken," he said. "They speak of spreading violence, of falling dominoes, and they hear the ominous echo—Vietnam. . . . I must oppose and vote against the President's request [for] increased military assistance to El Salvador. . . . As the situation worsens, will there be a call for more arms, more dollars, and more U.S. advisers?"[18]

Bad news for the administration continued to emanate from other quarters. Senator Kassebaum had returned from El Salvador in March 1982 with an upbeat assessment of the elections. Now, one year later, she proposed to cap 1983 military aid to El Salvador at $50 million (thereby approving less than one-fourth of the proposed increase), to freeze the number of military advisers, and to put the administration on record in favor of a political dialogue in El Salvador.[19] Kassebaum later joined with Democrats Inouye and Dodd in submitting the proposal as a formal amendment to pending foreign assistance

Subcommittee on Western Hemisphere Affairs, *Foreign Assistance Legislation for Fiscal Years 1984–85*, pp. 29, 60; U.S. Congress, House, Committee on Foreign Affairs, *Foreign Assistance Legislation for Fiscal Years 1984–85*, Part 2, Hearings, February 23; March 3, 10, and 23, 1983, 98th Cong., 1st Sess. (Washington, D.C.: U.S. Government Printing Office, 1984), p. 84.

legislation. As before, members of Congress were contesting policy with actual cutbacks in assistance. This time, however, the circle of administration opponents from both political parties had widened.

In the months after Reagan's speech to the National Association of Manufacturers, House and Senate committees and subcommittees amended, altered, and cut the president's requests. Only one Senate subcommittee approved the full amount; others, including the Republican-controlled Senate Foreign Relations Committee, cut the proposal in half and attached a string of new conditions. To add to the administration's woes, the House Western Hemisphere Subcommittee toughened the certification to require the achievement of certain objectives rather than simply progress toward them. The new language proposed by Representative Stephen Solarz required actual accomplishments: the achievement of "effective control" over military and security forces and the trial and discipline of "substantial numbers" of military and security force personnel responsible for abuses against civilians. [20]

The combined response to Reagan's March 10, 1983, speech on El Salvador was, in short, a political disaster for the administration. On top of the difficulties in Congress, a State Department memorandum for Secretary Shultz in April woefully noted that public support for maintaining U.S. advisers in El Salvador had declined over the past year, and that a majority of Americans opposed an increase in military assistance. [21] U.N. Ambassador Kirkpatrick received the dismal reports by trying to slay the messenger. In a *Washington Post* op-ed column, she lashed out at House Democrats whose opposition to policy made "the United States the enforcer of Brezhnev's doctrine of irreversible communist revolution" and later claimed that "there are people in the U.S. Congress . . . who would actually like to see the Marxist forces take power in [El Salvador]." [22] Kirkpatrick's remarks, the first of many subsequent administration attacks on the patriotism of policy opponents in Congress, helped further to destroy any incentive for compromise. In the eyes of the White House, the need for presidential intervention to rescue the policy expanded.

Nicaragua

Although the administration had faced rough going on Salvador policy in early 1983, the president's Nicaragua program took an even more severe beating. While Congress proved ready to give some aid to El Salvador to ensure the government's survival, opponents of Nicaragua policy sought to eliminate funds altogether to prevent the policy from going forward. An effort to bar funding for the contras gained momentum in the House throughout the spring. The move toward a contra aid ban had three sources: (1) confusion over the goals of the covert operation, particularly as the size of the insurgent force rose precipitously; (2) the extent or perception of the extent of administration compliance with the provisions of the Boland amendment passed in December 1982; and (3) the progressive alienation of House Intelligence Committee Chairman Boland, who was pushed to open, if reluctant, confrontation with the administration by members of his own party and by an administration that left him hanging out to dry.

Thus, factors both internal to the Congress (the prestige of a committee chairman) and external to it (the evolution of policy in the region) shared a common seam: the administration's willingness to operate within the constraints of the law.

Goals

Concern that the purpose of the contras was something other than arms interdiction had fueled the earliest stirrings of controversy around the policy. In early 1983 the hunches, reinforced by media reports, grew into conviction. In one national television broadcast, the face of "Comandante Max" of the FDN flashed across the screens, telling viewers that the rebels' fight was not "to solve the problems in El Salvador or to save El Salvador. . . . We have to be clear that we're fighting for Nicaragua."[23] A series of articles by *Washington Post* reporter Christopher Dickey underscored the prevalence of Somoza's former National Guardsmen in the rebel ranks. "The people who are fighting, they are not fighting to stop the weapons," a former National Guard sergeant nicknamed "Suicide" told Dickey. "We are fighting to liberate Nicaragua."[24] Such accounts not only provided key details about the contra program; they also stripped away the thin veneer of secrecy around U.S. actions.

The avowed goals of some of the forces receiving U.S. support suggested that the administration was being less than candid, or was simply confused, about its objectives in Nicaragua. Despite ongoing claims that the purpose of the covert operation was arms interdiction, the administration still refused to produce evidence that arms were actually being intercepted on their way to El Salvador. By simultaneously insisting that the arms flow from Nicaragua to El Salvador continued unabated and that the purpose of U.S. policy was to stop the transit of arms, the administration helped to undercut its own case for the covert operation. As in El Salvador, U.S. policy in Nicaragua appeared not to be working.

In addition, the size of the contra army continued to rise beyond any proportion that suggested a limited purpose. Only days after the adoption of the December 1982 Boland amendment, for example, the House Intelligence Committee was notified of significant increases in the size of the rebel force; between August and December 1982 the ranks of the rebel forces more than doubled, to about 4,000 men. By February 1983 the figure was between 5,000 and 6,000. By May, it was 7,000. According to a Republican member of the committee, William Goodling, "There is no question that the numbers increased far beyond what the committee anticipated. I think as the force increases and diversifies, controlling it would be an impossibility."[25]

Members of the House Intelligence Committee felt they were being trifled with, subsequently firing off a letter to the CIA listing several instances of administration testimony they thought was misleading. Trust was beginning to erode. The contras appeared less and less an instrument of policy than a policy in and of themselves. With political objectives ill-defined, skepticism grew about the purpose they were intended to serve.

Laws

Central to the brewing storm around the contras was the legal issue of whether the administration was complying with the Boland amendment of December 1982, which prohibited U.S. support for actions aimed at the overthrow of the Nicaraguan government. If the contras themselves declared their desire to oust the Sandinistas, then wasn't U.S. support for them a contravention of the law? Even if such support was in technical compliance with the law, what did the gap between U.S. and contra goals say about U.S. control of the rebel forces?

In March and April, House and Senate Democrats took the offensive to say that the law was being broken. Thirty-seven members of the House wrote President Reagan that support for anti-Sandinista elements in Honduras was a "violation of the Boland amendment" and urged him to act in "strict compliance" with the law. The letter stated that "press reports over the past year and a half have suggested that the Central Intelligence Agency has engaged in covert operations against Nicaragua and that these activities include the support of anti-Sandinista elements based in Honduras. We believe that U.S.-supported anti-Nicaraguan forces may be involved in the current hostilities."[26]

The ranking Democrat on the Senate Intelligence Committee, Daniel Patrick Moynihan of New York, said that a "crisis of confidence" was building between the Congress and the administration and that there was "evidence every night on television" that the law was being violated.[27] On the first day back from the 1983 Easter recess, Moynihan and Leahy, also a member of the committee, engaged in a colloquy on the Senate floor. The question, said Leahy, was not partisan division over Central America policy, but whether the administration "is within the letter and the spirit of the law."[28]

The administration's response to such charges fueled the controversy. According to Representative Barnes, CIA attorneys argued that U.S. aid to the contras was legal because the goal of U.S. agencies supplying money was not the overthrow of the Nicaraguan government, even if the goal of the insurgents was. "Not a jury in the country would accept this," retorted Barnes, "and the House will not accept it."[29]

The administration had found the Boland amendment acceptable in December 1982 principally because the CIA considered its operative provisions meaningless. By acting on that assumption, ignoring Congress's warning as well as its role in generating statutory limitations on executive behavior, the administration began to stumble into a trap of its own design.

Boland

In 1982 Boland had staked his prestige on an amendment designed to give the administration leeway in continuing covert operations in Nicaragua. He had sought to avoid a partisan clash over covert operations, carrying the administration's water in an effort to rein in Democrats of his own party who wanted to end the administration's program. As claims that the amendment was being violated reached a crescendo, Boland was left with two undesirable choices: to ignore the drumbeat within his own party that the law was being violated, thereby appearing indifferent to the statute that bore his name; or to toughen the restrictions, thereby making intelligence operations a subject of open, potentially partisan contention. Boland's decision to move in the latter direction was due to pressure by House liberals opposed to the contra program, who pushed Boland into the limelight in defense of his own amendment, and to the administration's cavalier attitude to the law, which deprived Boland of measures that he could use to rebuild confidence in the administration.

As in 1982, initiative in opposing covert operations came from liberals on and off the Intelligence Committee. In April, committee member Wyche Fowler returned from a six-day trip to Central America, charging that he had been "forced to conclude . . . that the law of the land as embodied in the Boland amendment is not being fully adhered to. . . . Congress has a clear responsibility to bring our government into compliance."[30]

Subsequent House actions focused further attention on Boland. On April 12 the House Western Hemisphere Subcommittee voted to cut off all U.S. support for the contras "unless and until" the Congress approved funding by joint resolution. The Foreign Affairs Committee was stepping into Intelligence Committee terrain. Then a core group of sixty-five Democratic liberals opposed to the Nicaragua program wrote Boland to commend him for "past efforts to see that U.S. aid for covert operations against Nicaragua would not go out of control," but asking for steps beyond continued oversight: the letter asked for a direct vote on the entire program or for Boland's assurance that no U.S. funds were being provided to the contras for "armed military, paramilitary, or sabotage actions in Nicaragua."[31] The letter and the Foreign Affairs Subcommittee action began to smoke the reticent chairman out of the shadows of bipartisan, cooperative intelligence oversight. An aura of inevitability about a public confrontation began to take hold.

Reluctantly, Boland began to speak out. On April 13, after a three-hour meeting of the House Intelligence Committee, Boland joined the chorus of those denouncing the administration's lack of compliance with the Boland amendment. He said that media and other reports indicated that the covert operation was "an apparent violation of the amendment. . . . I think we have a responsibility to see the spirit of the law and congressional direction fully adhered to."*

Perhaps even more than the pressure within his own party, what pushed Boland over the edge was the administration's unwillingness to heed the verbal, written, and statutory warnings that the committee had given in 1981 and 1982. By Boland's own account, by mid-1983 the number of fighters had increased dramatically and administration witnesses had broadened the scope of the program. Contra rebels were not occupied with efforts to intercept arms shipments but were engaging Sandinista military units in ever larger clashes. The Hondurans were being drawn into the spiral of violence.[32] The committee was told in 1983 that the contras were not going after economic targets in Nicaragua,

---

*Boland's comments contrasted sharply with those of Senate Intelligence Committee Chairman Barry Goldwater (R-Ariz.), who stated following a lengthy briefing with CIA Director Casey that the administration was "not violating the letter or the spirit" of the Boland amendment. Patrick Tyler and Don Oberdorfer, "Nicaragua Activities Questioned," *Washington Post*, April 14, 1983.

but that assurance ran counter to news reports and to the intelligence community's own internal summaries.[33]

In short, liberals were asking Boland for answers about the covert program, and he had none. "Eddie's a very proud person," recalled one of his colleagues. "He said to himself, 'I've tried to work with these fellas [in the administration], I've tried to keep a nonpartisan approach. It didn't work.' "[34]

"The reason this whole strategy . . . unraveled," said Representative George Miller (D-Calif.), "is that they decided to lie to Eddie Boland."[35]

On April 27, 1983, only hours before President Reagan was due to deliver a Central America policy speech to an unusual joint session of Congress, Boland and House Foreign Affairs Committee Chairman Clement Zablocki (D-Wisc.) introduced H.R. 2760, a bill "to prohibit United States support for military or paramilitary operations in Nicaragua."[36] The bill substituted an overt arms-interdiction program for covert paramilitary operations against Nicaragua, a way of saying that the administration's goals were legitimate but the contra policy was ill-suited to them. The administration's critical error in 1983 was letting Boland, with a reputation for shunning publicity, move into open opposition. Boland's stance meant that the credibility of the case against the contras was all but sealed, at least for the time being.

The President's Address

In an attempt to rescue the administration's Central America policies, Reagan's speech to Congress was both conciliatory and confrontational. The president stressed the themes of democracy and reform, drew a standing ovation when he pledged that "there is no thought of sending American combat troops to Central America" and promised to appoint a special negotiator to search for a peaceful resolution to the Central American conflict. But Reagan also insisted that:

> The national security of all the Americas is at stake in Central America. If we cannot defend ourselves there, we cannot expect to prevail elsewhere. Our credibility would collapse, our alliances would crumble, and the safety of our homeland would be put in jeopardy. . . . Who among us would wish to bear responsibility for failing to meet our shared obligation?[37]

Invoking a crisis atmosphere was intended as a warning, "to get more of a response than we've been able to get from individual congressional committees so far," in the words of National Security Adviser William Clark.[38] By telling the whole Congress and the American people of the priority he attached to Central America, and by hinting, more or less explicitly, at who would be blamed for failure, the president hoped to produce a legislative lineup behind his regional program.

It is difficult to measure the psychological impact of Reagan's speech, particularly since critics of the president's policies had long coupled an overall endorsement of Reagan's goals with an attack on policy means. What does stand out, however, is the regularity with which liberal critics appeared defensive, embracing the president's goals as well as some of his rhetoric. In the words of Wyche Fowler, "Everyone agrees with the objectives of the President. We all don't like communism. But it's the methods he's chosen to achieve the objectives that we are questioning." Or, in the words of Howard Wolpe (D-Mich.), a member of the Foreign Affairs Committee, "None of us wants Central America to become a base for Soviet operations in our hemisphere, yet none of us wants Central America to become another Vietnam, either."[39]

The effect of Reagan's speech on legislation regarding El Salvador was decidedly mixed. Both the House Foreign Affairs Committee and the Senate Foreign Relations Committee allocated slightly more aid than they had previously been willing to give. But both committees imposed new restrictions on U.S. policy—toughening the certification, limiting the number of advisers to fifty-five, and prohibiting the use of emergency drawdown procedures to transfer military aid to El Salvador by executive decree.[40] Because these measures contained new restrictions unacceptable to the administration, the State Department abandoned any attempt to promote floor passage of the foreign aid bill. In the absence of a strong congressional constituency for foreign aid, particularly among members of the president's own party, the effect of the administration's withdrawal was to kill the authorizing legislation.

The sheer volume of aid requests in 1983 meant that the process of compromise would produce higher levels of assistance to the Salvadoran army. But the amounts fell far short of what the administration said it needed. Consequently, in late May the Defense Department went around its own fifty-five-man limit on military advisers by sending an additional one hundred U.S. military personnel to train Salvadorans in Honduras. The administration dealt with congressional limitations by using executive privileges to go around them. This tactic frustrated congressional opponents of his policy but left them essentially powerless. "What do you do?" one Republican Senate aide asked rhetorically. "Send another letter?"[41]

Nicaragua:
The Sore That Festered

The focal battle over Central America policy in 1983—a House attempt to end covert operations in Nicaragua—indicated that the president had failed to convert the Congress by going before a joint session. By early May the objections to Nicaragua policy spread to the Senate Intelligence Committee, until then strongly supportive of administration policy. The committee voted 13–2 not to authorize funds for covert operations in Nicaragua unless the president submitted a new "finding" spelling out the purposes of the program and the new plan was approved by the committee.[42] The requirement allowed covert operations in Nicaragua to go forward, but it demonstrated that a broad spectrum of members now doubted that there was a coherent policy linking the program's stated objectives with the actual conduct of the war.

In the House, meanwhile, efforts to avoid a showdown on covert funding were undercut by the House leadership, which was unconvinced that compromise meant more than capitulation, and by the administration, which failed to offer concessions early enough to attract potential supporters. House Speaker Tip O'Neill, a strong opponent of Reagan policy in Central America since 1981, became more outspoken in response to the president's elevation of the prominence of the Central America issue. The Speaker publicly criticized attempts at a compromise on covert operations, saying that "the President of the United States broke the law and then laughed to the American people that he broke the law."[43] O'Neill's position reinforced that of Boland, his former roommate, in confronting the administration.

At the same time, however, critics of Reagan's policy in Nicaragua were reluctant to let the Sandinistas' increasingly restrictive domestic behavior become a political liability. In June, twelve House liberals and moderates wrote Nicaraguan Comandante Daniel Ortega, scoring the "conspicuous Cuban presence, serious human rights violations, and absence of democratic rights" in Nicaragua and calling for negotiations with Nicaragua's democratic opposition to "arrest the trend toward civil war, repression, and Cuban domination." The letter reflected distress over developments in Nicaragua as well as anger that the Sandinistas took for granted Reagan's critics in Congress. It suggested that opposition to the president's policy had begun to exact a political price: critics of Reagan's policies did not want to be seen as exercising a double standard with respect to El Salvador and Nicaragua, or worse, of being "soft on the Sandinistas."[44]

Rather than capitalize on concerns with the political evolution inside Nicaragua, the administration continued in its schizophrenic approach to collaboration with the Congress. On the eve of a House Intelligence Committee vote on proposed legislation to prohibit covert operations in Nicaragua, Assistance Secretary of State Enders visited the office of Intelligence Committee member Dave McCurdy (D-Okla.). A self-described "supporter of the President on much of his defense posture," McCurdy was one of several members of the Democratic Party's more conservative wing who were reluctant to oppose the president on national security policy. He shared the view that the "Sandinista government poses a clear threat to the security of its neighbors and to the United States."[45]

Belatedly, Enders recognized that members like McCurdy could help preserve majority backing for covert operations in Nicaragua. But McCurdy's support was not unconditional. A student of guerrilla warfare, he disputed the administration position that the contra operation had the ingredients for a successful insurgency: no political platform, too many indiscriminate attacks on civilians and economic targets, too many former National Guardsmen in the rebel leadership.

In a last-ditch attempt to erode what looked like a solid majority on the Intelligence Committee opposed to the covert war, Enders devised a last-minute compromise proposal that would limit the number of contra troops and emphasize reform of the contra leadership and the development of a political program. The plan was too little too late, and it coincided with Enders's worst difficulties within the administration. "The next time I heard from Tom Enders," recalled McCurdy, "he had been transferred [as ambassador] to Spain."*

The day after Enders's appeal to McCurdy, the Intelligence Committee voted 9–5 along straight partisan lines to support the Boland-Zablocki bill. Notably, the committee accepted the administration's central rationale for its policy, concurring in a report that the Salvadoran insurgency "depends for its life blood—arms, ammunition, financing, logistics and command and control facilities—upon outside assistance from Nicaragua and Cuba."

But, the committee said, the covert program was counterproductive. The

---

*Interview, January 28, 1987, Washington, D.C. Enders's removal as Assistant Secretary of State for Inter-American Affairs was announced on May 27, 1983, and he left the administration in July. McCurdy maintained that "on three separate occasions . . . the highest officials in the Administration rejected direct offers of compromise" (see p. 21 of the Intelligence Committee report cited in note 45 of this chapter). A senior administration official familiar with the negotiations disagreed that a compromise would have been possible. The official stated in an interview that "the relationship of trust between the Administration and the committee had eroded to the point where there was no obvious negotiated solution possible. Boland [said] that he just wouldn't believe any commitment Casey made to him."

"activities and purposes of the anti-Sandinista insurgents ultimately shape the program," it said. Those activities "point not to arms interdiction, but to military confrontation. . . . The violence of their attacks on targets unrelated to arms interdiction has grown. . . . These groups are not controlled by the United States."[46]

Soon after the Intelligence Committee's vote, the House Foreign Affairs Committee began its consideration of the Boland-Zablocki bill. There the debate demonstrated that the president's April speech to Congress had lifted the lid on partisan attacks against opponents of administration policy. Republicans accused Democrats of aiding Soviet strategy and abetting the spread of communism in the hemisphere. Representative Stephen Solarz (D-N.Y.) shot back that he had "never before" heard "members accused of promoting policies that would result in the selling out of America." And Representative Larry Smith (D-Fla.) said that he refused to be painted as a "Communist sympathizer" or one "who is soft on communism."[47] Over time, however, indignation would give way to queasiness as Reagan's popularity and commitment to the contra issue provided political cover to those who engaged in such attacks.

When the shouting died down, tiny cracks in the facade of Democratic unity on ending covert operations in Nicaragua suggested wider chasms the administration could exploit. Two members of the liberal Black Caucus opposed providing overt aid in place of covert aid, because they said it would militarize U.S. allies in the region for the dubious purpose of arms interdiction. Two other Florida Democrats voted to continue covert operations; another who opposed them indicated that he would seek out a consensus position with Republicans before the bill reached the House floor. Only one Republican supported the Boland-Zablocki bill. These small deviations from positions of straight partisanship suggested that the majority-party Democrats could not forge a winning coalition without unity in their own ranks or some Republican support and that the minority Republicans could not hope to prevail without picking up some members of the opposing party.

The struggle for the congressional "center"—liberal-to-moderate Republicans and moderate-to-conservative Democrats—was the critical one that would decide the fate of covert operations.

Floor Debate

Before the floor debate on the Boland-Zablocki bill began, House Democrats, Republicans, and top administration officials renewed efforts to find a compromise position on covert operations. The discussions testified to the uncertainty of both the president's supporters and his opponents that either could command a majority of the House. Ultimately, however, the talks broke down over the difficulty of finding a middle-ground position. The choice, in the words of Representative Lee Hamilton (D-Ind.) was, "Do you or do you not want the covert action to continue?"[48] The talks did identify a "swing" group of predominantly southern Democrats and moderate Republicans, whose votes two years later would give the president a decisive majority in favor of aid to the contras.[49] Understanding how this group, which was identifiable even in 1983, as well as eighteen members of the president's own party came to vote against the president is the key to explaining why a House effort to end covert paramilitary operations in Nicaragua was successful.

The two-day debate following an unusual secret session of the House was intensely partisan and bitter. Intelligence Committee member G. William Whitehurst (R-Va.) warned of a "Marxist triumph throughout all of Central America" if the Boland-Zablocki bill passed. "I do not want my name sullied with the irrefutable charge that I lost Central America," he said. Others charged that an end to covert operations would produce a "tidal wave of refugees, both feet people and boat people," echoing Reagan's admonition during a Republican fund-raiser in Mississippi that refugees would be "swarming into our country seeking a safe haven" if the "Soviet-Cuban-Nicaraguan axis" took over Central America.[50]

Opponents of the president's policy likened it to past U.S. interventions in Nicaragua and recalled the decades of U.S. support for the Somoza dynasty. Others declared that "we are literally playing with dynamite when it comes to the lives of another generation of young Americans," accusing the president of leading the country into another Vietnam.[51] Virtually all the speakers condemned the Sandinistas for the broken promises of their revolution, demonstrating that there was close to a consensus on the nature of the Sandinista regime in spite of deep divisions over what to do about it.

Only two Democrats had anything even remotely positive to say about the Sandinistas. Representative Studds compared Nicaragua to El Salvador, saying that "a political dissident, even in today's Nicaragua, may be ignored, he may be harassed, he may fear for his life, he may, accordingly, choose exile. But compare this to El Salvador where even according to President Reagan's own certification, political dissidents are simply killed."

Representative Harkin (D-Iowa) stated, "Those who say the Sandinistas are not Boy Scouts, I agree, they are not Boy Scouts. But compared to the Contras, whom we are supporting with this covert aid, they are Eagle Scouts."[52]

To a large extent, however, supporters and opponents of the bill talked past each other by failing to articulate underlying assumptions. Most Republicans, like the Reagan administration, argued implicitly that the Sandinista regime posed an irreconcilable threat to U.S. interests but declined to call openly for its overthrow or demonstrate how supporting the contras could change aspects of Sandinista behavior most objectionable to the United States. Most Democrats, meanwhile, rejected overthrow as a legitimate goal of U.S. policy but failed to make explicit the consequence of ending covert operations: accepting the existence of the Sandinista regime even while using diplomacy to promote changes in its behavior. Reluctance by both sides to lay bare their basic assumptions added to the intensity, if obscurity, of the exchange.

Central to the outcome of the debate was therefore not necessarily the arguments themselves but who was making them. Boland's reputation for bipartisanship, acknowledged even by his staunchest opponents, made his passionate opposition to the administration's Nicaragua policy all the more compelling. In opening his remarks against the bill, for example, the ranking Republican on the Intelligence Committee, Kenneth Robinson, praised Boland's "unwavering commitment to approach problems in a nonpartisan manner."[53] Moreover, there was a sense when Boland spoke that he knew more than everyone else, that if Boland were scared about the direction of U.S. policy, there was good reason to take heed.

"When we adopted the Gulf of Tonkin resolution" in 1964, he said, "we did not have all the facts. We could not—many of us could not—see where it would take us. Today the House does not suffer from that disadvantage. You have heard in secret session the numbers of fighters armed, the cost of the program, the plans for expansion. At the same time, you know the Sandinistas are not wearing white hats."[54] Knowledge, suggested Boland, was the key to avoiding disaster.

Boland enlisted the support of two others whose credibility, particularly among conservative Democrats, was critical to the case against contra aid. On July 26, at Boland's request, Dave McCurdy sent a "Dear Colleague" letter to a select list of Republican and Democratic moderates, expressing his support for legislation to cut off covert operations in Nicaragua.

"I reluctantly voted" to support the cutoff in the Intelligence Committee, McCurdy wrote, but "since that time, I have been troubled by the steady expansion and shifting of the Administration's justification for funding paramilitary activities within Nicaragua."[55] McCurdy's previous willingness to give the administration the benefit of the doubt on Nicaragua policy, and his support of a strong defense policy in general, made his appeal to swing voters all the more persuasive.

Finally, a strong endorsement from Majority Leader Jim Wright provided reassurance to conservative Democrats that the bid to end covert operations against Nicaragua was not solely the work of the party's outspoken liberal wing.[56] On the final day of impassioned speeches, Wright offered a substitute for the Boland-Zablocki legislation, which combined strong condemnations of Sandinista behavior with the operative provisions ending covert assistance. Wright's crafting of a substitute amendment provided cover for House moderates concerned that a vote against covert operations would be perceived as an endorsement of the Sandinista regime, and his skills as an orator capped the day for the Democratic opponents of contra aid.

Political blunders by the administration sealed the fate of contra aid in the House. A series of disastrous leaks about administration policy surfaced as the House debate opened, raising fresh concern about the administration's military plans for the region. One report held that the CIA sought presidential authorization to support 12,000 to 15,000 contra rebels, roughly twice the number two months before. Another report, based on a leaked internal document, showed that the administration proposed to increase military aid to the region by up to 40 percent in the coming year.[57]

By far the most damaging revelation, however, was that the administration planned two large military exercises off the Honduran coast, involving a U.S. Navy battle group with 16,000 sailors and 5,000 U.S. ground troops. The maneuvers were openly described by administration officials as designed to intimidate Nicaragua. In addition, however, they frightened members of Congress.

The decision to "send the fleet" can be seen as the culmination of the National Security Council's effort throughout 1983 to wrest internal bureaucratic power away from the State Department. As such, it heralded in the development of Nicaragua policy the beginning of the end of administration deference to congressional concern. Secretary of State Shultz was reported not to have been informed of the NSC's decision to launch the maneuvers, which had been under discussion for some time. That action was promoted instead by William Clark. Those with the closest day-to-day workings with Capitol Hill, who could have warned of the political costs of staging the maneuvers at the time of the House vote, were not involved in the decision. Shultz nonetheless had to travel to the Hill to defend the action before House Republicans, who were outraged at the ill-timed show of adventurism. In the words of House Minority Leader Robert Michel (R-Ill.), "This show of power turns off people who might be thinking of compromise." According to the chairman of the

Senate Foreign Relations Committee, "not one" congressional leader was informed of the maneuvers ahead of time.[58]

On July 28, 1983, the House voted 228–195 to end covert operations against Nicaragua. Eighteen Republicans joined with all but fifty Democrats to defeat the president on a key Central America policy. Forty-one of the fifty Democrats supporting contra aid were from southern states of the old Confederacy. Thirteen of the eighteen Republicans opposing the aid were from the Northeast; an additional three were from the Midwest.

The National Security Council, whose bid for internal power had cost Tom Enders his job and embarrassed the Secretary of State, triumphed in a bureaucratic struggle only to have its policy recommendations contribute to a major foreign policy defeat for the president. The rise of the NSC, later the seat of the Iran-contra scandal, was a quintessential pyhrric victory even from the beginning.

Reequilibrations II: El Salvador

Shortly before the House vote on covert operations, an administration interagency policy group finished work on a National Security Decision Directive (NSDD), a working document spelling out policy objectives and alternatives.[59] The document, unlike a similar assessment presented to the NSC one year before, was uniformly gloomy in its outlook for Central America. "It is still possible," the task force said, "to accomplish U.S. objectives without the direct use of U.S. troops (although the credible threat of such use is needed to deter overt Soviet/Cuban intervention), provided that the U.S. takes timely and effective action." U.S. policy faced "substantial opposition, at home and abroad," the document continued; "an increased effort would have to surmount even greater opposition."[60]

This mid-year policy review is critical as a point of departure for understanding a series of administration initiatives regarding El Salvador, culminating in a December 1983 visit by Vice President George Bush. Whereas in October 1982 U.S. Ambassador Deane Hinton had been reproached in Washington for delivering a harsh attack on right-wing violence, one year later the second-highest elected U.S. official was traveling to El Salvador for expressly the same purpose. Understanding what produced the shift—essentially a change in emphasis given to the issue of right-wing violence—reveals a series of interconnected factors critical in policymaking: the administration's own perception of what needed to be accomplished in El Salvador, the unwillingness of Congress to provide funds necessary for the purpose, and a series of precipitating events on the ground in El Salvador.

What stands out in unraveling these elements is the consistency with which policy debates on Capitol Hill furnished a steady reference point for administration and Salvadoran action, identifying not only "what needed to be done" in a policy sense but providing, through persistent debate, a constant source of motivation.

The pivotal center and driving force of all that took place from mid-1983 until the year-end Bush visit was the desire for increased military aid. "We knew Congress would be reluctant to take responsibility for providing no money," said a senior U.S. diplomat, "but would only give aid sufficient to keep the situation from getting worse, not better."[61] Periodic efforts to seek modest supplements, the July NSDD document warned, "may be perceived as incremental escalation to stave off defeat for the time being, without any clear strategy for success—an awkward parallel with Vietnam." To break the logjam, the administration working group responsible for the NSDD recommended a 40 percent jump in 1984 military aid. One way to procure a large increase in funding, the document argued, was to develop a "long-term strategy with improved chances of bipartisan support."

This desire for increased aid to El Salvador, particularly in light of persistent controversy over Nicaragua policy, helps explain the administration's decision to create a bipartisan commission to develop such long-term plans. On July 19, President Reagan had taken the suggestion of two prominent members of the Senate—Henry (Scoop) Jackson (D-Wash.) and Charles Mathias (R-Md.)—in appointing twelve members of a National Bipartisan Commission on Central America to seek a political consensus on U.S. policy in the region.[62] The commission—aimed at the congressional "center" of moderate to conservative Democrats and moderate Republicans—was intended to develop the ideological foundation for a bipartisan Central America policy, a way of furthering Reagan administration policy "without," in the words of the working document, "sacrificing our ability to attain fundamental objectives."[63]

Not everyone within the administration, however, viewed consensus-building as the way to induce Congress to support administration policy. "We're fed up with their interference on the one hand," a senior administration official told the press, "and their lack of support on the other and we intend to fight for what we think is a minimum American commitment to the region."[64] A group of officials—identified in press reports as including CIA Director Casey, Undersecretary of Defense Ikle, and NSC Director Clark—scorned attempts at negotiation with Congress, believing instead that Congress could be strong-armed into acquiescence with if not support for policy by blaming it for policy failures resulting from cutbacks in funds. The most notable public exponent of this approach was Ikle, who in a September speech to the Baltimore Affairs Council accused a "blocking majority in the House" of voting "to establish a sanctuary for the Sandinistas" by opposing covert aid. "As long as Congress keeps crippling the President's military assistance program," he said, "we will have a policy always shy of success. We will remain locked into a protracted failure."[65]

The administration thus attempted limited concessions in the spirit of bipartisanship as well as efforts to whip up a "who lost Central America" kind of fear to gain congressional backing. The result was a series of contradictory policy initiatives and statements that confused the administration's message to Congress and to allies and adversaries in the region. Divided against itself as well as against the Congress, the Reagan administration prolonged its own difficulties by its attempts to produce majority support for its policies.

Conciliation

Contained in the July NSDD was the recognition—as yet not publicly acknowledged—that the Salvadoran government's failure to reform underlay congressional reluctance to give aid. Salvadoran leaders, the document said, had "not been motivated to take the minimal actions required to help us sustain our support." The task force noted that "improved military and political performance in El Salvador" would have to be secured before Congress would be likely to increase its backing.[66]

The administration's July 20, 1983, certification to Congress on the human rights situation hinted at the growing State Department and embassy frustration with the Salvadoran military's commitment to reform. The certification said that "achievement of control over all elements of the armed forces has not yet been fully realized" and that "violations of human rights, including most importantly the right to life, continued to occur during the past six months." In its harshest language to date, the State Department wrote that "armed rightist terrorists, including some members of the government's security forces, bear responsibility for many deaths attributable to political violence."[67]

Like the certification that preceded it, the fourth certification was a notable departure from the administration's first. From denying that human rights abuses were prevalent, the administration admitted persistent problems. From attributing violence principally to the guerrillas, the administration laid blame on "armed rightist terrorists" connected with the security forces. From denying a 1982 government massacre at El Mozote, the State Department highlighted instances of civilian massacres by government troops and berated Salvadoran authorities for their failure to bring those guilty to justice.

Despite the critical stance, the administration refused to suspend military aid, as the law required. But the frankness took the edge off policy discussions, true to what Enders's replacement as assistant secretary, Langhorne (Tony) Motley, considered the "lily-pad theory of Congress." Motley, in the words of a State Department official, believed legislators "were just a bunch of bullfrogs croaking at you from the pond. Take away their lily pads and they sink to the bottom and the croaking stops."[68] The congressional response to the fourth certification was placid and even weary, a telling indication of what could have been the case had these shortcomings been admitted two years before.

Substantively, however, it appears that congressional concerns were slowly being incorporated into the State Department's view of what needed to change in El Salvador. By late 1983 the view that human rights improvements were essential to the Salvadoran government's capacity to consolidate its rule had begun to take hold.

Explaining the Bush Visit:
The View from Washington

Beginning in July 1981, when Enders gave a major policy speech supporting elections in El Salvador, the State Department had viewed the political quest for a legitimate government as central to a military effort aimed at defeating the guerrillas. "By the end of 1983," said a State Department official, "there was not a single policymaker who didn't agree that a legitimate election was the key to the right kind of political outcome in El Salvador. It was not just that you had to have an election or those guys on the Hill were never going to shut up. It was the key to winning the war."[69] In July, Salvadoran President Alvaro Magaña announced that national presidential elections would be held in early 1984 to continue the process of attempting to build a democratic system.

Political violence, however, could undermine the elections by calling into question the regime's ability to protect the citizenry and govern effectively. "If the death squads were rampant," the State Department official explained, "the elections could be considered illegitimate."*

*In July, on the eve of his departure from San Salvador, U.S. Ambassador Deane Hinton

The issue of legitimacy also inspired renewed Hill attention to the case of the U.S. churchwomen murdered in El Salvador. More than two and a half years after the nuns were killed, there was still no trial date set, let alone a serious investigation of leads against five National Guardsmen arrested for the crime in early 1982. "Support for aid was likely to collapse" in the absence of justice in the case, said a top aide to Senator Arlen Specter (R-Pa.). The case "was central to the credibility of aid to El Salvador."[70]

Specter, a former Pennsylvania district attorney, traveled to El Salvador twice in 1983, returning each time less confident of administration and Salvadoran government assurances that the case was going forward.[71] Unlike some Democratic opponents of aid to El Salvador, however, Specter had "no enthusiasm about threatening to cut off the money." Rather, he sought a formula that would give the Salvadorans incentive to undertake measures in their own self-interest. He devised an amendment tying 30 percent of 1984 military aid appropriations to a trial and verdict in the churchwomen's case. The provision became law in November with the passage of the year-end continuing resolution.

Congress set a cap of $64.8 million on military aid to El Salvador, more than double the amount of the previous year, but fully a third less than the administration had requested. Thirty percent of the aid could only be spent after "Salvadoran authorities have brought the accused to trial and have obtained a verdict."[72] Unlike the certification, which required movement toward a goal, Specter's amendment required a specific achievement. The administration's prediction that Congress would not support major increments in military assistance without "improvements" in Salvadoran performance was becoming more and more of a reality.

Explaining the Bush Visit:
The View from El Salvador

Congress's aid reductions provided the administration one incentive for more drastic action regarding political violence. Events in El Salvador provided

---

again scored the business sector for its silence on death squad killings: "when there are people [found] here in the parking lot of the Camino Real [hotel] strangled, with plaques saying 'we've killed them because we are the Secret Anti-Communist Army,' that is not acceptable and ought not to be acceptable for you." Quoted in Christopher Dickey, "Hinton Attacks Salvadorans for 'Silence' About Murders," *Washington Post*, July 14, 1983.

another. By the fall of 1983, death squad activity surged, targeting victims from the very sectors of Salvadoran society that the United States viewed as essential for reformist democracy: centrist peasant unions, the Catholic Church, university professors, and the Christian Democratic Party. One particularly disturbing event was the kidnapping, claimed by one of the death squads, of the third-ranking Salvadoran official in the Foreign Ministry.

In addition, rumors of death threats against the U.S. ambassador, almost routine since Bob White's days in 1980, began to pick up. "We were scared shitless," said one White House official. "It was obvious and clear," said another administration source, "that we had to do something tough and decisive."[73] That the increased violence coincided with a fall visit to El Salvador by members of the Kissinger Commission only intensified the pressure to deal with the killings.

Beginning in early November, the embassy began leaking to reporters the names of Salvadoran officials believed to be involved in the death squad activities—the heads of intelligence for the National Police and the Treasury Police, security officers in the Constituent Assembly connected with former Mayor D'Aubuisson, as well as two provincial army commanders.[74] In contrast to Assistant Secretary Enders's assurance to Congress earlier in the year that the death squads were a "phenomenon which is without a center," the naming of names suggested indeed a centralized network of killers run from the security forces.[75]

Publicly, Ambassador Thomas R. Pickering delivered a scathing critique to the American Chamber of Commerce in San Salvador, an echo of Hinton's speech to the same group one year earlier. Claiming that "the essential stumbling block to democracy in El Salvador remains extremist terror," Pickering lambasted the private sector for the "self-deluding belief that nothing is really known about the shadowy world of these individuals." Just as Hinton in mid-1982 had used congressional opinion to impress the Salvadorans of the need to keep D'Aubuisson out of the presidency, so Pickering reminded the group that Congress had cut aid by more than $20 million and set conditions for the rest.[76] As in the D'Aubuisson case, Pickering used the threat of a congressional backlash to bolster the credibility of his fight for a particular policy outcome.

Conflicting Signals

Despite a growing preoccupation with death squad violence, the administration was still divided over the source of the violence and Congress's role in stopping it. In early December, Reagan told a group of high school students that death squad murders might be carried out by the guerrillas knowing "the right wing will be blamed for it," a position specifically rejected by Pickering in his address to the American Chamber of Commerce.*

In addition, on November 30 the president pocket-vetoed an extension of the certification law by sitting on the legislation until it expired after Congress adjourned.[77] Opponents of the veto within the administration argued that the certification's provisions had become meaningless, and that failure to sign the bill would unnecessarily antagonize the Congress. These arguments were ignored. The veto predictably infuriated members of Congress. More important, it served to send conflicting signals to the Salvadorans about the relative importance the U.S. attached to human rights considerations.

A deteriorating military situation in El Salvador and a late-November shake-up of the Salvadoran High Command provided renewed impetus for a crackdown on the death squads. In three and a half months beginning in September, the guerrillas attacked more than 130 towns and held on to about 50, spreading fighting throughout the country. For the first time in the civil war, company-size guerrilla units traveled around in trucks rather than on foot; new Salvadoran recruits were fleeing from battle rather than putting up a fight.[78] In addition, a reshuffling of Salvadoran army command posts brought into key positions those with several years of battlefield experience. In the view of U.S. officials, their experience of waging war had underscored the need for popular support in a successful counterinsurgency, a recognition that the people "had to be with you, not just afraid of you," in the words of one State Department official.[79]

The Embassy felt it had a receptive group for a strong message emphasizing the need to curb the death squads. In late November, Pickering traveled to Washington to seek support for a crackdown.[80]

Domestic U.S. politics in a presidential election year provided a final rationale for immediate action on the death squad front. "Republicans didn't want to go into 1984 supporting a bloody kind of government," in the words of a top Senate Republican aide.[81] Bush was sensitive to that fact and was already planning to go to Latin America for the inauguration of Argentine President Alfonsín; a stopover in El Salvador could be easily arranged. Moreover, as former head of the CIA, Bush was a perfect candidate to deliver a tough, credible message to the

---

*Pickering had stated that "we know by their selection of victims and other information" that two of the most notorious death squads "are not guerrilla organizations." Pickering address, p. 10 (cited in note 76). Reagan's remarks are cited in Francis X. Clines, "Reagan Says Rights Reports Might Invite Salvador Strife," *New York Times*, December 3, 1983.

Salvadoran right. His presence would demonstrate that Ambassador Pickering was Ronald Reagan's man. On December 11, 1983, Bush paid a short visit to El Salvador.

At an official dinner presided over by President Magaña, he offered this blunt toast:

> Your cause is being undermined by the murderous violence of reaction-ary minorities. . . . These cowardly death squad terrorists are just as repugnant to me, to President Reagan, to the U.S. Congress, and to the American people as the terrorists of the left. . . . If these death squad murders continue, you will lose the support of the American people.[82]

Bush's public message was backed up by private meetings with top Salvadoran leaders. According to a Salvadoran present at one such meeting, the Bush delegation brought a list, written on a sheet of paper without letterhead, of Salvadoran civilians and military officers involved in the terror, demanding that they be exiled or expelled.[83] While the details of those encounters are still murky, Bush's message was clear. Almost three years after the Congress had begun insisting that human rights were the key to a successful policy in El Salvador, the highest levels of the Reagan administration had come around.

Nicaragua

The need for increased aid for El Salvador forced on the administration a policy of limited accommodation with the Congress. Nicaragua policy, however, displayed an opposite tendency: to defy Congress and pursue policy goals without regard for domestic consensus or the limits imposed by its absence. In the fall of 1983, a National Intelligence Estimate produced by the CIA concluded that the contra forces lacked the military capability and political support to overthrow the Sandinistas, and that the Nicaraguan government would not give up in a military confrontation with U.S.-supported forces.[84] This assessment did not deter the administration from expanding the covert war throughout the fall, a way of punishing the Sandinistas even if the far-off dream of ousting them was beyond reach.

Stiff resistance to the Nicaragua program in the House led the administration to deal more closely with allies on the Senate Intelligence Committee, who were willing to continue covert operations if the goals of the program could be brought into line with their policy preferences. In August, Casey briefed its members on the contents of a new presidential finding justifying covert operations, as required by the committee in May. When several objections were raised to the scope of the program, Casey came up with a new plan, returning with Shultz in September with a proposal that committee members viewed as scaled down.[85]

The new finding, signed by President Reagan on September 19, preserved the old emphasis on equipping and training paramilitary resistance forces, for what Thomas Enders had described as "turning inward"—pressuring the Sandinista government and diverting its resources until it stopped supporting subversion in other countries. This time, however, a new twist was added: "to bring the Sandinistas into meaningful negotiations and constructive, verifiable agreement with their neighbors on peace in the region." As in the case of El Salvador, Congress demanded, and the administration attempted to define, a legitimate political rationale for U.S. actions. In addition, the finding worked out with the Senate Intelligence Committee authorized the United States to "seek support of and work with other foreign governments and organizations as appropriate to carry out this program." Congress, it seemed in 1983, not only approved of but instructed the administration to broaden the number of backers of the contra movement.[86]

Undeterred by the process of "advise and consent" under way in the Senate, however, the House dug in its heels, voting twice more before the end of the year to end covert operations against Nicaragua. The September sabotage of Nicaragua's only coastal oil terminal and October attacks on oil storage facilities provided the first evidence of long-rumored maritime operations against economic targets in Nicaragua.* In apparent violation of assurances by the CIA that the contras would desist from attacking economic infrastructure, the October operation set huge fires resulting in the evacuation of civilians from the port city of Corinto. Evidence available to the committee suggested that the CIA not only helped plan the attacks, but that the CIA's unilaterally controlled latino assets (UCLAs) and CIA employees were directly involved, violating another

---

*On the eve of House debate on the Boland-Zablocki legislation to end covert operations, Representative Sala Burton (D-Calif.) placed in the *Congressional Record* a news report that "the CIA reportedly asked for detailed maps of three Nicaraguan ports as part of a covert plan to mine the harbors and intercept Soviet and Cuban weapons and supplies. The agency may have planned to give the mines to anti-Sandinista rebels who intended to sabotage one of the ports in May." John Wallach, *San Francisco Examiner*, in *Congressional Record,* July 21, 1983, p. E 3641.

assurance to the committee that no U.S. personnel would take part in covert attacks against Nicaragua.[87]

Following Boland's lead, the House voted again to end covert operations against Nicaragua during October consideration of the annual intelligence authorization. A margin of 227–194 in favor of the bill showed that there had been no slippage since the earlier votes in the summer. In early November the House included a similar prohibition in the bill appropriating funds for covert operations.

Both of these votes took place against a backdrop of world events that bolstered Reagan's foreign policy. The downing of a Korean Airlines plane by Soviet gunners in September hardened anti-Soviet sentiments, while the U.S. invasion of Grenada in late October demonstrated that swift, successful U.S. military action in the hemisphere could command broad popular support. Public enthusiasm for the Grenada invasion caused even disbelievers in Congress to embrace the show of force. But it was not at all clear that support for the tough U.S. action was transferable to Central America. On November 17 the House adopted a resolution supporting regional negotiations spearheaded by four Latin American nations—the "Contadora" group—a way of signaling the administration that despite Grenada it lacked a mandate for military intervention in Central America.[88]

The Senate, meanwhile, continued to support the administration on the issue of covert operations in Nicaragua following the drafting of a new finding in September. The vice-chairman of the Senate Intelligence Committee, Daniel P. Moynihan of New York, stated that the administration had listened to committee concerns about the scope of the program and scaled the plans back accordingly. "There was a response to our counsel," Moynihan said.[89] This attitude made a showdown on Nicaragua policy inevitable, as House-Senate differences would have to be resolved in a conference on one of the bills dealing with covert operations. That showdown came on the defense appropriations bill.

The conferees agreed to provide $24 million for the contras in the upcoming fiscal year. In exchange for giving in on the question of funding, the House exacted a prohibition on the use of CIA contingency funds or reprogrammings to add monies for the rebels. This meant that future appropriations would have to pass both houses, a way of preserving the House's blocking capability.[90] On this slender reed of a concession, Boland convinced House liberals to back the compromise.

While the conferees were wrangling over how much if any funding to give for the Nicaragua program, the administration expanded its activities, seemingly oblivious to the swirling controversies on Capitol Hill. In late 1983 the NSC approved an increase in the authorized strength of the contra rebels, up to a force of 18,000, unbeknownst to the oversight committees.[91] It was as if the bruising House fight over covert operations in 1983 had meant nothing, as if the administration could not see that early efforts to limit the covert war led to a broader clamor to shut it down. In contrast to a change in the emphasis of El Salvador policy, undertaken in part if not wholly in response to congressional concerns, the force that drove Nicaragua policy proved impervious to the tempering influence of congressional doubt. In the coming months, that failure of comprehension would prove the administration's undoing.

Chapter Six

1984:
Driving Policies to Conclusion

The Reagan administration intended 1984 to be the year of bipartisanship, the year in which the Kissinger Commission was expected to produce a consensus over Central America policy. Contrary to plan, however, the report of the Kissinger Commission only underscored the tensions between the Reagan administration and its critics over strategy.[1] While articulating the shared view that the United States had vital interests in Central America, the report failed to resolve the conflict over the correct policies to achieve agreed-upon goals.

Like many documents born of a process of political compromise, the commission report incorporated diverse views without reconciling opposing positions. In its section on El Salvador, the Kissinger Commission report recommended "significantly increased levels of military aid" (a proposal welcomed by the Reagan administration and its supporters) but suggested that it be strictly conditioned on human rights progress (a suggestion hailed by Reagan administration critics).[2] Recommendations for Nicaragua policy were even less suited to compromise. Stating that the majority of the commission's members "believe that the efforts of the Nicaraguan insurgents represent one of the incentives working in favor of a negotiated settlement," the commission gave backhanded endorsement to a policy of support for the contras.[3] With Congress still deeply divided over the contra issue, there appeared to be no middle ground between support for and opposition to U.S. funding for the rebels.

The irony of the Kissinger Commission's effort to forge a policy consensus is that the report's recommendations ultimately had little to do with congressional action on Central America in 1984. Rather, congressional action responded to two catalytic occurrences: the election of José Napoleón Duarte as president of El Salvador, and CIA participation in the mining of Nicaragua's harbors. Both these events served as turning points in congressional consideration of Central America policy: in El Salvador, toward the administration's position; in Nicaragua, down a road of increased confrontation and acrimony.

Duarte's election in El Salvador held forth the promise for democratic, reformist government, and as such convinced a congressional majority to support vast aid increases sought by the administration. The turnaround was especially dramatic in the Democratic-controlled House, for three and a half years the locus of bitter opposition to the Reagan policy.

Congress also came to a new agreement on Nicaragua policy, adopting a total prohibition on U.S. support for the contras. The involvement of the Central Intelligence Agency in the mining of three Nicaraguan ports triggered a political explosion in Washington that arguably outdid the damage to Nicaraguan commerce. When a majority of the Senate Intelligence Committee believed it had not been informed of the CIA role, what might have been simply a foreign policy blunder became a domestic crisis of major proportions. Outrage over the mining and the administration's perceived failure to report the mining to congressional oversight committees eroded support for the contra program from where it had been the strongest: in the Senate. The controversy provided the backdrop for a successful House-led effort at the end of the year to prohibit outright covert operations against Nicaragua.

What distinguishes 1984 from previous years in the Central America debate is the degree to which domestic political considerations mingled with events in foreign capitals in prompting congressional action. In El Salvador, for example, the holding of an election tapped a deeply held American political value—the right of the citizenry to choose its leaders. Just as Congress repudiated death squads, human rights abuses, and the foundering of an agrarian reform, it welcomed the 1984 election. The distinction between holding an election and constructing a democratic political system was less important than the fact that vast numbers of people voted. In Washington, the election was viewed as one evolutionary step on the way to building a Western-style democracy, free of the military domination of politics that had characterized Salvadoran history.

The impact of the election on key members of Congress—most prominently House Majority Leader Jim Wright—helped produce a Republican-Democratic majority that for the first time approved the administration's full requests for military and economic aid for El Salvador.

The political fury over the mining of Nicaragua's harbors, however, grew from a sense of trampled institutional prerogatives. Whether the Senate Intelligence Committee was informed of the mining or not, the perception of key committee leaders that they had not been informed became the relevant factor in a Senate-wide protest. Quite apart from the content of the policy, the administration's perceived failure to adhere to the rules governing consultation with the Congress over intelligence matters determined congressional action.

A further way that the 1984 Central America debate fell hostage to domestic considerations has to do with the administration's attitude toward a congressional role in determining Central America policy. Rather than broadening a Kissinger Commission-type effort at consensus, the administration accelerated its 1983 partisan attacks on the Congress. The attacks blamed Democrats in particular for their failure to support administration programs in Central America and insinuated that Congress would bear responsibility for any disasters that might befall the region.

The assaults resulted in increased partisanship and resistance to administration initiatives in the short run; if bipartisanship for the administration meant little more than a threat to do things the administration's way or pay the price with the public should the policy fail, Congress showed few signs of having been bludgeoned into submission. The administration then escalated the tension and in a multitude of small ways continued to place obstacles in its quest for bipartisanship under administration leadership. In seeking emergency supplementals for the region early in the year, for example, the administration bypassed key committee allies in a rush to pump more funding into the region. A major aid initiative—a request for an additional $21 million for the contras and $93 million for the Salvadoran army—thus became a referendum on proper procedure as well as on the merits of the request.

Over time, however, the administration's efforts to blame Congress for policy failures heightened the insecurity of some of its critics. By going and staying on the offensive, the administration played the preeminent role in defining the climate and terms of debate.

In a more profound way, the administration decision to play hardball with the Congress in 1984 contained the seeds of the greatest political debacle of the Reagan presidency: the Iran-contra affair. As congressional resistance to additional contra funding reached a crescendo, senior administration officials sought to enlist foreign governments and private individuals in a contra support effort that would not need congressional endorsement. These solicitations were technically within the law in 1984, because U.S. support for the rebels was not barred until the end of the year, and because the revised 1983 Nicaragua finding specifically encouraged the participation of other foreign governments. However, once a decision was made to back the contras regardless of any new legislative boundaries, it was only a short, and probably inevitable, path to disaster.

El Salvador

The Kissinger Commission recommendation for more but strictly conditioned aid was intended to mitigate the clash over policy. Instead, conflict deepened in the early months of 1984, as policy critics used the language of the report to justify tougher conditions than had previously been imposed. Moreover, the visit to El Salvador by Vice President Bush in late 1983 heightened the salience of the death squad issue, providing a context and creating an attentive public for new revelations about death squad activities to come.

Similarly, a series of guerrilla attacks around the New Year renewed Congress's perennial focus on the inability of the Salvadoran army to defeat the guerrillas, irrespective of increases in U.S. military aid. Devastating guerrilla attacks on a key northern military garrison on December 31, 1983, and the New Year's Day destruction of a main bridge linking eastern and western El Salvador elicited congressional responses that recalled the language and grammar of the "lessons of Vietnam" debate. "Having recently returned from El Salvador," wrote Representative Stephen Solarz in February, "I was struck by the sharp deterioration in the government's military position." While conceding that the armed forces faced some equipment shortages, Solarz concluded that "the real problems plaguing them are far more fundamental: ineffective leadership and inadequate motivation."[4]

Despite the inauspicious developments for administration policy, the executive branch did have some limited manifestations of progress to point to. As a result of the Bush visit in December 1983, two Salvadoran officers suspected of death squad activities were transferred abroad; another was dismissed from the army and a fourth relieved of his responsibility as security chief for the

Constituent Assembly.* The State Department submitted a human rights certification to Congress in January, even though no longer required to by law. That certification admitted that "continued abuse of human rights remains a central problem." But the State Department could rightly claim that "specific measures have been taken to control the death squads and to exert stricter discipline over members of the armed forces."[5]

A New Awareness: Death Squads and Official Murder

Instead of placating critics of El Salvador policy, administration admissions about death squad violence fueled an appetite for further progress—and greater restrictions on aid until it occurred. The transfer of Salvadorans, including military officers, implicated in the killing suggested not only that the problem existed, contrary to earlier administration claims, but also that Salvadoran authorities had the capacity to do something about it if sufficiently pressured. By claiming credit for curbing death squad murders, the administration thus lent credence to what members of Congress had maintained for several years—that there was official involvement in the hit teams and that the United States, to the extent that it failed to exert pressure, bore some responsibility for their continuation.

The administration's campaign against the death squads created a context for new allegations to be heard and raised questions about whether the Reagan administration had engaged in a cover-up of known death squad activities. In early February, former Ambassador Robert White told a House subcommittee that "from the first days in office the Reagan White House knew—beyond any reasonable doubt—that Roberto D'Aubuisson planned and ordered the assassination of Archbishop Romero."† White mentioned specific cables on right-wing

*Treasury Police Major José Ricardo Pozo and National Police Lieutenant Colonel Aristídes Alfonso Márquez were sent to posts abroad. Lieutenant Francisco Raúl Amaya Rosa, later identified by former Ambassador Robert White as a key figure in the murder of Salvadoran Archbishop Romero, was reportedly dismissed from the army. D'Aubuisson's crony, Héctor Antonio Regalado, was also reportedly removed as security chief of the Assembly. By 1988, Regalado was reportedly back in El Salvador helping to rebuild the death squads. Bernard Gwertzman, "Salvador Curbs Death Squads, U.S. Aides Say," New York Times, January 1, 1984; Robert McCartney, "El Salvador Confirms Loss of 100," Washington Post, January 4, 1984; Robert McCartney, "U.S. Lauds Drive to Halt Death Squads," Washington Post, January 8, 1984; Douglas Farah, "Salvadoran Death Squads Threaten Resurgence," Washington Post, August 28, 1988.

†White stated that D'Aubuisson presided over a meeting of twelve men and "supervised the drawing of lots for the 'honor' of carrying out the plot." He said that Amaya Rosa,

violence sent to Washington during his tenure as ambassador, which had been withheld from the Foreign Affairs Committee when it formally requested information on D'Aubuisson in 1982. White's allegations raised questions about the Congress's ability to obtain classified information from an administration unwilling to share it on matters of mutual concern. *

In March, a former Salvadoran intelligence official also accused D'Aubuisson of organizing and directing the death squads and the 1980 murder of Archbishop Oscar Arnulfo Romero. Senator Paul Tsongas (D-Mass.) and Representative Jim Shannon (D-Mass.) arranged several meetings between Colonel Roberto Santiváñez and members of Congress. Santiváñez alleged that a leader of one of the most notorious security forces in El Salvador was a paid CIA agent.[6]

The relentless publicity about death squads and D'Aubuisson had important ramifications for U.S. policy in early 1984. D'Aubuisson's announced candidacy in El Salvador's upcoming presidential elections raised an old specter: that the United States could end up having committed itself to support of a government whose leader had been implicated in organized murder. This concern made Congress reluctant to move on aid requests prior to a final election outcome in El Salvador. It also prompted the administration to intervene in the Salvadoran electoral process. In the words of a top Senate Democratic aide, "Everyone knew that if D'Aubuisson was elected it was all over as far as aid was concerned."[7] As it had at the time of the 1982 Salvadoran elections, the administration read the congressional apprehension as a mandate to keep D'Aubuisson out of office.

The Struggle Over Aid:
Old Questions, Stronger Remedies

When the Reagan administration unveiled in February an $8 billion aid package for Central America, including a fivefold increase in military aid for El Salvador,

---

one of the Salvadoran officials reportedly removed in January as a result of the Bush visit, had chosen the sharpshooter. Prepared Statement by Ambassador Robert White before the House Subcommittee on Western Hemisphere Affairs, February 2, 1984, pp. 1–11.

*Some cables had been provided to the Foreign Affairs Committee following a 1982 "resolution of inquiry" on D'Aubuisson sponsored by Representative Pete Stark (D-Calif.). Following White's testimony, the chairman and the ranking minority member of the Foreign Affairs Committee complained to Secretary of State George Shultz that "contrary to the assertions of [a State Department spokesman], the House Foreign Affairs Committee has *not* received all relevant cables" (emphasis in the original). Text, Letter from Representatives Fascell and Broomfield to Secretary of State Shultz, February 8, 1984.

it found that the Kissinger Commission had not laid the groundwork for a congressional leap of faith on Central America policy.[8] If anything, by recognizing the legitimacy of aid conditions tailored to Salvadoran government performance, the Kissinger Commission helped intensify debate on internal political conditions in El Salvador and the government's ability to prevail over the guerrillas without increased U.S. involvement.

As in 1983, centrists in the Senate led the charge against administration policy. In February, for example, Senator Bennett Johnston (D-La.) spoke for many who did not want to see a rebel victory in El Salvador yet who saw no formula for success: "It seems to me the situation is deteriorating, . . . that we are losing the war . . . because we are losing the war for the hearts and minds of the people. . . . And why is that? I think, perhaps because of the death squads, because of the lack of human rights in El Salvador."[9] A week later, Johnston was joined by Senator Inouye, who for the second time in less than a year went to the floor to denounce administration policy in Central America. "I fear that America is stumbling blindly toward the abyss," Inouye said of Central America. "[There are] signs which mark the way, yet those in power do not see them."[10]

While congressional critics seemed clear on what was wrong with El Salvador policy, they remained deeply divided over how to push the administration toward an alternative policy or, indeed, what that policy should encompass. The focus of congressional efforts, as they had been in the past, remained on the El Salvador aid package: reducing the overall amounts and placing new conditions on its disbursement.

Those conditions were more draconian than those in the now-defunct certification. In a move that structured debate in the House for the remainder of the year, the House Western Hemisphere Subcommittee approved a new certification requirement that mandated congressional approval of the certification by joint resolution. By taking tougher action, the House subcommittee reflected both a lack of faith in certifications by the administration and mounting impatience with the pace of reforms in El Salvador.

As soon became apparent, however, the proposals by the subcommittee did not reflect attitudes shared by the full House. The House Foreign Affairs Committee remained deeply divided over toughened legislation for El Salvador, and its new chairman, Florida Democrat Dante Fascell, was skeptical of any proposal that threatened the flow of aid to El Salvador. In mid-March the deadlocked committee voted to separate Central America from other portions of the foreign aid legislation. The action, taken so as not to tie up the entire bill, set the stage for a battle in the full House later in the year.[11] By postponing a decision, the Foreign Affairs Committee laid the groundwork for an El Salvador policy struggle in a wider, more contentious arena—the full House.

Despite the attempts to impose more stringent conditions on new El Salvador aid requests, the Congress lacked the capability and the clarity to force the administration's hand on an alternative approach. Negotiations toward a political settlement were the core of all congressional proposals for a substitute to the Reagan policy. As in 1981, however, members of Congress were confused as to the kind of settlement a negotiation would produce. While it is true that Congress could not force an administration to carry out negotiations in good faith, Congress itself lacked the political will to press ahead on the issue.

Central to the failure of nerve was the growing radicalization of neighboring Nicaragua. There the process of political evolution suggested that moderates in a coalition government gradually lost power to harder-line elements within it. Not only were members of Congress skeptical of the relative share of power held by nonguerrillas in the Salvadoran opposition coalition, they feared that negotiations with Salvadoran social democrats would result in a repeat of the Nicaraguan experience.

Even staunch opponents of the Reagan administration were unwilling to take the political heat should the worst occur. The administration deftly manipulated the charge that congressional proposals for a negotiated settlement were little more than calls for the integration of communist insurgents in a new government. Members of Congress became paralyzed by their own fears, including that of potential allegations that they were "soft" on communists in the hemisphere.

The absence if not elimination of a search for serious alternatives to Reagan policy in El Salvador by 1984 had several consequences. First, the debate remained technical, focusing on aid levels and on ways to finely tune conditions so that they would be enforced. Second, the definition of the terms of the debate was left almost entirely to the administration. Critics could raise the Vietnam specter as a logical consequence of blindly "staying the course" on Salvador policy, but when they backed off pressuring the Reagan administration and the Salvadoran government to negotiate, there were few alternatives short of disengagement. Finally, the lack of fresh ideas only added to battle fatigue. After going over and over the same ground for close to four years, members were tired of the Salvador issue and frustrated by the persistent difficulties in seeking solutions. In short, the El Salvador debate was becoming more and more an endurance contest. Convinced that the stakes were monumental, the Reagan administration had a decided psychological advantage in staying power.

To increase their advantage, and further narrow the terms of the debate, the administration submitted in March an "emergency" request for $93 million in military aid, attaching it to a bill for African famine relief that had already passed the House. The administration packaged the request in seemingly impenetrable wrapping, arguing that the Salvadoran army needed immediate funding to protect the upcoming March elections against guerrilla threats. The administration hoped to deflect attention away from the nature of the Salvadoran government, making support for elections a litmus test of democratic credentials. Debate was thus reduced to a series of stark questions defined by the administration: Would the Congress allow an elections process to be subverted for lack of adequate security? Would Congress defend the Salvadoran government against Marxist guerrillas dedicated to its overthrow?

To create the atmosphere of crisis necessary for swift action on the aid request, the administration campaigned vigorously on the theme of emergency. Shultz insisted to a House subcommittee that the Salvadoran army had to "husband their resources in order to string them out and they can't really do what they think is the right thing . . . in the name of their own security."[12] President Reagan told a group of Republican women officials that "the Salvadorans are out of U.S. military aid assistance funds, because my original request was not fully funded by the Congress."[13] A Defense Department "fact sheet" claimed that without the $93 million, "the ESAF [El Salvador Armed Forces] will either go back to the barracks or collapse."[14]

To punctuate its campaign for rapid action, the administration stepped up accusations that questioning the notion of urgency was tantamount to a sellout of U.S. interests in the hemisphere. Undersecretary of Defense Fred Ikle warned that Congress would be held accountable if they "wash their hands of Central America like Pontius Pilate. . . . We in the Administration don't sense an eagerness on Capitol Hill to take responsibility for communist victories in Central America." President Reagan told a group of Cuban-Americans at the White House that it was "naive or downright phony to express concern for human rights while pursuing policies that led to the overthrow of less-than-perfect democracies by Marxist dictatorships."[15] The message was a stark one: support our policy or accept responsibility for regional dominoes.

In fact, a preelection funding emergency did not exist, and the composition of the aid package itself suggested an effort to expand, rather than simply sustain, the Salvadoran army.[16] Nonetheless, the creation of the appearance of urgency paid early dividends for the administration, even while it distorted the debate. On March 14 the Senate Appropriations Committee voted to approve the entire $93 million request. While the proposal had a long way to go before clearing the entire Congress, this early victory provided an outer limit from which subsequent compromises would have to start.

Elections in El Salvador:
A Salvadoran—and Washington—Affair

The administration's efforts to cast the debate on its terms thus made inroads in early 1984. But scare tactics alone could not produce congressional support for sustained expansions in the Salvador aid program. Rather, as Assistant Secretary Enders had realized in mid-1981, developments in El Salvador would have to convince a majority of the Congress that the government warranted an increased U.S. investment. In 1984 the Salvadoran elections provided that reassurance, but only because the results—influenced directly by the United States—were consistent with a congressional desire to consolidate reforms and improve human rights.

On March 25, 1984, Salvadorans went to the polls to elect a president. Widespread confusion and disorganization plagued the voting day—a combination of administrative inefficiency and attacks by guerrillas determined that the elections not succeed.[17] But the results of the March election were themselves inconclusive. No candidate received a clear majority, paving the way for a May runoff between the two top contenders: José Napoleón Duarte of the Christian Democratic Party and Roberto D'Aubuisson of the Nationalist Republican Alliance (ARENA).

The mere process of holding elections in the midst of a war impressed a bipartisan group of nineteen congressional observers. Said Oklahoma Democrat Senator David Boren, "The right to vote, the privilege of voting, has taken on a new meaning for me because of what I saw." House Majority Leader Jim Wright, who had traveled to El Salvador after the 1982 Salvadoran elections, stated emphatically, "I'm going to do whatever is necessary to provide the means for the people of El Salvador to preserve a democratic society."[18]

The holding of the March Salvadoran election soon became a dominant factor in Senate consideration of the $93 million "emergency" aid request. For seven long days liberal senators offered amendment after amendment, reducing aid to El Salvador and tying it to a prosecution of the murderers of the U.S. churchwomen, eliminating funding for the contras, and requiring prior congressional approval before troops were introduced into Central America. But administration critics lost on all but a few minor changes in the law;[19] they were unable to hold the center of their own party and garnered only token support from Republicans. Key senators such as Inouye backed a compromise figure of $61.75 million in military aid for El Salvador, convinced that anything less would be rejected by a Senate majority favoring aid. The outcome served as a basic reaffirmation of Reagan's Central America policy.

Ignoring the Senate ratification of his policies, which had come with Democratic Party support, President Reagan intensified his campaign to blame Congress for its failure to support his policies in Central America. In an April 6 speech at Georgetown University's Center for Strategic and International Studies, Reagan lashed out at members of Congress who acted as if "their only task [was] to be vocal critics, and not responsible partners. . . . Either we help America's friends defend themselves and give democracy a chance or we abandon our responsibilities and let the Soviet Union and Cuba shape the destiny of our hemisphere."[20]

Coming in the wake of the Senate votes, Reagan's attack sharpened the atmosphere of conflict and recrimination in the Democratic-controlled House. "It's difficult to get a bipartisan foreign policy if you're reaching out with one hand and punching with the other," said Foreign Affairs Chairman Fascell. Majority Leader Wright excoriated the president for expecting "Congress to be a silent partner, to put up the money and keep its mouth shut and accept the blame whenever anything goes wrong."[21]

Once again the administration's tactics proved counterproductive to its goal of swift action on the emergency supplemental. In mid-April a determined House leadership sent the House into adjournment without having acted on the funds. During the congressional recess, the president retaliated, invoking emergency powers to send half of the aid—$32 million—thus bypassing the Hill. "I think it's wrong, wrong, wrong," said Representative Clarence Long, chairman of the Foreign Operations Subcommittee, who had agreed in principle to send some of the aid. The message from the administration was "go work your head off, but if we don't get exactly what we want, we'll bypass you." Speaker O'Neill called the president "untrustworthy."[22]

The president's tactics so angered members of the House that they voted overwhelmingly on May 2 not to go to conference with the Senate on the supplemental appropriations bill. They postponed the action until after the second electoral round in El Salvador. A showdown was building, with the runoff between José Napoleón Duarte and Roberto D'Aubuisson its centerpiece.

The House Turnaround—Duarte and the Salvadoran Electoral Process

In retrospect, it would have been surprising in 1984 if Duarte and his reformist platform had not triumphed in a country of impoverished campesinos and urban dwellers. The administration, however, wanted to take no chances. The United States feared not only the rapid political polarization and stepped-up violence a D'Aubuisson presidency would bring to El Salvador—a "bloodbath," in the word of a State Department official—but also that Congress would never be persuaded to expand aid to allow successful prosecution of the war unless there was a credible political component to U.S. policy.[23] "Everyone in the [U.S.] Embassy knew that if Duarte didn't win that was the end of Reagan's policy in El Salvador," said a State Department official close to the electoral process. "But everyone also knew we couldn't say that to the Salvadorans."[24]

Although senior U.S. officials professed neutrality in the upcoming electoral process, CIA polling experts kept a close watch on levels of support for each political party. The Christian Democrats were a largely urban-based party, and Duarte's weakness was in the rural areas. To win the election Duarte needed to beat D'Aubuisson in the countryside, picking up a majority of the votes that had gone to other parties during the first round. To further, if not guarantee, that outcome, the CIA between March and May expanded a program of covert assistance to centrist political parties reportedly begun in 1981, pumping funds into those political forces that had committed themselves to backing the Duarte candidacy. At the same time, the Agency for International Development worked with the Salvadoran Central Elections Council to set up a voter registration system that would minimize the chances for fraud.[25]

Rumors of the U.S. Embassy's role in funding the election began seeping out even before the May runoff. It was denounced first by ARENA on May 2, reportedly on a tip from the office of Senator Jesse Helms (R-N.C.).[26] In a floor speech on May 8, Helms alleged that "the United States provided funds for 400 precinct organizers for Mr. Duarte, set up a model press operation, provided radio and TV studios, gave technical advice and paid for the computer voter registration system that disenfranchise [sic] 20 percent of the voters the first time around." The State Department and the CIA "bought Mr. Duarte lock, stock, and barrel," Helms said. "[U.S. Ambassador to El Salvador Thomas] Pickering was merely the purchasing agent."[27]

State Department officials who had wanted to avoid CIA funding so that the elections would be "clean" were vindicated by subsequent events. After receiving several death threats, a U.S. AID employee detailed to the Salvadoran Central Elections Council was placed under twenty-four-hour Marine guard and shortly thereafter left El Salvador. Following the election, there were reports that the right plotted to assassinate U.S. Ambassador Thomas Pickering; D'Aubuisson was reported to be involved.[28]

The U.S. decision to bolster Duarte's candidacy may not have been decisive in his victory, but much uncertainty had surrounded the May 6 vote: Would the turnout be low? Would there be obvious fraud? Would the military accept the results? "It was a risky event, a watershed," recalled a State Department official. The outcome—a triumph for the Christian Democrats—was a "very, very happy surprise."[29]

A delegation of members of Congress who traveled to El Salvador as part of an official observer mission concurred. "It is our consensus that the election was fair and honest," they said in a statement. "The strong message of this election is that the Salvadoran people have declared their own political solution to the crisis that challenges the country. Three successful elections in two years are a clear repudiation of the insurgency."[30]

The statement of the observer mission—prominently led by Majority Leader Wright—set the tone for the House's upcoming debate on the foreign aid bill. On the surface, three alternatives were before the House: a liberal Democratic amendment making all aid contingent on a presidential certification approved by the Congress; a Foreign Affairs Committee proposal providing some aid "up front" and conditioning the rest on a presidential certification approved by Congress; and a Republican-sponsored proposal providing all the aid at once with minimal binding conditions. The debate on these different versions framed an immediate, practical question: Did the changes in El Salvador warrant a quantum leap in U.S. assistance, and if so, with or without the conditions Congress had insisted on since the beginning of the Reagan administration?

At a deeper level, however, the focus on Duarte and conditionality may have been a convenience masking the underlying perspectives of opposing sides. For some critics of policy, it was reform that should be the central issue in El Salvador; if reforms could not be achieved, no amount of U.S. aid could—or even should—save the country from defeat by the guerrillas. Arguing that aid conditions strengthened Duarte's hand in pushing for reforms was another way of saying that the United States had no business being in El Salvador if those reforms proved impossible. The consequences to U.S. security should a corrupt ally fall were not so overwhelming that disengagement should be ruled out.

For supporters of the president—some of whom might have been equally comfortable with a D'Aubuisson presidency—the central purpose of providing U.S. aid was to defeat communism, regardless of the political coloration of the surviving government. For some, Duarte's election was simply a convenience, a better way to justify aid that the United States should provide no matter which noncommunist party came to power.

Understood at this starker level, the debate had evolved little since 1981; what had changed was the way each side framed its arguments around the central new reality in El Salvador—the election of a civilian president.

Liberals distinguished between Duarte's formal and actual power in insisting on strong conditions: "There is no question [that] José Napoleón Duarte is a man with good intentions, but let us face the facts," said Representative James Shannon (D-Mass.). "When he was President before he did not run the country. It is the army which rules El Salvador." And Representative Howard Wolpe (D-Mich.) added that "it simply makes no sense to urge . . . that Mr. Duarte press for reforms . . . and then . . . tell the military . . . that they will be receiving all the guns and all the supplies they want."[31]

Conservatives argued that less than a total commitment to the battle against communism in El Salvador threatened U.S. security. "The country of El Salvador is 965 miles from the tip of Texas," said Representative Tom Loeffler (R-Texas). "We are so close that Central America's strategic posture automatically affects our own." A statement from the Republican Policy Committee accused Democrats of "turn[ing] America's back on growing threats to American and hemispheric stability. . . . If extreme Democratic partisans succeed in defeating the President's program for a free and stable Central America, the responsibility for the communization and destabilization of Central America rests with them."[32]

Less-strident proponents of the Republican package argued simply that "if we impose stringent measures, we may bring about a crisis rather than a recovery."[33] Added a Democratic supporter of the administration-backed amendment, burdening Duarte with "difficult restrictions . . . would make it impossible for him to act effectively. It may even send the wrong signals."[34]

What decided the House vote on May 10 may not have been the merits of the arguments made on either side but—as in the 1983 debate over covert operations in Nicaragua—who was making them. Two factors internal to the House, related to but not dependent on developments in El Salvador, thus became decisive in the final vote outcome. First, the advocacy of Majority Leader Wright in favor of the Republican-sponsored package was critical in splitting the Democrats and allowing a Republican victory. Second, the less-than-vigorous defense of the Foreign Affairs Committee plan by its chairman allowed undecided Democrats to gravitate toward Wright. Finally, some viewed the proposal by liberal Democrats to restrict aid to El Salvador as a ploy to stop aid altogether, a position with which Democratic Party centrists were uncomfortable.

Wright's colleagues pleaded with the majority leader not to make a floor speech in favor of the aid. But Wright ignored those calls and made the closing arguments of the tense afternoon. A quorum call immediately prior to his delivery brought virtually the entire House membership to the floor. Known as a skilled and impassioned orator, Wright spoke to a hushed chamber: "This is an agonizing moment for me," he began. "And yet, I feel so very strongly that I am impelled to speak out. . . . We need steady, emphatic commitment to freedom in El Salvador—not a tenuous, tentative, hesitant or begrudging commitment. . . . I have seen this country of El Salvador go through the travail and the birth pangs of a democracy. Let us not let that democracy be stillborn; nor die in its infancy." Wright argued that conditions proposed in the bill set up "a standard that we do not require of any other nation in the world. Why do we require it of our friends in El Salvador?"[35]

Giving added weight to Wright's remarks was the plea of newly elected President Duarte. In individual telegrams addressed to members of the House, Duarte reminded the representatives that "on three occasions now the people of El Salvador have defied all threats and freely voted in overwhelming numbers. . . . In order to avoid the disaster that has befallen our neighboring country which has seen its legitimate aspirations for democracy frustrated by a Marxist-Leninist takeover, we need adequate economic and military assistance. . . . Please help the people of El Salvador and contribute simultaneously to the security and stability of our hemisphere."[36]

Fascell, by contrast, spoke in favor of aid conditions. But a key element of institutional prestige—his desire to see the House pass a foreign aid bill in his first year as chairman of the committee—competed with his support of the committee version. "Fascell clearly wanted a foreign aid bill," said one of his top aides. "The Foreign Affairs Committee version was a little too harsh for him. It was expecting too much, too soon. He was looking for a policy that would force the Salvadoran government to clean up its act and a policy that would let aid flow."[37] Fascell's ambivalence—and, some alleged, private opposition to his own bill—gave permission to swing voters to oppose the committee chairman and support aid to El Salvador without conditions.

As the afternoon drew to a close, Republicans often opposed to foreign aid voted in favor of the bill in order to back Reagan on a key Central America policy issue. The president's supporters let out a cheer when the final vote tallies appeared on the lighted House scoreboard. By a margin of four votes, 212–208, the Republican amendment, known for its sponsor William Broomfield of Michigan, prevailed. Only eight Republicans broke with their party, while fifty-six Democrats, all but three of whom were from the South or Southwest, voted with the Republicans to create a winning majority. Wright had succeeded in bringing enough of his fellow Southerners to the president's side to eke out the slim margin of victory.*

In retrospect, it seems surprising, given Duarte's election and Wright's leadership, that the margin of victory was so narrow. But the vote was truly a turning point, the last time during the Reagan presidency that aid to El Salvador would be a subject of contention on the floor of either the House or the Senate. After the House vote of May 10, 1984, debate over El Salvador policy virtually evaporated. The vote thus testifies to the importance of events in the region as seen through the filter of U.S. political values and hopes. Duarte's election signaled for many members that political reform was progressing in El Salvador in a peaceful, evolutionary manner, an antidote to violent revolution.

"Before 1984," said former House Western Hemisphere Affairs Subcommittee Chairman Michael Barnes in an interview, "[Duarte] was seen as a tool of the colonels. Then [he became] a major democratic figure, a hero of democracy in the region."[38] Duarte's program—to end the death squads, carry through announced reforms, and open peace talks with the guerrillas—mirrored the issues skeptical members of Congress had been dwelling on for years. Duarte's announced commitment to reform, combined with his electoral mandate from Salvadoran voters, translated into a virtual political imperative in Washington to "give Duarte a chance."

Moreover, Duarte's own personal history and familiarity with the United States gave him broad personal appeal. "He had earned his bona fides," said Representative John Spratt (D-S.C.), referring to Duarte's 1970s political exile and subsequent comeback. In a meeting with House Democrats in May 1984, "[Duarte's] sincerity and genuine warmth and conviction about what he wanted to do for his country came across marvelously. . . . If you want a seminal event, a pivotal event when a politician made a speech that changed things, [that] was it."[39] "He was like Anwar Sadat [of Egypt]," said a Republican aide on the Foreign Affairs Committee, "tremendously popular outside of his country. He can do no wrong."[40]

Finally, the same battle fatigue that had produced a dearth of creative alternatives earlier in the year gave way to a collective sigh of relief that the ordeal might be over. "We're off the hook," said the staff director of the Western

---

*Wright astutely included several key Southerners in the official observer mission to the Salvadoran elections. All four of the election observers (in addition to Wright)—Roemer (D-La.), Montgomery (D-Miss.), Boner (D-Tenn.), and Pickle (D-Texas)—were from the South, and all four voted with Wright. Speaker O'Neill attributed the president's victory to members' fear of being blamed for the collapse of the Salvadoran government and a communist takeover.

Hemisphere Subcommittee, paraphrasing members. "We don't have to engage in this terrible fight with our own President and have him calling us communists. We can be on the same side."[41]

The desire—perhaps even the need—to claim success sent members scurrying away from the El Salvador issue in droves. Public opposition to policy, still located primarily in the churches, also diminished following another pivotal event in El Salvador: on May 24 a Salvadoran jury convicted five former National Guardsmen of aggravated homicide in the 1980 deaths of the four U.S. churchwomen. The episode that had most vividly brought violence in El Salvador before the American public was drawn to a close, and with it, the symbol that had galvanized resistance to U.S. policy throughout Reagan's first term was removed.

Through a series of votes throughout the summer the Congress reaffirmed its support for Duarte. By the end of the year it voted nearly 75 percent of the 1984 funds requested by the president and approved virtually the entire sum for 1985.[42] These funds permitted a vast expansion of the Salvadoran army's arsenal, with three main effects in El Salvador and the United States. First, the army was able to reverse the momentum of the war that had earlier seemed to favor the guerrillas, capitalizing on new air power to gain an advantage over the rebels. Second, the commitment of senior army officers to nominal civilian rule and elections grew, as Duarte proved to be the "key to the goose that laid the golden egg"—that is, the U.S. Congress.[43] As long as electoral politics were the sina qua non of congressional support, the army would surely tolerate, if not welcome, civilian rule. Finally, with Congress continuing to provide the funds, yet removed from the oversight of details as well as the broad contours of policy, the administration had a free hand to manage the counterinsurgency war. "You can't let Congress off the hook," said a key House aide in late 1984, "that they didn't vote for military victory in El Salvador."[44]

Nicaragua

If Congress and the administration had achieved positive consensus over El Salvador policy in 1984, no such consensus was forged over the contras. Dissension spread through Capitol Hill like the mines sowed in Nicaragua's harbors, breaking apart the fragile majority in favor of the president's policy. The mining episode began with a late-night announcement over a contra radio

station in Tegucigalpa, Honduras. On January 5, 1984, at 2:00 A.M., recalled
then-contra leader Edgar Chamorro,

> the C.I.A. deputy station chief, . . . the agent I knew as "George," woke
> me up at my house . . . and handed me a press release in excellent
> Spanish. I was surprised to read that we—the F.D.N. [the largest contra
> organization]—were taking credit for having mined several Nicaraguan
> harbors. . . . The truth is that we played no role in the mining of the
> harbors. But we did as instructed and broadcast the communiqué about
> the mining.[45]

The decision to mine Nicaragua's harbors seems to have been made in late
1983 and was consistent with an effort to disrupt the Nicaraguan economy as a
way of putting pressure on the Sandinistas. According to a top-secret memorandum from National Security Council aides Oliver North and Constantine
Menges, "Our intention is to severely disrupt the flow of shipping essential to
Nicaraguan trade during the peak export period. . . . It is entirely likely that
once a ship has been sunk, no insurers will cover ships calling in Nicaraguan
ports."[46] The mining was to have a psychological dimension as well, primarily
in Washington. "One of our problems all along," a U.S. official told the Los
Angeles Times, "has been to convince Congress that these guys [the contras] are
effective."[47] Blowing up ships heading into Nicaraguan ports was one way to
make a splash.

As Chamorro noted in 1984, the contras claimed credit for the mining but
did not themselves lay the mines. Rather, as subsequently leaked to the U.S.
press, Latin American commandos under the control of the CIA planted the
devices while operating from an agency "mother ship" off Nicaragua's coast.[48]
U.S. law governing intelligence operations required the administration to notify
Congress when a change in the "nature or scope" of an operation already under
way takes place. Whether and how extensively the CIA did or should have
reported the mining activity—and the CIA's role in it—to the House and Senate
oversight committees rests on how that law is interpreted; the CIA appears to
have made a minimalist interpretation of its obligation to inform the Congress,
a decision that triggered the agency's biggest crisis with Capitol Hill in the three-
year history of the contra program.

What did the intelligence committees know and when did they know it? The
question is critical to understanding the nature of the congressional reaction to
news of the U.S. role in the mining. A full picture of what the committees were
told may be available only when and if transcripts of CIA briefings to Congress

are declassified in future years. What we have now is a contradictory public record, with CIA officials claiming that they complied with an obligation to inform Congress just as vigorously as members of the Senate insist that they did not. The fact most relevant to policy, however, remains that members of the Senate Intelligence Committee behaved as if they had not been *fully* informed. That perception, above all, created the crisis with the administration.

Untangling the sequence of events following Chamorro's announcement highlights some of the weaknesses of the oversight process. First, even when informed of CIA activities, congressional oversight committees are not necessarily in a position to stop them. During a January 31, 1984, briefing, according to House Intelligence Committee Chairman Edward Boland, the CIA admitted that Puerto Sandino on Nicaragua's Pacific coast had been mined. When asked why the committee had not been informed in advance, intelligence agency officials responded that Puerto Sandino was an "anchorage" and not a harbor. "You couldn't get a straight answer," recalled a frustrated assistant.

In February the CIA extended the mining to Nicaragua's major port of Corinto, without informing the House Intelligence Committee. The committee learned of the expanded mining operation when it requested another briefing on March 27, 1984. But even with the information, the oversight committee could only offer its opinion as to the wisdom of the mining.[49]

Second, the Senate committee's preoccupation with the broader issues raised by the contra program—its relationship to U.S. goals in Nicaragua and the extent to which there were clear-cut goals—may have led senators to overlook the significance of new details even when presented. "The horizons are larger in the Senate," explained a former staff aide. "Senators tend to see things in shorthand. They don't have time for the details. They are preoccupied with the larger issues."[50]

When the Senate Intelligence Committee received a requested briefing on the Nicaragua program on March 8, 1984, moreover, they were less interested in the details of the operation than in a jurisdictional issue regarding funding for the covert war:* the CIA had bypassed the Senate and House Intelligence Committees in asking the Senate Appropriations Committee for an extra $21 million for the contras. The administration eventually referred the request to

---

*A delay in scheduling the Senate briefing appears not to have been solely due to CIA foot-dragging, as originally reported in the press. Committee supporters of the contra program were determined to have Secretary Shultz brief the committee alongside CIA Director Casey. Shultz's appearance was deemed vital at the briefing, even if his schedule was harder to arrange, because he had greater credibility with the members. Interview, September 28, 1987, Washington, D.C.

the Senate Intelligence Committee, but not after having "further undermined" the oversight process, in the committee's words.[51]

During the briefing on March 8, Director Casey mentioned the mining in the context of contra accomplishments, according to Staff Director Robert Simmons, thus apparently obscuring the CIA's role. Other congressional sources indicated that Casey notified the Senate committee about the mining on two occasions—on March 8 and at a subsequent briefing on March 13—when he said something to the effect that "mines have been placed."[52] If this account is accurate, Casey's use of the passive voice would indicate that a key element of the operation—the U.S. role—was withheld from the Senate Intelligence Committee. The vice-chairman of the committee, Daniel P. Moynihan (D-N.Y.), for one, claimed that Casey's notification of the mining was limited "to a single sentence in a two-hour Committee meeting [on March 8], and a singularly obscure sentence at that. This sentence was substantially repeated in a meeting on March 13. In no event was the briefing 'full,' 'current,' or 'prior' as required by the Intelligence Oversight Act."[53]

The habit of not volunteering information unless it was pried out of him seems to have been a hallmark of Casey's relationship with the oversight committees—recall the observation of Representative Norman Mineta (D-Calif.) that "Casey wouldn't tell you that your coat was on fire unless you asked him."[54] None of the senators who heard Casey's March 1984 briefings, however, seems to have raised further questions when the topic of mining was discussed. This led at least one Intelligence Committee member to fault not only the administration but the committee itself for less than vigorous oversight. "There was not enough due diligence," Senator Joseph Biden (D-Del.) told a Capitol Hill conference after news of the CIA's role in the mining broke. "We have lost the resolve to make the system work. . . . It would be nice to have an infusion of backbone, myself included."[55]

While briefings for congressional intelligence committees took place behind closed doors, bits and pieces of the mining operation began to filter out to a broader public. With greater and greater frequency throughout March, ships entering Nicaragua's harbors struck the mines, triggering explosions that damaged but did not sink the ships. First a Dutch vessel was damaged, then a Panamanian freighter. Smaller Nicaraguan fishing boats sank. A Soviet ship was hit on March 20, wounding five sailors. A Liberian tanker was damaged, then a Japanese ship carrying cotton. Speedboats armed with machine guns and explosive charges carried out two attacks on Corinto harbor. In response to the wave of attacks, the commander of the Sandinista navy charged that the speedboats "came from a vessel of large tonnage" anchored off Nicaragua's coast.[56]

Predictably, the mining began to raise eyebrows on Capitol Hill. Senators not on the Intelligence Committee began to demand information, particularly as the Senate opened debate on the supplemental funding bill, which included additional contra funding. As a result of these inquiries, the CIA informed the minority staff director of the Intelligence Committee, Gary Schmitt, that the mining was carried out by "unilaterally controlled Latino assets," an intelligence term indicating that the CIA directed the operation. Senate committee staffers were then briefed on the U.S. role on April 2, 1984.[57] They prepared a memo for members, already absorbed with the ongoing floor debate and with several amendments dealing with covert operations in Nicaragua.

Mining I: The Senate Debate

Thus, as debate on the Central America portions of the Fiscal Year 1984 Supplemental proceeded on the Senate floor, most senators knew from press reports about the mining, but few knew about the U.S. role. Members of the Intelligence Committee itself had little time to read the committee staff memo detailing the CIA's new revelation; most, in fact, seem to have overlooked it.[58]

One of the main reasons for this lack of attention was another mini-firestorm regarding the covert war. On March 29 an interview with President Reagan appeared in the *New York Times* in which he appeared to change the purpose of U.S. policy in Nicaragua and, by extension, the contra operation. Reagan said, "We've made it plain to Nicaragua—made it very plain that this [the war] will stop when they keep their promise and restore a democratic rule and have elections."[59] In other words, it was now the nature of the Nicaraguan government, and not its external behavior, that was the target of the contra policy.

The justification that had allowed the president to get Senate support for aid in 1983 had been spelled out in the finding presented to the Senate Intelligence Committee late in the year. It made explicit that the purpose of covert activities was to induce the Nicaraguan government to cease its support for neighboring insurgencies and to bring the Nicaraguan government into a regional peace process. The limited purpose of affecting the foreign policy behavior of the Sandinistas was now being broadened into the wider goal of changing the internal composition of the Nicaraguan government.

Moynihan had successfully defended the program in 1983 on the basis of its narrower purpose, and he was furious at Reagan's remarks. For the next several days, as the Senate debate on Nicaragua proceeded, he was absorbed with obtaining a clarification from the White House that would reaffirm the program's earlier, more limited goals. Attending to details of a CIA role in the mining was only a sideshow to the deeper purpose of returning the administration to its earlier commitments. As a result of Moynihan's protest, President Reagan delivered a last-minute letter to Majority Leader Howard Baker (R-Tenn.) disavowing any intent "to destabilize or overthrow the Government of Nicaragua; nor to impose or compel any particular form of government there." The letter repeated the objective of the revised 1983 intelligence finding, stating that the United States was trying "to bring the Sandinistas into meaningful negotiations . . . on peace in the region."[60] The day the letter was received, the Senate voted 60–31 to grant the additional $21 million for the contras. Moynihan voted with the majority in opposing an effort to strip the funds from the bill.

Intelligence Committee Chairman Goldwater and Vice-Chairman Moynihan led the fight to preserve the bipartisan Senate majority in favor of the administration's Nicaragua program. They opposed efforts by Democratic renegades to "play politics" with carefully crafted compromise positions of the Intelligence Committee, spearheading the effort to defeat several restrictions on Nicaragua policy posed by liberal opponents of the administration. When the Senate voted decisively to reject restrictions on the covert war, it appeared that the votes were just as much for a tradition of bipartisan intelligence oversight as they were in favor of covert operations.

Mining was a factor in the Senate floor debate but was not decisive in swaying opinion in either direction. Intelligence Committee member Durenberger (R-Minn.) noted the mining-related injury of five Soviet seaman, highlighting the inherent risks in paramilitary operations. Senator George Mitchell (D-Maine), another committee member, cited mining as an example of how the contras carried out their own agenda, regardless of the purposes for which U.S. covert aid was given. Senator Pell (D-R.I.) called the mining a "casus [sic] belli—a cause of war."[61] And Senator William Cohen (R-Maine), generally supportive of administration policy, said he was "troubled" by the mining, that "covert assistance should not be used for efforts to overthrow the government or to attack the economic infrastructure of the country."[62]

Both Moynihan and Goldwater, however, came to the administration's defense. Moynihan noted that reports of the mining had raised questions about the "legality and wisdom of the tactics" but that the State Department had provided him a legal analysis of mines and self-defense.[63] Intelligence Committee Chairman Goldwater also assured his colleagues that "the intelligence community is living up to its obligations under the law," claiming that "the right of individual and collective self-defense"—the ostensible justification for contra activities—were "specifically recognized by the U.N. Charter and the Rio Treaty." In remarks later stricken from the *Congressional Record*, Goldwater denied allegations that the United States had had a direct hand in the mining.[64]

Two days after the Senate vote to preserve funding for the contras, however, the *Wall Street Journal* revealed that the Reagan administration's role in the mining was larger than previously disclosed. "Units operating from a ship controlled by the Central Intelligence Agency in the Pacific participated in the operation," the *Journal* reported. "Though anti-Sandinista insurgents have claimed credit for the mining, a source . . . said that the units operating from the ship are self-contained, and are composed of Salvadorans and other Latin Americans from outside Nicaragua." Over the next two days other major papers carried accounts detailing the CIA's role in the mining.[65]

Mining II: The CIA Role

The revelations unleashed a tidal wave of protest, led by Moynihan and Goldwater. "They had put themselves out to defend the program and felt sandbagged," said a former Democratic aide who requested anonymity. "The Administration should have taken it upon themselves to know that members run the risk of embarrassment, through the exposure of something they didn't know about. The rule of thumb should be, make sure they're not surprised or sandbagged by something."[66]

Had the administration mentioned the mining to members and staff of the Senate Intelligence Committee on several occasions? Apparently yes. And committee members appear not to have probed further when mining was mentioned. But the administration's notification—particularly in briefings to the senators themselves—had been sketchy. Most important, the available record suggests that the administration left out the key detail outlining the precise U.S. role in the mining. Stricter committee oversight might have prevented the ensuing backlash, but only if a more forthcoming administration had taken more seriously its obligation to keep Intelligence Committee members "fully and currently informed."

Moynihan led the attack on the mining, and his vehement denunciations of the administration grew during the week following the *Wall Street Journal* revelations. He had waged a politically tricky fight for bipartisan support of the policy, tricky because the Nicaragua operation was unpopular in his own home state of New York and in the country at large. The basis for his advocacy had been that the policy was kept within limits, some of which he himself had helped design. Now there was a U.S. hand in the operation. Now the whole Vietnam scenario descended on the debate. Americans on a "mother ship." What if the Nicaraguans attacked and U.S. citizens were killed? Other members of Moynihan's own party had condemned the mining and tried to end funding for the covert war. He had stifled their efforts, splitting the Democrats and creating a bipartisan majority for the administration. Now it looked like the CIA had taken him for a ride.

"The mining must be stopped and it will be stopped," Moynihan said on April 7.[67] A week later he resigned as vice-chairman of the Intelligence Committee—"the most emphatic way," he stated, "I can express my view that the Senate Committee was not properly briefed on the mining of Nicaraguan harbors with American mines from an American ship under American command."[68]

Goldwater whipped off a stinging letter to CIA Director Casey, complaining, "I am forced to apologize to the members of the Intelligence Committee because I did not know the facts on this. At the same time, my counterpart in the House did know."[69] Later, on the Senate floor, Goldwater elaborated that he had been left in an untenable position:

> A member of my committee came to me [during the debate on the $21 million] to ask if I had seen a document which indicated that the President ordered the mining of selected harbors in Nicaragua. I responded . . . by saying that I had seen no such document and that I could not believe the President could have approved such a program since our committee had not been so briefed. Nor had I received any such briefing. . . .
>
> This afternoon CIA Director Casey appeared before my committee in closed session. . . . I learned to my deep regret that the President did approve this mining program, and that he approved it almost two months ago. . . . I have written Director Casey that this is no way to run a railroad.

"It is indefensible on the part of the Administration," Goldwater later retorted, "to ask us to back its foreign policy when we don't even know what is going on because we were not briefed pursuant to the legal requirements."[70] More than two years after the incident took place, Goldwater was still annoyed. In remarks at an award ceremony at which he received the CIA's Agency Seal Medallion,

Goldwater reiterated his irritation at the way the mining issue was handled, according to an official present.

With the Intelligence Committee leadership thrown into disarray, resolutions condemning the mining passed by wide majorities in both houses of Congress. In the Senate, the Republican leadership made no effort to defend the administration, and Majority Leader Howard Baker joined forty-one Republicans on April 10 in an 84–12 vote to condemn the mining. The House vote on April 12 was 281–111 against the action.[71] "It was one thing for Nicaraguans to be killing Nicaraguans," explained a senior House aide, reflecting concern about the harm to U.S. allies. "It was another thing for Nicaraguans to be blowing up Dutch sailors."[72] The mere existence of a new debate illustrated that members of Congress made a fundamental, if arbitrary, distinction between mining carried out by the U.S.-backed contras and mining undertaken with the United States directly involved.*

The Reagan administration stuck to its guns throughout the controversy on Capitol Hill, insisting that it had lived up to its legal obligation to inform the committees. Casey asserted that the CIA had "fully met all statutory requirements for notifying our Intelligence Oversight Committees of the covert action program in Nicaragua . . . [and] complied with the letter of the law in our briefings . . . [and] with the spirit as well."[73] National Security Adviser Robert McFarlane told an audience at the U.S. Naval Academy that "every important detail" of U.S. covert operations in Nicaragua and El Salvador, including the mining, was "shared in full by the proper congressional oversight committees."[74]

But faced by a mutiny in the Republican-controlled Senate, Casey was forced to apologize. On April 26, in a closed meeting with the Senate Intelligence Committee, Casey "apologize[d] profoundly." At the conclusion of the briefing, the committee stated that "it was not adequately informed in a timely manner of certain significant intelligence activity in such a manner as to permit the Committee to carry out its oversight function. The Director of Central Intelligence concurred in that assessment."[75]

Despite the appearance of reestablished harmony, the mining incident had a profound impact on the administration and on Congress. Both branches felt that their trust had been betrayed, but their responses were diametrically

---

*New York Times columnist Tom Wicker ridiculed this distinction: "Senators and representatives were either deluding themselves or averting their gaze if they actually thought there was a real distinction between (a) voting funds that the C.I.A.-trained and -supported contras used to mine Nicaraguan harbors, and (b) voting the same funds for the same contras to mine the same harbors under C.I.A. direction." Tom Wicker, "The Senate Wakes Up," New York Times, April 13, 1984.

opposite. For the Senate Intelligence Committee the public scandal and its own embarrassment spurred an effort to tighten the rules governing prior notification, a reform intended to clarify the reporting requirements that seemed to have been skirted in the mining episode.

For the CIA, however, the public dressing-down broke a "gentleman's agreement" in which the agency would furnish information to the Congress, provided only that the secrets were kept and the committees bought off on most covert activities.[76] Following the mining uproar, and with the $21 million supplemental request in deep freeze in the House, the CIA accelerated efforts to find backing for the contras which would neither require congressional approval nor, necessarily, its knowledge.

The Congress: Tightening the Rules

The Senate Intelligence Committee attempted to refine the rules governing the reporting of covert activities. On June 6, 1984, Moynihan, Goldwater, and Casey signed what came to be known as the "Casey accords," a new set of guidelines for keeping the Intelligence Committee "fully and currently informed" of covert activities. According to Moynihan, "the understanding provided that the DCI [Director of Central Intelligence] would notify the Committee of all covert action activities for which higher authority or Presidential approval was required (a working definition of 'significant') and that this notification would occur *prior to* implementation of the actual activity" (emphasis added).[77] The written agreement had several expanded requirements:

- That the Senate Intelligence Committee be provided with the text of new presidential findings concerning covert actions
- That the committee be informed of "any other planned covert action activities for which higher authority or Presidential approval has been provided, including . . . approvals of any activity which would substantially change the scope of an ongoing covert action"
- That the committee be informed of activities "of such a nature that the Committee will desire notification . . . prior to implementation, even if the activity does not require separate higher authority or Presidential approval"[78]

The last provision in particular was a catch-all covering almost any covert activity. In short, the Casey accords posited a new operative guideline for the intelligence community: share with Congress any activity requiring presidential approval, as well as everything you might think Congress would want to know. As the events of the next two years demonstrated, however, the accords were honored in the breach. Even before Casey signed the agreement, the administration had taken steps to subvert its meaning.

The Administration:
Heading Out and Around

In May, just after both houses of Congress had passed resolutions condemning the mining, U.S. officials traveled secretly to Central America to deliver a simple message to the contras: that political outcries in Washington did not spell an end to President Reagan's commitment to their cause. As former contra leader Edgar Chamorro recalled, "We were repeatedly assured by the [CIA] station chief [in Honduras] and his deputies, in the strongest possible terms, that we would not be abandoned and that the United States Government would find a way to continue its support." According to Chamorro, those assurances were delivered by two U.S. officials, including Lieutenant Colonel Oliver North, an aide on the National Security Council.*

Behind the promise of political and financial backing was a new political reality. The administration had already begun to explore third-country alternatives for the contra funding Congress was unwilling to provide.[79] In January 1984, CIA Director Casey met with a South African government official and had him briefed on the situation in Central America by the Nicaragua task force chief, Duane "Dewey" Clarridge. Later Casey told NSC chief Robert McFarlane that the Israelis in 1983 has provided $10 million worth of equipment and that, according to press reports, the South Africans were a possible source of equip-

*Edgar Chamorro, affidavit before the World Court, September 5, 1985, Washington, D.C., pp. 19–20. A 1986 investigation by the President's Intelligence Oversight Board "failed to yield any corroboration of Chamorro's allegations." See Bretton G. Sciaroni to Kenneth E. DeGraffenreid, "Allegations by Edgar Chamorro Concerning Potential Violations of Law by Employees of the Central Intelligence Agency," May 19, 1986, p. 6. According to North's testimony before the Iran-contra committees, he began in the spring of 1984 to support the "Nicaraguan resistance . . . as part of a covert operation, . . . when we ran out of money, and people started to look . . . for some sign of what the Americans were really going to do." North said he was introduced to the contra leadership by CIA operative Duane "Dewey" Clarridge. Testimony of Lieutenant Colonel Oliver L. North, quoted in his *Taking the Stand* (New York: Pocket Books, 1987), pp. 104, 124.

ment and training. Following the April mining controversy, however, other CIA officials warned against involving South Africa "in [the] already complicated Central American equation." Casey's plan to involve the South Africans apparently did not come to fruition.[80]

Even before the mining controversy, Casey had recognized "possible difficulties in obtaining" additional contra funding from Congress. He therefore instructed NSC adviser McFarlane to "explore funding alternatives," indicating that "two such alternatives" were under consideration. Casey also recommended approaching a "private U.S. citizen to establish a foundation that can be a recipient of non-government funds which could be disbursed" to the contras.[81]

The most lucrative of those alternatives appears to have been the Saudi Arabian government. In May or June 1984, according to McFarlane, a "foreign official," later identified as Prince Bandar bin Sultan of Saudi Arabia, offered to donate $1 million a month in "personal funds" for the contras. In early 1985 that contribution was increased to $2 million a month.[82]

The decision to pursue third-country funding alternatives was made at the highest level of the Reagan administration. According to minutes of a June 25, 1984, meeting of the National Security Planning Group, top officials including President Reagan, Vice President Bush, CIA Director Casey, National Security Adviser McFarlane, Chairman of the Joint Chiefs of Staff Vessey, Secretary of State Shultz, and Secretary of Defense Weinberger discussed the subject of third-country military support for the contras. (By this time, according to other documents, Casey had already arranged for a $10 million shipment to the contras of arms captured by Israel from the PLO, and he and McFarlane had agreed to approach Israel for more. McFarlane had also "encouraged" Saudi Arabia to support the contras.)

Shultz voiced the opinion that White House Chief of Staff Jim Baker believed that such solicitations would constitute an "impeachable offense." Bush commented that the "only problem" in seeking third-country support might be "if the United States were to promise to give these third parties something in return" so that the deal was interpreted as "an exchange." The topic was deemed so sensitive that McFarlane cautioned against making any of the discussion public. Reagan himself remarked that "if such a story gets out, we'll all be hanging by our thumbs in front of the White House until we find out who did it."

During the meeting, White House counselor Edwin Meese proposed that the Justice Department be instructed "to find the proper and legal basis" that would permit third-country financing, because "you have to give lawyers guidance when asking them a question." Such a determination was quickly made, because by mid-July Casey was urging CIA and State Department officials to "get moving" on third-country financing on the basis of the Attorney General's recent conclusion "that raising the funds in this manner would not be an impeachable offense."[83]

In August 1984, Reagan and others discussed a plan attributed to Secretary of State Shultz by which the United States would provide military assistance to El Salvador, "which in turn would provide lethal aid to the Resistance." This would permit Congress to "wink" at lethal contra support. During the Iran-contra hearings, Shultz portrayed himself as out of the loop of administration decision-making on third-country military support to the contras.

Documents released by the court also show that Salvadoran President José Napoleón Duarte cooperated with the U.S. effort to get aid to the contras from El Salvador and worried that the disclosure of Salvadoran participation would result in a congressional cutoff of the Salvadoran aid program.[84] When Duarte visited the United States in October 1986, Oliver North recommended and John Poindexter approved a request by the Salvadoran ambassador to the United States for a "photo opportunity" for Duarte with President Reagan. "Given the active support for the Nicaraguan democratic resistance provided by El Salvador," North advised, "such a brief meeting is highly appropriate."[85]

These early- to mid-1984 fund-raising efforts on behalf of the contras were not illegal, but they reflected an attitude that would later plunge the Reagan administration into a deep political crisis: if Congress presented obstacles to the execution of Central America policy, go around the obstacles and then dissimulate before congressional oversight committees. In the fall of 1984, Assistant Secretary of State Motley and CIA official Clarridge briefed the House Intelligence Committee about non–U.S. government support for the contra effort. Motley and Clarridge stated that they "did not know where the support was coming from," despite the now extensive administration efforts to find alternatives to fund the rebels.* Given the pattern of deception being established, it is not difficult to see how the administration would continue to circumvent Congress, even after it passed a law prohibiting U.S. Government involvement with the contra rebels.

There was thus a certain irony accompanying congressional attempts in the

---

*Motley and Clarridge stated that it was "obvious that the FDN did indeed have significant financial support," and that "this further limited our control" of the rebels. Clarridge said that "the support was likely coming from individuals and countries worldwide who feel strongly about the cause of anti-communism." Oliver L. North, Memorandum to Robert C. McFarlane, "Subject: HPSCI/SSCI Hearings on U.S. Private Citizens Support to Nicaraguan Resistance Forces," September 13, 1984 (Iran-contra committees Exhibit DRC #24).

spring and early summer of 1984 to decelerate covert operations against Nicaragua. During Senate consideration of a defense bill in mid-June, Intelligence Committee member Daniel Inouye offered an amendment that would provide limited funds for the "safe and expeditious withdrawal" and resettlement of the contras. Rather than prohibit covert activities in Nicaragua outright, Inouye was proposing a mechanism for winding down the war.[86]

The administration was so worried that Inouye's proposal would pass that Vice President Bush, dressed in a tuxedo and straight from a White House dinner, arrived to preside over the Senate debate.[87] Inouye's proposal was never voted on. But the Senate Intelligence Committee narrowly split, 7–8, to defeat a procedural motion that would have allowed a vote on ending the contra war altogether. The close margin demonstrated that the mining episode continued to reap a whirlwind. Senators Moynihan, Huddleston, Bentsen, and Inouye, all past Democratic supporters of the administration, and Republican Senator Cohen, all publicly broke with the administration in refusing to support the covert war. As an Intelligence Committee report later explained, "The consensus built in the Fall of 1983 had been fractured."[88]

Symbolic actions in the Senate were soon followed by concrete blows. Since April, the House had steadfastly refused to approve the administration's supplemental request for contra funding. The deadlock between the House and the Senate over this one issue meant that the entire supplemental spending bill was in limbo. Rather than continue to hold up the bill, which also contained funds for politically popular domestic programs, the Senate voted 88–1 in late June to separate the contra request from the supplemental. The move effectively killed the administration's bid for increased contra funding.

The contras were out of U.S. funds. Within several days of the congressional action, however, the first of more than $20 million contributed by the Saudis was deposited in contra bank accounts.[89] Third-country funding was now a major source of contra support. The administration had lined up its new financial sources just in time.

Counterattack

While administration attempts to raise non-U.S. Government funds for the contras remained covert, there was a strident, overt part to its strategy on behalf of the rebels. Beginning in July, the administration renewed its propaganda offensive around Sandinista arms shipments to the Salvadoran guerrillas and the totalitarian nature of the Sandinista regime. The publicity offensive was the outgrowth of the administration's 1983 decision to launch a public outreach program to generate support for administration policies. It was a way of raising the cognitive dissonance between assessments of the Sandinistas and opposition to administration policy. This propaganda did succeed in making administration critics more defensive, even while fundamentally distorting the basis on which policy was calculated.

On July 18, 1984, for example, the administration released a report on "Nicaragua's Military Build-up and Support for Central American Subversion." The paper said that there had been a "steady" flow of arms from Nicaragua to the Salvadoran guerrillas. A draft copy of the report circulated on Capitol Hill several weeks earlier, however, had said that such an arms flow was "sporadic."[90]

In early August, moreover, an alleged Nicaraguan government defector told the Senate Labor and Human Resources Committee Subcommittee on Drug Abuse that Nicaraguan "government officials at the highest level, in their individual capacity," including Nicaraguan Defense Minister Humberto Ortega, were involved in smuggling drugs into the United States. According to the Drug Enforcement Administration (DEA), however, no firm evidence implicated Sandinista officials in the drug trade.[91]

In one of the most notable examples of propaganda aimed at U.S. domestic opinion, an unidentified U.S. official announced following Ronald Reagan's reelection landslide in November 1984 that Soviet MiG fighters were on their way to Nicaragua. The announcement proved patently false—Secretary of State Shultz said that whoever leaked the information "engaged in a criminal act"— but politicians across the political spectrum denounced the delivery of MiG's and endorsed U.S. military action to remove the security threat.* The administration played on its distinct advantage to frame issues, create perceptions, and even foment crises. By 1988, investigators for the House Foreign Affairs Committee concluded that the "extensive involvement" of covert-operations and psychological-operations experts from the CIA and Defense Department in these propaganda efforts was a "contravention of U.S. laws and regulations."[92]

---

*Seven years later, twenty-four-year CIA veteran Melvin A. Goodman charged that the CIA slanted intelligence on several issues of importance to CIA Director William Casey, including Nicaragua. As an example of the pandering to Casey's agenda, Goodman cited the suppression of CIA reports making the case that the Soviet Union would not deliver MiG fighters to Nicaragua. U.S. Congress, Senate, Select Committee on Intelligence, *Nomination of Robert M. Gates*, Hearings, Vol. II, September 24, October 1, 2, 1991, 102nd Cong., 1st Sess. (Washington, D.C.: U.S. Government Printing Office, 1992), p. 152.

Denouement I:
The Second Boland Prohibition

It is no small indication of the depth of opposition to the contra program that administration critics were able to end contra aid in late 1984, even in the face of concerted administration pressure. The lessening of Senate willingness to defend the administration in the wake of the mining episode, and the unrelenting opposition of House Intelligence Committee Chairman Edward Boland, provided a backdrop for the House position of no aid to prevail. The administration's refusal to compromise on the issue, meanwhile, left its would-be allies in Congress without the necessary flexibility to prevent an all-out demise of the program.

In a now familiar pattern, Congress resolved policy questions under pressure to clear a year-end omnibus spending bill, the continuing resolution, or CR. The House-passed version of the CR included a total prohibition on aid to the contras. When the Senate opened debate on the CR, Senator Inouye again proposed an amendment that would have prohibited all funds for the contras except for a limited amount for their "orderly and humanitarian withdrawal and resettlement."[93] Inouye's amendment failed 57–42, but the margin reflected a loss of strong bipartisan backing for the covert war. The stage was set for a showdown in the House-Senate conference on the omnibus spending bill.

For more than a week the House and Senate remained deadlocked over the Nicaragua provisions of the CR. Boland led the fight to end contra aid, insisting that "the House voted four times to stop this war" and pledging not to let the issue get away from him now.[94] The White House floated a proposal to drop contra funds in the bill if the House would lift a ban on the CIA's use of its contingency fund for that purpose. But Boland refused to substitute one source of funding for another.

The logjam was broken in the early evening of October 10, when Senate conferees accepted the House position on contra aid. In a way, it marked the end of an endurance contest, but it was also the Senate negotiators' way of saying to the administration, "You didn't keep your end of the bargain with us. Now don't expect us to fight your battles for you." Exhaustion and disillusionment, rather than new consensus, characterized the resolution of the contra aid issue.

Senators on the conference committee were able to exact one concession. The compromise ended contra aid immediately but allowed the administration to make a new request on or after February 28, 1985. New funding could go forward only if approved by both houses of Congress, and the House was unlikely to approve a renewal of contra aid. By inviting the administration to make a new pitch, however, congressional negotiators ensured a reopening of the congressional debate.[95] Given President Reagan's commitment to the contra cause, a new request was virtually assured.

When Boland took the compromise back to the House floor for a final vote, he was jubilant. "The compromise provision clearly ends U.S. support for the war in Nicaragua," he said. Indeed, the operative provision appeared impermeable:

> No funds available to the Central Intelligence Agency, the Department of Defense, or any other agency or entity of the United States involved in intelligence activities may be obligated or expended for the purpose or which would have the effect of supporting, directly or indirectly, military or paramilitary operations in Nicaragua by any nation, group, organization, movement, or individual.[96]

"Let me make very clear," Boland said during the floor debate, "that this prohibition applies to all funds available in fiscal year 1985 regardless of any accounting procedure at any agency. . . . The prohibition is so strictly written that it also prohibits transfers of equipment acquired at no cost."[97]

Boland's remarks before the final vote made congressional intent clear. The provision was written "as a Catch-22," said its principal author. "If you are engaged in support of the contras, you are involved in intelligence activities. So you are covered" by the ban.[98] "No one," wrote Democratic Majority Whip Tom Foley (D-Wash.) in defense of the ban, "appears to have had any doubt about [the Boland amendment's] meaning. *It meant the end of United States assistance to the contras*" (emphasis in the original).[99]

As subsequent events demonstrated, however, the administration interpreted the law as not covering the National Security Council. This was despite a 1981 executive order defining the NSC as "the highest Executive Branch entity that provides review of, guidance for and direction to the conduct of all national foreign intelligence, counterintelligence, and special activities, and attendant policies and programs."[100] Moreover, the administration gave no indication to members of Congress that the National Security Council was exempt from the Boland amendment. "I was never told at any time that it was the position of the National Security Council that Boland did not apply to them," said Representative Lee Hamilton, who chaired the House Intelligence Committee from 1985 to 1986. "I had plenty of reason to believe they believed it did apply to them."[101]

A meeting in CIA Director William Casey's office within weeks of the congressional ban, however, reveals the lengths to which the administration was willing to go in order to evade Congress and to establish deniability for its efforts. On November 9, 1984, Casey summoned NSC aide Oliver North and CIA Central America Task Force chief Alan Fiers to his office.

According to Fiers, the conversation went like this: "The Director [Casey] looked at Ollie and said, Ollie, Alan tells me you're operating in Central America. Is that true . . . Ollie, are you operating? And Ollie looked at the Director and said, no sir, I am not operating [in Central America]. . . . The Director said, good, I want you to understand you are not to operate in Central America."

Afterward, CIA Deputy Director of Operations Clair George took Fiers aside. George said, according to Fiers, "You have got to understand what happened in that meeting just now. . . . Sometime in the dark of the night Bill Casey has said, I will take care of Central America, just leave it to me. And what you saw go on in there was a charade."

"Jesus Christ, Clair," Fiers replied, "if that is true then this will be worse than Watergate, if it ever comes out in the open." Fiers testified, "And Clair just shook his head and he said essentially, that is not a problem."[102]*

---

*At least ten countries, including Israel, Honduras, Guatemala, Taiwan, El Salvador, Saudi Arabia, China, South Korea, Panama, Costa Rica, and several unnamed others, cooperated with the contra military effort between 1983 and 1986, providing funds, weapons, airfields, and territory in response to requests from U.S. officials, contra leaders, and private intermediaries. Some of the countries were promised specific favors, particularly aid, in return. See Affidavit, *United States of America v. Oliver L. North*, Criminal No. 88-0080-02-GAG, United States District Court, District of Columbia, undated, pp. 1–42.

Chapter Seven

1985–1986:
The Triumph of
Presidential Power

In the two years after his landslide 1984 reelection victory, President Reagan achieved a major goal of his presidency: securing congressional backing, first for humanitarian, then lethal assistance to the contra rebels fighting in Nicaragua.* Coming so quickly on the heels of the total defeat of the contra program in late 1984, the turnaround was dramatic: after voting no less than six times since 1983 to deny funds for the covert program, the House of Representatives approved a program of $27 million in overt nonlethal aid in June 1985. Within a year, the House crossed another threshold, providing $100 million in military aid to be administered by the CIA.

*Congress used the term "humanitarian" aid to distinguish it from lethal military assistance, even though the aid was going to troops engaged in an insurgency. Humanitarian assistance distributed by international relief agencies normally does not go to active combatants.

In achieving those victories, the Reagan administration accomplished two things. It convinced enough moderate Democrats and Republicans that there was a sound basis for supporting administration policy, and it so raised the political costs of opposing the president that moderates feared the consequences of voting against him. Through a renewed effort to dominate the political debate and heighten the perceived domestic costs of opposition, the administration convinced a majority of the Congress to back President Reagan on a policy that remained highly unpopular with the public at large.

Some members believed, for example, that administration policy had been modified through a series of concessions and that reforms in the contra movement made it more representative, but these considerations do not entirely explain the House votes in 1985 and 1986. Statements made at the time of the congressional turnarounds, as well as in subsequent interviews, reveal that domestic political concerns—the fear of being branded "soft on communism" or weak on defense, or of appearing out of stride with an enormously popular president—played an important role in the vote shifts of a number of members of Congress. This was particularly true of Republicans and of those coming from conservative areas of the country, most notably the southern United States.

The years 1985 and 1986 were culminations in more than one sense. At one level they represented the years in which Ronald Reagan was at the peak of his presidential power, his overwhelming victory against the Democratic Party in a 1984 general election now paving the way for legislative victories on the extremely controversial contra aid issue. At another level, however, it would be during those two years that the Reagan administration became overconfident of its mandate and determined to pursue its policies in Central America at any cost. The series of actions that became known collectively as the Iran-contra affair meant for Nicaragua that administration officials during this period, particularly at the National Security Council, maneuvered secretly to keep the contras together "body and soul," despite the October 1984 congressional prohibition on aid to the rebels. This was done despite an August 1985 NSC memorandum recognizing that "the legislative intent of the [Boland] Amendment is to end funding in support of paramilitary operations in Nicaragua."[1]

Whether or not U.S. Government actions in support of the contras were direct violations of the law or only violations of its spirit and intent, there can be little question that these actions built on prior administration decisions to execute Central America policy free of congressional interference. Administration efforts surely distorted the congressional debate over whether to resume aid to the rebels, as such debates were based on the false notion that contra troops without any backing struggled against a Soviet-supplied Sandinista army.

The extent of administration deception of Congress regarding contra support activities spills off the pages of the final report of the congressional committees investigating the Iran-contra affair. According to the report, from 1985 to 1986 (the period of the congressional restriction on U.S. military assistance to the contras) President Reagan and officials of the National Security Council secretly raised $34 million for weapons and other support from third countries and another $2.7 million from wealthy U.S. citizens. An "enterprise" of private businessmen and former U.S. officials coordinated by the NSC used its own airplanes, pilots, operatives, and Swiss bank accounts to continue the covert contra aid program. All the while, the administration denied to members of Congress and oversight committees that such actions were taking place, despite repeated inquiries based on press reports alleging extensive U.S. involvement.[2]

The exposure of contra support activities following the passage of the Boland amendment suggests an important, if unanswerable, question: Would Congress have behaved differently regarding the contras in 1985 and 1986 had it known the full extent of administration actions on their behalf? Such a question is virtually impossible to answer in hindsight, but it suggests another, more accessible one: Why, based on what it knew at the time, did Congress vote to renew contra aid?

The answer to that is found in domestic as well as foreign policy considerations: mounting congressional dissatisfaction with the Sandinistas and changes in the composition of their contra opponents; apparent compromises by the administration in both the composition of contra aid and the objectives it was intended to serve; the perceived lack of alternatives to administration policy; presidential powers to shape and control the political debate, reinforced by vigorous lobbying by conservative groups supporting the president; the foreign policy "lessons" drawn by Democrats following the 1984 presidential landslide; and the persuasive powers of Ronald Reagan himself. In fact, nowhere do the domestic and foreign policy aspects of congressional decisions better come together than in the 1985 and 1986 votes to provide assistance to the contra rebels.

Backdrop to Victory:
A Landslide Second Term

In terms of the contra debate, the end of 1984 might be characterized as "the tale of two elections." In Nicaragua, Daniel Ortega led the Sandinista Party to victory with more than 60 percent of the popular vote; but by election day the major opposition candidate, Arturo Cruz, and other important opposition parties had pulled out, denouncing the Sandinistas for political restrictions that impeded a fair ballot.

Explanations for Cruz's withdrawal were as widely polarized as the contra debate itself. But his nonparticipation meant that the Sandinistas failed to achieve what had been one of the major objectives of the election: legitimizing the regime not only in the eyes of Nicaraguans but also in the view of world opinion.[3] Cruz, moreover, was catapulted into the role of the regime's preeminent critic and, as he had been since first arriving on the Washington-Nicaragua scene in 1980, a symbol of the Sandinistas' tolerance for and commitment to democracy and pluralism.

In the United States, Ronald Reagan trounced his opponent Walter Mondale, carrying forty-nine of fifty states and attracting one out of every four Democrats to the Republican ticket. Reagan made impressive gains among southern voters, making the South, at least in presidential politics, one of the most reliably Republican regions in the nation.[4]

In the Congress, there was further indication that political dominance in the South was slipping from the Democratic Party. Of the fourteen seats Republicans picked up in the House, eight were from the South. What looked like a surge of Republican victories in a traditional bastion of Democratic strength had a psychological impact that may have put many Southerners on the defensive, regardless of comfortable margins of victory in their own districts. "They see a wave of people changing parties down there, officeholders," commented House Speaker Tip O'Neill, "and they're deeply concerned about that."[5] Southern Democrats accounted for the bulk of those who switched their position on contra aid.

One aspect of Reagan's landslide victory was particularly relevant to the issue of contra aid—that during his first term the president was consistently more popular than his policies. Dependable majorities of the U.S. public liked Reagan personally, while less than half favored his particular stands on issues.[6] This divergence may help explain why Congress voted to support the contras, despite opinion polls registering opposition to the Reagan policy.

"I don't think there was ever a lot of support . . . for the contras," observed a Senate Republican aide, "except you had a very popular president saying, 'I want it, I need it.' " Or, in the words of a House Democratic switcher, "Nationally, there is basic opposition to this [contra] policy. The thing that overrides [it] is Reagan's deep personal appeal."[7]

A Bold New Policy

As in 1981, the president himself and his closest advisers saw the electoral sweep as a broad political mandate. "I feel the people of this country made it very plain that they approved what we've been doing," Reagan said a few days after the election. And he intended to use his popularity to "make them [members of Congress] feel the heat if they won't see the light."[8]

From the beginning of his second term, the words and deeds of administration officials demonstrated that U.S. support for the contras—not just in defiance of Congress but with the support of Congress—was a key priority. On January 15, 1985, Lieutenant Colonel Oliver North of the NSC was already proposing to his superiors a plan to seek congressional approval for contra funds "adequate to achieve victory." Later that month North wrote that "with adequate support the resistance could be in Managua by the end of 1985." The "primary goal," he suggested in talking points drawn up for discussion with House Minority Leader Robert Michel, was to lift the Boland restrictions of October 1984.[9]

To overcome congressional opposition, however, the administration needed to create a new basis of legitimacy for its policy. North's comments suggested that the central goal of the administration was still the overthrow of the Sandinista government, a goal the Congress had implicitly rejected during previous debates over contra aid.

A key part of any victory strategy, then, had to be the construction of a different political rationale for the contra program, one capable of joining congressional moderates with conservatives. That was accomplished by shifting the focus of U.S. policy to the internal composition of the Nicaraguan regime and by outwardly rejecting the goal of overthrowing the Sandinistas while leaving that goal implied in U.S. strategy. In this intellectual reorienting, the administration was aided by Democrats who shared the belief that "pressure" on the Sandinistas could lead to internal changes but who were distrustful of the administration and searching for a goal short of the violent overthrow of a neighboring government. The uneasy marriage of the administration and these Democrats provided the backdrop for a renewal of congressional backing for the contras.

Understanding the ambiguities of the Reagan approach begins with a look at the president's 1985 State of the Union Address, the first explicit articulation of what was subsequently dubbed the "Reagan Doctrine." In early February President Reagan told the Congress: "We must not break faith with those who are risking their lives on every continent, from Afghanistan to Nicaragua, to defy Soviet-supported aggression and secure rights which have been ours from birth.

. . . Support for freedom fighters is self-defense. . . . The struggle [of democratic forces] is tied to our own security."[10] In other words, anti-Soviet insurgencies were by their very nature democratic and important to U.S. security. But what Reagan did not get into in this first expression of the Reagan Doctrine was whether offending regimes supported by the Soviet Union could be reformed or whether they needed to be replaced altogether.

In the early months of 1985, pro-administration intellectuals elaborating on the president's theme, at times elevating strands of administration thinking to the status of doctrine, did indeed get into this question. "Why can't the Administration give it straight?" asked neoconservative columnist Charles Krauthammer. "Say it supports the contras because there is no other conceivable way to move Ortega's Nicaragua to pluralism. . . . A pluralist Nicaragua is the only conceivable guarantor of peace in the region. . . . The objective need not be overthrow."[11]

This was a step in a new direction, one that focused U.S. energies on transforming the internal nature of the Sandinista government, not just on modifying its external behavior. The idea of exerting pressure for a regime to democratize was not new—and indeed had first been expounded by liberals concerned about human rights abuses in authoritarian countries. What was different in the Nicaraguan case was the notion that this purpose could also be accomplished through military force.

The administration had the makings of a legitimate basis for its policy, capitalizing on an American ethos of promoting democracy. But there were still inconsistencies in the administration's approach, born of the ambivalence of the president and his supporters as to the end purpose of U.S. policy. "The successful overthrow of Communism by indigenous forces in even one country might do incalculable damage to Communism's historicist mystique," wrote a proponent of the Reagan Doctrine, for example, indicating that overthrow remained the ultimate objective of supporting freedom fighters if the Sandinistas refused to give up power.[12] "The Reagan Doctrine proclaims overt and unashamed American support for anti-Communist revolution," declared Krauthammer in an article credited with giving the new policy its name.[13] Abandoning the quest for freedom, argued Secretary of State Shultz, "would be conceding the Soviet notion that communist revolutions are irreversible while everything else is up for grabs."[14]

The concept that Soviet gains could be overturned appeared to resolve the central dilemma posed by Jeane Kirkpatrick in her seminal essay "Dictatorships and Double Standards." If Kirkpatrick had lamented the seeming permanence of a totalitarian government once it consolidated, here was the promise of replacing totalitarianism with democracy, of proclaiming, in Kirkpatrick's words, the "revolutionary" superiority of democratic institutions by pledging assistance to "freedom fighters . . . defending themselves against incorporation into a great warrior empire."[15] The Reagan Doctrine was thus as much a hope as it was a policy, providing new emotional encouragement that communist countries might not be forever "lost."

The original purpose for the covert war against Nicaragua—stopping an arms flow from Nicaragua to El Salvador—soon became a thing of the past. The original goal of punishment—striking against the "Cuban presence and Cuban-Sandinista support structure in Nicaragua and elsewhere in Central America"—was replaced by one of promise: freeing Nicaragua from the oppression of its domestic political structures. It was as if the administration and its supporters breathed a collective sigh of relief. Now the United States would stand tall for democracy.

To the April Vote

The 1984 law prohibiting contra aid had provided a window for the administration to seek additional rebel funding by permitting the president to make a new request on or after February 28, 1985. Although a formal proposal was not introduced until April 4, much of the administration's time was spent during the first months of 1985 paving the way for the next congressional vote.

Early indications from the Congress were that the path to renewed rebel funding would be arduous. In January, Senate Foreign Relations Chairman Richard Lugar (R-Ind.), a key administration supporter, had predicted that Congress would probably deny further aid to the contras and that the program was no longer "viable because it is no longer covert."[16] Incoming Senate Intelligence Committee Chairman David Durenberger called covert military support for the contras an "illogical and illegal absurdity" and said that provisions of U.S. law held American action "hostage to an ill-timed vote on an ill-planned program in support of a policy which no one understands."[17]

Leading Democrats, meanwhile, went further, challenging the premises that underlay U.S. support for anticommunist insurgencies. "I don't think we have any call to appoint ourselves as God's avenging angels," said House Majority Leader Jim Wright, "and reform by force any government with whom we disagree." The new House Intelligence Committee chairman, Lee Hamilton, suggested that "the heart of our policy should be the negotiation of an agreement with the Sandinistas, the key provision of which would be our promise to 'live and let live' in exchange for Sandinista concessions in important areas of their foreign policy."[18]

Early in the year, however, events in Nicaragua hardened congressional opinion of the Sandinistas. Following the 1984 elections, the Sandinista leadership stepped up its harassment of political opponents and imposed more stringent press censorship—a way, perhaps, of punishing the opposition for its failure to remain in the presidential elections. Members of Congress who questioned these policies during trips to Nicaragua were given long lectures about the external threat faced by the Sandinistas and the U.S. responsibility for it. What one Democratic member called the "Ortega ass-hole factor," the sense that dialogue was fruitless and communication impaired, began to take hold. "Personal factors are very important," he said. "Why go out on a limb for a jerk?"[19]

For their part, the Sandinista leadership grew "sick of liberals who come down for 24 hours and tell them what to do."[20] Less than three months after Congress had voted to shut down the contra program, Sandinista leaders in Managua appeared convinced that nothing they could do could reverse the tide of opinion against them in Washington. The correlate of that attitude—that their actions were as irrelevant to congressional deliberations as they had been to administration strategy, and that currently low opinions of their government could not lower further—could not have proved more erroneous.

About the same time that attitudes against the Sandinistas hardened, estimations of their opponents improved. In early January 1985, Arturo Cruz took yet another step on his political journey away from the Sandinistas, saying that it would be a "terrible political mistake" for the United States to end support for the contras before the Soviet Union ended its support for the Nicaraguan government. Two months later Cruz signed a joint statement with contra political leaders, an act formally identifying him with the rebels. The San José Declaration, hammered out in a Miami hotel room with NSC operative Oliver North, called for political objectives such as a national dialogue and the "establishment of a political system which guarantees a real separation of powers, authentic pluralism and a just, efficient mixed economy." Part of the administration's task, in North's words, was to "convince the U.S. Congress that the opposition was led by reasonable men."[21]

The attempts to reform the contras' image paid early dividends. Potential contra supporters such as Representative John Spratt (D-S.C.) admitted the presence of former Sandinistas such as Cruz in the contra leadership "represented to me a genuine opportunity for social democracy in Nicaragua."

"These people were not talking overthrow," recalled Representative Dave

McCurdy (D-Okla.). "They were talking some opening of the political process."[22]

Leaders of the FDN, meanwhile, continued to express their goal of ousting the Sandinistas. "We will defeat the Sandinistas militarily" in 1985, claimed contra leader Indalecio Rodríguez, in direct counterpoint to Cruz's stated aims. The year 1985 "will be the year of freedom's triumph and Nicaragua's new independence."[23]

The actions and statements by Nicaraguans posed both opportunities and limitations for the administration's campaign: on the one hand, mounting congressional disaffection with the Sandinistas and growing interest in the views of a prestigious recruit to the contra cause; on the other hand, a contra military leadership interested primarily in overthrow, rather than reform, of the Sandinista government. In its ambivalence about the purpose of its policy, the administration remained in part a prisoner of its own zeal to defeat the Sandinistas. It was unable in the short run to make the best of a congressional current moving increasingly in its direction.

One need only examine the language used by the administration in early 1985, when the White House launched its public campaign to generate support for the contras, to show why members of Congress remained skeptical of administration ambitions. In mid-February, President Reagan called the contras "our brothers" and compared them to "freedom fighters" like Lafayette and Simón Bolívar. An administration official claimed that "our objective in Nicaragua is to achieve a pluralistic and fully democratic government," but the president later stated at a press conference that the goal in Nicaragua was to have the Sandinista government "remove[d] in the sense of its present structure," not overthrown, he insisted, but made to "say, 'Uncle.' " Later, Reagan told a group of conservative supporters that the contras were "the moral equal of the Founding Fathers."[24]*

By employing such hyperbole, the administration attempted to posit a moral dimension to the contra fight. Enough evidence from previous years, however, and fresh reports from the field indicated that important contra leaders were former members of Somoza's National Guard, and that troops regularly committed atrocities against civilians, especially Sandinista supporters. By overstating its case in support of the contras, the administration defined the debate for its

---

*A somewhat more jaded view of contra leader Adolfo Calero was expressed by a U.S. official several decades earlier. In 1969, a foreign service officer described Calero as the "manager of the Coca Cola plant. Not a very useful contact but good to put on guest lists when you need a businessman who speaks English." Confidential memorandum from Jack White, July 24, 1969.

opponents. "Who are the contras?" and "How do they conduct themselves in the field?" became central issues for Reagan's critics.[25]

The efforts to present the contras in glowing terms, moreover, had a darker underside. Resurrecting themes from Reagan's first term, administration officials charged or implied that dissenters over the contra policy were dupes of the Soviet Union or promoting its goals. In mid-February, Shultz told the House Foreign Affairs Committee that contra opponents wanted to "enact the Brezhnev doctrine into law," to validate the Soviet claim that "what's mine is mine, and what's yours is up for grabs." Days later President Reagan alleged that a worldwide "disinformation campaign" was under way to discredit administration policy. At one point, the National Security Agency, the Central Intelligence Agency, and the Federal Bureau of Investigation intercepted telephone calls or eavesdropped on meetings between representatives of the Sandinista government and about half a dozen members of Congress and their staffs. Administration officials considered the conversations to be breaches of security and proposed prosecuting those who engaged in them.[26] In one case, CIA Director William Casey apparently tried to intimidate leading contra aid opponent Michael Barnes into muting his criticism of policy by confronting him with information about a conversation between one of Barnes's aides and Sandinista representatives.[27] Insinuations about the motives of contra opponents added more heat to an overcharged atmosphere, prompting accusations of "McCarthyism" by outraged Democrats and emboldening supporters of the administration to engage in similar attacks.[28]

Overt Propaganda, Covert Efforts

In addition to the succession of public statements by high-ranking officials, the administration engaged in extensive public relations lobbying. The State Department's Office of Public Diplomacy, according to its director, Otto Reich, aimed at denying "the critics of the policy any quarter in the debate" and at driving home the message that "attacking the President was no longer cost free."[29] While there is nothing unusual about an administration pursuing an informational strategy to achieve its policy goals, the Reagan administration took efforts to shape the political debate one step further: making Congress and the public targets of what the General Accounting Office called "prohibited, covert propaganda" on behalf of the contras. "If propaganda is a portrayal of reality that is not balanced," said one State Department official critical of Reich's operation, "then it is true that there was a lot of propaganda . . . in the stuff that Otto Reich's people cranked out."[30]

One of the endeavors involved a " 'white propaganda' operation" to discredit the Nicaraguan regime and bolster the democratic credentials of contra leaders. State Department official Johnathan Miller described to White House Communications Director Patrick Buchanan a series of actions undertaken by the State Department's Office of Public Diplomacy. These included collaborating with a university professor in the preparation of an article about the Soviet arms buildup in Nicaragua, while concealing the U.S. government role. Administration consultants prepared op-ed pieces that appeared under the signatures of contra leaders and set up appointments for them with major media through a "cut-out," also a covert action term. Officials of the Office of Public Diplomacy also maintained a close working relationship with Citizens for America, "a nationwide grass roots organization engaged in lobbying and fund raising activities on behalf of Nicaraguan Contra causes."[31]

In the seven weeks preceding the April contra vote, pro-contra lobbying efforts aimed at Capitol Hill included the following: a Citizens for Reagan activist packet "to convince Congress to support the Freedom Fighters in Nicaragua"; a five-part series in the *Washington Times* attacking groups lobbying against contra aid; visits by 180 Central Americans in a "Spirit of Freedom" campaign sponsored by the Jefferson Educational Foundation; a Citizens for America day-long conference in a Senate office building on "Central America: Resistance or Surrender," featuring National Security Adviser Robert McFarlane; text of a pro-contra speech by Jeane Kirkpatrick, circulated by Free the Eagle; a series on "Central America: Freedom or Slavery," distributed by the Christian Broadcasting Network; a State Department-Defense Department report on the "Soviet-Cuban Connection in Central America and the Caribbean"; and a copy of "Comandante Bayardo Arce's Secret Speech before the Nicaraguan Socialist Party," circulated by the State Department. A week-by-week blitz coordinated primarily by the Office of Public Diplomacy and the National Security Council from February 21 to April 21, 1985, projected over seventy publications, conferences, briefings, and meetings with editorial boards to further the contra cause.[32]

The effect of the barrage was to distort and polarize the contra debate even further. Opponents of contra aid simply could not counter the depth of negative information put out by the administration and its supporters, and consciously chose not to do so. "The American public will never know much about Nicaragua," explained a Democratic aide: "Here was Reagan with a 60 percent approval rating saying 'they're communists.' There was no use to debating the nature of the government. Why fight on your opponents' turf?"[33] In addition, by raising the visibility of the contra issue, conservative groups created an atmosphere of apprehension, if not fear, on Capitol Hill. "If you cross him [the President]," observed a Senate Republican aide, "they're going to carve you up publicly. . . . Public opinion polls showed one thing. But organization and money speak loudly, too."[34]

While the administration struggled to put a political message before the Congress that would reverse the ban on contra funding, it worked just as hard behind the scenes to keep the contra military effort alive in the field. Fundraising from third countries for contra military supplies accelerated in early 1985, particularly as the Saudi government doubled its contribution from the 1984 pledge of $1 million a month. In February, Lieutenant Colonel North (under the alias "Steelhammer") wrote to FDN leader Calero (alias "Friend") asking him to keep the increased Saudi donation quiet. "Please do *not* in any way make *anyone* aware of the deposit," North cautioned. "We need to make sure that this new financing does *not* become known. The Congress must believe that there continues to be an urgent need for funding" (emphasis in the original).[35]

In February 1985, notwithstanding Bush's cautionary words at the June 1984 National Security Planning Group meeting about providing "something in return" to third countries, an administration Crisis Pre-Planning Group composed of senior and mid-level officials from the CIA, NSC, Joint Chiefs of Staff, and State and Defense Departments agreed to provide "enticements to the Hondurans for their continued support to the resistance." These included expedited deliveries of military aid, the release of withheld economic aid, and "increased support from the CIA on several projects" in Honduras.

The group agreed that the message to the Hondurans should not be contained in a written document, but rather that President Reagan should send a letter to Honduran President Roberto Suazo Córdova indicating U.S. support, followed by a "visit of an emissary who will verbally brief the 'conditions.' " Reagan personally authorized the plan as outlined to him in a memo from McFarlane on February 19, 1985.

North and an NSC colleague were especially worried about "unauthorized disclosure of a direct request to the Hondurans" because by that time Congress had banned contra aid. They wrote McFarlane that "to date, all administration officials have been able to state to the Congress that we have not approached any other government to support the resistance" and that it was "very clear from the colloquy during the debate" over the 1984 Boland amendment "that the legislative intent was to deny *any* direct or indirect support for the military/ paramilitary operations in Nicaragua" (emphasis in the original).

Bush met with Honduran President Suazo Córdova on March 16, 1985, and told him that President Reagan had directed expedited delivery of military aid, the release of economic aid, and the enhancement of other programs.[36]

By mid-March, North notified his superior, Robert C. McFarlane, that the contras' needs were being met. The "current funding relationship which exists between the resistance and its donors," North wrote, "is sufficient to purchase arms and munitions between now and October—if additional monies are provided for non-military supplies."[37] Less than two weeks later, Assistant Secretary of State Langhorne Motley publicly assured Senator Christopher Dodd (D-Conn.) that the administration was complying with the restrictions of the Boland amendment prohibiting contra aid. "It does not have to be written by any bright young lawyers," Motley said.[38]

The Uphill Battle

Public confrontations marking the first months of 1985 masked an evolving receptivity among moderate Republicans and conservative Democrats for some form of contra aid. "The Nicaraguans in the FDN," said Senator Durenberger, "are the original revolutionaries against Anastasio Somoza. . . . They had their revolution stolen by fellow revolutionaries who belong to the Sandino party." Durenberger added that he had no objection to aiding the FDN. "My only position is, don't do it through the CIA."[39]

If the contras were legitimate revolutionaries trying to hold Nicaragua's leaders to their original promises, then the political question was how U.S. policy could help them in that goal. Such a prescription was provided by Senator Sam Nunn (D-Ga.), a contra supporter and leader of the conservative wing of the Democratic Party on defense issues. "The end of all aid for the contras," Nunn told the hawkish Coalition for a Democratic Majority in April, would be perceived as "a victory for the Sandinistas." Nunn proposed "honoring our commitment to the democratic forces in Nicaragua" by approving humanitarian aid—food, clothing, and medical support—while intensifying political and economic forms of pressure. One of the options Nunn recommended was an economic embargo.[40]

The nature of these Senate proposals suggested that the Reagan administration was making inroads. While still rejecting the stridency of the president's approach and the ambiguities of pressure *cum* overthrow, influential members of the Congress were accepting his characterization of the conflict in Nicaragua, the appropriateness of maintaining the contra force as an inducement toward internal reform, and the desirability of achieving a democratized Nicaragua as a precondition to the fulfillment of U.S. security objectives.

The Reagan administration lost the first round of contra votes in 1985 because its ardor to succeed prevented leading policymakers from perceiving the subtle attitude shifts on Capitol Hill. Administration supporters in Congress tried to warn the president that a bid for military assistance to the contras would be doomed. "Without any change in formulation of policy there," House Minority Leader Robert Michel told Reagan on April 3, "we're dead in the water for the moment in the House."[41]*

Nonetheless, Reagan unveiled his request for $14 million in military aid the next day, attaching it to a "proposal for peace" that would provide only humanitarian aid for sixty days while the Catholic Church attempted a contra-Sandinista dialogue. The proposal was significant in that it recognized Congress's preference for a negotiated solution; but other elements—particularly a provision that allowed the president unilaterally to revert to military funding after the sixty-day period—made the concessions look more cosmetic than substantive. Senator Durenberger called the plan an "apple with a razor blade," while House Speaker O'Neill denounced the concession as a "dirty trick played by the Reagan Administration" because "they knew they didn't have the votes."[42]

In fact, the administration deliberately concealed from Congress the extent of the contra funding that was under way. Lieutenant Colonel North himself had recommended seeking funding for "non-military supplies" because the military needs of the contras were being met by third-country donors. Reagan's assertion on April 4 that the contras "are close to desperate straits" was patently false. From July 1984 through April 1985, North wrote McFarlane on April 11, the contras had received a total of $24.5 million, of which more than $17 million had "been expended for arms, munitions, combat operations and support

---

*Four Republican representatives—Bob Stump, Bob Livingston, Henry Hyde, and Bill McCollum—met with National Security Adviser Robert McFarlane on March 4, 1985. According to Oliver North's handwritten notes on the meeting, Stump told McFarlane "[We] don't have the votes for 'covert' program." In an indication that at least some members of Congress knew the White House was considering continuing contra funding regardless of what Congress did, North's notes show that McFarlane informed the four congressmen of six options being considered by the president. These included "3d country support" for the contras and "center[ing] the activity in the White House." Oliver North, notebooks, entry for March 4, 1985.

activities." The FDN had grown "nearly twofold since the cut-off of USG funding," North continued. It had "well used the funds provided and has become an effective guerrilla army in less than a year."[43]

The administration's talk of peace was overshadowed by an escalation of harsh rhetoric. "If we provide too little help," Reagan said on April 4, "our choice will be a communist Central America with communist subversion spreading southward and northward." One hundred million people, he warned, "could come under the control of pro-Soviet regimes and threaten the United States with violence, economic chaos, and a human tidal wave of refugees."[44] The administration's refrain was a familiar one: that the choice was support for the president or abandonment to the communists.

What shaped the arguments of Reagan's critics was less the hyperbole than other indications of the administration's intentions in Nicaragua. Although the extent of covert military financing for the contras was still secret, parts of the classified annex accompanying the president's April request bore little resemblance to the peace proposal. On April 17, only days before the scheduled aid votes, the New York Times published portions of a leaked copy of the document. In it the president asserted that "direct application of U.S. military force . . . must realistically be recognized as an eventual option, given our stakes in the region, if other policy alternatives fail." The document revealed plans to expand the rebel forces to between 20,000 and 25,000 in the north and between 5,000 and 10,000 in the south. Then the "size and effectiveness" of the insurgent forces would rise to a point "where their pressure convinces the Sandinista leadership that it has no alternative but to pursue a course of moderation."[45]

For members of the House leadership, the contents of the classified annex were taken as confirmation that the president was committed to sending U.S. troops to fight in Nicaragua. The April contra vote became a Gulf of Tonkin-type confrontation.

For Speaker O'Neill in particular, the memory of Congress's passivity as the United States entered deeper into the Vietnam War was a bitter one. In the words of a House leadership aide, "He was determined not to let that happen again. It was not appropriate for us to be taking sides in a military way when the opportunities for negotiation hadn't been taken advantage of. There was a sense that reasonable alternatives were being foreclosed. . . . Once you put contra kids in a position of grave danger, how do you cut it off? How do you pull the plug? There was the fundamental sense that this was the wrong policy."[46] Later, another assistant recalled that he hadn't seen the Speaker work so hard on a vote in ten years. "You could hear the sound of elbows crunching," he recalled, as swing voters and freshman members were called into O'Neill's office for one-on-one encounters with the Speaker.[47]

Despite the apparent thirst for a showdown with the president, however, several liberal and moderate Democrats were concerned that contra opponents be able to vote for a policy alternative and not just against the administration. The search for "what to do about the Sandinistas"—as much a quest for political cover as for a positive policy—began before and in anticipation of the president's formal request for $14 million. When finally unveiled, a bipartisan alternative (known as Barnes-Hamilton, for two of its principal drafters) had as its center-piece support for regional negotiations undertaken by the Contadora group, and provided $14 million for refugee assistance and Contadora treaty implementation.[48] No funds were to go to contra troops in the field, a proposal Reagan decried as "shameful surrender."[49]

The Senate Debate

The Senate voted 53–46 to approve the request on April 23, but not by the wide margin the administration needed to claim bipartisan victory. Ten Democrats, mostly from the South, supported the president, while nine Republicans, predominantly from the East and Northwest, deserted him. Intense negotiations between Senate Democrats and the administration prior to the vote failed to produce an alternative to the administration's April 4 proposal; but Reagan made several concessions in order to broaden its appeal.

In a letter to Senate Majority Leader Robert Dole only seventy-five minutes before the final vote, for example, the president dropped his request for military aid and agreed to "provide assistance to the democratic resistance only for food, medicine, clothing, and other assistance for their survival and well being." Reagan affirmed his intention to "resume bilateral talks with the Government of Nicaragua," a key demand of Democrats preferring diplomacy over military action. The president also addressed concern over human rights abuses by contra troops by stating that "the U.S. condemns atrocities by either side in the strongest possible terms."[50]

While the Senate had never voted against funding the contra program, the reasons senators gave for supporting the last-minute concessions were noteworthy. The promises in Reagan's letter to Dole represented genuine concessions, according to Senator Nunn. The president "has taken at least three steps backwards," he said, reducing the emphasis on military actions and increasing the focus on political and economic pressure.

The president should be taken at his word, argued Senator David Boren (D-Okla.). "I hope I never see the day," he said, "when any of us stand up and say we cannot accept the word of the president of the United States, no matter what party we belong to."

For Senator Bennett Johnston (D-La.), the absence of an alternative policy left no recourse but to back the president, "I am personally not willing to walk away and abandon the contras," Johnston stated. Defeat of the aid request, said Senator William Cohen (R-Maine), would "hand [Nicaraguan President] Ortega a victory," while nonmilitary aid allowed diplomatic and economic pressures to be pursued.[51]

Presidential credibility, concessions, and the lack of a perceived alternative led the Senate to support President Reagan's contra aid request. Ultimately, the same forces would help to reverse House opposition to the contra program.

The House Debate

While the defeat of the president's request for military aid was virtually a foregone conclusion in the House, the nature of the debate itself showed that administration campaigning, aided by the Sandinistas' own actions, had made substantial inroads. For the first time since public debate on the contra issue began in the House, Democrats were divided over whether or not U.S. policy should pursue changes in the internal structure of the Sandinista government or only seek to modify its external behavior. Remarks by several Democrats illustrate the shifting positions. In opposing the president's request, for example, Representative Dave McCurdy stated: "The Sandinista regime is an obstacle to the growth of democracy. It is also a dictatorship that is doomed to fail unless it is kept alive by outside help. There is growing internal opposition to the economic and militaristic policies of the Sandinistas. . . . In my opinion, to relieve the outside pressure on the Sandinistas would be a mistake."[52] Similarly, Representative Bill Richardson (D-N.M.) opposed contra aid that would "undercut the Contadora process," but praised the president's willingness to compromise by providing humanitarian aid.[53] Although the House resoundingly defeated the president's request 248–180, some administration officials found grounds for optimism. "I was saying, 'Listen to these great speeches! This is terrific,' " recalled Lawrence L. Tracy, a Pentagon official detailed to the State Department's Office for Public Diplomacy. "Everyone thought I was nuts, but I knew that was it. After that it was just a matter of time."[54]

The day after the defeat of the president's proposal, House actions demonstrated the accuracy of Tracy's predictions. After voting down the contra aid request, the House took up the bipartisan alternative emphasizing the Contadora negotiations. It passed by a comfortable margin of 219–206. But another key proposal—a Republican alternative providing $14 million in humanitarian assistance through the Agency for International Development—lost narrowly, 213–215. The slim two-vote margin meant that the Democratic leadership might have won a temporary battle against the administration's contra policy, but it had begun to lose the war.

House debate ended with an anticlimax that shaped—if not determined—options for the future. On April 24, Republicans and Democrats together defeated the contra aid bill on final passage; it contained the bipartisan alternative and no aid—military or otherwise—for the contras. An odd coalition of political forces joined together to send the bill to defeat. Liberal Democrats voted no, to prevent the bill from going to conference with the Senate, which had approved some aid, while a majority of Republicans voted no to register their anger at the overwhelming defeat for the president. The demise of the aid package, however, spelled disaster for the Democrats. Without a positive alternative to the president's position, embodied in the Barnes-Hamilton proposal, centrists in the party felt exposed and deceived. "I was just livid," recalled Dave McCurdy. "That very night a bunch of us—Andrews, Spratt, Cooper, Coleman, Skelton—sat on the floor; we had felt a little betrayed, a little co-opted. We had made a good-faith effort within the party to make a regional policy. We wanted something that made some sense. I had taken these guys out on a limb electorally [by opposing the President and working for the bipartisan alternative]. . . . When they [the liberals] backed off, we said, the hell with them. That very night we were drafting the basis for the $27 million [in humanitarian aid]."[55] "It was a great mistake to end up with nothing," echoed fellow Oklahoman Representative Jim Jones. "If you vote Reagan down without an alternative, and something goes wrong, you're going to get the blame."[56]

The absence of a policy thus appeared to have both domestic and foreign policy consequences, increasing the perceived political vulnerability of those who had voted against the president while leaving others without the sense that they were contributing to a solution.

The June Switch

Within less than two months, the House overwhelmingly reversed its opposition to contra aid, voting 248–184 on June 12 to approve $27 million in humanitarian assistance for the rebels. Given the House's narrow defeat of a similar humanitarian aid proposal in April, perhaps the only surprises were the size of the margin and that a second opportunity to revisit the issue of contra aid came so closely on the heels of the president's defeat. The reversal of three years' opposition to President Reagan's Nicaragua policy reveals how presidential power, divisions within the Democratic Party, and regional events combined to effect change in the House's longstanding position.

On April 24, the second day of House debate on the president's contra aid package, the Information and Press Directorate of the Nicaraguan government announced that President Daniel Ortega would depart for the Soviet Union on a working visit. News of the trip made quiet rounds on the House floor during the debate but appeared in the Washington press only the day after the House had voted down the contra aid bill.[57] Nicaraguan leaders had traveled to the Soviet Union many times since taking power, but the timing of the visit, coupled with the raw emotions following a bruising fight with the president, produced an uproar among members of Congress who had labored to defeat Reagan's request. "For him to be going to the Soviet Union at this time," fumed Senator James Sasser (D-Tenn.), "indicates that the Sandinista leader is either naive, incompetent or not as committed to negotiations as recent statements would indicate."[58]

Ortega's action undercut the position of Democrats who had argued that adverse trends in Nicaragua, including the government's increasingly close ties to the Soviet Union, were products in part of U.S. pressures caused by the contra war. The trip to Moscow, however, seemed evidence that the Sandinistas sought the Soviet relationship by choice rather than necessity and were willfully indifferent to U.S. sensitivities. "He embarrassed us, to be perfectly truthful," said House Speaker O'Neill. "I took it as an intentional slap at the Congress and a slap at those of us who had gone out on a limb to come up with something," retorted Representative Butler Derrick (D-S.C.), who voted for contra aid in June. "The trip undercut enormously the position of the leadership," added an O'Neill aide, commenting on the degree to which Nicaragua had become a sensitive political issue in the United States. It complicated the task, he said, "not to give [members] votes that could defeat them in an election."[59]

While it is clear that liberals opposed to contra aid felt politically exposed by the Moscow trip, the impact of Ortega's visit on moderates who ultimately switched their votes on contra aid seems less important. "Ortega's trip was just a smoke-screen," said Representative Jim Cooper (D-Tenn.), who changed his vote in June. "The deciding factor [in the House switch] was the way liberals sabotaged the very policy they had voted for."[60] In public comments after the

April votes, McCurdy coincided in that assessment: "It is often said that the Ortega visit to Moscow was the reason that many people in the House changed their minds about aid. That is just not the truth. Our meeting [to draft a contra aid package] occurred before that trip actually took place, nor would that trip have made a difference."[61]

By making the House leadership feel vulnerable, however, Ortega's trip helped assure that moderate Democrats drafting a contra aid alternative would be given a chance to offer their proposal on the House floor. "It allowed the whole thing to coalesce," in the words of a Democratic leadership aide.[62]

If Ortega's trip provided immediate shock value, more subtle currents transformed "the lust members feel to strike out against Communism" into a coherent intellectual position.[63]

The first idea grew out of perceived policy successes in El Salvador. There, the logic went, Democrats had collaborated rather than collided with the administration by providing aid but insisting on human rights and social reforms; the result was a Reagan policy ultimately forced to abandon death squads and to foster democracy. Duarte's election, and improvements in overall political and social conditions within the country, were products of bipartisan cooperation rather than obstructionism, according to the emerging view.

Applied to Nicaragua, the analogy suggested that Democrats working with the administration could recast the goal of U.S. policy from military overthrow to the pursuit of democracy; Democrats could encourage that process, furthermore, by insisting on reforms within the contra movement (including an end to human rights abuses against civilians and the purging of military leaders who served in Somoza's National Guard), and by offering the Nicaraguans incentives such as the end of U.S. military maneuvers and other forms of U.S. pressure.[64] Only by working with rather than against the administration, the logic went, could the Congress contribute to a successful policy.

The comments of members of the swing group on contra aid suggest that the El Salvador analogy was relevant to their thinking about Nicaragua. "Seeing what we did there [in El Salvador]," said Representative John Spratt, "gave the Administration some credibility." McCurdy added that Duarte's election in 1984 was "absolutely key."[65]

The second notion was that if the presence of the contras was used to pressure rather than replace the Sandinista government, this could improve the chances for a negotiated settlement. Moderates expressed faith in the compatibility of force and diplomacy, judging that the administration either shared their goal or could be compelled to do so. "George Shultz came and met with us," recalled

Representative Spratt. "He said, 'Look, I'm an old labor negotiator. If you want me to negotiate with the Sandinistas, I have to have something to trade with. I have to go to the table and meet their force with my force.' If that's what he wants the force for, to make the best deal he could, then I'm prepared to give it to him." Providing humanitarian aid, in Spratt's view, gave the United States the ability "to maintain the contras as a fighting force, without the wherewithal to step up the violence dramatically. It gave Shultz the leverage for negotiations. It gave us a way to stay involved."[66]

The basis for providing nonlethal aid to the contras had a subjective as well as rational side. Some members found the analytic arguments persuasive; for others, according to a House leadership aide, "the political side of the 'pressure' argument was that if we don't do this, these people will all die. The intellectual justification was to keep the pressure on. The real issue was, 'I don't want to be responsible for having [the contras] exterminated.' "[67] In a nutshell, members felt that their vote on the issue could have electoral consequences.[68] Although opinion polls showed public opposition across the nation to the contra policy, members relied on their own perceptions rather than concrete data. "They think as politicians," said a Democratic aide. " 'What won't I be able to defend one and a half years from now? What is something I can't answer?' "[69] Or, in the words of one anti-contra lobbyist, "The public was fickle, the President was popular, polls unreliable, . . . and the examples of Senators Clark and Church chilling."*

Moreover, some Democrats believed that toughness on the issue of Central America was important for them and for the Democratic Party. The division among Democrats over the question of contra aid as thus both a political and a philosophical dispute—between those groping for a party answer to Reagan's 1984 landslide and those who believed in the need for a stronger U.S. defense posture. Senator Sam Nunn hinted at both dimensions when he observed that "Central America is a great testing ground for our nation and also for the Democratic Party."[70]

Others sounded more defensive. "I thought it was critical," said Representative

---

*Interview, Susan Benda, American Civil Liberties Union, January 21, 1987, Washington, D.C. Senator Frank Church (D-S.D.) and Senator Dick Clark (D-Iowa) were both defeated in the 1980 election. Church, chairman of the Senate Foreign Relations Committee, had also headed the Senate's inquiry into CIA misconduct during the mid-1970s, which resulted in the establishment of the Senate Intelligence Committee. Clark, a liberal foreign policy activist, had sponsored the "Clark amendment" ending U.S. covert operations against Angola.

Bill Richardson, "for the Party not to be the typical no response, don't intervene in any country [party]. There was a division in the country. We had just taken a terrific beating with Mondale defeated."[71] On June 12, the day of the House turnaround on contra aid, Representative Dan Daniel (D-Va.) had this warning for his colleagues:

> Last fall, we were trampled at the polls in the Presidential election. The score for the states was 1 to 49. Post-election polls indicated that one of the reasons for that political loss was the perception that the Democrats were soft on defense. If we now fail to oppose the spread of communism in this hemisphere, and we are once more perceived to be soft on defense, and communism, then we could be shut out completely in the next election.[72]

One of the lessons of 1984, then, was that foreign policy issues had domestic consequences; for some members the contra votes posed a critical test before the U.S. electorate of Democrats' willingness to employ military force in fulfilling U.S. global objectives.

President Reagan exploited the Democrats' sense of vulnerability as he made good on his promise to return to Congress "again and again" until it approved contra aid.[73] Embarking on a series of Republican fund-raisers in the South in June, the president stepped up attacks on the Nicaraguan government and on contra aid opponents. Touching an especially raw nerve, Reagan reminded one southern audience that "as the refugees come flooding out of Nicaragua, it becomes harder and harder not to hear their cries of anguish."[74]

The adoption of a southern strategy paid off. Although opinion polls showed a majority of Southerners opposed to contra aid, Reagan increased the pressure on southern Democrats by painting the issue starkly in terms of being for or against communism. "Our constituency tends to be more pro-military, pro-intervention, and pro-anti-communist," said John Spratt of South Carolina. "On top of the pro-military attitude," observed Representative Jim Cooper, "there is a strong consensus in the deep South for the President's policy. . . . A more primary determinant of how they vote is the presence or fear of Central American immigration."[75]

Of the twenty-six Democrats who switched on contra aid from April to June 1985, only five were not from the South. All the Democrats from Alabama and South Carolina, and two-thirds of those from Texas, supported the president.

By turning the campaign for contra assistance into a kind of holy crusade, the president invited, if not spearheaded, a degeneration of political discourse in

Washington. "I get the impression that our colleagues on the other side of the aisle feel like we should cower in a corner while the Communists march on around this world taking country after country," said Representative Dan Burton (R-Ind.) during the House debate in June. "My friends, don't be soft on communism." Representative Newt Gingrich (R-Ga.) called a vote restricting military aid to the contras a "vote for the unilateral disarmament of the side that favors freedom in Central America." Minority Leader Robert Michel picked up the president's warning about a flood of refugees, observing that "down South, the streets are filling up. It's a fact of life."[76]

House Majority Leader Jim Wright described the assaults as "to some degree" reminiscent of McCarthyism, and Boland observed that in his thirty-two years in the House, he had never heard more "frenetic rhetoric" than that on the issue of contra aid.[77] But by giving members from conservative districts a taste of what they could expect by continuing to oppose the president, the subtle and not so subtle red-baiting added to the pressures to vote with the administration.

What finally tipped the balance in 1985 in favor of contra aid was a last-minute display of presidential conciliation engineered by Democrats. On the eve of the June House vote, Reagan dispatched a letter to Representative McCurdy that had been dictated to the White House by McCurdy himself and by a pro-contra human rights lobbyist.* In it the president promised to "pursue political, not military solutions in Central America":

> Our policy for Nicaragua is the same as for El Salvador and all of Central America: to support the democratic center against the extremes of both the right and left, and to secure democracy and lasting peace through national dialogue and regional negotiations. We do not seek the military overthrow of the Sandinista government or to put in its place a government based on supporters of the old Somoza regime.
>   . . . I take very seriously your concern about human rights. The U.S. condemns, in the strongest possible terms, atrocities by either side. †

*McCurdy stated in a January 1987 interview, "I dictated letters to Bud McFarlane that came back with the President's signature." According to lobbyist Bruce Cameron, human rights and negotiations provisions of the humanitarian aid amendment had been removed during marathon drafting sessions among House moderates, Republicans, and the White House. The letter was one way of getting the president on record in support of those aspects of U.S. policy, short of writing them into law. See Bruce Cameron, "The Making of a Liberal Apostate—1985" (manuscript), pp. 1–19.

†President Reagan sent identical letters to Representatives McCurdy and Michel, which

The letter softened the edges of harsh presidential rhetoric delivered only days before, allowing wavering members of Congress who wanted to support the president to do so on a basis other than intimidation. "I think the administration has made some significant movement," said Representative Mike Andrews (D-Texas) shortly after casting his vote in favor of aid; there were "some significant about-faces."[78]

Less than six months after the House approved humanitarian aid, the administration renounced in private what had been publicly stated to obtain aid. When North traveled to Central America in December with incoming National Security Adviser John M. Poindexter, he wrote that one of "the messages we need sent" was that the United States intended to "pursue a victory" and reassure a Central American country that it "will not be forced to seek a political accommodation with the Sandinistas."[79]*

The Vote's Aftermath:
Political Beachheads and Back-Channel Operations

The 1985 House vote was thus an important landmark. It not only legitimized the contra force as an instrument of U.S. foreign policy but also provided the administration a political beachhead from which to wage a campaign for full funding of the rebel movement. Within a year of the humanitarian aid vote the House crossed another threshold, providing military aid to the contras through the CIA. A process, described by North as "bite off a little at a time and start moving back toward full support," had been set in motion.[80]

In late February 1986, the president unveiled the military aid request. The

---

were circulated to the House as Dear Colleague letters under the separate signature of each, June 11, 1985, pp. 1–3. The letter was similar to one sent to Senate Majority Leader Robert Dole before the April Senate vote.

*In late October 1985, a year after Congress had banned military aid to the contras, a North memorandum sought Reagan's approval for an "extraordinary" and "expensive" intelligence operation to airdrop information and weapons to contra units to sink ships carrying arms to Nicaragua. John M. Poindexter, then assistant to McFarlane, signed for Reagan in the space marked "Approved" and then added the words "President Approves." There is no indication in the document as to whether or not the operation ever took place. George Lardner Jr., "Reagan Apparently Approved North Plan for Airdrop, Trial Told," *Washington Post*, March 17, 1989; David Johnston, "North Trial Challenges Image of Aloof Reagan," *New York Times*, March 20, 1989.

proposal for $100 million in military aid to be distributed by the CIA represented a quantum leap in U.S. backing. As in 1985, Congress debated the aid package unaware that the administration had accelerated its actions to improve the military effectiveness of the contras. By June 1986, for example, the NSC and private operatives had established air resupply operations to the principal contra front operating in northern Nicaragua and had worked to procure arms and other assistance for the opening of a second front in the south.[81] These activities went beyond the narrow confines of the 1985 legislation, which permitted an office of the State Department to distribute only nonlethal aid.*

The loss of a majority opposed to contra aid in the House, meanwhile, had several consequences. First, it enhanced the institutional power of McCurdy and others of his "swing group," letting a minority of Democrats and a handful of Republicans define the parameters of any contra aid proposal or alternative that could carry the whole House. Second, it served as a psychological disincentive for liberal Democrats to oppose the administration, since they knew that they might not have the votes to win a showdown. The task of the House Democratic leadership was thus reduced to a series of narrow tactical maneuvers: how to come up with alternatives to the president's policies that could hold enough swing voters without compromising an anti-contra position so far as to push the liberal wing into open rebellion. The assignment the leadership set for itself, to "build a wall against military aid," was a quintessentially defensive one.[82]

Understanding that defensive mentality explains in part why early congressional efforts to expose the contra military resupply operation were unsuccessful. By August 1985 a steady stream of press reports hinted at the NSC's role in circumventing congressional restrictions on aid to the contras.[83] On the basis of these reports, House Intelligence Committee Chairman Lee Hamilton and Western Hemisphere Subcommittee Chairman Michael Barnes separately wrote to National Security Adviser Robert McFarlane in the fall asking for information

---

*The Fiscal Year 1986–87 foreign aid bill authorized $27 million in humanitarian aid for the contras while prohibiting the CIA and the Defense Department from distributing it. The intelligence authorization later that year broadened the definition of humanitarian aid to include radios and transportation equipment and allowed the CIA to share certain types of information with the rebels. But it still prohibited CIA participation in training or any other activities "that amount to participation in the planning or execution of military activities by the Contras." In mid-January 1986 a new covert-action finding authorized the CIA to engage in the activities funded by Congress. Remarks of Representative Lee Hamilton, *Congressional Record*, November 19, 1985, p. H 10294; Report of the Congressional Committees (see note 1 for this chapter), p. 64.

and other documents relating to North's contacts with the rebels. Apparently in response to the congressional inquiries, the president's Intelligence Oversight Board was asked to write an opinion regarding the 1984 Boland amendment's applicability to the National Security Council. Board counsel Bretton G. Sciaroni, without being shown key documents indicating North's role in contra fund-raising and weapons purchases, arrived at the opinion that the Boland amendment did not apply to the NSC.[84]

In written correspondence with House committee chairmen and in private meetings with Senate Intelligence Committee leaders, McFarlane flatly denied any NSC involvement. He offered Chairman Barnes a chance to review a stack of documents at the White House, without staff and without making copies. Barnes turned down the offer as insufficient, deciding later in consultation with the House leadership that documents should be turned over to the Intelligence Committee. Hamilton, meanwhile, accepted McFarlane's written assurances that "at no time did I or any member of the National Security Council staff . . . solicit funds or other support for military or paramilitary activities either from Americans or third parties."[85]*

Administration officials were misrepresenting their actions to members of Congress; Congress lacked the will—as well as possibly the legal authority—to compel the release of information by an office of the White House. "That was the problem," said Barnes. "The NSC came to believe 'we can do anything we want and no one can touch us.' " Equally significant, however, was the unwillingness of congressional Democrats to press the issue. "They [the administration] wanted to play hard ball," explained a staffer, "and we weren't willing to pursue . . . a constitutional confrontation."[86]

The March Vote:
Snatching Defeat from the Jaws of Victory

The administration, however, seemed to have endless energy for its fight with Capitol Hill. That excess, in part, led to yet another major political defeat for

---

*Hamilton conveyed McFarlane's assurances to Common Cause, a public interest group that had pressed the Intelligence Committee to investigate the allegations about North's private network. "The Committee was impressed by Mr. McFarlane's willingness to discuss this matter and his response to our questions," Hamilton wrote. "He told the Committee that he had conducted a thorough review of all of the allegations that had appeared in the press about Colonel North. I judge the Committee is willing to accept those responses barring new evidence that might contradict them." Lee H. Hamilton, letter to Fred Wertheimer, November 7, 1985.

the president in March, when the House voted down his bid for $100 million in military aid. As in 1985, however, the president's setback was temporary: opponents of contra aid could hold a majority on a straight up-or-down vote on the president's proposal, but they could not prevail on an alternative crafted by moderate Democrats that included some contra aid and policy restrictions. What made 1986 different from the previous year was that even the Democratic alternative failed, as the House voted in June to approve a Republican package providing the $100 million.

The White House began its bid for the $100 million with a stream of exaggerations and outright misrepresentations. Despite the administration's role in military resupply of the contras, President Reagan exhorted Republican leaders, "You can't fight attack helicopters piloted by Cubans with Band-Aids and mosquito nets." Later he told a group of Jewish professionals that ignoring the strategic threat posed by Nicaragua would result in a "map of Central America covered in a sea of red, eventually lapping at our own borders."[87]

Images of abandonment and Soviet beachheads, and terrorists and subversives "just two days' driving time from Harlingen, Texas," filled the newspapers and airwaves.[88] Intended to step up a pressure campaign, the rhetoric alienated many who shared the president's preoccupation with Nicaragua's behavior.

Blatant red-baiting by the administration and its supporters accompanied the barrage of harsh statements. Writing in the *Washington Post*, White House Communications Director Patrick Buchanan charged that by blocking contra aid, "the national Democratic Party has now become, with Moscow, co-guarantor of the Brezhnev doctrine in Central America. . . . With the vote on contra aid, the Democratic Party will reveal whether it stands with Ronald Reagan and the resistance—or Daniel Ortega and the communists."[89] The National Conservative Political Action Committee (NCPAC) announced that it was targeting for electoral defeat the "Ortega 33," members of Congress who consistently voted against the president's policies in Central America.* Citizens for Reagan placed ads in the Florida district of Representative Buddy MacKay asking "Whose Buddy is he? . . . Your Congressman and communist Nicaragua." Other newspaper ads targeting Representative John Spratt (D-S.C.) warned that if contra aid were defeated, U.S. borders would be flooded with "refugees, spies, criminals and terrorists."[90] One House Democratic leader remarked that

---

*Democratic Congressional Campaign Committee chairman Representative Tony Coelho (D-Calif.) discounted NCPAC's intentions, however, noting that a January 1986 financial disclosure statement showed $3.6 million in debts and only $59,000 in cash on hand. Thomas D. Brandt, "NCPAC Targets Ortega Backers," *Washington Times*, February 20, 1986.

the attacks were like one giant boot to the groin and then a lot of discussion afterward about whether or not it was a good idea.

While some such attacks may have intimidated some members of Congress, they emboldened others. MacKay fumed that "they can take their out-of-state ad campaign and shove it," and abandoned the president on subsequent contra votes. "Members become defiant when the nuts get on them," McCurdy said. "When you apologize for votes, that's when you get in trouble."[91] Even Republicans who voted for aid decried the tactics. Durenberger called the attempt "to portray every senator and congressman who votes against lethal aid as a stooge of communism" as "outrageous," while Kassebaum lamented the loss of "any hope of a reasoned and rational debate."[92]

The administration tactics were responsible in large part for the House vote to defeat the president's military aid request. By giving the Democrats the moral high ground in the debate, red-baiting provided the excuse for wavering members to oppose the president's package. Speaker O'Neill, in a rare floor speech just before the vote, made the tactics a centerpiece of his bid to defeat the aid request. "There is a difference," he said, "between debating the effects of policy and questioning the motives of those who advocate those policies. . . . My conscience dictates that I vote 'nay,' not only for the Administration policy but to its tactics as well."[93]

Developments in the Contadora peace process also had a significant impact on the March 1986 vote. In mid-January, leaders of the Contadora group issued an explicit plea for the "termination of external support to the irregular forces operating in Central America."[94] Hoping to create breathing room for the ongoing negotiations, a group of thirty-one Democrats, including twenty-five who had voted for contra aid in 1985, wrote President Reagan in early February. They asked him to withhold any new aid request until after an upcoming regional summit meeting, and to meet with the Contadora heads of state to explore ways in which the United States could be supportive of the negotiations. Within days of the congressional letter, eight Latin American foreign ministers met with Shultz, insisting that "the end of external support for irregular forces operating in the area is an indispensable contribution to peace."[95] By requesting aid in defiance of the pleas of swing Democrats and Contadora leaders, the administration defied its stated commitment to pursue a nonmilitary solution in Central America.

The defeat of the president on March 20 held within it, however, the promise of future aid. By the time of the vote, a majority of swing Democrats still favored some form of contra assistance; many, however, were unwilling to provide it on the administration's terms. As the price of staying with the Democratic leadership on the March vote, these Democrats exacted a promise for another chance to offer a contra aid alternative on a legislative vehicle that would pass the House.

Two days before the March 20 vote, McCurdy and key members of his core group of swings—Chapman, MacKay, Spratt, Lloyd, Tallon—met with the Speaker. O'Neill was opposed to all forms of aid to the contras, yet he saw that he needed the votes of the Democratic moderates to beat the president's proposal. He promised them a chance to offer an alternative package shortly after the vote in March. Upcoming consideration of a supplemental appropriations bill in April was the vehicle of choice.

Once the agreement had been made, members of McCurdy's group voted with the leadership, virtually without exception. Even with the Senate voting in favor of a modified version of the $100 million proposal, the president's proposal was dead.

The Vote's Aftermath

As expected, Reagan condemned the House action and repeated his vow to "come back, again and again, until this battle is won."[96] Unlike in 1985, the threat this time carried with it the possibility of ultimate success. The House had already accepted in principle the concept of aiding the contras. And the Democratic leadership's commitment to a second vote on an alternative meant that it was only a matter of time before the House approved some form of contra aid. The March vote margin—a mere twelve votes—meant also that only seven members had to be turned around in order to achieve a presidential victory. The administration returned to Capitol Hill with seemingly unflagging determination. Ultimately, the accumulation of political pressure generated by repeated votes proved too much for the opposition to bear.[97]

Immediately after the House vote, for example, the administration played up the significance of a Sandinista incursion into contra base camps in Honduras, using the occasion to increase military aid to Honduras, airlift U.S. troops to the border zone, and blame Congress for the action by failing to approve contra aid. At the time, the incident looked like a replay of Daniel Ortega's trip to Moscow, "unjustified and stupid" in the eyes of Democratic Whip Tom Foley; while Ortega was a "bumbling, incompetent, Marxist-Leninist communist," in Tip O'Neill's words.[98]

Only years later did Congress and the public learn that the White House and the CIA ignored State Department estimates discounting the significance of the raid in order to blame Congress for it, and that U.S. Ambassador to Honduras John Ferch had told the Hondurans they "don't have a choice" about requesting emergency aid.[99] Able to conduct secret diplomacy and retaining the advantage in shaping public perceptions of foreign incidents, the administration continued to define a foreign policy climate congenial to its interests.

Congress, meanwhile, faced a policy vacuum. Again and again, aid opponents emphasized the danger that support for the contras would lead to U.S. intervention in Central America and pressed for a regional negotiated solution. But such arguments appeared less and less forceful in their repetition, particularly as regional events provided less and less basis on which to believe them.

Eventually, both sides in the contra debate talked past each other, marshaling different sets of issues to justify their position. Aid opponents focused on details of contra corruption, drug and gun running, and human rights abuses;[100] administration supporters, meanwhile, emphasized the broken promises of the Sandinista revolution and the dangers of communism on the U.S. doorstep. Having long ago abandoned a challenge to the Reagan administration's definition of what was at stake in Nicaragua, moreover, the Democrats' calls for negotiations could only look weak against the president's call for military pressure. In the words of one House Democratic aide, "We got left in the dust on the big arguments. We lost the high road."[101]

Legislative Interlude: The April Vote

As Speaker O'Neill had pledged, the House prepared in mid-April for a second contra aid go-around. The contra aid alternative drafted by McCurdy and his colleagues provided $30 million in humanitarian aid for the contras, with an additional $70 million in military aid to be available after a second vote of the Congress. The second-vote provision was designed to give regional negotiations in Central America a chance to succeed and to give Congress an institutional role in deciding whether to release the additional funds.

Republicans, however, objected to any agreement placing contra aid on the supplemental appropriations bill, which Reagan was almost certain to veto for budgetary reasons. In addition, the Republican leadership rejected the rules under which the House would consider McCurdy's proposal. Devised by a Democratic-controlled Rules Committee, the procedures specified a complex series of amendments engineered virtually to guarantee passage of the McCurdy restrictions. When the contra aid package was brought to the floor, Republicans surprised the House leadership and sabotaged a vote on McCurdy's aid package.* Through deft parliamentary maneuvering, the issue of contra aid was separated from the supplemental, a key objective of Republican strategists.

The continuing postponement of contra aid emboldened the White House in its search for alternative funding. According to National Security Adviser Poindexter, President Reagan stated in early May, "If we can't move the Contra package before June 9, I want to figure out a way to take action unilaterally to provide assistance." Poindexter told a deputy, "The President is ready to confront the Congress on the Constitutional question of who controls foreign policy. . . . We have to find some way and we will not pull out." To eliminate the need "to endure further domestic partisan political debate," administration officials agreed at a May 16, 1986, meeting of the National Security Planning Group to step up the solicitation of third-country sources.†

Regional Negotiations

Events in the region continued to affect congressional calculations, albeit indirectly, by playing upon the incentives of swing voters to support the president.[102] By June 1986 the Contadora peace process was at an impasse, and evidence available suggested that the Sandinistas were responsible. In early April the Nicaraguan government refused to sign any peace treaty requiring it to reduce its military forces or expel foreign military advisers unless the United States ended its support for the contras and military maneuvers in the region. Three congressmen who attended Contadora talks in Panama reported back that "Nicaragua is being intransigent, that the Sandinistas' commitment to peace is suspect."[103] The failure of the latest round of the peace talks further undercut the position of contra aid opponents, who posited regional negotiations as the alternative to administration policy.

*Ironically, the Republicans did this by voting en masse for an amendment offered by Representative Lee Hamilton that provided no aid for the contras. Under the rule, passage of the Hamilton amendment precluded votes on subsequent amendments. See *Congressional Record*, April 16, 1986.

†During the Iran-contra hearings, Secretary of State George Shultz portrayed himself as unaware that North and his superiors had raised tens of millions of dollars for military aid for the rebels. Report of the Congressional Committees (see note 1 for this chapter), pp. 69–71.

To be sure, the administration's own commitment to regional peace was still a matter of dispute. Reagan's Central American envoy, Philip Habib, had written Representative Jim Slattery (D-Kans.) in April that the administration interpreted the Contadora treaty as "requiring a cessation of support to irregular forces and/or insurrectional movements from the date of signature."[104] Conservative Republicans demanded Habib's recall, and the outcry reached such a level that Assistant Secretary of State for Latin America Elliott Abrams was called in to assure conservatives that Reagan would not forsake the contras through a diplomatic settlement. Abrams disavowed Habib's letter, agreeing that it "was in error" and calling it "imprecise."[105] The public undercutting of Habib was matched by private commitments within the administration to support objections to the treaty by U.S. Central American allies "while denouncing the Sandinistas," in Poindexter's words, "for refusing to negotiate."[106]

Though the promise to pursue a peaceful settlement in Nicaragua had helped convince the Congress to renew contra funding in 1985, the administration appeared to have no real commitment to that goal. By 1986, however, that too seemed not to matter, as substantive issues declined in importance and enough swing members of Congress retained their belief in the efficacy of military force to exact concessions from the Sandinistas.

The McCurdy Proposal and Its Mirror Image

The content of the two major proposals for House consideration in June also determined vote outcomes. At the suggestion of several Central American presidents, McCurdy broadened the focus of U.S. policy beyond Nicaragua by including $300 million in economic aid for the region. It was a sign, McCurdy thought, that the U.S. supported development in Central America rather than just military action.

While McCurdy and his group struggled to maintain the support of Democratic liberals and at least some Republicans, other Republicans and solidly pro-contra Democrats drafted their own counterproposal. Representative Mickey Edwards (R-Okla.) and Representative Ike Skelton (D-Mo.) abandoned the administration's earlier partisan attacks and drew from the McCurdy proposal some of its most attractive elements. Democratic policy analysts and lobbyists were reportedly important in taking the edge off the adversary relationship between the administration and members of Congress. "Republicans in general are not good at dealing with Democrats," observed Robert Kagan, head of the

State Department's Office of Public Diplomacy. "There had to be a reaching out to Democrats."[107]

When finally unveiled in June, their plan looked like a mirror image of the Democratic alternative; it offered $300 million in economic aid for the region, divided the release of aid into installments and delayed actual delivery of weapons and ammunition until after September 1, and required reports on issues such as contra reform and progress in peace negotiations. The main difference between the McCurdy and Republican-sponsored proposal was thus narrowed to a procedural one: whether Congress would cast a second vote on or after October 1 in order to release military aid.

In retrospect, McCurdy himself was forced to admit that scheduling a second vote so close to the November election was a strategic error. "The second vote in October was probably what killed it," he observed after the House approved the administration's plan. "People don't want to vote on this in October, before the election. They want to get it behind them."[108]

Presidential Lobbying

With the March bid for contra aid lost by only twelve votes in the House, the White House was able to narrow its lobbying. Sixteen Republicans who had sided against the president were targets of particularly heavy pressure. The White House stressed the importance of party unity, while the House Republican leadership issued veiled threats to withhold desired committee assignments and opportunities to rise in the Republican leadership if members continued to oppose the administration.[109] In mid-April a coalition of thirty conservative groups wrote GOP presidential candidates and Republican National Committee Chairman Frank Fahrenkopf Jr. asking them to withhold support for any House member who voted against contra aid.[110] Instances of overt "horse trading"— offering a member support for a program in his or her district—did not publicly surface, but the selective targeting paid off in the end. Five Republicans switched in June to support the president. *

In a demonstration of Republican determination to win the June vote, Minority Leader Robert Michel made sure that Representative George O'Brien

*The five Republicans who switched were Wylie (Ohio), Frenzel (Minn.), Hopkins (Ky.), Rowland (Conn.), and Snowe (Maine). On previous contra votes, at least one Democratic switcher admitted in an interview that he had been offered, through another member of Congress, federal support for a project important to his district.

(R-Ill.) was on hand to cast his ballot on June 25. O'Brien, stricken with cancer, entered the House chamber in a wheelchair. To a standing ovation, he pulled himself to the microphone and spoke only briefly, without mentioning the contras.

There was some irony in O'Brien's presence. Almost nine years earlier to the day, he had played a key role during a floor fight to restore military aid to the regime of Anastasio Somoza Debayle.

Final credit for reversing House votes lay with Ronald Reagan himself. Combining the personal appeal that had kept his overall approval ratings high for six years and the prestige of the office of the presidency, Reagan called potential switchers to the White House for a bit of personal attention. In the words of Carroll Hubbard, a Kentucky Democrat who changed his vote:

> It was a real thrill to meet with him. . . . I was leaning toward changing my position prior to meeting with the President, but I must admit his taking about 15 minutes of his time . . . was persuasive upon me to help him out, to go along with him and trust his judgment. . . . I've always liked and admired him. I'm a Democrat, he's a Republican, but he's also my president.

A similar assessment of Reagan's easygoing personal style was offered by fellow Kentuckian, Republican Larry Hopkins:

> I'm from Wingo, Kentucky. I never thought I was ever going to be in the Oval Office much less even see a president. You're overwhelmed by that but this president, I think, puts you at ease. . . . He's the kind of guy you just want to help. One of the better things that's happened in my life is the opportunity to visit with him just for a brief time. I'm proud to stand in his shadow.[111]

These complimentary accounts bolster an impression held by Democratic opponents of contra aid: that when a president as popular as Ronald Reagan made an issue his primary foreign policy goal, it was just a matter of time until he got what he wanted. "The guys in the middle just got tired of being beaten up on by both sides," observed Representative Michael Barnes. "They knew Reagan was going to come back and back and back on this. He was obsessed by it. . . . He just wore everybody out."[112] Even so committed an opponent as House Speaker O'Neill acknowledged Reagan's substantial skills of persuasion. "The power of the President is absolutely awesome," he said. "When you are talking to the President, the most powerful man in the world, you can't deny" his ability to persuade.[113]

The Aftermath of the Vote

A series of delaying tactics in the Senate kept congressionally approved military aid from flowing to the contras until late October 1986.[114] But by that time North's private network was conducting regular air drops of military equipment and supplies to the contras' northern and southern fronts. Assistant Secretary of State Elliott Abrams solicited an additional $10 million in nonlethal assistance from the government of Brunei in August and then gave what he described as "misleading" testimony to congressional committees about his activities.[115] The Reagan administration continued its flat-out denials before congressional investigating committees that the U.S. Government, and particularly the NSC, had any involvement in contra support activities, statements that North later conceded were false.[116] In the face of categorical denials, members of Congress dropped efforts to pursue the issue of illegal funding any further.

The situation began to change in the fall. On October 5, 1986, Sandinista troops shot down an airplane loaded with 10,000 pounds of ammunition and gear for contra forces in northern Nicaragua. Three crew members, including the pilot and copilot, were killed; another, the "kicker," parachuted to safety and was captured by Nicaraguan soldiers. The captured American, Eugene Hasenfus, carried identification issued by the Salvadoran air force saying he was an "adviser," as well as a business card belonging to a U.S. official involved in getting nonlethal supplies to the contras. One of the dead airmen had an ID card issued by Southern Air Transport, a former CIA proprietary and principal in North's resupply operation.

As noted by the committees investigating the Iran-contra affair, "Virtually every newspaper article on the incident in the days after the downing would quote senior Government officials, including the President himself, denying any U.S. Government connection with the flight." Yet, according to later testimony by Lieutenant Colonel North, "I was the U.S. Government connection."[117]

The press corps went after the Hasenfus story like piranhas in bloody waters. For the first time the names of those to whom North had delegated responsibility for the support operation surfaced regularly in news accounts.[118] Yet in a mad scramble to prevent exposure of the government-led contra resupply operation, a host of administration officials knowingly lied to congressional committees about their knowledge of the support network. Within days of the crash, for example, Oliver North informed CIA Central America Task Force Chief Alan Fiers that the downed aircraft was part of North's contra effort. Nonetheless, Fiers assured members of the House Intelligence Committee on October 14, 1986, that he had "no idea" whose plane it was that had crashed; "as to who was flying the flights and who was behind them we do not know," said Fiers.[119]

Fiers pleaded guilty in mid-1991 to two misdemeanor charges of withholding information from Congress. He revealed that his boss, CIA Deputy Director of Operations Clair George, had instructed him to lie to Congress. Fiers said that George ordered him not to include in prepared testimony references to an airbase in El Salvador that was part of North's resupply operation or other information that would "put the spotlight" on the U.S. Government connection to Hasenfus's flight.[120]

Fiers and Assistant Secretary of State Elliott Abrams were present when George assured the Senate Foreign Relations Committee on October 10 and the House Intelligence Committee on October 14 that the CIA had no role "directly or indirectly in arranging, directing, or facilitating resupply missions" to the contras.[121] George told the Senate committee, "We did not provide any form of assistance to or facilitate these flights in any way."[122]

George was tried and found guilty in December 1992 of making two false statements to Congress, one of which was having assured the House Intelligence Committee on October 14, 1986, that he did not know the identity of a former CIA official involved in the operation.[123]

Abrams, meanwhile, became the administration's most public spokesman after the Hasenfus plane was downed. He falsely asserted in an open hearing of the House Subcommittee on Western Hemisphere Affairs that "the flight in which Mr. Hasenfus took part was a private initiative. It was not organized, directed, or financed by the U.S. Government."[124] Five years later, Abrams pleaded guilty to charges that he "unlawfully withheld material information" from Congress about the Hasenfus affair.[125]

What could have remained just another episodic revelation of the workings of the covert war against Nicaragua soon mushroomed into a full-scale political scandal. In early November the press revealed that the United States had sold arms to the government of Iran to secure the release of U.S. hostages in Lebanon. In investigating that allegation, the Justice Department uncovered a memo written by North indicating that $12 million of the "residual funds" from the Iran arms sales were to be "used to purchase critically needed supplies for the Nicaraguan Democratic Resistance Forces."[126] Here, apparently, was direct evidence that the Reagan administration had funded the contras beyond the levels approved by Congress. The memo was the tip of the iceberg of what had been suspected by many on Capitol Hill and always denied by the administration.

Who saw the memo and whether it ever reached the president's desk became key issues in ensuing administration and congressional inquiries. And two controversial foreign policies—Iran and Nicaragua—became entangled, plunging the Reagan administration into its most serious political crisis in six years. As in the Hasenfus affair, senior administration officials lied to Congress about their knowledge of the diversion and of the contras' covert support network. CIA official Alan Fiers told the Senate Intelligence Committee on November 25, 1986, that "the first I knew" of the diversion was when it was reported on CNN earlier that day. In fact, Fiers had been told by Oliver North about the diversion in late summer of 1986 and had then told two of his superiors, including Clair George. George also lied several days later when he told the Senate Intelligence Committee that he "had never laid eyes on" a retired U.S. general who was a key figure in the Iran-contra network. [127]

CIA Director Casey must have known how explosive the revelations about the diversion were when he telephoned Fiers the day after Attorney General Meese's press conference. As Fiers recalled it, Casey said, "Don't worry. Everything is going to be okay, we haven't done anything illegal, you understand that?" Fiers answered, "Yeah, boss, I understand that."

"Good," Casey replied. "Now remember that, we haven't done anything illegal." [128]

Ultimately, the administration's most intense efforts on behalf of the contra rebels would shake the foundations of its crusade to ensure U.S. Government backing of them. But not enough to compel Congress to shut off contra aid altogether, or compel the administration to seek a nonmilitary settlement of its differences with Nicaragua.

Chapter Eight

1987–1988:
The Policy Collapses

After several preliminary investigations, a joint House-Senate panel convened in May 1987 to investigate the sale of arms to Iran and the diversion of profits to the contra rebels. Four months of televised hearings produced 250 hours of public testimony, while the committees themselves heard testimony from thirty-two public officials and private individuals. As in the Watergate affair, the media and members of Congress searched intently for the "smoking gun," some evidence that President Reagan had known of or authorized the diversion of profits to the contras. According to Senator Daniel Inouye, Chairman of the Senate Iran-contra committee, the committee cared only about President Reagan's knowledge of the diversion, an act that would have constituted an impeachable offense.[1] Most of the momentum of the investigation was thus lost when National Security Adviser John Poindexter testified in mid-July that "on this whole issue, you know, the buck stops with me."[2]*

Before the first whirs of the television cameras, the Democratic majority on the committee, still wary of attacking a popular president, decided not to use the hearings as a fractious referendum on the merits of the contra policy. The Democrats had regained control of the Senate in 1986, but House and Senate Democrats alike seemed determined to avoid any suggestion of a head hunt with overtly partisan overtones. The hearings focused instead on the flawed governmental processes that led to this policy disaster. The efforts at nonpartisanship, however, were one-sided. While House Democrats appointed the chairmen of standing committees to serve on the Iran-contra panel, the Republican leadership named some of the most ardent supporters of the contra cause. Republicans on the committee launched spirited defenses of administration policy, inviting witnesses to explain and justify their actions. The hearings *cum* morality play reached their height when NSC aide Oliver North testified in uniform, bedecked with combat medals, captivating a national audience with a proud defense of his actions in the name of patriotism and national service.[3] By the time the hearings were over, all semblance of being above the political fray was gone. Eight of the committee's eleven Republicans denounced the "hysterical conclusions" of the majority report, as well as the "supposedly 'factual' narrative" on which it was based.[4]

The immediate impact of the Iran-contra affair on Congress's support for

---

*In his 1991 book *Under Fire: An American Story*, Oliver North assserted that "I have no doubt that he [Reagan] was told about the use of residuals for the contras, and that he approved it. Enthusiastically." North also wrote that "President Reagan didn't always know what he knew. I believe he was told about the transfer of funds to the contras, but that doesn't mean he paid attention to it or remembered it."

In mid-1990, investigative journalist Seymour Hersh accused the committees of failing to pursue key leads, including testimony from a White House aide that two memoranda detailing the diversion of proceeds from the Iranian arms sales to the contras had been drafted by North, for review by Poindexter and approval or disapproval by President Reagan. The aide, James R. Radzimski, was never scheduled to testify in public. According to Hersh, the committees also scaled back their investigation in order to finish their inquiry before the 1988 election year and because President Reagan was about to enter into strategic arms talks with the Soviet Union. According to Hersh, the committees were "shellshocked" by the public's enthusiastic reception of North's testimony. Chief counsel for the Senate Iran-contra committee Arthur L. Liman denied the charges. David Johnston, "North Says Reagan Knew of Iran Deal," *New York Times*, October 20, 1991; Seymour M. Hersh, "The Iran-Contra Committees: Did They Protect Reagan?" *New York Times Magazine*, April 29, 1990, pp. 47, 61, 64, 67, 70, 77; and Arthur L. Liman, Letters to the Editor, *New York Times Magazine*, May 20, 1990, pp. 12, 14.

Nicaragua policy was subdued. Before the hearings began the House cast a symbolic vote to hold up unspent portions of the $100 million approved in 1986 until the administration fully accounted for the money. The same "moratorium" was defeated in the Senate, however, and even the House vote merely served to avoid a direct up-or-down ballot on cutting off the contras.

One effect of the scandal, however, was unmistakable. By stripping the mantle of invincibility from President Reagan, the Iran-contra affair weakened what had been one of the administration's strongest suits in dealing with the Congress: the president's own powers of persuasion. According to polls taken after the scandal broke, Reagan's public approval ratings were the lowest of his entire presidency, registering a 21 percent drop—the sharpest ever recorded in a public opinion poll on presidential performance. About half the public believed Reagan was "lying" when he insisted that he had not been told of the diversion of funds, and the public by a two-to-one margin trusted Congress, rather than the president, "to make the right decisions on foreign policy."[5] Even the administration's own Special Review Board convened to investigate the affair, chaired by former Texas Senator John Tower, scored the president's management style and portrayed him as out of touch with the national security policies conducted in his name.[6]

The final report of the Iran-contra committees, delivered on November 18, 1987, contained a scathing critique of administration policymaking. The report, signed by all the committee's Democrats and three of its Republican senators, found that the common ingredients of the Iran and contra policies were "secrecy, deception, and disdain for the law." It described a "seriously flawed" policy process characterized by "pervasive dishonesty." And it charged the president—even if he had not known of the diversion of funds to the contras—with allowing a " 'cabal of the zealots' " to take over key aspects of foreign policy, something for which he bore "ultimate responsibility."[7]

After the hearings ended and the final report was issued, House opponents of the contra program could almost taste the prospects for cutting off the contras once and for all. The mood of these liberals—and their possibilities for success—were not lost on the administration. During the summer of 1987, officials began to cast about for some basis on which to maintain long-term congressional funding.

In the Congress, too, there were those who saw an abrupt end to rebel funding as disadvantageous. Chief among them was House Speaker Jim Wright, who had labored intently as early as 1980 for an economic aid plan that would enhance the prospects for political pluralism in Nicaragua. "Junking contra aid wouldn't have achieved any objectives," Wright explained. "A cut-off of aid would be the abandonment of policy, not an alternative."[8]

In July, administration lobbyist and former Texas Republican congressman Tom Loeffler approached Wright with an idea for a peace plan for Nicaragua. It held forth the possibility of an end to U.S. support for the contras in exchange for Nicaraguan concessions on its domestic and foreign policies. To Wright the plan seemed like an opportunity to commit the administration to a peaceful settlement in Nicaragua, through negotiations instead of warfare. When formally unveiled on August 5, the Wright-Reagan proposal called for a ceasefire in the Nicaraguan war, an end to outside military aid to both sides in the conflict, and a process of national reconciliation and dialogue within Nicaragua.

Wright cut a deal with the administration without involving other key House leaders, gambling that the administration was sincere in its desire for peace. The plan was immediately condemned, however, by contra aid supporters and opponents alike. Supporters feared the Sandinistas would make token concessions—enough to erode the basis for contra aid but not enough to threaten their own power. Aid opponents, including other members of the House Democratic leadership, thought the proposal was a trap, designed to be rejected by the Sandinistas, thereby paving the way for continued aid. Ultimately Wright proved his liberal critics wrong, not in small part because, despite the Wright-Reagan accord, members of the administration remained hostile to a peace process that spun quickly out of its control.

No sooner was the ink dry on the Wright-Reagan plan, for example, than Central American leaders signed a peace accord of their own. Meeting in Guatemala City on August 7, the five Central American presidents called for cease-fires, steps toward democratization and reconciliation, and an end to outside support for regional insurgencies. The plan was a variant of a proposal presented in February 1987 by Costa Rican President Oscar Arias Sánchez. It differed from the Wright-Reagan plan by permitting outside military aid to governments in the region and by not requiring elections in advance of those already scheduled in each country.[9]

Speaker Wright immediately embraced the Arias plan and thought the administration would do the same thing. It did not. In September the president deemed the Arias plan fatally flawed because it did not deal with the issue of Soviet aid to the Sandinistas.* And that same month, Secretary of State Shultz

---

*Nor did the plan proscribe U.S. military assistance to its allies in El Salvador and Honduras. The Wright-Reagan proposal would have linked an end of U.S. aid to the contras to an end of Soviet military support for the Sandinistas.

announced to the Senate Foreign Relations Committee that the administration would ask for $270 million in new contra aid. The request stood in harsh contrast to the Arias plan's call for an end to outside support for regional insurgencies.

The Speaker, meanwhile, took up the cause of Central American peace as if it were a personal crusade. Wright invited President Arias to address a session of the House Democratic Caucus, to which senators and Republicans were invited, because the administration blocked the convening of a formal joint meeting of Congress, a courtesy usually extended visiting heads of state.*

At the administration's request, Wright then met with contra leaders, but he infuriated the administration by also meeting privately in Washington with Nicaraguan President Daniel Ortega, whom the State Department had refused to see. Stepping up his personal involvement in bringing the opposing sides in Nicaragua together, the Speaker sought to convince Nicaraguan Cardinal Miguel Obando y Bravo to serve as mediator between the Sandinistas and contra rebels. At the invitation of the Vatican's envoy in Washington, Wright was present when Ortega offered Cardinal Obando a government proposal for a cease-fire and negotiations with the contras.

Administration officials were outraged at what they thought was the Speaker's improper involvement in diplomacy and complained that Wright had not even kept them informed of his discussions. One senior official, later identified as Assistant Secretary of State Elliott Abrams, anonymously charged that the Speaker's activism constituted "guerrilla theater" that was "screwing up" the peace process.[10] Wright requested a White House summit with Reagan and Shultz to clear the air. "They resented my being interested," Wright claimed. "But they had asked me to be involved."[11]

On November 17, Wright and Shultz held a press conference to patch up their differences and reaffirm a joint commitment to regional peace. But the appearance of reestablished harmony could not mask the fact that as a result of the Iran-contra affair, the Arias plan, and Speaker Wright's activism, the initiative in Nicaragua policy no longer lay with the administration.

Central American presidents and House Democrats became the key judges of Nicaraguan compliance with the peace accord and the desirability of further contra aid. In a break with the past, U.S. allies in El Salvador and Honduras went so far as to ask the United States to refrain from bringing up contra aid

---

*According to two House Democratic aides, the administration did not even want Arias to speak in the House chamber, preferring instead the Caucus Room of a nearby House office building.

while the peace process was still moving forward. The Sandinistas themselves moved further and more quickly than expected; by January 1988 they had lifted the state of emergency, allowed exiled critics to return, freed some political prisoners, and agreed to a direct dialogue with the contra rebels. With an eye on Congress and hopes for a cutoff of contra funding, the Sandinistas made concessions in the context of a Central American agreement that they had vowed never to make to the United States.

Despite Arias's repeated admonitions that contra aid from the United States hurt the peace plan, the administration insisted that contra pressure led to Nicaraguan concessions and that only further pressure could guarantee full compliance. In October 1987 the president vowed before the OAS to "speak and work, strive and struggle" for contra aid "as long as there is breath in this body."[12] To swing voters and perennial critics in Congress, it looked as if the administration was trying to undermine the peace accord.

Unsure of enough congressional support, the administration stepped back from introducing a massive contra aid request in the fall. Nevertheless, swing voters in Congress, fearful that a total cutoff of aid would remove an important incentive for the Sandinistas to negotiate further compromises, helped win congressional approval of more than $14 million in nonlethal aid before the end of the year.

By the time the administration did introduce a request for contra funding, in late January 1988, it asked for a fraction of the initial amount—only $36 million; and of that, only a tiny portion—$3.6 million—was for military aid.[13] The administration repeated the mistakes of past years, however, ignoring pleas from key swing voters to delay the request pending further progress in the peace talks and to give Congress a role in deciding whether to release military aid. Those errors cost the administration valuable support with the very group it had won over on previous contra aid votes.

On February 3, 1988, the House voted down the entire package of contra aid. In a vivid and embarrassing reflection of the tattered state of Reagan's presidency, all three major television networks refused to broadcast his speech in defense of contra aid, saying that it contained no news.

The February defeat in the House was testimony to the president's utter loss of initiative. But other factors also explain Reagan's congressional debacle. First, as Nicaraguan actions in January appeared to demonstrate, the Arias plan was yielding concrete results. Florida Democrat Dan Mica, a supporter of the contras who now opposed Reagan, observed, "We spent seven years trying to get Ortega to the peace table. I don't think we should shoot ourselves in the foot when we finally get him there."[14]

Second, President Arias himself had publicly insisted that *any* contra aid undercut the peace process, and his prestige soared when he won the Nobel Peace Prize in 1987. On the eve of accepting the award, Arias said that "as long as there is an aggression" [Daniel Ortega] was "going to use it as an excuse" to avoid democratization. "The contras, from my point of view," he said, "are the problem and not the solution."[15]

Third, as on previous occasions, the Democratic leadership promised to sponsor a contra aid alternative if the president's plan was defeated. Swing voters thus felt assured that the Congress would not eliminate contra aid altogether. The Reagan proposal lost in the House, 219–211.

The following day, however, the Senate approved Reagan's request by three votes. Even though it was the smallest margin of any Senate vote on rebel funding, the February votes showed that Congress remained divided on contra funding, even with the Democrats in control of both houses.

In a repetition of a now familiar pattern, House Democrats brought a contra aid alternative before the House on March 3. It contained more than $30 million in nonlethal aid, almost half of which was for child survival programs. The alternative passed by a slim five-vote margin, only to go down when the House failed to approve final passage of the bill. The coalition that sank the bill was reminiscent of 1985 and 1986. All but five Republicans voted against the bill because it represented a defeat of their administration-supported plan; fifteen liberal Democrats who had supported the Democratic alternative to please the leadership voted against final passage to register opposition to all forms of contra aid. The demise of the contra aid proposals showed the exhaustion of intricate designs to maintain a bipartisan majority in favor of rebel funding, even as it spelled the beginning of the end of the contras as an effective fighting force against the Sandinistas.

Congress's refusal to enact contra aid had immediate effects on the ground in Central America. On March 23, 1988, the Sandinistas and the contras met in the town of Sapoá near the Costa Rican border and signed a sixty-day cease-fire. The accord granted a gradual amnesty for former National Guardsmen in prison and committed the Sandinistas to open up the political system and grant press freedoms; the accord also permitted "exclusively humanitarian aid" to be channeled to the rebels through neutral organizations while talks toward a permanent cease-fire were under way.[16] Months of political negotiations then ensued, only to break down in June 1988 with both sides charging the other with bad faith. The Sandinistas responded by instituting a harsh crackdown against domestic opponents, arresting dozens of opposition leaders at a rally in July. Then, charging that the United States fomented opposition political activity in Nicaragua, the Sandinistas expelled the U.S. Ambassador and several embassy employees. The State Department retaliated in kind. Earlier hopes that the slackening pace of the war would have induced the Nicaraguan regime to make political concessions seemed dashed in a whirl of mutual recriminations between the United States and Nicaragua and between the regime and its opposition.

But the March 1988 cease-fire accord, coupled with Congress's unwillingness to renew military aid, also threw the contra movement into disarray. Rebel military and civilian leaders openly bickered over whether or not and under what conditions to abandon armed struggle and reenter a political process in Nicaragua. The contras' image suffered further when they were widely blamed— in the press and by other contras—for the breakdown in cease-fire talks in June. According to one report, the contras deliberately broke off the negotiations in order to provoke a crisis that might pave the way for further military aid.[17]

But Congress was unwilling to consider such an alternative. Most of what took place for the remainder of 1988 constituted the fitful gasps of a dying policy. The administration withdrew to the sidelines. Few in Congress seemed particularly enthusiastic about contra aid, but just as few seemed willing to disband them while the Sandinista commitment to democracy remained untested. The Sandinista crackdown in July elicited harsh resolutions of condemnation that passed by wide majorities in both the House and the Senate. In late September, Congress passed another installment of nonlethal aid. As a result of pressure from contra supporters, the legislation allowed Reagan to request the release of military equipment stockpiled in Honduras, if approved by both houses.

As on numerous other occasions, the year-end patchwork compromise reflected domestic realities as much as, or more than, foreign ones. Having lost a key battle in February, Republicans were reluctant to force the issue of military aid to the contras. But the Democrats were just as reluctant to end aid altogether. Reflective of the divisions over policy, the 1988 Democratic presidential ticket was split between an opponent of contra aid (Michael Dukakis) and a supporter (Senator Lloyd Bentsen). Republican presidential candidate Vice President George Bush, meanwhile, avoided campaigning on the contra issue. This was because his campaign manager, James A. Baker III, believed there was no public support for the policy.[18]

The contra policy, so long a centerpiece of the Reagan administration's foreign policy, thus died with a whimper, not a bang. What the Iran-contra affair took from the administration in credibility and trust, the Arias plan replaced with hope and opportunity. The unstable majority in favor of contra aid, built less on consensus than on a rare confluence of domestic circumstances, proved unsustainable once Ronald Reagan had lost his magic and the region presented a viable-looking plan for dealing with the Sandinistas. The Reagan administration sacrificed on the altar of zeal what it could not obtain in the crucible of compromise. There has hardly been a script for a more self-defeating foreign policy than that of the Reagan administration's approach in Nicaragua.

El Salvador

For most of Reagan's second term, Congress left untouched the crown jewel of his Central America policy achievements: the establishment of bipartisan support for the Duarte government. But late in Reagan's second term, that support began to wear thin. The Arias plan's emphasis on ending guerrilla insurgencies served to underscore that the war showed no signs of abating, despite confident predictions by senior military strategists in 1984 that "80 to 90 percent of the country" would be under the military's control within two years.[19]

Equally troubling was that the far-right ARENA party won control of El Salvador's National Assembly in March 1988, putting former Major Roberto D'Aubuisson, suspected mastermind of the assassination of Archbishop Romero, in a key position of power.[20] President Duarte, himself suffering from incurable liver cancer, seemed to personify the multiple ills of his administration. Economic austerity measures had taken a devastating toll on the party's urban base, eroding popular support for the regime. Violent abuses by the army and death squads were resuming an upward spiral, prompting Duarte to decry the "extremist death squads that seem to be coming back to life."[21] The Christian Democrats themselves were badly divided over who should succeed Duarte as candidate in the 1989 presidential elections.

Against this backdrop, ranking Senate Appropriations Committee Republican Mark Hatfield (R-Ore.) and Subcommittee on Foreign Operations member Tom Harkin (D-Iowa) attempted to refocus congressional attention on the recipient of what then amounted to more than $3 billion in overt U.S. aid.[22] They offered a modest amendment to the foreign aid appropriations bill for fiscal year 1989, holding back 50 percent of military aid for six months and requiring the administration to report on "efforts" to find a negotiated solution to the war and reduce human rights abuses.[23]

The amendment was adopted in subcommittee, only to be defeated, by one vote, when the full Appropriations Committee took up the foreign aid bill on June 22, 1988. Hatfield's appeal to his colleagues to make clear their "support for a negotiated end" to the war was undercut by a poignant, if not pitiful, one-page letter to Senator Robert Kasten (R-Wisc.) from the ailing Duarte, who was in Washington for cancer treatment. With Walter Reed Hospital printed on the stationery as his return address, Duarte urged Kasten not to "let my friends undermine my legacy. . . . For me and my country, please move to strike this proposal."[24] The Hatfield-Harkin amendment lost when Chairman John Stennis (D-Miss.) cast an unusual vote to break a 14–14 tie. Aid to El Salvador went forward without conditions.

Denouements

While neither the contra nor the El Salvador debates unfolded in 1988 with the same passion or intensity of earlier years, the final months of Reagan's presidency defined limits for the next administration. Congress's embrace of the Arias plan foreclosed new military aid for the contras, shifting attention instead to internal political changes in Nicaragua that would permit an unarmed challenge to Sandinista rule. But even if the Arias plan were to have failed utterly in moderating Sandinista behavior internally or externally, it was unlikely that Congress would ever resume rebel funding in the wake of the Iran-contra affair.

In El Salvador, the renewed indications of congressional concern had failed to redirect policy. But the problems that prompted the attention—a stalemated war, a failing economy, surging death squad killings, and a right-wing bid for power—suggested deeper problems that any new administration could ignore only at its peril.

It is to the credit of the incoming administration of George Bush that it perceived the need for a fresh approach in Nicaragua. But it would take the near collapse of the Salvadoran government during a guerrilla offensive in late 1989, and the appalling murder of six well-known Jesuit priests, their housekeeper, and her daughter, to force a change of policy in El Salvador.

Chapter Nine

1989–1992: The Bush Years

Defining the Bush administration's overarching vision for extricating the United States from Central America's conflicts is difficult essentially because there was none. The collapse of the Cold War removed anticommunism as the driving motivation for U.S. policy in Latin America, leaving an eclectic policy based on reflexive impulses and domestic politics. In both El Salvador and Nicaragua, guerrilla wars that had raged for a decade came to an end through political mediation. Rather than stand on the sidelines of multilateral efforts to seek peace or firmly oppose them, as had Reagan, the Bush administration became actively involved in the search for negotiated solutions. In the case of Nicaragua, that meant making peace first with Congress, whose opposition to the contras during the final year of the Reagan administration gave the incoming president few realistic options for continuing the war. In El Salvador, too, the administration's options were limited when congressional impatience with the war and repudiation of prominent cases of political murder led to sharp curtailments in military aid.

Several dynamics explain the shift from military to political confrontation. First, from its earliest days in office, the Bush administration seemed eager to move beyond the fierce ideological struggles over Central America that had defined the Reagan years. Even if some in his administration remained deeply committed to the anticommunist struggle in the region, Bush and his secretary of state, James A. Baker III, shared little of Reagan's ideological fervor regarding communism in the Western Hemisphere. The desire to disengage stemmed partly from a reading of sentiments on Capitol Hill, but it also reflected the desire of senior administration officials to restore the emphasis in U.S. foreign policy to "larger" issues—growing political and economic integration in Europe, the steady rise of Japan as a global economic power, and the process of political and economic reform under President Mikhail Gorbachev in the Soviet Union. The recognition of new world complexities was also a departure from the Reagan era, in which the East-West conflict defined a framework as well as a balance sheet for virtually every foreign policy struggle.

A March 1989 "bipartisan accord" over contra aid offered the first evidence of Bush's new approach to Central America. The agreement with Congress allowed modest funding for the contras to continue while shifting the focus of U.S. policy to the 1990 Nicaraguan presidential elections. In late 1989, Congress approved a substantial aid package aimed at bolstering the Nicaraguan opposition's chance of defeating the Sandinistas at the polls. The triumph of opposition candidate Violeta Barrios de Chamorro, and the subsequent demobilization of the contra army, allowed both the administration and critics in Congress to declare victory in Nicaragua and to disengage, even if fundamental problems of the distribution of power remained.

Second, the end of the Cold War dramatically shifted the global context for Central America policy discussion. The first year of the Bush presidency saw the fall of the Berlin Wall, the reunification of Germany, and the toppling of dictators throughout Eastern Europe by mass-based popular movements. By the summer of 1991 the Soviet Union itself was in the process of breaking up into autonomous republics. Such world-historical events, virtually unimaginable for two generations of postwar policymakers, undermined the central rationale for U.S. involvement in Central America: that it was necessary to defeat communism there in order to deny the Soviets a toehold on the North American continent. Just as important, and as a result of domestic and regional turmoil, the Soviets joined the Bush administration in the search for political solutions in Central America.[1]

The demise of the Cold War had its most pronounced impact on El Salvador policy. But even there, the Bush administration was slow to relinquish what the Cold War had implied: unswerving support for the Salvadoran government. The Bush administration responded timidly when Alfredo Cristiani of the rightist ARENA party won the presidency in March 1989; the administration moved simultaneously to emphasize human rights issues and to embrace far-right leaders such as Roberto D'Aubuisson in the name of political realism. The policy of backing the Salvadoran army continued unabated, even as the corollary of that policy—supporting centrist political evolution—was compromised by the election of an overtly rightist government.

The events of November 1989 riveted attention on El Salvador in a way not seen since the beginning of the decade. The largest guerrilla offensive of the war brought thousands of rebel fighters to the capital, sweeping away any illusions that they had lost the capacity to mount a serious challenge to government forces.* The murder of six Jesuit priests and two women on a university campus during the offensive shocked even the staunchest defenders of U.S. policy. The administration made several efforts initially to blame the murders on FMLN guerrillas. But evidence of the military's involvement—leading to the indictment of nine members of the Salvadoran army—undercut a central claim of U.S. policymakers: that the military's behavior had fundamentally changed as a result of U.S. engagement.

The guerrilla offensive and the Jesuit murders shaped U.S. policy in two essential ways. First, by demonstrating the hopelessness of a military victory by either side, the offensive underscored the need for a negotiated political settlement. From April 1990 through December 1991, representatives of the Salvadoran government and FMLN held a series of meetings under the auspices of the United Nations. While broadly supportive of the notion of a political settlement, the Bush administration remained so critical of the U.N.'s handling of the process and of FMLN stances that it appeared at times to undermine the talks.

Second, the unique horror of the Jesuit murders made an adequate investigation and punishment of those responsible central to the continuation of U.S. support for the Salvadoran government. Throughout the 1980s, the Reagan administration and Congress accepted large quotients of political murder in

---

*In April 1989, for example, Representative Dave McCurdy (D-Okla.), a member of the House Armed Services and Intelligence Committees, wrote that "the growing political isolation of the hard left appears to be matched, contrary to popular wisdom, by its declining military capability." Dave McCurdy, "Help for El Salvador," *Washington Post*, April 6, 1989.

order to achieve a broader goal defined in national security terms. As the anticommunist glue of U.S. policy melted away, however, human rights concerns came to the fore with new intensity. The prominence of the victims and the army's involvement raised a host of questions about the nature of "our" side in the Salvadoran struggle.

In a highly unusual step that emphasized the centrality of human rights in a post–Cold War era, the House leadership created a special task force to monitor the Salvadoran government's investigation of the Jesuit murders. A steady stream of damaging revelations from the task force—first that the army high command had participated in a cover-up, and eventually that senior officers had ordered the murders—led to a profound questioning of U.S. policy. In 1990, Congress cut military aid by half, sending a dramatic signal that defeating the FMLN was no longer a sufficient rationale for continuing support for the Salvadoran government.

A final, albeit less driving incentive for resolving Central America's conflicts lay in domestic politics. By 1989, the Salvadoran struggle alone had cost the United States close to $4 billion in overt aid.[2] The ability of the Bush administration to sustain large foreign aid commitments came under constant challenge as the U.S. economy sank deeper into recession throughout Bush's term. Foreign assistance, never popular in the best of times, became more difficult for members of Congress to justify to constituents hurt by unemployment and painful cutbacks in domestic spending and services. It is important not to overstate the budget issue as a motivation behind U.S. disengagement from Central America. Nevertheless, the tangible costs of U.S. policy served as yet another irritant for Congress and thus as a reminder to the administration that conflicts in Central America could not be sustained forever.

To the Bipartisan Accord

The earliest months of the Bush administration were devoted in no small measure to making peace with the Congress over Nicaragua. Even in their initial contacts with Capitol Hill following the 1988 election, Secretary of State–designate James A. Baker III and President Bush himself sought suggestions for an acceptable alternative to contra aid. Late in 1988, newly elected Senate Majority Leader George Mitchell told Baker point-blank not to begin his administration "with a big fight over an initiative he can't win."[3] Bush traveled to the Capitol to meet with House Speaker Jim Wright, who accepted an invitation to work out jointly a new bipartisan policy.[4]

One Republican Hill staffer involved in the subsequent discussions bluntly explained why the administration sought a contra aid deal. "They could count," he said, referring to previous votes to cut contra aid. The eight-vote margin by which the House had defeated the Reagan administration's request for contra funding in February 1988 showed no signs of narrowing.[5] Baker thus called for a "different approach" in Central America and stressed bipartisanship in his confirmation hearings in January. He called the Arias plan "a good platform for peace,"[6] indicating that the administration might be willing to mold U.S. policy around the regional solution sought by U.S. allies.

Whatever the administration's initial desire to seek a resolution of the conflict over Nicaragua, it soon found itself outpaced by events in Central America. At a February 14, 1989, meeting in El Salvador, the five Central American presidents agreed to devise within ninety days "a joint plan for the voluntary demobilization, repatriation or relocation in Nicaragua and third countries of Nicaraguan Resistance members and their families."[7] The presidents also set an earlier date for elections in Nicaragua as part of the peace plan's emphasis on internal democratization.

These provisions broke new ground in the Central American peace process. Whereas previous agreements had called in principle for the end of insurgent activity, the accord signed at Tesoro Beach set a specific timeline for phasing out the contras. Moving the date for the elections from November to February also offered a benchmark by which to gauge Sandinista promises to open up its political system.

The agreement caught U.S. officials by surprise[8] and was followed by several weeks of intense negotiations between the State Department and Capitol Hill over a graceful exit from the contra war. The current appropriation for nonlethal contra aid expired at the end of March 1989, giving added urgency to the discussions. State Department negotiators sought to keep the contras intact as a fighting force* in order to pressure the Sandinistas to make good on their electoral promises. They also sought to avoid any charge by congressional supporters of military aid that the Bush administration was abandoning the rebels while getting nothing concrete in Sandinista concessions in return.

---

*During negotiations with congressional leaders, Baker vehemently opposed any designation of funds for relocation and resettlement of the contras as called for in the Tesoro Beach accord. According to a senior Senate aide, Baker believed that explicitly funding resettlement would put too much pressure on the contras during that stage of the negotiations.

Administration officials thus suggested placing military aid in escrow while preparations for the February 1990 Nicaraguan elections were under way.

Meanwhile, opponents of any contra aid sought assurance that the administration's refusal to disband the contras immediately was not merely an excuse for attempting to maintain a discredited policy. House Chief Deputy Majority Whip David Bonior, reflecting the skepticism of Democratic liberals, insisted that Congress retain some control over any additional appropriated funds. "We have had eight years of rancor and bitterness," he said, so "the distrust level is quite high."[9] Eventually, State Department negotiators led by Secretary Baker acceded to a demand that any one of four congressional committees could stop the aid after November 30, 1989. It was understood at the time, however, that Congress would not block the aid after November as long as the administration remained committed to its policy of disengagement from the contra war.[10]

The bipartisan accord on contra aid was unveiled by President Bush and House and Senate leaders at a White House ceremony on March 24, 1989. The accord reflected Congress's unwillingness to cut off the contra movement entirely and thereby be open to blame for subsequent developments in Nicaragua; the accord continued nonlethal assistance at the existing rate of $4.5 million a month until just after the Nicaraguan elections. But the compromise reflected a clear departure for the Bush administration. It sought a way out of a losing policy inherited from its predecessor, and it did so by seeking the cooperation of opponents in Congress.

In striking contrast to the Reagan administration, Bush administration officials conceded to congressional liberals the centrality of the Central American peace accords. The agreement gave explicit support to "the goals of the Central American Presidents embodied in the Esquipulas Accord," and, echoing the agreement at Tesoro Beach, specified that additional funding provided by Congress could be used "to support voluntary reintegration or voluntary regional relocation by the Nicaraguan resistance."[11] Unlike President Reagan, who had wanted to "remove . . . the present structure" of the Sandinista government and make its leaders "say 'Uncle,' " President Bush publicly, if not somewhat disingenuously, disavowed any "right to order the politics of [Nicaragua]."[12]

Forced by circumstance, the bipartisan accord thus both scaled back and clarified U.S. objectives.* It set the upcoming elections as the focus of U.S.

---

*Congress formally approved the bipartisan accord on April 13, voting to provide $49.74 million in nonmilitary contra aid through the February 1990 elections. The accord also prohibited any additional aid unless specifically authorized by Congress and included funds for the repatriation of contra rebels and leaders to Nicaragua. John Felton, "Hill policy. And in a gamble for the Bush administration, the accord implied a softening of the U.S. attitude if the Sandinistas won in a fair ballot. As the coming months would show, however, the United States was less than fully prepared to leave the political playing field entirely to Nicaraguans. Despite Bush's pledge to leave the ordering of Nicaraguan politics to Nicaraguans, the United States became deeply involved in efforts to shape the electoral outcome.

Electoral Aid

After the signing of the bipartisan accord, Bush administration policy in Nicaragua centered on promoting and maximizing the chances for a Sandinista defeat at the polls. The administration itself was divided over whether that might be possible, given Sandinista control of the state apparatus and the weakness and divisions within Nicaragua's internal opposition. The lack of a vigorous political opposition was itself a consequence of Reagan administration policy, which had largely discounted political means as a way of getting rid of the Sandinistas.[13]*

Gives Contra Package Bipartisan Launching," *Congressional Quarterly*, April 15, 1989, pp. 832–36.

*Even though the amount spent on the contra military effort—$350 million over a nine-year period—dwarfed the amount spent on political activities, the United States had not entirely abandoned the Sandinistas' internal opposition. Throughout the 1980s, several covert programs had channeled funds to opposition parties and the Catholic Church as a parallel track to the contra military effort. By one report, the CIA spent $10 million to $12 million from a "political" account earmarked for Nicaragua's internal opposition. According to documents released at the 1992 trial of CIA official Clair George, contra political leaders meeting in Miami in August 1986 stressed the need for a "well orchestrated and far reaching political and propaganda campaign" to be launched when the $100 million in contra military aid approved in 1986 became available. A specific description of the "non-paramilitary, covert project in support of the Nicaraguan resistance" was excised from the released document.

In a separate document, excisions of discussions of "nonparamilitary covert project[s] in opposition to the Sandinista regime" were suggestively made in the context of reporting on the Catholic Church and the Nicaraguan Democratic Coordinator (CDN), a coalition of opposition political parties. That same document spoke of a "coordinated CIA-State effort" in support of Brooklyn Rivera, a Miskito Indian leader. See "U.S. Aid to Contras, Fiscal Years 1982–90," *Congressional Quarterly*, April 15, 1989, p. 834; Brian Barger, "Policy Shifts to Support Internal Nicaraguan Opposition," UPI, August 7, 1988; Alan D. Fiers (CIA official), "Weekly Central America Covert Action Situation Report," August 19, 1986, p. 1; and Alan D. Fiers, "Weekly Central America Covert Action Situation Report," July 8, 1986, p. 1.

As a result, the only well-organized political party in Nicaragua was the Sandinistas'. Despite the odds, key State Department officials, including Assistant Secretary of State for Inter-American Affairs Bernard Aronson, believed that the Sandinistas could be defeated if the fairness and the secrecy of the voting were ensured.[14]

For most of the spring and summer of 1989, however, the administration could not agree on the form of U.S. electoral support in Nicaragua. It sought to preserve the option of sending covert funding to the Sandinista opposition, the purpose of which, according to a senior State Department official, was "to keep the Sandinistas guessing."[15] Congressional critics of covert aid argued that it would "compromise the integrity of the electoral process"[16] and pressed the administration to state publicly that it would refrain from covert electoral financing. The administration initially refused. At an April Senate hearing, acting Assistant Secretary of State for Inter-American Affairs Michael Kozak would not assure Senator Tom Harkin (D-Iowa) that the CIA would not covertly aid the opposition. Secretary of State Baker and Assistant Secretary Aronson also refused to give assurances that the United States would refrain from covert assistance.[17]

Convinced that covert aid would sully the entire elections process, Harkin introduced legislation to prohibit "covert actions for the purpose of influencing, directly or indirectly, the electoral campaign."[18] In the House, liberals pressed Intelligence Committee Chairman Anthony Beilenson (D-Calif.) to add language in the intelligence authorization that would "strictly prohibit" any covert support for political parties or the elections themselves.[19]

The growing resistance to covert aid tore at the bipartisanship so assiduously cultivated earlier in the year. In response, the administration floated a proposal to openly finance opposition political campaigns through the National Endowment for Democracy (NED), a government-supported foundation whose stated goal was to strengthen "democratic institutions throughout the world."[20] Between 1984 and 1988, the NED had openly channeled $1.9 million to non-Sandinista political parties, private sector and religious groups, trade unions, and the media.[21] Congress earmarked funds for the Nicaraguan opposition on a number of occasions beginning in 1987, based on the somewhat lackluster belief that Congress should substitute political action for war as the contra policy withered under the glare of the Iran-contra scandal.

By mid-1989, Congress had directed $3.5 million to the NED for the nonarmed opposition to the Sandinistas.[22] But directly financing campaigns or candidates for political office would have violated the NED's charter.[23] Ultimately, the administration's proposal to fund the elections through the NED was withdrawn, not in small measure because of protests by NED officials themselves.[24]

The pressure within the administration to decide on the form of electoral assistance intensified in early September, when the Nicaraguan opposition nominated Violeta Barrios de Chamorro, widow of a renown newspaper editor assassinated by the Somoza regime and herself a member of the Sandinista government in 1979.* As the opposition coalesced around Chamorro's candidacy, members of her National Opposition Union (UNO) traveled to Washington in September in search of U.S. support. They requested $9 million in aid, a sum inflated in part to compensate for a requirement in Nicaraguan law that 50 percent of any foreign financing go to Nicaragua's Supreme Electoral Council overseeing the election.[25]

The State Department adopted the $9 million figure and, on September 20, 1989, formally asked Congress to support it. The purpose of the money, according to Secretary Baker, was to "support democratic institutions" and "level the playing field" between "an under-financed democratic coalition" and an "authoritarian state."[26] A fact sheet circulated by the administration indicated that $5 million would go to the NED for election monitoring, voter registration, and "building party infrastructures," while another $4 million would go for "additional non-partisan technical support."[27] The State Department compared the program to NED efforts in Chile, Poland, and the Philippines, overlooking that the amount proposed for Nicaragua was almost double what was spent in all three countries combined.†

With voter registration in Nicaragua taking place during several weekends in October, the administration sought rapid congressional approval of the assistance. The pressure to act brought the question of covert assistance to the fore.

---

*Adding to the sense of urgency was an agreement signed by the Nicaraguan government and the opposition political parties in early August. The forty-point accord repealed a repressive "Law for the Maintenance of Order and Public Security," guaranteed press freedom, and contained detailed regulations for carrying out the elections. The stakes were further raised by an August 1989 decision by the Central American presidents meeting in Tela, Honduras, to reject the U.S. linkage between contra demobilization and democratization in Nicaragua. The presidents called for the demobilization, repatriation, and relocation of the contras by the end of the year.

†In the Philippines, a country of 50 million people, the NED spent $890,000 on the election. In Chile, a country of 12.1 million people, the NED spent $1.5 million. In Poland, a country of 35.8 million people, the NED spent $2.8 million. The administration proposed spending $9 million in Nicaragua, a country of 3 million people. *Congressional Record*, October 17, 1989, p. S 13530.

Congressional liberals, many of whom opposed any U.S. support for the elections in Nicaragua, sought explicit assurances that the CIA would not intervene in the elections. In response, Baker conveyed promises to several congressional leaders in late September. According to Chairman of the Senate Intelligence Committee David Boren (D-Okla.), he got "absolute assurances" that the CIA would not be involved in the elections. "It's not going to happen," he said. "There's not a glimmer, not a crack, not a loophole of any kind . . . that would allow anything to go on."[28]

Democrats in the House, however, were less willing to take the administration at its word. Under pressure from House liberals, the House Intelligence Committee included a restriction on covert funding for the elections in the 1990 intelligence authorization bill. The bill contained no funds for the purpose of supporting opposition parties or candidates in the Nicaraguan election and ruled out use of the CIA's contingency reserve for that purpose.[29] As the legislation headed for the House floor, Intelligence Committee Chairman Beilenson publicly assured members of the Rules Committee that "the only way the administration could obtain funds for such covert aid would be by a reprogramming procedure." Pressed as to whether the bill authorized funding for any programs to assist the Nicaraguan political opposition, Beilenson flatly stated "No."[30]

On the basis of assurances from congressional leaders and the administration, former President Jimmy Carter, who was leading one of the delegations to observe the Nicaraguan elections, told President Ortega that the CIA would not interfere in the campaign.[31]

Controversy erupted in 1991, however, over whether the Bush administration had violated both its private assurances and the law. According to a report in *Newsweek* magazine, the CIA spent at least $500,000 to $600,000, beginning in the summer of 1989, on a Nicaraguan Exile Relocation Program (NERP) designed to encourage approximately one hundred contra leaders based in Miami to return to Nicaragua.[32] That the administration had sought to phase out the contras' Miami operations as early as March 1989 was a matter of public record.[33]* But covert support, which the press indicated was for the purpose of

---

*Following the signing of the bipartisan accord on contra aid in the spring of 1989, the Bush administration began cutting the subsidies paid to contra leaders in the United States. Contra leaders recalled being told by an agent of the Central Intelligence Agency that "whoever doesn't go to Managua will end up like the dinosaurs. They will vanish like an extinct species." Christopher Marquis and Alfonso Chardy, "2 Ex-Contras Now Battle Chamorro," *Miami Herald*, October 14, 1992.

getting exile leaders to participate in the elections, was allegedly not phased out entirely.

When *Newsweek* revealed the NERP program in October 1991, administration officials insisted that funds were spent solely for contra repatriation. "The administration's idea was to get the contras into Managua so that the contra army wouldn't screw up the elections," explained a State Department official.[34]

But other officials contended that the program was to get the exiles to go back to work in the Chamorro campaign. As many as eleven of the one hundred exiles funded by NERP became candidates in the February elections. Two embittered ex-contras who said they refused the money also maintained that it was secretly used to promote Chamorro's campaign.[35] The competing claims about the purposes of NERP funding ultimately were impossible to reconcile: when the congressional intelligence committees tried to investigate how NERP money was spent following the article in *Newsweek*, they found that inadequate record-keeping made it impossible to trace how exactly the funds had been distributed.

Members of Congress, however, believed that the door to covert electoral funding had been shut when they considered the request for $9 million in overt assistance. While the administration had originally made a distinction between assistance to Chamorro's campaign and assistance to ensure a fair election, the explicit message of Bush and others at the time of the debate was that the United States supported and sought an opposition victory. Bush wrote Minority Leader Robert Dole that presidential candidate Chamorro "has told us that the opposition needs our assistance desperately, and that only by receiving help can it make a real contest of this election."[36] Chamorro herself referred to the proposed funds as the "program of assistance to the National Opposition Union of Nicaragua."[37] Though liberals continued to argue that the United States was trying to "buy an opposition victory,"[38] both the House and the Senate approved the aid by substantial margins in October 1989.[39]

Chamorro trounced Ortega, 55 to 41 percent, on February 25, 1990. But the impact of U.S. funding on the vote outcome is difficult to assess. Delays in the U.S. aid bureaucracy, and intentional foot-dragging on the part of the Sandinistas, kept all but several hundred thousand dollars from reaching Nicaragua until just weeks before the election. Nevertheless, U.S. funding did help train poll-watchers and finance election observer delegations, both of which created greater confidence in the secrecy and fairness of the balloting. The fact of U.S. funding may also have had a psychological impact, conveying the clear message that the United States preferred an opposition victory and implying that relations between the United States and Nicaragua would normalize with the Sandinistas out of power.[40]*

Members of Congress fell over themselves to claim credit for Chamorro's victory, some ascribing the outcome to the contra war, and others to efforts to end it. The competition for credit was so fierce that the Senate was unable to pass a resolution praising the outcome; lawmakers simply could not agree on whom to congratulate.[41] The reaction of relief, however, was nearly universal. "It's almost as if a dark cloud has passed us by," said Senator Christopher Dodd.[42] Even more than the bipartisan accord negotiated the previous year, the Sandinistas' electoral defeat signaled that Nicaragua might get off the policy agenda once and for all.

Following Chamorro's triumph, senior Bush administration officials sought to ensure a smooth transition in Managua by removing any pretext for a Sandinista refusal to cede power. This meant pressuring contra rebels to give up their military struggle and return home to participate in political life. "There is no reason at all for further military activity from any quarter," Bush said the day after the election. Secretary Baker was more succinct, telling the Senate Budget Committee on February 28, 1990, "The war is over."[43]

U.S. officials equated the electoral results with the advent of democracy in Nicaragua. They explicitly attributed the outcome to the contras' military struggle and attempted to convince skeptical fighters that Chamorro's election represented a victory even though the Sandinista army remained intact. In the two months preceding Chamorro's April inauguration, an array of administration officials traveled to contra base camps in Honduras to push the rank and file to demobilize. Vice President Dan Quayle, the administration's standard-bearer with the U.S. political right, met with contra leaders in Washington. He, too, delivered the message that the war was over. President Bush lifted the 1985 economic embargo, doing so before the Sandinistas left office in a gesture of goodwill. Over a period of several months, large contingents of rebels surrendered their arms in official ceremonies. By year's end, some 22,000 troops and

---

*Bush and Chamorro met at the White House, for example, on November 8, 1989, during the Nicaraguan electoral campaign. The meeting stood in stark contrast to the refusal of both Reagan and Bush to meet with President Ortega. A written statement released by the White House at the time said "the United States would be ready to lift the trade embargo and assist in Nicaragua's reconstruction" if Chamorro won. "Statement by Press Secretary Fitzwater on the President's Meeting With Violeta Chamorro of Nicaragua," *Public Papers of the Presidents of the United States, George Bush*, Book II, July 1 to December 31, 1989 (Washington, D.C.: U.S. Government Printing Office, 1990), p. 1484.

supporters had turned in their weapons to verification teams run by the Organization of American States and the United Nations.[44]

After Chamorro's election, the administration sought swift congressional approval of an "urgent" $300 million aid package for Nicaragua. The goal was to jump-start the country's economy and provide assistance for demobilized guerrillas.[45] President Bush made the request in mid-March 1990 even before Chamorro took office, and he coupled it with a request for $570 million for Panama in the wake of the December 1989 U.S. invasion. But Congress took its time, using the supplemental as a vehicle for shifting several billion dollars from the Pentagon to domestic programs as part of a "peace dividend" from the end of the Cold War.

The bill containing the Nicaragua funds got further bogged down in unrelated debates over federal financing for abortions. And House liberals attempted to tie up the legislation until the administration ceded more ground in a burgeoning fight over conditions on military aid to El Salvador. By the time the aid request cleared Congress on May 25, the supplemental totaled $4.3 billion.[46] Bush signed the bill the same day, making the funds for Chamorro available one month after she took office.

After describing the situation in Nicaragua as "critical" and the government "absolutely bankrupt," however, the Bush administration held up the disbursement of the funds. Almost a year after she took office, barely one-third of the funds earmarked for her government had been disbursed.[47] Chamorro's decision to keep Sandinista commander Humberto Ortega as chief of the armed forces, and her policy of seeking accommodation with the Sandinistas, angered many in the UNO coalition and the State Department, who had hoped for a more definitive break with the past.[48] Chamorro made an official visit to Washington in April 1991, but her speech before a joint meeting of Congress was attended by only about 100 out of 535 congressmen and senators. Apathy, dissatisfaction, and a desire to forget about Nicaragua now that the war was over characterized the mood on Capitol Hill.*

During the remainder of the Bush administration, Nicaragua receded into the deep background of policy concerns. On several occasions, however, the smoldering embers of previous controversies ignited small fires. In one prolonged

---

*Noticeably absent from Chamorro's speech were large numbers of liberal Democrats, who associated Chamorro's election with the contra war, and conservative Republicans, angered over continued Sandinista power in the government and alleged involvement in the murder of contra leader Enrique Bermúdez in February 1991. Author's interviews, April 16, 1991; Carroll J. Doherty, "Chamorro Asks Joint Meeting for Long-Term Aid Pledge," *Congressional Quarterly*, April 20, 1991, p. 1001.

episode, Senators Dodd and Jesse Helms (R-N.C.) sat on the nominations of State Department officials Michael Kozak and Joseph Sullivan to be ambassadors to El Salvador and Nicaragua, respectively. The two officials had overseen Central American programs when the State Department instituted the covert NERP program prior to the 1990 election.[49] Helms was apparently angered at State Department support for Chamorro over other more conservative candidates in the UNO coalition.[50]

Dodd, however, had deeper objections. For him, the October 1991 revelation of the NERP program served as evidence that the Bush administration had learned little from the Iran-contra affair. In March 1989, Congress had prohibited the administration from spending any money on the contras beyond what was specifically authorized by law. Dodd himself, over Secretary Baker's objections, had insisted that the bipartisan accord over contra aid include funds for the repatriation of contras to Nicaragua. The existence of NERP appeared as evidence that the Bush administration had spent money beyond the amounts approved by Congress. To Dodd, it appeared that Bush, like Reagan, was willing to defy Congress and the law in the pursuit of policy goals.

The State Department escalated the fight with Dodd and Helms by refusing to cooperate with an audit of the NERP program by Congress's investigative arm, the General Accounting Office. Instead, the Department carried out its own review, which concluded that the State Department officials had done nothing improper and that the NERP program "was lawful when developed and initially implemented in early to mid-1989."[51] Ultimately, however, the State Department withdrew Sullivan's nomination in September 1992 when the stalemate could not be broken. By the end of the year, Kozak had still not been confirmed. The feud left El Salvador and Nicaragua without ambassadors for all of 1992, a year of key political developments in both countries.

A second skirmish over Nicaragua involved a White House incursion into the politics of foreign aid. In mid-1992, before the U.S. presidential elections, the administration allowed Jesse Helms and other Republican senators to hold up the disbursement of $104 million in economic aid to Nicaragua, even though authority to block aid funds once they have been appropriated by Congress is normally accorded only committee chairmen, not members of the minority party.[52]

At issue for Helms were Chamorro's failure to return properties confiscated by the Sandinistas from U.S. citizens, and U.S. taxpayer support for a government that a senior aide described as "full of Sandinistas."[53]* At issue for the White

*In late August, Helms released a 144-page staff report on Nicaragua denouncing

House were electoral issues: Helms's influence with the right wing of the Republican Party, whose support Bush needed to shore up, and Helms's prominence in a state that the Republicans hoped to carry in the November election.

The White House's courting of Helms dovetailed with the interest of State Department and embassy officials in pressing the Chamorro government to institute a number of reforms.[54] Following the suspension of aid, and in response to subsequent U.S. pressures, Chamorro announced several changes in the police in September 1992, named a prominent commission to look into cases of political murder, and intensified negotiations on property issues. Within weeks, Bush reportedly sought Helms's opinion on whether or not to release the aid. Helms said no, and the aid suspension remained in effect.[55] Bush and Helms later campaigned together in North Carolina, which the Republicans carried in the November presidential campaign.

Less than a month after Bush's defeat at the polls, however, the State Department released half of the withheld aid. According to a State Department official, "There was no way they [Helms's office] can retaliate against a dying administration."[56]

If the episode demonstrated the way in which U.S. electoral politics can intrude on foreign policy decisions, it also illustrated the leverage the United States could wield in small countries receiving U.S. assistance. In contrast to its actions in Nicaragua, however, the Bush administration resisted Congress's efforts to use aid to effect change in El Salvador. As during the Reagan administration, resistance to congressional involvement in foreign policy was as much a matter of divergent policy goals as it was a matter of protecting executive branch prerogatives.

El Salvador

If President Bush had worked deftly to salvage the wreckage of Nicaragua policy inherited from his predecessor, the departure from Reagan policy in El Salvador

---

rampant government corruption, Sandinista control of the military and government ministries, and a "systematic campaign to assassinate" demobilized contra rebels and leaders. State Department spokesman Richard Boucher called the report's charges "far-reaching and disturbing" and announced that an official delegation would leave for Managua to look into the allegations. See U.S. Congress, Senate, Committee on Foreign Relations, *Nicaragua Today*, Republican Staff Report (Washington, D.C.: U.S. Government Printing Office, 1992), pp. 1–144; U.S. Department of State, Office of the Assistant Secretary/Spokesman, "Senate Republican Staff Report on Nicaragua," September 1, 1992, p. 1.

was slow and hesitant and forced upon the administration by events beyond its control. As Bush took office, political violence and polarization in El Salvador were on the upswing. The rightist ARENA party stood poised to win the presidential elections scheduled for March 1989. For a period of several months, the guerrillas had increasingly brought the war to the capital, staging several major assaults on urban military installations and launching a grenade attack on the residence of the U.S. Deputy Chief of Mission in January. A January 1989 State Department report pessimistically noted that economic conditions had "deteriorated drastically," that respect for human rights remained "uneven," and that "the general level of violence" had increased slightly over the last year.[57]

The Bush administration addressed the deteriorating conditions by making for the most part only minor adjustments in the Reagan policy. One exception, however, surfaced in January 1989, when the FMLN offered to participate in the upcoming elections if they were postponed for six months. The State Department and the U.S. Embassy urged President Duarte to consider the proposal, which he had initially rejected out of hand.[58] An agreement for FMLN participation was never worked out, but the State Department recognized the significance of the FMLN's offer, the first time the guerrillas had formally indicated their acceptance of elections as a path to achieving power. The administration's effort to bring the FMLN into the elections won approval with congressional critics of Reagan administration policy, who sent a letter to Bush praising the move.[59]

In addition, the administration sought to place renewed emphasis on human rights, given the prospect of heightened repression if ARENA took power and its most fanatical elements took over key positions in the government. At the request of the U.S. Embassy in San Salvador, Vice President Dan Quayle made a one-day visit to El Salvador en route to the inauguration of Venezuelan President Carlos Andrés Pérez. Quayle raised the September 1988 army massacre of ten peasants in the town of San Sebastián, a case that U.S. Ambassador William Walker called the "key test" of El Salvador's justice system and the military's human rights performance.[60] Shortly after Quayle's trip, the military detained three officers and four enlisted men for their role in the killings. All but one were later released.[61] And the case dropped from the administration's sights altogether following the Jesuit murders later that year.

The ARENA party candidate, Alfredo Cristiani, did win the March 1989 elections. Conscious of what a Salvadoran diplomat called ARENA's "image problem" in the Congress, Cristiani traveled to Washington within weeks of his victory.[62] There he impressed lawmakers with his emphatic insistence on a political solution to the fighting. Cristiani promised that rightists such as Roberto

D'Aubuisson, whom many in Washington associated with the death squads and threats on the life of a former U.S. ambassador, would not dominate his administration.*

Following the visit, most members appeared inclined to "give Cristiani a chance," just as they had President Duarte after his election in 1984. Senator Dodd, chair of the Senate's subcommittee on the Western Hemisphere, was impressed by Cristiani's commitment to seeking a negotiated settlement of the war. But liberals remained deeply suspicious of the extremist elements within ARENA and frustrated with the failure of U.S. policy to end the war. Senators Mark Hatfield (R-Ore.) and Tom Harkin had reintroduced their bill to hold back half of El Salvador's military aid for six months, until the State Department reported on efforts to end the war and political killings. The conditions were mild compared with those adopted by Congress a year later. But they served notice that the consensus over El Salvador policy was beginning to wither the longer the war dragged on.

In the months after Cristiani's election, members of the House and Senate made several attempts to toughen the conditions governing aid. Modeling its approach on provisions of the bipartisan accord on contra aid, one House subcommittee passed an amendment giving four congressional committees the power to block aid every six months. Undersecretary of State Lawrence Eagleburger called the provision "simply not acceptable to the administration."[63] Representative Matthew McHugh (D-N.Y.) attempted to attach even stiffer conditions when the foreign aid bill came before the House in June. He proposed that aid could be provided after six months only if Congress voted affirmatively to continue it. McHugh's amendment failed overwhelmingly, however, 185–233. The vote signaled the House's reluctance to revive full-pitched battles over El Salvador in the absence of serious missteps by the government.

Efforts to condition aid also failed in the Senate, as Cristiani made good on his commitment to engage the FMLN rebels in political dialogue.† At Cristiani's

---

*D'Aubuisson met with Vice President Quayle during his February trip, although the U.S. Embassy pulled photos of the two men from the batch sent back to Washington. D'Aubuisson and other far-right leaders were subsequently invited to Ambassador Walker's residence for a July 4th party. The invitations were justified in the name of pragmatism. In a 1993 report, the United Nations Commission on Truth for El Salvador confirmed that D'Aubuisson had given the order to assassinate Archbishop Romero in 1980. (See Chapter Two.)

†In his inaugural address on June 1, 1989, Cristiani affirmed that "we consider the basic challenge to be the search for a solution to the armed conflict. Nobody in his right mind wants this fratricidal and unjust war to be prolonged." Cristiani called for the formation

initiative, and through the efforts of several opposition party leaders, members of the Salvadoran government and the FMLN met in mid-September in Mexico City, in the first face-to-face meetings in nearly four years. While the talks were mostly procedural, Cristiani made his gesture in the face of opposition from the military and elements within his own party.

The initiation of dialogue killed the effort in Congress to condition aid to El Salvador. Less than a week after the Mexico City meetings, the Senate opened consideration of the foreign aid appropriations bill. The legislation contained an amendment written by Harkin and Hatfield that divided military aid into three segments and allowed four congressional committees to block the final install-ment.[64] Led by two liberals, Dodd and John Kerry (D-Mass.), the Senate voted not only to remove the conditions but also to increase the amount of military aid to the Salvadoran government.

The votes identified chief protagonists in the congressional debate whose alliances would shift over time. Senator Patrick Leahy (D-Vt.) argued against signing another "blank check" for El Salvador that would provide no incentives to the military to support the dialogue.[65] Dodd, however, countered that restrictions "will assist those who want to undermine the negotiating process" by signaling a lack of trust in President Cristiani.[66] Senator Kerry echoed that the Mexico City discussions "point out that there are real hopes for solution now, . . . hopes that are based on the current aid."[67] The Senate voted 68–32 to table, and thereby kill, an amendment by Senator Leahy to retain conditions in the bill. The Senate then voted, 82–18, to remove the conditions altogether and to increase military aid to $90 million, $5 million more than the administration had requested.

Within weeks, however, the consensus in favor of "giving Cristiani a chance" was assaulted by dramatic and violent developments in El Salvador. Peace talks resumed in mid-October. But on October 31 a powerful bomb exploded at the headquarters of the left-wing trade union FENASTRAS, killing nine people, including a top union official, and wounding dozens of others. Cristiani condemned the attack and promised an investigation, but the bombing was widely assumed to have been carried out by members of the military or the far-right opposed to any dialogue with the guerrillas.* The FMLN pulled out of the

---

of a dialogue commission to contact the FMLN. San Salvador Domestic Service, "Alfredo Cristiani Delivers Inaugural Speech," *Foreign Broadcast Information Service,* June 2, 1989, p. 17.

*In the wake of the attack, Secretary Aronson and the head of the U.S. Southern Command made an emergency trip to San Salvador. Aronson publicly blamed "a violent negotiations within days and stepped up preparations for a long-planned military offensive. Some senior rebel leaders viewed an offensive as enhancing their leverage in the peace talks. Other rebel leaders sought to spark a popular uprising and take power.[68]

On November 11, just as jubilant demonstrators halfway around the world tore down the Berlin Wall and marked the end of one of the Cold War's most bitter episodes, the FMLN launched a nationwide military offensive. Thousands of fighters streamed into San Salvador for the first time in nearly a decade of war, taking up positions in densely populated poor neighborhoods around the city. The guerrillas held on to portions of the capital for several days, calling for a general uprising among the population that did not materialize.

Bush administration officials sought to minimize the impact of the offensive, calling the push a "desperation move" and insisting that "there is no threat to the Salvadoran government."[69] Secretary Baker condemned what he said were "acts of terror, pure and simple."[70] But the situation, as perceived by Salvadoran officers, was close to desperate. At stake was losing control of the capital or seeing it divided, Beirut-style, into zones held by different warring factions. Senior officers meeting at army headquarters on November 15 decided to use increased firepower and air attacks against rebel command posts in the urban areas. It was "them or us," according to one of the colonels present.[71] At the end of the meeting, the officers stood up, held hands, and asked for God's help in defeating the insurgents.[72]

It was in the heat of this offensive that a handful of senior officers led by Defense Minister René Emilio Ponce made a decision to murder Jesuit priest Ignacio Ellacuría, rector of El Salvador's Central American University (UCA), and to leave no witnesses.[73] The army and members of El Salvador's conservative elite viewed the Jesuits as the intellectual authors of revolution; for more than two decades Jesuits had been threatened and murdered and their academic institutions attacked.[74] Ellacuría had been one of the foremost proponents of a negotiated political solution to the war. But his periodic contacts with the FMLN were viewed as proof of his guerrilla leanings, even though Ellacuría had been supportive of President Cristiani in his negotiating effort. Shortly before

---

left and a violent right" for their willingness to use terrorism. But the message to the military, according to a senior U.S. official, "was that whoever is doing this stuff is doing the work of the guerrillas for them. It doesn't matter where it is coming from, it has to be stopped." Douglas Farah, "3 Salvadoran Politicians Found Dead," *Washington Post*, November 8, 1989.

his death, Ellacuría had been asked by Cristiani to serve on an official commission investigating the FENASTRAS bombing. *

Crack troops of the army's notorious Atlacatl Battalion crept onto the UCA grounds in the early morning hours of November 16 to carry out the murder mission. Four priests in a small dormitory were taken to the garden outside their quarters, forced to lie face down, and then shot through the head with high-powered assault rifles. Two others were killed in their sleeping quarters. The Jesuits' housekeeper and her daughter, who had taken refuge on the university campus during the offensive, were discovered in a nearby bedroom. They were riddled with bullets as they sat huddled on the floor. The soldiers then simulated a fire fight and retreated, leaving behind a banner scrawled with the message, "The FMLN has executed the spies who turned on them. Victory or Death. FMLN."[75]

The murder of the Jesuits marked the beginning of a tectonic shift in U.S. policy. Ellacuría and two of the other murdered priests were well known to scores of members of Congress who had traveled to El Salvador over the course of the decade; several of the Jesuits had also frequently visited Washington. As news of their deaths spread through official circles, shock and grief mingled with the disbelief that, after ten years of U.S. involvement in El Salvador, crimes as hideous as the murder of six priests could still take place. "The horror is what captivated people's attention," said a senior Senate aide. "That these peaceful, cultured men could be hauled out in the dead of night and brutalized almost beyond words, . . . in ways no other event had done, it encapsulated the horror of what people in El Salvador were capable of doing to one another."[76]

Administration officials took pains not to ascribe responsibility for the killings to the Salvadoran government, although the identity of the victims and the audacity of the crime during an army-imposed curfew suggested military involvement. During an emotional hearing of the Senate Foreign Relations Committee

---

*A U.S. Embassy cable the day of the Jesuit murders noted that Ellacuría "had recently publicly disapproved of FMLN positions and even grudgingly approved of some of Cristiani's policies." The same cable called Ellacuría "a leading leftist intellectual who often sympathized with FMLN positions." A harsher view was expressed by a U.S. military adviser who received advance warning of the murder plot. "I just knew he [Ellacuría] was dirty," said U.S. adviser Eric W. Buckland in a statement to the FBI. Asked whether he would have accepted the killings as a necessary thing, Buckland replied, "I either accepted as necessary and I really understood it." AmEmbassy San Salvador to SecState WashDC, "Jesuit Rector of UCA Shot Dead; Seven Others Killed," November 16, 1989, p. 2; "Transcript of the Video Declaration of Major Eric Warren Buckland," Washington, D.C., pp. 8 and 12.

the day after the killings, Assistant Secretary of State Aronson carefully avoided any mention of the armed forces, venturing that "it is more likely that [the killing] was from the violent right than the left."*

Others, however, were less circumspect. Dodd, who had supported aid only two months before, now predicted that U.S. support would be "restricted and eventually eliminated." Kerry, who had also supported aid, declared that "not a dime of military aid should go to El Salvador" until the armed forces were purged of those who abused human rights. "It's our money," he said. "We have a right to decide what to do with it."[77]

Little remarked at the time of the hearing was Secretary Aronson's passing reference to the need for negotiations to end the war. "Many will try to exploit Father Ellacuría's memory and name," Aronson said on the fourth page of a five-page written statement. But the only "fitting memorial" was "to mobilize whatever resources and pressures can be brought to bear to negotiate an end to the conflict in El Salvador and guarantee safe space in the democratic process for all."[78]

Aronson's statement marked the first time a U.S. official had explicitly gone on record favoring a settlement to the war through political negotiations. The remark implied recognition that U.S. policy, founded on counterinsurgency and attempts to build representative democracy, needed to change course. But for the next two years, U.S. policy would lurch between recognition of the need for a new approach and the Cold War moorings of the last decade. In an exchange emblematic of the resistance to change, two women hecklers interrupted President Bush several days after the Jesuit murders to ask, "Why are we supporting El Salvador?"

"Because it had certifiably free elections," Bush retorted. "President Cristiani is trying to do a job for democracy, and the left-wing guerrillas must not take over."[79]

---

*"Though I would say," continued Aronson, "the FMLN is every bit capable of murdering their own if they thought it would be in their interest." In his prepared remarks, Aronson called those responsible "murderers and barbarians." Aronson's statements were no doubt based on an embassy cable that ascribed responsibility to "extremists on either the right or left." The cable also speculated that "FMLN extremists may have murdered Ellacuría et al. in order to salvage their hoped-for popular uprising." Senate Foreign Relations Committee, Transcript of November 17, 1989 hearing, p. 123; testimony of Bernard W. Aronson, Assistant Secretary of State for Inter-American Affairs, before the Senate Foreign Relations Committee, November 17, 1989, p. 3; AmEmbassy San Salvador to SecState WashDC, "Jesuit Rector of UCA Shot Dead," p. 2.

As fighting from the offensive temporarily abated in late November, Congress, too, showed that it was not prepared to change course precipitously in El Salvador. House Democrats made a final attempt to condition military aid when a foreign aid bill conference report came to the floor on November 20. "Let us not allow these holy men to have died in vain," Representative Joe Moakley (D-Mass.) said passionately. But the House defeated, 215–194, a procedural motion over whether to allow a vote on a proposal to withhold 30 percent of military aid for six months. [80]

A similar proposal to restrict military aid in the Senate also failed, with opponents arguing that any cut would reward the FMLN for provoking "internal anarchy." [81] Both the House and the Senate passed resolutions condemning the FMLN for launching the offensive and expressing the "strongest revulsion" at the "heinous murder" of the Jesuits and the two women. [82] The message from the Congress to the Salvadoran government and the FMLN, at least for the time being, was, in Senator Leahy's words, "a pox on both your houses." [83]

In the days and weeks after the Jesuit murders, however, the Bush administration committed a series of political errors from which U.S. policy never fully recovered. Ambassador William Walker, for example, appeared to justify the Salvadoran military's harassment and imprisonment of church and humanitarian workers, comparing the church raids to U.S. internment of the Japanese during World War II. [84] Furthermore, U.S. attempts to downplay the significance of the rebel offensive appeared woefully out of touch. Days after Salvadoran and U.S. officials had described the offensive as a "sign of weakness" and "stunning military defeat" for the guerrillas, [85] scores of rebel fighters infiltrated one of the wealthiest neighborhoods of the capital. They inadvertently trapped twelve U.S. military advisers during a takeover of the Sheraton hotel. * After a tense standoff, the guerrillas evaded Salvadoran troops and slipped away. The episode demonstrated, said one U.S. journalist, that "large numbers of leftist insurgents can enter and leave the capital at will, even under intense government scrutiny and bombardment." [86]

By far the most serious administration missteps involved the Jesuit case. A sequence of words and actions conveyed the impression that the United States was more interested in providing cover for the Salvadoran government and armed forces than in finding out the truth. First, the U.S. Embassy attempted

---

*The advisers were engaged in a training exercise with the commando unit of the Atlacatl Battalion that later carried out the Jesuit murders. Speaker's Task Force on El Salvador, "Interim Report," April 30, 1990, p. 15.

to discredit the only known eyewitness to the murders, who told the Jesuits, and then FBI and Salvadoran investigators, that the killings were carried out by soldiers wearing camouflage uniforms and carrying rifles.* "The fact that she saw five guys in camouflage suits doesn't prove army involvement," said Walker after details of the witness's testimony became known.[87]†

Walker's attempt to exonerate the army contrasted sharply with the common-sense assessments of others in the administration. "In El Salvador," said one official, "the simplest explanation is probably the right one. If you hear hoofs outside your door, it's probably horses, not zebras."[88]

The version that the FMLN was responsible persisted even after contrary information became available. On December 27, 1989, the U.S. Embassy reported to Washington that the Salvadoran investigation "continues to focus on the armed forces" and on members of the army's Atlacatl Battalion in particular.[89] Notwithstanding that report, Walker told Representative Joe Moakley, who had recently been appointed to head a special House task force on the murders, that they had probably been committed by the FMLN.

As Moakley recalled it, Walker "was not sure that the Salvadoran military was involved" and, by claiming that the FMLN sometimes stole army uniforms, "made arguments to the effect that it could have been the rebels."[90]

"You'd have to be deaf, dumb, and blind to come away from that briefing not thinking the Embassy thought the FMLN did it," recalled Moakley's senior aide on the task force.[91]

Within five days of Moakley's meeting with Walker, however, President

---

*According to the Lawyers Committee for Human Rights (which served as counsel for the Jesuits), witness Lucía Cerna was flown to Miami and interrogated for four days by two FBI agents and a Salvadoran lieutenant colonel. Grilled by the investigators and convinced that they didn't believe her, Cerna eventually changed her story to say that she had seen nothing. She then failed a polygraph test. U.S. officials familier with the questioning of Lucía Cerna admit to "mistakes" regarding her handling but deny that the U.S. Government was trying to make her change her story or to prove her a liar. FBI interrogators "didn't understand the significance of the [Jesuit] case until the shit hit the fan" regarding Cerna's treatment in the United States, said a U.S. Embassy official. (Lawyers Committee for Human Rights, "The Jesuit Murders: A Report on the Testimony of a Witness," December 15, 1989, pp. 1–37; interview, September 24, 1992.)

†A cable from Walker to the State Department on December 11 expanded on that view: "In a number of occasions in the offensive, FMLN fighters have worn military uniforms . . . [the witness's] statement does not provide a direct link or conclusive proof that the ESAF [El Salvadoran Armed Forces] was involved in the murders." AmEmbassy San Salvador to SecState, WashDC, "Demarche on Nicaraguan Subversion," December 11, 1989.

Cristiani stated that "some elements of the armed forces" were involved in the murders.[92] Cristiani announced the names of nine army suspects on January 13, 1990. The highest ranking was Colonel Guillermo Alfredo Benavides, the head of the Military Academy. All but one of the suspects were taken into custody.

The events that prompted Cristiani's announcement of military involvement proved further damaging to the Bush administration's credibility. A U.S. military adviser stationed in El Salvador, Eric W. Buckland, informed his superiors on January 2, 1990, that he had learned from a Salvadoran military colleague in mid-December that Colonel Benavides had confessed his role in the crime to a top Salvadoran investigator. Buckland came forward, he said, "because the investigation was not progressing," even though he felt troubled about betraying the trust of his Salvadoran counterpart.[93]

The Embassy's handling of Buckland's revelation called U.S. intentions into question. Instead of protecting Buckland's Salvadoran army source, embassy officials brought him and Buckland before officers of the army high command. When asked to repeat what he had told Buckland, the Salvadoran officer denied the account entirely. "It was a dumb mistake to take Buckland immediately before [Minister of Defense] Ponce," said a senior U.S. official in retrospect.[94] The damage, however, was done. The U.S. Embassy "burned" a Salvadoran source, thereby signaling to others in the armed forces that the United States was not to be trusted.

The episode cast U.S. motives into doubt: were they to break the case or to break those who came forward? In a further display of ineptitude or outright malice, State Department and embassy officials withheld from Salvadoran investigators the detailed account that Buckland gave the FBI.[95] A transcript and videotape of Buckland's questioning indicated that he and his Salvadoran source said that they had prior knowledge of the plot to kill the Jesuits.[96]

The details regarding what the Bush administration did or did not do regarding the Jesuit case acquired relevance because the House leadership had appointed in early December 1989 a special Democratic task force to monitor the investigation of the case. Never before had Congress assigned a special group to investigate an abuse of human rights in a foreign country. The fact that the House did so in the Jesuit case was testimony to the prominence of the victims, to the elevation of human rights concerns in the wake of the Cold War, and to the massive level of U.S. involvement in El Salvador over the course of a decade.

Speaker Tom Foley named Representative Joe Moakley as task force chairman and appointed nineteen other Democrats with liberal to conservative views. Moakley was personally acquainted with several of the slain Jesuits, principally through previous sponsorship of legislation that suspended the deportation of

Salvadoran refugees in the United States. Moakley's close relationship with the House Democratic leadership and chairmanship of the powerful Rules Committee made him a powerful force within the House. His tenacity and commitment earned him the respect of even those in the Bush administration most threatened by his effort to get to the bottom of the case.

Containing the Damage

The Salvadoran government's January announcement that military officers were the principal suspects in the Jesuit murders fueled a congressional appetite to restrict or eliminate military aid. At the same time, the rapid dissolution of communist regimes in the Eastern bloc throughout the fall of 1989 punched gaping holes in the central rationale for U.S. policy in El Salvador—that U.S. security depended on defeating left-wing insurgents. Deprived of its anticommunist bottom line, U.S. policy appeared deeply flawed, dependent on an army that murdered Catholic priests. An editorial in *Time* magazine captured the shift in public and congressional opinion. "Washington should cut off military aid unless travesties like the killing of the six Jesuits are stopped," said an editorial. "El Salvador's armed forces, nourished by American dollars, bear primary responsibility for the country's scandalous human rights record."[97]

Cristiani traveled to Washington in early February 1990 to contain the damage occasioned by the Jesuit murders. Predictably, he encountered greater congressional reluctance to hold its collective nose and vote for aid. "We understand what he's putting up with the FMLN," said Representative John Miller (R-Wash.). "But he has just got to do something about human rights. It's not a blank check."[98]

Congress Responds

Within days of Cristiani's visit, Senator Christopher Dodd introduced legislation that became the blueprint for congressional efforts to restrict aid over the next two years. The bill sought to promote both a negotiated settlement and a resolution of the Jesuit case by applying aid conditions to both the Salvadoran government and the FMLN. Military aid would automatically be cut by 50 percent unless the FMLN blocked progress toward a negotiated settlement or threatened the survival of the government. Aid would be cut in full if the government refused to negotiate in good faith or failed to make progress in the Jesuit and other human rights cases. Dodd, who had angered his colleagues in the fall of 1989 by voting against aid restrictions, noted "a growing sense of fatigue" in Congress because of the abuses.[99]

The Bush administration, while putting out firm signals that it favored a negotiated settlement of the war, opposed the aid restrictions. "The only path to peace is at the negotiating table," Secretary Aronson told a House subcommittee on January 24.[100] But he defended the military, saying that the armed forces had "cooperated fully" in the Jesuit investigation and downplaying the role of the U.S.-backed Atlacatl Battalion. "I don't think it indicts the armed forces if a unit committed an atrocity," he said. "I don't think it is the norm."[101]

Bush also condemned the effort to cut aid. It would send "negative signals, especially to the armed groups," he said after a February meeting with Cristiani, indicating that he, like Reagan, preferred carrots to sticks in dealing with the Salvadoran military.[102]

In the spring of 1990, the administration made a half-hearted attempt to negotiate a bipartisan compromise on El Salvador similar to the March 1989 accord on Nicaragua. But the talks in the House fell through when the State Department rejected any linkage between El Salvador and its priority aid package for Nicaragua and Panama, a linkage that House Democrats saw as a key point of leverage with the administration. In late April, and in defiance of personal appeals by Secretary Baker, the House Foreign Affairs Committee voted to cut military aid to El Salvador in half. Against the administration's wishes, the restrictions were attached to the supplemental bill containing funds for Nicaragua and Panama.[103]

The administration's uphill battle to avoid a substantial aid cut got steeper on April 30, when the Moakley task force issued its first comprehensive report on the Jesuit murders. The investigation and prosecution of the case were at a "virtual standstill," the task force reported, and Salvadoran investigators had made "almost no effort" to determine whether officers other than those indicted had had a role in ordering or covering up the crime. Taking issue with U.S. and Salvadoran government attempts to portray the murders as the act of individuals and not an indictment of the armed forces, the task force charged that "it is both."[104]

Not even the staunchest supporters of U.S. policy took direct issue with the report's findings. Moakley's inquiry had been conducted "in a balanced and professional manner," Baker said. Bud Shuster (R-Pa.), the senior Republican to have accompanied the task force to El Salvador in mid-February, described most of the report as "fair."[105]

The House Takes Action

Even as it became clear that the Jesuit case alone would provide grounds for restricting aid, there was movement in the effort to negotiate an end to the war. In early April 1990, the FMLN and the Salvadoran government met in Geneva, this time under United Nations auspices. The following month, the two sides met again to establish a formal agenda for the talks. The process envisioned a series of political agreements on needed reforms to lead ultimately to a cease-fire and further talks on ways to integrate the FMLN back into society.[106] The Bush administration welcomed the talks. But officials viewed the agenda as largely set by the FMLN and expressed impatience and frustration with the pace of the talks and the style of the senior U.N. negotiator.[107]

Initial progress on the negotiations front proved too limited to brake Congress's momentum toward cutting aid. Moakley gained powerful allies on the task force, most notably conservative Democrat John Murtha (D-Pa.), who proved critical in reaching members outside liberal circles. On May 22, 1990, the House overwhelmingly adopted a Moakley-Murtha amendment to cut military aid in half. The amendment allowed the administration to restore aid under a number of conditions, including if the FMLN refused to negotiate, received significant weapons shipments from abroad, or murdered civilian noncombatants. The debate itself showed how far sentiment had shifted following the Jesuit murders. And with the Sandinistas out of office in Nicaragua, the old security arguments held less sway.

Republican references to "vicious communist terrorists" fighting a "duly elected government" seemed anachronistic, especially with El Salvador's Christian Democrats breaking with their past and supporting the aid cut.* Even a Republican substitute offered by Representative William Broomfield reduced military aid by 25 percent, one of the largest proposed cuts in the history of the war. But that substitute failed, 175–243.

---

*Secretary General of the Christian Democratic Party Fidel Chávez Mena endorsed "freezing half the military aid, as proposed by Congress." Invoking the name of former President Duarte, Chávez Mena wrote that "a combination of international pressure and support is beneficial to the negotiating process." *Congressional Record*, May 22, 1990, p. H 2667.

"Enough is enough," Moakley insisted passionately. "They killed six priests in cold blood. I stood on the ground where my friends were blown away by men to whom the sanctity of human life bears no meaning—and men who will probably never be brought to justice."[108]

The damage occasioned by the Jesuit case was beyond repair. Thirty-one Republicans voted for the Moakley-Murtha amendment, which passed by a margin of 250–163. Only twenty-eight Democrats opposed it. Speaker Tom Foley rightly called the vote a "watershed" in U.S. policy toward El Salvador.[109]

Initially, however, the aid cut was merely symbolic. Some Democrats wanted more time for further negotiation with the administration over a possible bipartisan compromise on El Salvador policy. Employing tactics that had been used against him on a 1985 contra aid vote,[110] Moakley Task Force member Representative Dave McCurdy (D-Okla.) rounded up scores of his fellow Democrats to oppose final adoption of the bill containing the Moakley-Murtha language. The administration itself lobbied heavily against final passage, and the bill was defeated, 244–171.

Ultimately, however, the Moakley-Murtha formula for reducing aid survived. Administration officials and senior members of both parties in the House carried out intense negotiations over a compromise position in June, but without results. On June 27, 1990, the House incorporated the 50 percent cut into the foreign aid appropriations bill. Recognizing the strength of sentiment for a large reduction, Republicans made no attempt to delete or alter the provision on the House floor.

The administration redoubled its efforts to negotiate a compromise in the Senate, proposing both a smaller aid reduction and a different set of conditions for restoring aid.[111] But Senate leaders showed no interest in ceding ground. Even worse for the administration, Dodd joined forces with Leahy in sponsoring the 50 percent cut when it became clear that the only Senate action on foreign aid would be on the appropriations bill.

Aware that progress in the Jesuit case was critical in averting further congressional action, the administration dispatched Assistant Secretary Aronson to El Salvador in mid-July to seek greater cooperation from the armed forces.[112] And it was soon evident why. On August 15, Moakley issued a withering statement blasting the army high command for its involvement "in a conspiracy to obstruct justice." Salvadoran military officers had "withheld evidence, destroyed evidence, falsified evidence and repeatedly perjured themselves in testimony before the judge," Moakley said.

"The High Command's goal, from the beginning, has been to control the investigation and to limit the number and rank of the officers who will be held responsible for the crimes."[113] As a sign of its own frustration with the army's cover-up, the administration in August quietly ordered a slowdown in the delivery of military aid.*

Aid Is Cut . . . and Restored

President Cristiani returned to Washington in late September in a last-ditch attempt to lobby the Senate to vote against the Dodd-Leahy legislation. "Cutting aid will not end the war quickly," Cristiani wrote in the *Los Angeles Times*. "The FMLN guerrillas are looking for a signal that the United States will abandon its earlier resolve."[114] Secretary Aronson attempted to preempt congressional action, writing in the *Washington Post* on the eve of the vote that "either justice will be done or military aid will be cut."[115]

Aronson, along with Secretary Baker and Deputy Secretary Lawrence Eagleburger, intensely lobbied swing members of the Senate to oppose the Dodd-Leahy provision and support an alternative offered by Senators Bob Graham (D-Fla.) and John McCain (R-Ariz.). That substitute would have allowed the administration to restore military aid unless the guerrillas and the government achieved a cease-fire in sixty days. Designed to put pressure on the FMLN to negotiate a swift end to hostilities, the amendment ignored the linkage established in the U.N. talks between a cease-fire and prior agreement on reforms.

On October 19, the Senate voted overwhelmingly, 74–25, to adopt the Dodd-Leahy amendment. It then rejected the Graham-McCain substitute, 58–39. The extent of the margins showed not only the depth of sentiment regarding the Jesuit case but also the reluctance to underwrite the Salvadoran military in the absence of Cold War justifications. People are "fed up," Dodd said after the vote.[116]

The aid cut formula adopted by the Congress and signed by the president on November 5, 1990, broke a logjam around previous attempts to reduce assistance. Rather than punish only one side in the conflict, the restrictions applied to both the FMLN and the government, specifying a complex set of circum-

---

*A staff memorandum following the August 15 statement came close to pinning blame for the murders directly on the high command. According to the staff, "some members of the armed forces believe that the High Command is responsible for the murders" as well as for obstructing the investigation. See Jim McGovern and Bill Woodward, Memorandum to Hon. Joe Moakley, "Staff Trip to El Salvador," September 14, 1990, p. 2.

stances in which FMLN actions could result in a restoration of aid to the Salvadoran government, and government actions could result in the elimination of all assistance.[117]

But the conditions still empowered the administration to decide whether and when to release aid or to restrict it further. Using the authority conveyed on it by the Congress, the administration restored aid on January 15, 1991, a scant two months after the aid cut had been written into law.[118] Throwing a bone to critics in Congress, the White House promised to suspend release of the aid for sixty days in order to further the negotiations.

Precipitating the administration's action was the FMLN's downing of a U.S. helicopter on January 2, 1991, and the subsequent murder of two surviving crew members. The administration formally stated that its decision was based on the FMLN's targeting of civilians during a late 1990 military offensive. But the execution of the U.S. servicemen provided an opportunity to reward the Salvadoran government when criticism of the FMLN was at its height. Moreover, as the United States prepared to go to war in the Persian Gulf, State Department and Pentagon officials gambled that few in the Congress would mount a protest over El Salvador as tens of thousands of U.S. troops stood poised for combat against Iraq.

They were only half right. Moakley condemned the restoration of aid as "unbalanced" and "ill-timed" and said it was based on a "selective use of the facts" to punish the FMLN while the military stonewalled on the Jesuit case.[119] Dodd decried the decision as "unwarranted and dangerous," sending the "wrong signal" about U.S. insistence on a negotiated solution and resolution of the Jesuit murders.[120] Angered at the seemingly casual way in which congressional intent had been flouted, Dodd began writing a tougher version of the aid cut that would give Congress the authority to decide whether or not to release aid in the upcoming fiscal year.

A direct personal message was delivered to the Salvadoran government by Representative Murtha, Moakley's key ally on the Speaker's task force. On a short visit to San Salvador in early January 1991, Murtha met with Cristiani, Defense Minister Ponce, and Lieutenant Colonel Manuel Antonio Rivas, the army official in charge of the investigation.* Murtha told them that they were in danger of losing aid if they made no progress on the Jesuit case. The United

---

*The report of the U.N. Truth Commission implicated Rivas, who headed the U.S.-backed Special Investigative Unit (SIU), in the cover-up of the murders. The report said that Rivas advised Colonel Benavides to destroy the barrels of the guns that had been used, in order to prevent their identification through ballistics tests. United Nations, *De la Locura a la Esperanza*, p. 48.

States was going to war, Murtha said, and he had other things on his mind. But the Salvadoran government should make no mistake about the importance Congress attached to bringing the Jesuit killers to justice. Stressing the end of the Cold War and the huge U.S. budget deficit, Murtha reminded the Salvadoran leaders that other priorities competed for U.S. attention. Moreover, he said, the U.S. Embassy shared the opinion of congressional investigators that the murders might have been ordered by senior military officers that had not yet been charged.[121]*

Such private diplomacy was unusual but not unprecedented for a member of Congress. Because of the administration's stated interest in seeking justice in the Jesuit case, it could not publicly oppose, and some officials even welcomed, the behind-the-scenes involvement.

The Gulf War did dominate U.S. foreign policy concerns in early 1991, but El Salvador did not disappear from the congressional agenda. In early March, 116 members of the House and 34 Senators, including Majority Leader George Mitchell (D-Maine) wrote President Bush requesting that military aid not be restored when the sixty-day waiting period expired.[122] Wary of picking a fight with the Hill, and facing resistance to a resumption of aid from the U.S. Embassy in San Salvador, the administration delayed releasing aid until June.

The Push for Negotiations

The sense that Congress was bailing out of its decade-long support of the Salvadoran government had a decisive impact on the administration's search for a negotiated solution. "We could not sustain a majority in Congress supporting the assistance absent real progress toward a settlement," said a senior U.S. official reflecting on the aid cuts of 1990.[123]

"What the FMLN was not winning on the battlefield it was winning in Congress," said another official. The State Department's nightmare was that Congress would enact a full cutoff, leading the Salvadoran government to "go for a full Guatemala" solution of unmitigated repression.[124] In the ensuing

---

*A U.S. Embassy cable on Murtha's visit was released under the Freedom of Information Act with more than half its contents deleted. The cable states: "Murtha told Ponce that as a longtime friend and supporter of El Salvador, he wanted to emphasize that the persons responsible for the murders had to be found, even if they were members of the ESAF." All of Ponce's reply was excised. AmEmbassy, San Salvador to SecState, WashDC, "CODEL Murtha Wrap-Up," January 4, 1990, pp. 1–4.

climate of polarization, administration officials feared, the FMLN could take over.

United Nations mediation of the peace talks, however, provided both an opportunity and an obstacle for U.S. policymakers. The fact that the United Nations, the "Mother Teresa of international affairs,"[125] was involved gave the talks broad legitimacy. But the involvement of the United Nations robbed the United States of its status as principal international arbiter of Salvadoran affairs. U.S. officials made no effort to conceal their dislike and distrust of senior U.N. negotiator Alvaro de Soto, whom they accused of pandering to the FMLN. In a rare display of public hostility, an unnamed "senior administration official" told the *New York Times* in late January that de Soto "accede[d] to the guerrillas' delaying tactics" and was "less than energetic in pursuing the peace process."[126] Over the coming months, the administration made the swift entry into a cease-fire the sina qua non of FMLN seriousness in the talks, continuing to ignore the formula accepted by both the Salvadoran government and the FMLN that put agreement on substantive reforms ahead of an end to military hostilities.

Throughout 1991, Democrats who had led the fight for aid conditions struggled with the impact of a renewed battle over military assistance on the peace talks. Regardless of provisions of the 1990 bill that covered FMLN behavior, it was clear that the 50 percent cut had been a serious blow to the government, not to the guerrillas. Adding to congressional uneasiness was the FMLN's January 1991 murder of the two U.S. servicemen and the sense that the guerrillas, too, should pay a price for their conduct. State Department officials lost no opportunity to equate the killings of the servicemen with the murder of the Jesuits, portraying the murders as the FMLN's "Jesuit case."[127]

Following a direct request from U.N. negotiator Alvaro de Soto to "freeze things right where they are" in terms of congressional action, the House leadership agreed in early June 1991 to delay any consideration of further El Salvador conditions until September.[128] The idea was to put pressure on both sides in the talks by keeping them guessing as to what Congress would do. The two foreign aid bills that passed the House in June contained no language specific to El Salvador.

At the same time that they exercised restraint, Moakley and ninety-eight other members of the House made a special plea to President Bush to refrain from reinstating the aid withheld under the 1990 law. Their plea to "join us in not rocking the boat at this delicate stage in the peace process"[129] was ignored, however, when the administration announced on June 27 that it would deliver half of the previously frozen funds to the Salvadoran Army but limit goods to nonlethal items.

Moreover, what House leaders viewed as restraint in postponing an aid vote the State Department saw as Congress's incipient neutralization. State Department officials began to "relentlessly work" the Senate in order to prevent any conditions from being adopted in future laws. The administration achieved a key victory when the Senate Foreign Relations Committee in mid-June failed to adopt Dodd's proposal to withhold 50 percent in military aid and give Congress a role in its release. Assistant Secretary Aronson personally lobbied members of the committee, ultimately convincing southern Democrats Terry Sanford (D-N.C.) and Charles Robb (D-Va.) to vote against aid conditions, which were tabled by a 10–9 vote.

The defeat in committee forced Dodd, now joined by Senator Leahy, to take the amendment to the Senate floor in late July. Arguing that existing conditions had "worked effectively," Dodd urged the Senate to keep and strengthen them in the upcoming year.[130] Dodd and Leahy defeated by a wide 56–43 margin an attempt by Senate Minority Leader Robert Dole to table their amendment. But Senator John McCain (R-Ariz.) began an administration-supported filibuster of the entire bill. Aid opponents lacked eight of the sixty votes needed to end the filibuster. Dodd and Leahy were forced to withdraw their amendment, a move the State Department viewed as a "huge victory" in its effort to block further action by the Congress.[131]

Despite the postponement or defeat of efforts to condition aid in 1991, Congress retained some influence over events in El Salvador and administration policy. Throughout the summer, Moakley continued to pummel the army high command for covering up the Jesuit murders. During a guest appearance on the UCA campus in July, he took previous allegations one step further by charging that "the murders were ordered by senior military officers" not currently indicted. Expanding on a previous theme, he blasted the institution of the armed forces "not only for the murders but for the failure of the investigation, thus far, to uncover the whole truth."[132]

During that same visit to El Salvador, and over the explicit objection of the State Department, Moakley traveled to the town of Santa Marta in FMLN-controlled territory. "It was important to go . . . and say, 'we want to end this thing,' " said Moakley aide Jim McGovern. "We looked at it in terms of the symbolism, of building a bridge."[133] Ambassador Walker, who had accompanied Moakley, offered embassy cooperation on development projects to civilians living in the zone.

FMLN leaders engaged in the peace talks saw the trip as a sign of goodwill. "It was really clear," said an FMLN source close to the negotiations, "that very powerful sectors of the Congress were pushing for negotiations and bringing the administration along."[134] Walker returned to Santa Marta on August 31, this time with an entourage that included U.S. Military Group Commander Mark Hamilton, an aide to Senator Paul Sarbanes (D-Md.), and an official of the Salvadoran land bank. During an overnight visit, the group met with Raúl Hercules, the *nom de guerre* of one of the FMLN's top *comandantes* inside the country.

"I can't tell you how many times the FMLN mentioned Santa Marta as showing we thought they were people we could deal with," said a senior U.S. official.[135] FMLN commander Joaquín Villalobos later told Moakley that the trips to Santa Marta were turning points for the FMLN, signaling a new U.S. willingness to treat the rebels as legitimate participants in Salvadoran political life.* Just as important, the gesture of goodwill was reciprocated. "The trips had a big impact at the U.N.," said a U.S. official. "The FMLN started treating us as part of the solution."[136]

In a stroke of what may have been only dumb luck, the trips to Santa Marta did coincide with major progress in the peace talks.[137] By August, negotiators had made significant headway in devising an alternative to direct FMLN participation in the armed forces, by fleshing out proposals for rebel participation in a newly created police force. Negotiators also made progress in discussions of a forum for political participation; the National Commission for the Consolidation of Peace (COPAZ) would give representatives of the government, opposition political parties, and the FMLN a role in overseeing the implementation of a peace accord prior to elections scheduled for 1994.[138]

Given breakthroughs in these two critical areas, U.N. Secretary General Javier Pérez de Cuéllar invited the Salvadoran government and the FMLN to New York in September, where the talks could continue under his direct supervision. Pérez de Cuéllar's term as U.N. Secretary General expired at the end of 1991, adding a new element of pressure on all sides. By the fall, it had become increasingly evident that failure to conclude a peace accord by December meant that there might not be one at all.

On September 25, Salvadoran government and rebel negotiators concluded

---

*According to the FMLN's top military strategist Joaquín Villalobos, the FMLN was discussing at the time "the possibility of a unilateral cease-fire, a key step to push negotiations forward. Some were opposed to taking such a definitive step, but when we saw Walker in Santa Marta, we felt conditions were really different. We knew the trip made the military furious, and we were impressed. But had we known it was an individual gesture, not a policy statement, I doubt we would have called the cease-fire." Douglas Farah, "Salvadoran Ex-Rebel, Key to Peace Pact, Tries Centrist Politics," *Washington Post*, November 12, 1992.

the New York Accord, which Pérez de Cuéllar asserted untied the "Gordian knot" blocking a final treaty.[139] The accord set out procedures for purging and reducing the size of the army and described in broad terms the formation of a new National Civil Police to replace existing security forces. It was the first detailed agreement in more than eighteen months of talks that went to the heart of the most difficult issue—military reform.

Pressure on the armed forces in the peace talks accelerated as a five-person jury in San Salvador delivered a verdict in the Jesuit case, only three days after the signing of the New York Accord. Colonel Benavides was found guilty of murder, the first time in Salvadoran history that a senior officer was convicted for a human rights crime. Another lieutenant was found guilty of the murder of the housekeeper's fifteen-year-old daughter. But all other seven defendants, including the self-confessed triggermen, were acquitted. The irrationality of the verdict suggested a fix, something to which Moakley alluded when he called the outcome a "terrible injustice" and revealed that one of those who was acquitted had threatened to talk if he had been found guilty.[140]

After allowing the Salvadoran judicial system to work its way through the case, Moakley went public with information given to him by Salvadoran military sources. Moakley said that the decision to murder the Jesuits was made at a small meeting of officers held at the Salvadoran Military Academy. Those present included then-chief of staff General René Emilio Ponce, deputy defense minister General Juan Orlando Zepeda, former Air Force chief General Juan Rafael Bustillo, and head of the army's First Brigade, Colonel Francisco Elena Fuentes. According to Moakley, "the initiative for the murders came from General Bustillo, while the reactions of the others ranged from support to reluctant acceptance to silence."[141]

The officers named vehemently denied Moakley's charges. But in Washington, the administration and its congressional supporters largely remained silent, a tacit admission that the charges were essentially true. When pressed by reporters, however, the State Department referred to Moakley's report as containing "charges but no direct evidence," a surprising locution given the number of U.S. officials who concurred with Moakley's judgment.[142] The subsequent findings of the U.N. Truth Commission for El Salvador—that General Ponce had given the order—confirmed Moakley's charge that the decision to murder the Jesuits originated with the high command.

But once more at year's end, the Congress acceded to administration pressure and declined to include restrictions on aid to El Salvador in the omnibus spending bill called a Continuing Resolution. In exchange for passing a bill with no conditions, Acting Secretary of State Lawrence Eagleburger pledged that the administration would withhold 50 percent of military aid unless there was a "radical change" in the military situation. Eagleburger noted that congressional "cooperation"—its inaction on previous bills—had "helped create the conditions in which the peace process has advanced."[143]

Still, a bipartisan group of House members sought to hold a sword of Damocles over the Salvadoran government and the FMLN, as well as the Bush administration. In mid-November, leading Democrats including Moakley, Majority Leader Richard Gephardt, Foreign Affairs Committee Chairman Dante Fascell, and Foreign Operations Subcommittee Chairman David Obey introduced a bill to restrict all disbursements of military aid unless approved by four congressional committees. The bill proposed to transfer military aid to a Demobilization and Transition Fund for former combatants in the event of a cease-fire and sought to pressure the FMLN to turn over the killers of the two U.S. servicemen to U.S. or Salvadoran authorities.[144]

Because the Continuing Resolution approved in October 1991 covered only the first six months of the fiscal year, Moakley and others felt confident that they could force a vote in March 1992 to tie up all aid. They also were sure they could win in the wake of Moakley's revelations regarding the involvement of the high command in ordering the Jesuit murders. "We made it clear" to the administration, said Moakley aide Jim McGovern, that "it was all over. There was going to be a massive cut."[145]

With the clock ticking closer to the end of Pérez de Cuéllar's term, Salvadoran negotiators met in marathon sessions at the United Nations in December. On New Year's Eve, and under intense pressure from U.S. and Latin American officials, five commanders of the FMLN and four representatives of the Salvadoran government put the final touches on a comprehensive peace settlement. The FMLN agreed to disarm its combatants by October 15, 1992, in exchange for sweeping reforms in Salvadoran institutions and some economic measures, including land reform. The government and the FMLN signed the accord in an emotional ceremony in Mexico on January 16, 1992. A formal cease-fire went into effect on February 1.

The country where Reagan administration officials had vowed to "draw the line" against communism had what U.N. mediator Alvaro de Soto now called a "negotiated revolution."[146] The solution was possible not only because both sides in the Salvadoran conflict came to believe that the war was unwinnable, but also because the United States came to accept negotiations as a way of securing its interests in El Salvador. Following the murder of the Jesuits, and after the electoral defeat of the Sandinistas, Congress indicated that it was prepared to back away from its decade-long commitment to the Salvadoran government.

The breaking of the consensus in favor of aid provided the political space for the U.N. negotiations to move forward.

Ironically, in attempting to silence the Jesuit priests, the Salvadoran high command made more compelling their call for dialogue and reconciliation.

Conclusion

If the process of making peace in El Salvador was contentious, the process of implementing it was at times excruciating. Senior U.N. officials traveled to El Salvador repeatedly in 1992, attempting to break deadlocks between the government and the FMLN over interpretations of key provisions of the accord. The guerrillas disarmed the last of their troops on December 15, 1992, bringing the war formally to an end. But the army then refused to carry out a purge of its ranks at year-end, thereby violating one of the peace agreement's most central provisions.[1] Under pressure from the military, President Cristiani allowed a core of eight senior officers, including the Defense Minister and his deputy, to retain their posts and transferred another seven to diplomatic posts abroad. U.N. Secretary General Boutros Boutros-Ghali stated flatly in early January 1993 that the Salvadoran government's measures were "not in compliance" with the peace accord and urged the government to fulfill its commitments under the agreement.[2] By April 1993 Cristiani delivered to the United Nations a plan for carrying out the purge over a period of several months. In July 1993, the minister and vice-minister of defense finally stepped down.

The event that prompted Cristiani's renewed effort was the March release of the report of the U.N. Commission on the Truth for El Salvador. Established in the peace agreement, this commission was charged with investigating "grave acts of violence" carried out over a decade of war.[3] The Truth Commission's report established responsibility for some of the most notorious cases of political murder in El Salvador. It named Defense Minister René Emilio Ponce and four other officers as having ordered the 1989 murder of the Jesuits. It laid at the army's doorstep the "deliberate and systematic" massacre of more than five hundred civilians in and around the town of El Mozote in 1981, a massacre that had been denied by Salvadoran and U.S. officials at the time (see Chapter 4). The Commission named onetime presidential candidate and founder of the ruling ARENA party Roberto D'Aubuisson as having ordered the 1980 assassination of Archbishop Romero, and it implicated former Defense Minister General Carlos Eugenio Vides Casanova in the cover-up of the 1980 murders of the four U.S. churchwomen (see Chapter 3).[4] Top FMLN leaders, meanwhile, were named as responsible for a string of murders of civilian mayors in the mid-1980s and for the murder of four U.S. Marines and nine civilians in San Salvador's "Zona Rosa" in 1985, among other cases.

The commission scrupulously avoided comment on U.S. policy in El Salvador,* but its findings amounted to a stunning indictment to anyone who could read between the lines. The commission confirmed that current or former defense ministers who had served as the linchpin of U.S. strategy either ordered or covered up spectacular killings. Of the 22,000 complaints the commission registered, 85 percent involved government forces, paramilitary groups, and death squads.[5] These judgments contrasted starkly with U.S. official assurances that the army's human rights performance, while flawed, was adequate to warrant the continuation of U.S. assistance and that the FMLN bore principal responsibility for abuses against Salvadoran civilians.

The release of the Truth Commission report resulted in predictable calls on

---

*The report did, however, state that the U.S. Government "tolerated" betwen 1979 and 1983 the actions of Salvadoran exiles in Miami who "directly financed and indirectly helped direct" some of the death squads. The report made note of the "ambiguous statements" of Secretary of State Alexander Haig and U.N. Ambassador-designate Jeane Kirkpatrick regarding the U.S. churchwomen (see Chapter 3) and noted that the weapons used by the Salvadoran army in the El Mozote massacre were of U.S. origin. Comisión de la Verdad para El Salvador, *De la Locura a la Esperanza: La guerra de 12 años en El Salvador* (San Salvador and New York: United Nations, 1993), pp. 63, 122, 144.

Capitol Hill for a U.S. version of truth-telling, with liberal Democrats denouncing primarily the Reagan administration for distorting and covering up the human rights record of the Salvadoran armed forces.[6] What members of Congress did not bring up, however, was the role of their own institution in carrying out U.S. policy. If anyone could claim vindication from the Truth Commission's report, it was congressional liberals who had sought to eliminate or reduce aid until the Salvadoran army's human rights performance improved or there was serious progress toward a negotiated settlement of the conflict.

Throughout the twelve years of the Salvadoran conflict, a majority in Congress shared the Carter, Reagan, and Bush administrations' objective of preventing armed leftist guerrillas from seizing power from a U.S. ally, a goal consistent with the long-standing policy of containment. Pursuing that goal in practice meant an alliance with El Salvador's repressive forces, even if the nature of that alliance—whether the U.S. tolerated abuses or exerted pressures to end them— became a matter of great controversy.

The Carter administration, for example, supported socioeconomic change in El Salvador and pressed the armed forces to curb political murder. But the notion that violence emanated principally from the extreme right and the extreme left, not from government forces, originated with the Carter administration. Members of Congress agonized over that characterization in mid-1980 when the administration sought to resume a small program of nonlethal military aid, but most, including some liberals, supported the request. When evidence of Cuban and Nicaraguan support for the FMLN surfaced in the last weeks of Carter's term, the State Department modestly expanded U.S. military aid to help the government beat back a rebel offensive.

The El Salvador policy debate was over the means of policy, not the ends. The principal conflict between the Congress and the administration arose when Congress sensed that the shared objective of defending the Salvadoran government against an armed insurgency was being undermined by the very policy means adopted by the Reagan administration.

Sending large quantities of military aid and advisers, and downplaying or ignoring issues of human rights and social reform, suggested to important segments of the Congress that the Reagan administration was fundamentally wrong in its reading of the situation in El Salvador. Underlying the debate over policy means, then, was a core congressional-executive disagreement over the roots of the Salvadoran conflict—whether it was primarily a home-grown insurgency born of poverty, repression, and the absence of political and social opportunity, or whether it resulted from direct or indirect Soviet aggression in a traditional U.S. sphere of interest. Uncertainty over the capacity of the Salvadoran military to defend itself, coupled with exaggerated statements of the U.S. stakes in the conflict, conjured up images of Vietnam and made it appear that the United States was on a path to direct military intervention. It is notable in the self-defeating nature of Reagan administration policies in El Salvador that so many battles with the Congress were not over ultimate purposes but over the most desirable way to meet shared objectives.

From the beginning, prior U.S. foreign policy debates informed congressional deliberations over El Salvador and posed limits on both the Congress and the administration. On the one hand, the intensity of the backlash against the administration's rhetoric and emphasis on military aspects of the crisis suggested that Vietnam was still a powerful metaphor for how not to get involved in Third World conflicts, despite a 1980 Republican electoral victory on themes of reasserting American military power. The debate itself—augmented and largely impelled by organized opinion in the churches—sent a powerful message that there was no domestic political mandate for deeper U.S. military involvement.

On the other hand, the Reagan administration was successful in getting Congress to go along with its goal of preventing a left-wing victory, even if it meant an alliance with repressive forces. The administration moved the 1970s debate over human rights away from an exclusive focus on promoting human rights and over to a two-faceted effort to promote human rights within a context of maintaining internal stability. The debate over El Salvador demonstrated that some liberal attitudes toward military assistance could be moved away from cutting aid until a regime's behavior improved to using military aid as a lever toward constructive transformation. The fear that El Salvador would become "another Nicaragua," and the sense that that outcome would have both foreign policy and domestic repercussions, in large measure underlay the shift.

The fact that Congress and the administration shared bottom-line objectives in El Salvador had implications for Congress's choice of measures to influence or restrict administration policy. The adoption of a certification requirement meant that Congress would not attempt to block the administration's ability to implement policy but, rather, through a series of legislative conditions, would force the administration to pay attention to issues they were seen as ignoring. The adoption of a human rights certification was thus less a repudiation of policy than an attempt to reorient it away from a focus on issues of external subversion and East-West conflict and closer to those of internal reform and development.

The very process of compromise leading to passage of the certification, however, meant that the impact of the certification process would be limited. Congress imposed certification rather than accept responsibility for cutting off aid as a way of forcing changes, asking the administration to supply information about the situation in El Salvador and depriving itself of a veto over the administration's assessment. The only issue left was the lengths to which the administration would go in defending and justifying its decision to certify human rights progress. The wide gap between what the administration said and what private groups reported about the situation in El Salvador gave rise to heated and often emotional debate.

The use of certification as a procedural mechanism for influencing policy would have had meaning only if the decision to certify or not certify was an open question. In the case of El Salvador, however, once the administration made the basic political decision that providing military aid to ensure the survival of the Salvadoran government was vital to U.S. interests, the certification amounted to little more than putting the best face on a bad situation. Moreover, the United States limited its own ability to exercise influence over Salvadoran behavior by making it clear that the U.S. commitment to the war effort against the guerrillas was not negotiable.* Administration critics in Congress, however, lacked the votes to impose tougher measures, a fact that repeatedly gave the administration the upper hand in dealing with aid conditions imposed by Congress.

In the early 1980s, dissatisfaction on Capitol Hill with the pace of reforms in El Salvador and the orientation of administration policy translated into cutbacks in assistance. These usually were a matter of conscious effort, but at times they occurred as the inadvertent result of a failure to complete action on foreign aid legislation. Because the driving force of administration policy, up through and including 1984, was for ever-higher levels of military aid, Congress's power over appropriations compelled the administration to heed some of its concerns. This was especially true when the administration's vital center of support—moderates from both parties in the Republican-controlled Senate—began to erode and when levels of funding were tied to specific events in El Salvador, such as the repeal of aspects of the agrarian reform or failure to prosecute the killers of the American churchwomen.

---

*The same conclusion was reached in a report on death squads by the Senate Intelligence Committee: "The leverage which the United States can exert . . . declines when the United States is perceived by those whom it is attempting to influence to be constrained by independent policy considerations (e.g., the effort to limit Communist influence in Central America) that restrict its freedom of action." See U.S. Congress, Senate, Select Committee on Intelligence, Report, *Recent Political Violence in El Salvador*, October 5, 1984, 98th Cong., 2nd Sess. (Washington, D.C.: U.S. Government Printing Office, 1984), p. 17.

Congressional debates over human rights and socioeconomic reforms, for example, helped resolve an initial debate inside the Reagan administration over whether to pursue an "Argentine solution" of unmitigated repression; the congressional debates also provided a reference point for later adjustments in policy, including Vice President Bush's visit in December 1983 to curb death squad activity and other pressures to stop the more egregious forms of mass killing and torture. It would be important, however, not to overestimate the impact Congress had on the administration and the Salvadoran government. By backing ever-higher levels of military aid throughout the decade, Congress signaled that its shared determination to fight the war would override other concerns.[7]

The extent of Congress's impact on administration policy and on the human rights situation in El Salvador is easy to overstate, simply because the basis of departure was so low. Over the two-year period in which the certification was in effect, the administration gradually moderated its denial that the Salvadoran armed forces were responsible for any abuses of human rights. The fourth certification issued in July 1983, for example, highlighted instances of civilian massacres and acknowledged persistent problems in bringing the killers of civilians to justice. But it still deflected attention from the government's central role in abuses by ascribing much of the political violence to "armed rightist terrorists." Whatever evolution there was in the emphasis of the certifications can only be counted as progress when measured against claims made at the time of the first certification that the "killers of the majority [in El Salvador] are the true phantoms of this struggle."

The record also shows that U.S. officials either tolerated the practices of abusive officers who were deemed effective at prosecuting the war or chose simply not to learn of abuses.[8] "These were the guys we were working with day in and day out, and we did not want to create a hostile situation," a senior U.S. official admitted in 1993. "We were here to fight the guerrillas, they were the enemy, and we did not go around investigating our friends."[9]

Moreover, a number of officials who did speak out were undercut by the actions of their superiors. For example, at the same time that Vice President Bush traveled to El Salvador to press for an end to death squad killings, President Reagan publicly claimed in Washington that guerrillas were carrying out death squad murders in order to smear El Salvador's reputation, because "the right wing will be blamed for it."[10] The failure of the administration to speak with one voice necessarily diluted the message that human rights improvements were central to U.S. policy.

The debate in Congress did have the effect of convincing a majority of Reagan administration officials responsible for Central America policy that a political quest for legitimate government in El Salvador was central to the military effort to defeat the guerrillas. The 1984 elections took place partly as an outgrowth of the Washington debate over human rights. Nonetheless, both Congress and the administration too readily equated the holding of elections with the advent of democracy, ignoring such cornerstones as civilian authority over the armed forces and the rule of law. President Duarte found his power to move forward in a number of areas—from bringing to justice the perpetrators of human rights violations to carrying out a political dialogue with guerrillas—constrained by elements in the army and by conservative political parties. And even with expanded U.S. aid, the army proved incapable of moving beyond a military stalemate with the guerrillas.

Congress removed itself from oversight of policy following Duarte's election, allowing the worst trends in El Salvador to proceed unchecked. Until late 1989, a majority in Congress believed—or simply chose not to dispute—the Reagan administration view that fighting the war while seeking to consolidate political reforms was capable of bringing stability to El Salvador.

The Bush administration initially continued the Reagan policy, despite some renewed emphasis on human rights and a greater willingness to explore possibilities for the incorporation of the FMLN into the political system. The November 1989 guerrilla offensive and the murder of the Jesuits, however, undercut U.S. policy in two ways: by demonstrating that the war was far from being won and that the military, after a decade of U.S. tutelage, was still capable of stunning atrocities. The blow to U.S. policy was intensified by the fact that soldiers from an elite U.S.-trained battalion carried out the Jesuit murders, thereby undermining the premise that U.S. military training contributed to improved human rights performance.

The intensity of the congressional reaction to the Jesuit murders no doubt took the Salvadoran army by surprise, given that U.S. funding had continued and even expanded throughout the previous decade of political violence. What the military apparently did not comprehend was that the end of the Cold War had contributed to the beginnings of a fundamental shift in congressional attitudes toward Central America. The dissolution of the Soviet empire in Eastern Europe, internal difficulties in the Soviet Union itself, and the defeat of the Sandinistas in free elections made the imperative to fight communism on the U.S. doorstep less compelling. Stripped of its anticommunist bottom line, U.S. policy was forced to confront the nature of a key ally in the global struggle against totalitarianism. In this warmer spotlight of a Cold War thaw, Congress saw the practices of the Salvadoran military as appalling and began to cut aid accordingly.

If the Jesuit murders laid bare the military's most brutal instincts, the FMLN offensive also illustrated the lack of widespread popular support for the guerrillas and their willingness to place civilian lives at risk as an essential part of military strategy. In addition, the offensive demonstrated the futility of pursuing what the Pentagon called in 1981 a "victory strategy" in the misguided belief that it would take only a few years. The Bush administration captured a central lesson of the November 1989 offensive—that neither side stood a chance of winning the war—and called for political negotiations to end it. The call for meaningful dialogue as a way of ending the Salvadoran conflict was a radical shift from the Reagan policy.

For the better part of two years, however, the Bush administration cast doubt on the depth of its commitment to a new approach. Public and private criticisms of the U.N. role in the peace talks, and opposition to aid cuts imposed by Congress in the wake of the Jesuit murders, appeared as continued defense of the Salvadoran government at any cost. In reality, threatened or actual aid cuts—structured by Congress to influence Salvadoran government as well as FMLN behavior—signaled the administration and the Salvadoran government that a solution had to be found because support in Congress was drying up. Aid reductions, which the Bush administration fought, indicated that the war— which the Salvadorans perceived as being in El Salvador's and the United States' *mutual* interest—had become a one-sided affair.[11]

The administration appeared divided as well over how vigorously to press the Salvadoran government on the Jesuit murders. The designation of a House task force to monitor the investigation illustrated that issues of military accountability and human rights had become central to U.S. policy in the twilight of the Cold War. Numerous administration missteps, including early attempts to implicate the FMLN in the killings, the burning of several Salvadoran military sources, the harassment of a witness, and the suppression of information from a U.S. military adviser who knew about the murder plot, made it appear that at least some elements of the administration were not interested in a full airing of the truth.

The work of the Moakley task force also demonstrated how fully Congress could deploy its powers of oversight and investigation, even in the face of executive branch resistance. The experience of the task force suggested that some of what Congress claimed not to have known in the early days of Reagan policy was a matter of its own choosing.

Nicaragua and the Roots of the Iran-Contra Affair

Congress's involvement in El Salvador policy suggested that influence over both Salvadoran events and U.S. Salvadoran policy was a product more of confrontation than of bipartisan collaboration with either the Reagan or Bush administrations. The Nicaraguan experience, until U.S. policy ran aground on the shoals of the Iran-contra affair, underscored the limits of influence through either conflict or compromise.

During the Reagan years, key officials of the administration sought to execute policy free of congressional interference. That determination was the product of two attitudes: first, that foreign policy was the prerogative of the president and that Congress had no right to intrude; and second, that the stakes in Nicaragua were high enough to justify exceptional means in combating the communist threat. In both its ideological orientation to Nicaragua policy and its practical attitude toward congressional involvement in policy formation, the Reagan administration operated without regard for a domestic consensus on the ends and means of policy and without exercising the restraint that would have been warranted by the absence of consensus.

The roots of the Iran-contra debacle, then, lie perhaps less in the specific obstacles to contra funding posed by the Congress (particularly the 1984 cutoff of funds) than in deeper tendencies in the Reagan administration. Beginning in 1981 the strident campaigns about communist interference in El Salvador suggested that policy responded not only to regional events but also to broader foreign policy impulses: the placing of local conflicts within the larger framework of U.S.-Soviet competition, and the desire to free the country from the shackles of post-Vietnam anti-interventionism. Once events in peripheral areas of U.S.-Soviet competition assumed such transcendent domestic and international proportions, a certain disengagement between policy prescription and local reality was virtually assured. The supplanting of pragmatism by ideology was one necessary precondition for policy decisions outside the norms of foreign policy decision-making. This was as true for the administration's single-minded determination to secure a change of the Sandinista regime as it was for the commitment to "draw the line" in El Salvador against further communist advancement.

Still, it would be a mistake to view the Reagan administration as uniformly committed to an ideological interpretation of Central America's conflicts. Indeed, a good part of the history of the Reagan administration's first four years reveals persistent internal conflicts: between embassies in the field with an understanding of local problems, and Washington policymakers slow to abandon geopolitical fixations; between those who accepted congressional activism in foreign policy as a legitimate part of the governmental system, and those who rejected it as improper meddling; between those who viewed domestic consensus as something to be built through discussion and compromise, and those who sought it by coercion. A second precondition for the unfolding of the Iran-contra affair, then, was the resolution of internal policy struggles in favor of a group of individuals less interested in the normal give-and-take of policy formation than in the implementation of Reagan's agenda in the hemisphere at any cost.

That internal shift in the balance of power occurred most decisively in mid-1983 with the ouster of Assistant Secretary of State Thomas Enders. Enders had privately advocated negotiations with the Nicaraguan government over security issues as a way of capitalizing on pressures exerted by the contras; after his removal, the idea of negotiating a settlement with the Sandinistas disappeared from serious consideration, even though pursuit of such a settlement remained a stated objective of Reagan policy.

The National Security Council wrested internal bureaucratic power away from the State Department at the height of difficulties in implementing regional policies and in securing congressional support. As President Reagan himself stepped into the forefront of policy promotion, these obstacles were seen less as the product of the wrong policies and more as a failure to pursue them with enough vigor and resources. A symbolic turning point in administration deference to congressional sensitivities was the staging of large-scale military maneuvers in the region on the eve of a congressional vote to end covert operations against Nicaragua. The White House's new sense of urgency and redoubled commitment led to recklessness, even as it began its successful attempt to dominate policy discussion and transform the Central American imbroglio into a key issue of domestic political concern.

Once the administration determined that the nature of the Sandinista regime, rather than the nature of its policies, posed an irreconcilable threat to U.S. interests, it felt compelled—indeed, entitled—to act on that conviction. A constantly shifting set of rationales was put forward as justification for U.S. sponsorship of the contras, but in Senator Richard Lugar's words, "In your heart of hearts you [the Reagan administration] really have the overthrow of the Nicaraguan government in mind."[12] In approving contra aid in 1985 and 1986, Congress fell victim to the administration's rhetorical ability to describe its purposes in ways that were politically palatable. A core group of moderates actually believed in the administration's newfound moderation, even if the rationales masked a deeper objective that the majority of Congress and the

American public rejected. Consider, for example, the words of contra leader Adolfo Calero:

> First we are told that the official cover story for the armed opposition is that we're helping to interdict arms traffic from Nicaragua to leftist guerrillas in El Salvador. OK, so we went along with the story. Why not? Then the story became that our struggle was to force the Sandinistas to restore democracy. Then the story was that we were fighting to force the Sandinistas to negotiate with the opposition, including with us, the opposition in exile. In the end, we don't know what the administration wants us to fight for. [13]

The constantly shifting rationales suggested not a genuine change of purpose in response to congressional skepticism, but rather political expediency, if not genuine confusion within the administration over the goals of its Nicaragua policy.

Despite its apparent conviction about the need to replace the Sandinistas, however, the Reagan administration was never able to get Congress to go along with that objective. At first, members of congressional intelligence committees voted funds for a program ostensibly aimed at arms interdiction, in light of what it viewed as convincing evidence that the Sandinistas were providing support to Salvadoran revolutionaries.* From the earliest days of U.S. involvement in the contra war, however, the administration provoked considerable debate over the

---

*Those views would radically change with time. In 1992, Representative Lee Hamilton, a member of the House Foreign Affairs Committee and former chairman of the Intelligence Committee wrote: "During the early 1980s . . . several members of Congress, including myself, knew that U.S. intelligence did not support President Reagan's claim that Nicaragua's Sandinista government was shipping 'a flood of arms' to communist guerrillas in El Salvador, but we were unable to respond to the president's assertions because the information was classified." In a similar post–Cold War revelation, former Senate Intelligence Committee Vice-Chairman Daniel Moynihan said that in December 1983 he began to press the CIA on the issue of Sandinista arms smuggling to El Salvador. "Show us one, I would ask. I mean one shotgun. They couldn't produce a shotgun shell. (They did come up with an infrared film, taken from the air, of a small boat landing on the Salvadoran coast. It looked like two amoeba mating under a microscope.) It became clear that the administration was lying." Lee H. Hamilton, "The Costs of Too Much Secrecy," *Washington Post*, April 13, 1992; Daniel Patrick Moynihan, "System of Secrecy Has Served Liars Well," *Albany Times Union*, May 3, 1992, reprinted in Center for National Security Studies, *First Principles*, vol. 17 (July 1992), pp. 11–12.

means of U.S. policy. Drawing on the memory of prior failed covert operations, members of Congress questioned whether a trained exile force was succeeding in interdicting arms, whether such a large-scale undertaking could remain secret, and whether a secret foreign policy was consistent with domestic values and democratic practices.

These doubts heightened when the behavior and statements of contra troops suggested that *their* aim was the more expansive one of overthrowing the Sandinistas; members of Congress then questioned not only the means of U.S. policy but also the ends—whether the Reagan administration also harbored dreams of replacing the Nicaraguan government. It is noteworthy that the administration was not able to convince Congress to support contra funding until it abandoned rhetoric of forcing the Sandinistas to "say uncle" and began speaking of positive goals, such as bringing democracy to Nicaragua or enhancing the prospects for a negotiated solution. Even then, however, it was less than clear how democratic pluralism would emerge in Nicaragua from the ashes of the contra war.

Ultimately, confusion in the Reagan administration's approach helped prove the undoing of the contra program. The administration attempted simultaneously to maintain that the purpose of arming the contras was to pressure the Sandinistas into making concessions to their neighbors and internal opponents and that negotiations with Marxist-Leninists were pointless because they would not negotiate in good faith and would use discussions only to buy time to consolidate their power. The lack of consensus within the Reagan camp that negotiations were the desired end of U.S. policy left administration officials in the unenviable position of claiming that whatever concessions the Sandinistas made were always insufficient.

However, many if not most of the congressional swing voters who came to support President Reagan on Nicaragua policy believed in the validity of negotiations as a way to resolve U.S. differences with Nicaragua. Even where the president was able to convince a segment of Congress of the need for a military component to U.S. policy, he was not able to erase the preference for diplomacy as a means of resolving international disputes. This became especially clear in the Congress's wide embrace of the Arias plan, particularly as it began to produce results. Hence, even if a critical group of congressmen believed that the use of force in international politics could lead an opponent to make concessions, that same group also believed that force was an instrument, rather than an end in itself. The Reagan administration never reconciled these opposing views, ultimately relying on the contras as a middle ground between negotiations with the Sandinistas, constrained by divisions internal to the administration, and stronger measures to oust the Sandinistas—by direct U.S. intervention—which were limited by the lack of domestic support.

Still, the success of the Reagan administration in garnering support for the contra policy testified to certain boundaries implicit in U.S. domestic debate during the Cold War. The virtual syllogism in American politics that "if you are Marxist you have to be bad,"[14] and the endurance of anticommunism as a fundamental component of a postwar foreign policy consensus, created a strong reserve of sympathy for a tough policy toward the Sandinistas. The Reagan administration's success in dominating the debate, moreover, meant that policy discussions often consisted not of what members believed but of what they felt they could say. Similarly, the constant search for congressional alternatives—as much to provide political cover for Reagan opponents as to contribute to successful policy—attested to a perceived imperative to "do something" about Nicaragua, regardless of the logic of a proposed course. Repeated infusions of what Congress called humanitarian contra aid, for example, had less to do with a coherent policy alternative than with the political imperative not to get blamed for abandoning the contras. The House in particular tried to have it both ways, posing as a brake on Reagan administration policy out of Vietnam-era fears that the United States was being drawn into a deeper conflict in Nicaragua, while giving the president most of what he wanted in order not to be vulnerable to the "soft on communism" charge.[15]

Reagan dominated the debate—both over the nature of the Sandinista regime and over U.S. stakes in the conflict—because congressional opponents found it intuitively more expedient not to fight the administration on its turf. This said as much about the perceived limits of domestic political tolerance as it did about the convictions of administration critics.

Because of the limits posed by domestic politics and the strength of the Reagan presidency, the debate over Nicaragua during Reagan's two terms took place over incidentals or over the politically "safe" insistence that Democrats shared all the administration's stated goals in Nicaragua but had a better way to accomplish them. Thus, two central questions of post-Vietnam foreign policy—how to interact with those states having undergone revolution, and whether those states posed such a threat that U.S. interests could only be guaranteed with their removal—dropped from the congressional agenda. Advocates of the Contadora regional negotiations, for example, implicitly argued that U.S. security interests could be satisfactorily addressed through negotiations, spearheaded by Latin American allies, leading to a verifiable treaty. What these advocates failed to say, even though they rejected the administration's view, was that radically altering the internal structure of the Nicaraguan regime was not a precondition to settling security issues—that is, that only through transforming the nature of the Nicaraguan government could U.S. interests be secured.

The position that the internal configuration of states was of inherent interest to the United States and that the United States had a moral and universal interest in the way governments treated their citizens had been a cornerstone of the liberal argument for the centrality of human rights considerations in U.S. foreign policy. The Reagan administration thus borrowed from liberal concerns and took them one step further, positing that the internal nature of the Sandinista regime was the rightful object of U.S. policy and that an interest in democracy justified the sponsorship of armed insurgency. In convincing a segment of the Congress that military force should be deployed to bring about democracy, the Reagan administration dramatically altered the political debate. In contrast to prevailing attitudes in the 1970s, members of Congress who came to support the contra policy seemed to be saying that not all killing was objectionable; the central question was whether U.S.-sponsored violence was likely to achieve stated goals.

The blending of security concerns with a more idealistic, if not transcendent, purpose to American policy was not unique to the Reagan approach; precisely such a combination was credited with containment's long survival as a cornerstone of postwar foreign policy.[16] But in the Western Hemisphere there has perhaps been no greater historical disjuncture than between the stated idealistic purposes of U.S. policy and the actual result of U.S. involvement. Reagan administration policy in Nicaragua was no exception to this pattern. The notion that a society could be made democratic by means of an armed rebellion was cast in doubt by the insurgent leaders' very lack of democratic credentials, by their pervasive abuses in the conduct of the war, and by authoritarian measures the Sandinistas themselves justified by the existence of an external threat.[17] Indeed, these are the reasons that Reagan administration critics viewed the Reagan Doctrine not as a new global policy but as little more than a much needed justification for the ravages of U.S. policy in Central America.[18]

Ultimately the Reagan administration's expansive view of the presidency carried within it the seeds of its own destruction. Sooner or later the secret effort on behalf of the contras would be exposed to public scrutiny, because operations of such scale and duration are difficult to keep covert indefinitely. Disclosure of the administration's deception in carrying out Nicaragua policy invited Congress to take drastic measures to restore equilibrium between the two branches, if only to reassert the primacy of law in a constitutional government.

The holding of the Iran-contra hearings demonstrated that presidential power was relative, not absolute, and that even national-security policy had to operate within the limits defined by political culture. The notions that governments in a democracy must be accountable to the governed as well as to the governors, that the public has a right to know, and that the United States has presidents and not kings, accounted for the widely felt shock over actions that were clearly within the power of the president to take. The very convening of the hearings was its own remedy of sorts, a deterrent against future temptation at misconduct. Recalling John Poindexter's insistence that he did not tell President Reagan of the diversion of funds to the contras, Representative Lee Hamilton observed, "It's going to be a long time before you hear a National Security Adviser say 'the buck stops with me.' "[19]

President Bush took office determined to drain the Central American poison from the U.S. political system. The scenario he inherited was not a politically attractive one. Congress had cut off military aid to the contras in the wake of the Iran-contra scandal, and guilty pleas and pending indictments of several Reagan officials issued by the office of independent counsel Lawrence M. Walsh illustrated that the Reagan policy had been not only controversial but also illegal. With the prospects for resuming the contra war virtually nonexistent, Bush sought the most graceful exit he could by striking a deal with Congress. The bipartisan accord over contra aid protected both the president and Congress from charges of having abandoned the contras altogether, while narrowing policy objectives. Centering its approach on provisions of the Central America peace plan, the Bush administration turned its attention to the promotion of a free election in Nicaragua. Democracy, which had served as a banner of war during one stage of the contra effort to overthrow the Sandinistas, was quickly hoisted as the banner of defeat.[20]

The 1990 electoral victory of Violeta Barrios de Chamorro sent contra supporters and opponents alike rushing to claim credit for the outcome. Supporters of the Reagan policy argued that without contra pressure on the Sandinistas there would have been no elections, while critics maintained that elections were possible only because President Bush declined to seek military support for the rebels and sought a regional, negotiated settlement.[21] The reality, however, was more complex. If the contra war created the need for a Central America peace plan in the first place, it was not clear that only war could have produced free elections. Moreover, the elections that were a cornerstone of the Arias peace plan were never a contra or Reagan administration goal.

The Sandinistas did view elections as a means of increasing their legitimacy and contributing to international pressures to end the contra war.[22] But holding the elections in February 1990 was not necessarily a concession to internal opponents or to the United States. (Elections had been scheduled for November of that year.) The Sandinistas not only firmly believed that they would win the election but also wanted international observers present in order to ratify and authenticate that victory.* International legitimacy was particularly important as Soviet economic and military aid dropped off in 1989 and the Sandinistas sought financial backing elsewhere, particularly in Western Europe.[23]

If the Sandinistas came to view the 1990 elections as a way of legitimizing their own rule and thereby of ending the war, they perhaps shared the analysis of Reagan administration officials, who rejected elections for precisely that reason. The architects of the contra policy believed that a military victory would be possible after Congress approved contra military aid in 1986 and that it was fruitless to use democratic means to defeat the Sandinistas. Those convictions help explain not only the efforts in 1984 to convince the Nicaraguan opposition to withdraw from the presidential elections, but also the widespread hostility to the Central America peace plan and its emphasis on internal democratization.

To demonstrate the Reagan administration's lack of faith in anything but military force, one need only recall Reagan's dire warning in March 1988 that "those who led the fight against our package of assistance to the democratic resistance cannot escape responsibility for what happened"[24] or the words of Elliott Abrams, who described progress in the peace process in early 1989 as a "step backward on the road to democracy and peace": "Does anyone really believe that an election conducted with the full Sandinista military and police apparatus of repression intact would be truly free?"[25]

Support for the elections was one of the only realistic options available to the Bush administration given the domestic rancor and bitterness occasioned by the Reagan policy. Shifts in tone, style, and substance created a basis for cooperation with the Congress to continue an anti-Sandinista policy. The administration openly sought, and Congress provided funds to help ensure, an opposition electoral victory. The funding of one side in the Nicaraguan election demonstrated how partisan involvement in the domestic politics of another country could be justified politically in the name of supporting democracy, even if such support would be illegal if pursued in a U.S. context.[26] Once again, however, part of Congress's motivation was defensive. Opponents of Reagan's policy in

---

*Consider, for example, the remarks of Sandinista commander Dora María Téllez: "Sandinism governed with a perspective of eternal power, in part due to known historical experiences. Revolutionary forces, once they had taken power, would be there forever. We were convinced, and we convinced others outside the country, that we were going to win the elections. We didn't realize the opposite; even on February 25, [1990], we didn't understand it clearly." Quoted in "El Socialismo Pasa Por la Solución del Problema Nacional," *L'avispa*, April–May 1991, pp. 8–23.

Nicaragua who supported electoral funding under President Bush did so partly to avoid being blamed if the opposition lost to the Sandinistas.

The results of the 1990 Nicaraguan election, however, lent themselves to something less than Bush's triumphant view that "free elections brought democracy to Nicaragua."[27] As in the case of El Salvador, President Bush equated the holding of an election with the advent of democracy, ignoring questions of civilian control over the armed forces and accountability under the law. The deep polarization of Nicaraguan society after the ravages of the contra war and a decade of Sandinista authoritarianism left little room for optimism that democratic practices would flourish. Rather, polarization, intensified by the economic ruin explicitly sought by U.S. policy, seemed to head Nicaragua into new rounds of confrontation and violence. One of the most true lessons of the contra war may be that once a small, impoverished country had been brought to its knees[28] the task of resurrecting its economy and fostering political pluralism posed the greater challenge. By then, however, both the administration and the Congress appeared to have lost interest.

The Domestic Legacy

The decade of Central American wars brought economic devastation and massive loss of life to El Salvador and Nicaragua. It also injected cynicism and distrust into U.S. political life. In order to pursue policies they deemed vital to the national interest, Reagan administration policymakers withheld information from Congress, committed perjury, and obstructed justice. These acts formed the core of the Iran-contra scandal. The domestic deception—rather than the foreign policies that deception obscured—formed the basis for criminal convictions and indictments of several senior officials. During a six-year period and at a cost of more than $31 million, Independent Counsel Lawrence Walsh secured convictions of four Reagan administration officials for lying and withholding information from Congress.*

*Former CIA Deputy Director for Operations Clair E. George was convicted in December 1992 on two counts of lying to Congress. Former Assistant Secretary of State for Inter-American Affairs Elliott Abrams pleaded guilty in October 1991 to two counts of withholding information from Congress. Former Chief of the CIA's Central America Task Force Alan D. Fiers Jr. pleaded guilty in July 1991 to two counts of withholding information from Congress. Former National Security Adviser Robert C. McFarlane pleaded guilty in March 1988 to four charges of withholding information from Congress.

On December 24, 1992, and as he prepared to leave office, President Bush issued pardons of six Reagan administration officials, including the four who had been convicted and two others, including former Defense Secretary Caspar Weinberger, scheduled to go to trial in early 1993. In issuing the pardons, Bush stated that he objected to the "criminalization of policy differences" and said that those differences "should be addressed in the political arena."[29] Special Prosecutor Walsh countered that the pardons "undermine[d] the principle that no man is above the law" and charged that "the Iran-contra coverup . . . has now been completed."[30] Walsh charged that Bush had concealed his own notes of official conversations from the Iran-contra days, implying that the president had issued the pardons in part to avoid being implicated in the scandal.[31]

Whatever Bush's motive, he issued the pardons without specifically stating that what had taken place was wrong. He thereby seemed to affirm that the executive branch was free to lie and mislead Congress in defense of policy goals, thereby undermining our own democracy. Even if policy differences did lie behind some of the illegal acts, political controversy did not require official deception. Indeed, according to House Majority Leader Richard Gephardt, the secrecy protected "ill-founded foreign policy decisions that never would have been made in the light of day."[32]

Gephardt's comment raised a central question: whether Congress would have acted differently toward Nicaragua and El Salvador if members had had the information concealed by the administration. In the case of Nicaragua, the answer is almost a certain yes. By passing a law banning support for the contras in 1984 Congress meant for the program to end. The resumption of nonlethal aid in mid-1985—necessary because, the administration said, the contras were in desperate straits—might never have occurred had Congress known of the administration's orchestration of an extensive private and third-country network of contra military support. It is true that the chairmen of relevant congressional committees were timid in exploring press reports of the private support network, but perhaps those members can be forgiven their belief that, when they posed a direct question to administration officials, they were entitled to a truthful answer. *

Former Secretary of Defense Caspar W. Weinberger and former CIA official Duane R. Clarridge were scheduled to go to trial in 1993, on charges of perjury and making false statements to Congress.

*At times, the congressional efforts to get information were quite precise and the administration lies quite blatant. Following the October 1986 downing of the Hasenfus plane carrying supplies to the contras, House Intelligence Committee Staff Director Tom Latimore and Counsel Michael O'Neil were briefed by CIA Central America Task Force

In the case of El Salvador it is more difficult to judge whether Congress would have ended or significantly restricted military aid had the full extent of Salvadoran government involvement in political violence been acknowledged. The regime's miserable performance on human rights matters throughout the 1980s was a matter of public record. But the congressional majority acceded to the administration's requests to increase aid in order to secure a quintessential Cold War goal: forestalling a guerrilla victory. Moreover, some members of Congress had access to classified U.S. reports that admitted Salvadoran government complicity in brutal acts. Greater truthfulness might have altered the balance in May 1984, a key moment when the House decided to send unrestricted aid to the Duarte government by a mere four-vote margin. Even then, however, debate would have continued over the means but not the ends of policy. At a minimum, greater disclosure could have spared Congress and the public the corrosive effect of a debate based on a whitewash of Salvadoran government practices. It could also arguably have saved lives in El Salvador.

Who Runs Foreign Policy

The distinctions over what might have happened are important because critics of congressional involvement in Central America policy asserted that an "imperial Congress" improperly tread on presidential prerogatives or left a public record that was so contradictory and imprecise that the executive had to take matters into its own hands.[33] In fact, the record of congressional involvement with El Salvador and Nicaragua showed that Congress acted timidly at first in opposing administration policy, challenging administration officials in open hearings, sending letters of concern, and adopting mild legislative restrictions such as the certification and the first Boland amendment. The attitude that the

---

chief Alan Fiers and three other CIA officials. According to a CIA memo on the meeting, O'Neil noted that "the Agency had no problem reporting on information it received regarding the private aid effort, but it did not follow up by finding out who ultimately was behind the aid effort." O'Neil told the CIA officers that "the members will not believe that the Agency does not know where the money to finance the private aid was coming from." Fiers responded with a deliberate distortion, saying that "it is extremely difficult to track down the source of funding" and that if the Saudis or the Israelis were behind it, "it would be almost impossible to trace the money back to them." In fact, the United States had arranged the Saudi and Israeli involvement some years before. CIA, Memorandum for the Record, "Subject: HPSCI Staff Briefing on Crash of C-123 in Nicaragua," October 16, 1986, p. 2.

president ran foreign policy, and that if one intended to challenge him it had better be for good reason, dominated early discussions of Central America policy.

Congressional activism accelerated, however, as the administration pursued policies outside the mainstream of opinion and then failed to accommodate congressional concerns. The increasingly restrictive measures adopted by the Congress throughout 1983 and 1984 illustrated that presidential authority depended less on a sense of his constitutional mandate than on sound policy and styles of leadership. "The hackneyed lament that there are now 535 congressmen aspiring to be secretary of state is not true," observed former Senate Foreign Relations Committee Chairman Richard Lugar.[34] Rather, by viewing conflicts with the Congress as a zero-sum game, President Reagan heightened confrontation over both the style and substance of his leadership.

Within Congress, meanwhile, the need for compromise in order to obtain a majority often resulted in legislation reflecting more the correlation of political forces in the United States than coherent policy judgment. This tendency was exacerbated by the deep policy divisions among administration opponents in the Congress and by the need to reconcile House and Senate versions of the same bill. The end result of negotiation was at times a combination of the disadvantages of several approaches, while important policy issues were submerged. Legislation providing aid to the contras, in which the precise composition of nonlethal aid or the appropriate agency of government to deliver it were principal subjects of debate, exemplified this problem.

The struggle to define the proper roles for Congress and the executive in foreign policy did not begin with the Central America debate, nor did it end there. The rules of engagement spelled out in the U.S. Constitution are themselves vague, inviting conflict over relationships of power. In an equally basic sense, disputes will endure because they are inherently political, deriving from judgments over correct policy. Indeed, some of the arguments over Congress's proper foreign policy role would not exist absent the more substantive political struggles.

The effort to enact legislation as a more permanent corrective to the abuses constituting the Iran-contra affair met with only limited success during the Bush years. In late 1990, President Bush pocket-vetoed provisions of the Intelligence Oversight Act that would have required the president to report to Congress any "request" to a third party to carry out a covert action on behalf of the United States. The bill also contained a requirement that Congress be informed within a few days, without exception, of the initiation of a covert operation, thereby limiting the existing provision that Congress be notified in a "timely fashion."*

A compromise bill signed by the president in August 1991 contained such significant loopholes that it was difficult to say whether congressional oversight had been strengthened. The president had to inform Congress if a third party participated "in any significant way," but the law did not require that the party be named. Similarly, Congress stated its belief that notification of covert operations in a "timely fashion" meant within a few days, but recognized that the president could invoke constitutional authority to withhold notification for a longer period.[35] At the end of Bush's term, and six years after the Iran-contra scandal erupted, Congress had failed to take any significant step to alter the balance of power in the conduct of foreign policy. This signified that basic foreign policy roles, with the president leading and the Congress reviewing and advising, continued with only minor adjustments.

Congress and Central America:
The Meaning of the Conflict

This inquiry began with a twin observation: that for a period of time President Reagan was able to prevail in obtaining congressional backing for his policies in El Salvador and Nicaragua, but that the difficulty encountered by the adminis-tration and the intensity of the conflict with the Congress was exceptional, particularly given executive branch advantages over the legislature in carrying out foreign policy. The Central America crisis of the 1980s illustrated the enduring power of the presidency to set a foreign policy agenda and, over time, secure the necessary congressional backing to implement it.

The Central America conflict was far more, however, than a simple contest

---

*The president's Memorandum of Disapproval stated that he "cannot accept the broad language" requiring notification of any " 'request' by the United States to a foreign government or a private citizen to conduct a covert action on behalf of the United States." Bush also said that the requirement to notify Congress "within a few days" of the beginning of covert operations "would unconstitutionally infringe on the authority of the President and impair any administration's effective implementation of covert action programs." George Bush, The White House, November 30, 1990, quoted in Gary M. Stern, "Bush Vetoes Post Iran-Contra Intelligence Oversight Legislation," *First Principles*, vol. 15 (December 1990), p. 9.

over the right to exercise foreign policy prerogatives. During the Reagan years, it took on more essential meaning, involving a redefinition of the purposes of American power and the objectives for which it is deployed. As much as the Reagan administration might have wanted to use Central America as a vehicle for fashioning a new foreign policy consensus, the results of that effort were decidedly mixed. In the 1970s the Vietnam War had shattered an existing consensus over the extent of U.S. interests and the desirability of using military force to protect such interests as were worthy of defense. In regard to Central America, the public's resistance to sending troops indicated that the central feature of the "Vietnam syndrome," an unwillingness to pay in blood to determine who would run a foreign country, endured. Reagan administration attempts to overcome that resistance failed in light of the ongoing conviction that military involvement in Central America would be costly and protracted, on behalf of uncertain allies, and in pursuit of nebulous goals.

Moreover, administration efforts to turn the Vietnam analogy on its head—to suggest that failure to support administration policy would lead to the very interventions the public feared—succeeded not in drumming up support for administration initiatives but in reviving suspicions that the administration intended to deploy military force. The persistence of a post-Vietnam reluctance to intervene in Central America was all the more remarkable given the history of U.S. involvement in the region, a history built on assumptions of predominance and on enthusiasm for curtailing communist influence or simply maintaining control.

It is over Nicaragua policy that the departure from a post-Vietnam context was most pronounced. Members of Congress did not dispute the desirability of preventing the Sandinistas from exporting their revolution or allying itself more closely with the Soviet bloc, because those ends were consistent with preserving U.S. security through a policy of containment. Yet a segment of the Congress was willing to go further, to fund the application of indirect military force for the purpose of producing reforms in the internal nature of the Sandinista government. Congress and the Reagan administration differed over what such pressure was intended produce—capitulation at the bargaining table or the demise of the Sandinista regime. But the Reagan administration was at least partially successful in relegitimizing the covert and even overt destabilization of foreign governments and in getting Congress to support it through military, albeit non-U.S. military means.

Congress's willingness to fund the contras may have represented only a temporary shift in elite attitudes toward the purposes of American power. The persistence of bitter, partisan debate, the slender vote margins, and the prominence of domestic factors in producing congressional turnarounds indicated that circumstances at least as much as conviction played a key role in administration victories. Nonetheless, President Reagan sparked a debate that would have been unthinkable in the years immediately after Vietnam, when Congress was bent on curtailing U.S. covert operations and when nonintervention was a foreign policy, if not moral imperative.

The demise of the Cold War removed the central anticommunist rationale for U.S. interventions but did not appear to have expunged the Vietnam syndrome from the American consciousness. Had the Bush administration's December 1989 invasion of Panama turned from a blitzkrieg into a protracted, bloody affair, there is little doubt that domestic debate would have forced a revision of military strategy and possibly U.S. withdrawal. Moreover, the extensive congressional debate prior to the 1991 war in the Persian Gulf was testimony to the deep reluctance to engage abroad militarily. That Congress authorized the use of force prior to the war with Iraq suggested that policymakers could be convinced that some goals were worth fighting for, as long as those goals were spelled out in advance and embodied some compelling notion of the national interest. The 1992 deployment of troops to Somalia appeared to meet both those conditions, reflecting both the urgency of humanitarian tasks and the sense that the cost in U.S. lives could be kept to a minimum.

To draw sweeping conclusions about the demise of the Vietnam syndrome during the Bush administration or to take credit for such a demise would thus be a mistake. Neither Reagan nor Bush transformed a proscriptive injunction not to intervene militarily in the developing world into a shared consensus over the circumstances in which such intervention would be warranted. The end of the Cold War removed one pretext for the debate, simultaneously revealing the enormous complexity of issues facing the post–Cold War world. The intractability of underdevelopment, racial intolerance, and tribal and ethnic conflict—at times made worse by the imposition of superpower competition—showed just how inadequate the East-West prism had been for viewing, let alone solving, foreign policy problems.

Central America at the Crossroads

In September 1979, during the Carter years, then-Assistant Secretary of State for Inter-American Affairs Viron P. Vaky told a congressional subcommittee that Central America stood at a crossroads. Violence, poverty, and demands for social equity made change inevitable, he said. "The central issue . . . is not whether change is to occur but whether that change is to be violent and radical, or peaceful and evolutionary, and preserving individual rights and democratic values."[36]

But change in the late 1970s and 1980s was violent, in part because prior U.S. administrations had ignored demands for change until they had come to a boil. And once those wars erupted over issues of economic justice and an end to institutional violence, they quickly became matters of U.S. national security. The tragedy for Central Americans was not only the interposing of superpower conflict on their struggles for economic and political modernization, but also the particular vehemence with which U.S. Cold War ideology was applied.

Accept, for the sake of argument, that preventing the FMLN from taking power in El Salvador and preventing the Sandinistas from spreading their revolution and consolidating an authoritarian system were appropriate U.S. goals. It does not follow that whitewashing the record of the Salvadoran government was necessary, or that an alternative solution in El Salvador based on political negotiations would not have been possible much earlier in the decade. The refusal of the Reagan administration to consider anything other than a negotiated surrender of the FMLN made such negotiations impossible, just as its defense of indefensible army conduct prolonged army abuses.[37] Similarly, the exaggerated demonization of the Sandinista regime was intended to foreclose nonmilitary options as the contra war in Nicaragua became an end in itself. But that war promised little more than unending bloodshed even if the contras had emerged victorious and the Sandinistas had retreated to the hills to wage their own renewed guerrilla struggle.[38]

It is not clear even with hindsight that alternative policies toward El Salvador or Nicaragua would have borne fruit. But that does not absolve the Reagan administration for never having tried, or for standing in the way of regional allies who sought peaceful solutions long before Bush did, however halting and inconsistent his efforts.

The March 1993 release of the U.N. Truth Commission's report on El Salvador momentarily refocused U.S. attention on Central America. But the lack of interest in helping Central Americans rebuild their shattered lands contrasted starkly with the single-mindedness of U.S. efforts to wage war in the 1980s.[39] Given that proving the United States's consistency as an ally served as a key rationale for U.S. involvement in the region a decade ago, the disregard can at best be called ironic.

Under the Clinton administration, the relative inattention was also a question of resources. Pressing domestic needs initially overshadowed the interest in foreign policy, except for urgent crises, such as those in the former Soviet Union or the former Yugoslavia, that could not be ignored. The pattern of U.S. involvement in Central America thus appeared to be coming full circle, with the region retreating to its traditional obscurity as long as the threat of upheaval remained in check.

Hopefully, the Clinton administration would find that contributing positively to reconciliation and reconstruction was as much a matter of consistent focus and diplomatic engagement as it was of financial commitment, and that smaller amounts of aid properly directed could help alleviate some of the root causes of the conflict. Unless political energies are directed at overcoming polarization, and economic resources are aimed at rebuilding, the United States may someday find that it has bought time but not peace in the region. Neglect could lead to new cycles of instability and violence. And that would only compound the enormous suffering Central Americans have already endured.

Epilogue

The report of the United Nations Commission on the Truth for El Salvador, published on March 15, 1993, reopened a policy debate in the United States over U.S. involvement in the Salvadoran war. Secretary of State Warren Christopher, speaking for a new Democratic administration and noting that he was "deeply shocked" by the report, appointed a small panel to "examine the activities and conduct of the [State] Department" during the period covered by the Truth Commission report.[1] One reason for the panel, Christopher said, was "to make sure that our human rights reporting was not in some way stifled by political considerations."[2] Christopher appointed two retired foreign service officers, George Vest and Richard Murphy, to head the inquiry.*

*The panel's review was to include "responsiveness to congressional and public inquiries, human rights reporting, and the degree to which we encouraged State Department

In addition, and in response to a specific congressional request, President Bill Clinton agreed to declassify documents relating to thirty-two cases of political violence investigated by the Truth Commission. Clinton wrote members of Congress on June 7, 1993, that the State and Defense Departments had set a September deadline for reviewing documents for declassification and that the CIA would review documents on an "expedited basis." Clinton promised "to provide the maximum possible material" while protecting intelligence sources and methods.[3] Reflecting the administration's desire to make public as much as possible, Christopher told a Senate subcommittee in late March 1993 that "embarrassment is not a national interest."[4]

After a three-month inquiry, the State Department Panel on El Salvador issued its report on July 15, 1993. It found overall that U.S. Embassy officers "performed well on human rights issues" and that the State Department and foreign service personnel "performed creditably—and on occasion with personal bravery" in advancing human rights in El Salvador. The panel noted the contribution of U.S. ambassadors in pushing their staffs to prepare "honest, detailed human rights reports for Washington" and did not find evidence overall that information had been withheld from members of Congress. Nor did it find that the change in administrations in 1981 "sent ambassadors and reporting officers scurrying to trim their sails." Although limiting its evaluation to issues of human rights performance, and not to overall U.S. policy toward El Salvador, the panel did characterize the policy's basic lines: "Support for a moderate but shaky government's economic and political reform efforts, assistance to the Salvadoran military to defeat the FMLN, and efforts to improve the country's human rights and social conditions."[5]

The panel coupled this overall praise for State Department conduct with a number of criticisms. Annual human rights reports to Congress were tailored to bolster policy by "limit[ing] the scope of condemnations of rightist actions and add[ing] details on abuses by the leftists." Policy advocacy on occasion "spilled over into statements that were perceived as misleading Congress or conveying 'disinformation,' " even though the panel said it found "no instances of officials intentionally lying" to Congress. Certain "egregious statements" in the early 1980s, however, "conveyed a message of callousness that the public media magnified." Moreover, the panel said, U.S. officials spent as much time

---

officers to conduct a full and independent inquiry of abuses by both sides in the civil conflict." Office of the Assistant Secretary/Spokesman, "Statement by Secretary Christopher," March 24, 1993, in U.S. Department of State, *Dispatch*, vol. 4, no. 13, March 29, 1993, p. 188.

attempting to counter the arguments of human rights organizations as in "finding ways to work together."[6]

The toughest criticism in the report was directed at the handling of the 1981 Salvadoran army massacre at the town of El Mozote (see Chapter Four of this book). The panel found that administration officials drew selectively on embassy reporting to discount reports of a major massacre and to counter critics, something that "left the Department vulnerable when it did not have all the facts." Exhumations carried out in 1992 showed that "the Department had been wrong."* The panel also criticized former Secretary of State Alexander Haig for his assertion that the U.S. churchwomen murdered in El Salvador in 1980 might have been killed while trying to run a roadblock (see Chapter Three). Said the panel: Haig's statement "was a clear mistake which should have been labeled as such immediately."[7]

These criticisms aside, the bulk of the panel's report accepts the State Department's own view that officials and foreign service personnel pressed vigorously on human rights matters. The report thus paints a distorted picture.

First, the report underestimates the effect in El Salvador of the Department's admitted "pulling of punches to support the policy." Annual human rights reports to Congress "put a more positive gloss" on the human rights situation than was warranted, said the report, emphasizing FMLN abuses while minimizing abuses by the government. Human rights certifications to Congress compelled officials to demonstrate that a "bad situation was indeed getting better . . . since it quickly became obvious that the Administration was not about to yield to critics by cutting off aid."[8]

Nowhere did the panel discuss, however, how the diminishing of Salvadoran government abuses for the purposes of policy advocacy sent the message to Salvadoran forces that Washington would defend them regardless of their behavior. The panel failed to recognize the trade-off between public defense of government actions and the effectiveness of private pressures on human rights

---

*According to the panel, U.S. Ambassador to El Salvador Deane Hinton complained in a February 1982 cable that he was uncomfortable with the way officials in Washington were characterizing his position on the massacre. "Additional evidence strongly suggests," he wrote, "that something happened that should not have happened and that it is quite possible Salvadoran military did commit excesses."

Elsewhere, the panel's report states that the "circumstances of this lapse on El Mozote were not typical, they were the exception." Nonetheless, the handling of El Mozote "damaged the Department's credibility and that of the Administration as a whole." U.S. Department of State, "Report of the Secretary of State's Panel on El Salvador," July 1993, pp. 21, 34–35, 57.

matters. Because of the upbeat public portrayals of the human rights situation, the principal message the Salvadoran military *received* was that they could count on a steady stream of aid no matter what. The message sent by the State Department and other U.S. agencies during the period of the worst abuses—that the Salvadoran government's effort to defeat the FMLN was vital to U.S. security—undercut any private insistence that human rights improvements were central to U.S. policy.

Second, throughout the 1980s, the Carter, Reagan, and Bush administrations sought to characterize political violence as emanating from extremes of the left and right, thereby deflecting attention from abuses committed by government soldiers. The report continued this pattern, asserting that "violence came from both the left and the right" but that "human rights violations by the right were particularly blatant" in the early 1980s.[9] The report's continuing failure to emphasize the government's central role in human rights abuses showed how deeply ingrained that attitude was within the State Department and foreign service. The flawed characterization was even more striking in light of the U.N. Truth Commission's finding that the vast majority of human rights violations were carried out by government forces and death squads allied with them.[10]

The report admitted to policy differences between the State Department, the CIA, and the National Security Council but implied that it was other agencies, not the State Department, that failed to perform on human rights matters. The Defense Department and intelligence agencies "had prosecution of the war (i.e. not human rights issues) as their primary mission," according to officials interviewed by the panel.[11] This assertion both underplayed State Department responsibility for the failure to promote human rights and highlighted a central limitation of the panel's inquiry.

The panel's mandate did not permit it to investigate other U.S. government agencies involved in policy toward El Salvador, and it was not empowered to evaluate overall U.S. policy. Nonetheless, the panel made repeated characterizations of U.S. policy along the lines of what State Department officials themselves maintained: that policy was designed to promote human rights, to prosecute the war, and to build Salvadoran democracy and institutions. Without taking into account the numerous instances in which the U.S. government sent conflicting signals on human rights matters, including on issues of such overriding importance as the death squads (see Chapter Five), the panel should have avoided policy judgments altogether. By not examining the multiplicity of policy actors, the report's characterizations of policy are inaccurate.*

*The report does note one of the most egregious episodes of mixed signals, that involving

The report gives false credit to embassy and foreign service personnel for pursuing high-profile human rights cases and reporting voluminously on them. Congress required evidence of progress in the investigations of many of these cases as a condition of U.S. aid. Moreover, public and private *démarches* about the centrality of these cases to U.S. policy were undercut by the administration's admitted tendency to paint government behavior in glowing terms and by its quest for ever-expanding levels of U.S. military assistance.

Finally, the report was also curiously silent on the State Department's own contribution to the polarization of debate and overheated rhetoric of Reagan's early years in office. It views as "mistakes," or exceptions to a rule, what in fact formed a pattern. Secretary of State Haig's insistence that international terrorism would replace human rights as the dominant focus of U.S. foreign policy, the State Department's public campaigns around a "white paper" showing El Salvador to be a "textbook case" of communist aggression in the hemisphere, Haig's references to the murdered U.S. churchwomen as "pistol-packing nuns," Assistant Secretaries of State Thomas Enders's and Elliott Abrams's denials of the massacre at El Mozote, and attempts to soft-pedal information about rightist leader Roberto D'Aubuisson's death squad connections were essential, not incidental, elements of the Reagan administration's approach. *

The report soft-pedaled the Reagan administration's all-out assault on the credibility of Salvadoran and U.S. human rights monitoring groups; in one of its grossest understatements, the report noted blandly that Assistant Secretary Abrams "did not effectively cultivate" critics of U.S. policy "as a constituency on El Salvador."[12] The concerted attacks throughout the decade on those who challenged the administration's portrayal of the human rights situation were an integral part of its effort to defend the Salvadoran government in order to ensure a steady stream of congressional funding.

In short, the report of the Panel on El Salvador was limited and disappointing. Liberal critics in Congress called it "basically a whitewash" and evidence of the

---

National Security Adviser William Clark's disavowal of U.S. Ambassador Deane Hinton's strongly worded speech to a Salvadoran business group in October 1982. (Clark is left unnamed in the panel's report.) The report also acknowledges that the State Department "watered down the Ambassador's language" when it circulated copies of Hinton's speech in Washington (see Chapter Four). Ibid., p. 13.

*Viewing these actions and statements as exceptions, and ignoring the Reagan administration's fixation with the East-West and security dimensions of the Salvadoran conflict, led the panel to assert a false continuity between Carter and Reagan administration policy. The view that there was such continuity is a favorite of former Reagan administration officials.

inability of the foreign service to investigate itself.[13] The panel thus failed in one of its stated tasks: to "make a small contribution to reconciliation among Americans who anguished over Salvador."[14] Instead, the debate continued, and the cleavages remained basically the same.

In one regard, however, the El Salvador panel may contribute to a settling of policy differences. The panel added its voice to those asking for the "declassification of the vast bulk of the record," adding that the majority of State Department documents "could be declassified in toto."[15] It remains to be seen, however, whether the documents released, as President Clinton has promised, will paint a comprehensive picture of U.S. policy in El Salvador as carried out by the full range of agencies involved, or whether the documents will suggest only a sanitized version of that history.

Appendix
Major Government Figures Prosecuted as a Result of the Iran-Contra Affair

Major Prosecutions

The following is a summary of the major prosecutions of U.S. Government officials stemming from the investigation of Iran-contra independent counsel Lawrence M. Walsh:

Elliott Abrams, former Assistant Secretary of State for Inter-American Affairs
> October 7, 1991
>> Pleads guilty to two misdemeanor counts of withholding information from Congress about secret efforts to support the contras.
> November 15, 1991
>> Sentenced to 100 hours of community service, fined $50, and placed on two years' probation.

Duane R. "Dewey" Clarridge, former head of the CIA's Latin American and European Divisions
> November 26, 1991
>> Indicted on seven felony counts of perjury and making false statements to Congress; two counts later dropped. Trial date set for March 1993.

Joseph F. Fernandez, former CIA station chief in Costa Rica
> June 20, 1988
>> Indicted on five counts of conspiracy and making false statements to Congress and other investigators; charges dismissed on a technicality on October 19, 1988.
> April 24, 1989
>> Reindicted on four felony counts of making false statements to Congress.
> November 24, 1989
>> Case dismissed when the Justice Department, exercising its powers under the Classified Information Procedures Act, blocks the declassification of documents Fernandez said he needed for his defense.

Alan D. Fiers Jr., former head of the CIA's Central American Task Force

July 9, 1991

Pleads guilty to two misdemeanor charges of unlawfully withholding information from Congress about contra support efforts.

January 31, 1992

Sentenced to 100 hours of community service and one year of probation.

Clair E. George, former CIA Deputy Director for Operations

September 6, 1991

Indicted on ten counts of perjury, making false statements to Congress, and obstructing congressional and federal investigations into the Iran-contra affair. Three obstruction of justice charges subsequently dropped and two new ones filed in May 1992.

August 26, 1992

Judge declares a mistrial when jurors remain deadlocked over the verdict on each count.

December 9, 1992

Convicted after a second trial on two felony counts of perjury and making false statements to Congress. Acquitted of five other counts of obstruction and making false statements to investigators.

Robert C. McFarlane, former National Security Adviser

March 11, 1988

Pleads guilty to four misdemeanor charges of withholding information from Congress.

March 3, 1989

Sentenced to two years' probation, 200 hours of community service, and fined $20,000.

Oliver L. North, former National Security Council aide

March 16, 1988

Indicted on sixteen counts including conspiracy, theft of government property, making false statements to and obstructing Congress, and destroying official documents; four counts of conspiracy to defraud the government later dropped.

May 4, 1989

Convicted of three felony counts of destroying documents, accepting an illegal gratuity, and obstructing Congress; acquitted on nine other counts.

July 5, 1989

Sentenced to a three-year suspended prison term, two years of probation, 1,200 hours of community service, and fined $150,000.

July 20, 1990

Federal appeals court overturns North's conviction on the charge of destroying classified documents and sets aside the remaining two convictions pending a review by the trial court to determine whether North's trial was tainted by testimony he gave Congress under a grant of immunity.

May 28, 1991

Supreme Court declines review of the case, thereby upholding appeals court ruling.

September 16, 1991

Case dismissed on the grounds that the trial was tainted by North's immunized testimony before Congress.

John M. Poindexter, former National Security Adviser

March 16, 1988

Indicted on seven counts of conspiring to defraud the United States, obstructing congressional inquiries and making false statements to Congress; two of the counts involving wire fraud and theft of government property later dropped.

April 7, 1990

Convicted on five felony counts of obstructing Congress, making false statements to Congress, and conspiracy.

June 11, 1990

Sentenced to six months in prison.

November 15, 1991

U.S. Court of Appeals overturns the convictions, saying that the trial may have been tainted by Poindexter's testimony to Congress given under a grant of immunity.

January 18, 1992

Independent prosecutor Lawrence M. Walsh says he will ask the Supreme Court to reinstate Poindexter's five-count conviction.

December 7, 1992

Supreme Court declines to review the case, letting stand the appeals court decision overturning Poindexter's conviction.

Caspar W. Weinberger, former Secretary of Defense

June 16, 1992

Indicted on five counts of perjury, making false statements, and obstructing Iran-contra investigators by denying that he had kept notes about his activities during the unfolding of the Iran initiative. Charge involving the withholding of his notes dismissed in September.

October 30, 1992
> Four days before the U.S. presidential election, indicted on additional charge of making a false statement to Congress. Additional charge dismissed in December.

January 5, 1993
> Case scheduled to go to trial.

On December 24, 1992, President George Bush granted presidential pardons to Elliott Abrams, Duane R. "Dewey" Clarridge, Alan D. Fiers Jr., Clair E. George, Robert C. McFarlane, and Caspar W. Weinberger, describing the pardons as a response to the "criminalization of policy differences." Independent Counsel Lawrence M. Walsh denounced the pardons for "undermin[ing] the principle that no man is above the law."

Other Iran-Contra Prosecutions

Carl R. "Spitz" Channell, contra fund-raiser
> April 29, 1987
>> Pleads guilty to one count of conspiracy to defraud the government by using a tax-exempt foundation to raise money for the contras.
> July 7, 1989
>> Sentenced to two years' probation and fined $50.

Thomas G. Clines, former CIA agent
> February 22, 1990
>> Indicted on four felony counts related to tax evasion and falsification charges.
> September 18, 1990
>> Convicted on all four counts.
> December 13, 1990
>> Sentenced to sixteen months in prison and fined $40,000.

Albert A. Hakim, businessman who organized the finances for Oliver North's Iran-contra network
> March 16, 1988
>> Indicted, along with North, Poindexter, and Secord, on five counts of conspiracy, fraud, and theft of government property.
> November 21, 1989
>> Pleads guilty to a misdemeanor charge of providing an illegal gratuity to Oliver North.

February 1, 1990

Sentenced to two years' probation and fined $5,000; agrees to drop his claim to $7.3 million out of $9 million in profits from the Iranian arms sales.

Richard R. Miller, head of a Washington, D.C., public relations firm

May 6, 1987

Pleads guilty to a misdemeanor charge of conspiring to defraud the government by raising money for military aid to the contras through a charitable organization.

July 6, 1989

Sentenced to two years' probation and 120 hours of community service.

Richard V. Secord, retired U.S. Air Force Major General, chief operative in Oliver North's Iran-contra network.

March 16, 1988

Indicted, along with North, Poindexter, and Hakim, on six counts of conspiracy, theft of government property, and mail fraud.

May 11, 1989

Indicted on nine additional charges including obstructing and making false statements to Congress. Charges later consolidated to twelve.

November 8, 1989

On eve of trial, pleads guilty to one felony count of making false statements to Congress, in exchange for dismissal of eleven remaining charges.

January 24, 1990

Sentenced to two years' probation.

Sources: *New York Times; Washington Post; Congressional Quarterly*; Office of the Independent Counsel, "Fact Sheet," December 1992, in Peter Kornbluh and Malcolm Byrne, *The Iran-Contra Scandal: The Declassified Record* (New York: New Press, 1993), Document 90. Compiled with the assistance of Carlos Sánchez.

Notes

Chapter One. Central America and the Post-Vietnam Congress

1. U.S. Congress, House Select Committee to Investigate Covert Arms Transactions with Iran and Senate Select Committee on Secret Military Assistance to Iran and the Nicaraguan Opposition, *Testimony of Richard V. Secord*, Joint Hearings, 100th Cong., 1st Sess., May 5–8, 1987 (Washington, D.C.: U.S. Government Printing Office, 1987), p. 2. (Hereafter cited as Joint Hearings, Secord.)
2. Ibid., pp. 1, 3.
3. See, for example, Daniel Schorr, "A Whiff of Watergate?" *Washington Post*, November 12, 1986; Haynes Johnson, "A Scandal, But Not a Watergate," *Washington Post*, December 4, 1986; David Ignatius and Michael Getler, "This Isn't Watergate—But the Moral Is the Same," *Washington Post*, March 1, 1987.
4. Control of foreign policy is a shared responsibility under the U.S. Constitution. Article 1, Section 8, specifies that "the Congress shall have power To . . . provide for the common Defence and general Welfare of the United States . . . To regulate Commerce with foreign Nations . . . To declare War . . . To raise and support Armies . . . To provide and maintain a Navy." Article 2, Section 2, specifies that "the President shall be Commander in Chief of the Army and Navy. . . . He shall have Power, by and with the Advice and Consent of the Senate, to make Treaties, provided two-thirds of the Senators present concur; and he shall nominate, and by and with the Advice and consent of the Senate, shall appoint Ambassadors, other public Ministers, and Consuls . . . he shall take Care that the Laws be faithfully executed."

   Presidential scholar Richard Neustadt has written that the Constitution created "separated institutions sharing powers," while constitutional scholar Edwin Corwin has called the Constitution an "invitation to struggle for the privilege of directing American foreign policy." See Neustadt, *Presidential Power* (New York: Signet Books, 1964), p. 42, and Corwin, *The President: Office and Powers, 1787–1984* (New York: New York University Press, 1984), p. 201.
5. *Public Papers of the Presidents: Ronald Reagan 1983*, vol. 1 (Washington, D.C.: U.S. Government Printing Office, 1984), p. 363. See also Piero Gleijeses, "Tilting at Windmills" (Washington, D.C.: Johns Hopkins University School of Advanced International Studies, Foreign Policy Institute, 1982), pp. 2–7.

6. Electoral considerations were only part of this domestic equation: although public opposition to Reagan's Central America policies remained fairly constant throughout his two terms in office, surveys conducted since the Vietnam War have shown that the American public gives low priority to foreign policy issues in relation to other policy matters. See, for example, John E. Reilly, ed., *American Public Opinion and U.S. Foreign Policy, 1979* (Chicago: Chicago Council on Foreign Relations, 1979).

7. John Felton, "On Foreign Policy, Navigating the Mainstream," *Congressional Quarterly*, September 1, 1984, p. 2160; Charles McC. Mathias Jr., "Congress Will Meddle," *New York Times*, April 15, 1984.

8. For a discussion of the role of convictions and assumptions in suggesting appropriate courses of action, see Michael Hunt, *Ideology and U.S. Foreign Policy* (New Haven: Yale University Press, 1987).

9. See, for example, Arthur Schlesinger Jr., "Foreign Policy and the American Character," *Foreign Affairs*, vol. 62 (Fall 1983), pp. 4–6.

10. President James Monroe stated in his 1823 State of the Union Address that "the American continents, by the free and independent condition which they have assumed and maintain, are henceforth not to be considered as subject for future colonization by any European power. . . . We should consider any attempt on their part to extend their political system to any portion of this hemisphere as dangerous to our peace and safety." Quoted in Dexter Perkins, *A History of the Monroe Doctrine* (Boston: Little, Brown, 1963), p. 28.

11. See Margaret Daly Hayes, "U.S. Security Interests in Central America," in Bruce M. Bagley, ed., *Contadora and the Diplomacy of Peace in Central America*, vol. 1 (Boulder, Colo.: Westview Press, 1987), p. 5; and Lars Schoultz, *National Security and U.S. Policy in Latin America* (Princeton: Princeton University Press, 1987), p. 118.

12. John D. Waghelstein, "Choices in Central America," *New York Times*, August 7, 1984.

13. Schoultz, *National Security and U.S. Policy*, pp. 109–22, identifies 1954 as the year in which the Monroe Doctrine was "multilateralized," with Secretary of State John Foster Dulles's declaration that the "domination or control of the political institutions of any American state by the international Communist movement, extending to this hemisphere the political system of an extra-continental power, would constitute a threat to the sovereignty and political independence of the American States" (p. 119). Schoultz argues that Reagan administration perceptions of the conflict in Central America stemmed from these postwar notions of U.S. security.

14. See *Congressional Quarterly Almanac 1954*, pp. 285–86; *Congressional Quarterly Almanac 1962*, pp. 331–40; and *Congressional Quarterly Almanac 1964*, pp. 331–32.

15. *Congressional Quarterly Almanac 1965*, p. 516.

16. Ibid., pp. 514–18. Fulbright's claims were based on evidence presented at closed hearings of the Senate Foreign Relations Committee. For Fulbright's view of the Dominican intervention and other revolutions in underdeveloped countries, see J. William Fulbright, *The Arrogance of Power* (New York: Vintage Books, 1966), especially part 2, "Revolutions Abroad."

17. Lee Riley Powell, *J. William Fulbright and America's Lost Crusade: Fulbright's*

Opposition to the Vietnam War (Little Rock, Ark.: Rose Publishing Company, 1984), pp. 177–80.

18. See Clark Clifford, "A Vietnam Reappraisal," *Foreign Affairs*, vol. 47 (July 1969), pp. 601–22. Clifford stated that "the forces we have deployed and the human and material costs we are now incurring have become, in my opinion, out of all proportion to our purpose."

19. Following the passage of the 1964 Gulf of Tonkin Resolution, neither Presidents Johnson nor Nixon sought congressional approval for the expansion of U.S. troop commitments or the geographical extension of the war. In 1970 Nixon sent U.S. troops into Cambodia; in 1971 he authorized U.S. air support for the South Vietnamese invasion of Laos; in 1972 Haiphong harbor was mined; and in December 1972 the massive bombing of North Vietnam was undertaken. *Congressional Quarterly Almanac 1975*, p. 296.

20. Quoted in I. M. Destler, "Executive-Congressional Conflict in Foreign Policy: Explaining It, Coping with It," in Dodd and Oppenheimer, *Congress Reconsidered*, 3rd ed. (Washington, D.C.: Congressional Quarterly Press, 1985), p. 348.

21. The War Powers Act, passed over President Nixon's veto, provided for congressional oversight of the decision to intervene, by stipulating that the president had to report to the Congress within forty-eight hours of sending U.S. soldiers oversees into "hostilities" or situations of "imminent hostilities," and gave Congress the power, after sixty days, to require the president, by joint resolution, to withdraw U.S. troops from hostilities abroad. A 1983 Supreme Court ruling would appear to make the second provision (a legislative veto over presidential action) unconstitutional. In mid-1988, a bipartisan group of Senators introduced legislation to revise the War Powers Act, claiming that its provisions were unworkable and damaging to U.S. interests during a crisis.

22. Quoted in Diane Granat, "Whatever Happened to the Watergate Babies?" *Congressional Quarterly*, March 3, 1984, p. 500.

23. In 1973 the House Democratic Caucus decided to submit committee chairmanships to a secret vote of the entire party membership, rather than have chairmanships determined by seniority. In 1975 the "Watergate babies" joined with more senior colleagues to depose the aging chairmen of three major committees—Armed Services, Banking, and Agriculture. The attack on seniority spread to the subcommittee level as well, opening subcommittee chairmanships to the congressional rank and file. Other regulations prohibited committee chairmen from chairing more than one of their committee's own subcommittees, while members on the Appropriations, Rules, and Ways and Means Committees were prohibited from serving on other permanent committees.

24. Former Carter administration official Anthony Lake has suggested that "no more Vietnams" was likely to be as unsuited to future foreign policy crises as was the "no more Munichs" imperative following World War II. He has characterized prevailing post-Vietnam attitudes as follows: "The United States should avoid foreign wars not by nipping them in the bud, but by staying out of them." Lake, ed., *The Vietnam Legacy: The War, American Society, and the Future of American Foreign Policy* (New York: New York University Press, 1976), p. xvii.

25. U.S. policies in Vietnam also gave rise to the notion that the United States had not

only ignored human rights abuses but had contributed to them. In 1970 a congressional delegation to Vietnam that included then staff aide Tom Harkin discovered that political prisoners at Con Son prison were kept in tiny confinement cells called "tiger cages." The United States had provided funds to Con Son through AID's Office of Public Safety. Subsequent investigations into the U.S.-funded Phoenix Program in Vietnam revealed that U.S. funds had gone for "assassinations, ambushes, kidnappings, and intimidation," according to a former Phoenix operative. Over 26,000 South Vietnamese civilians were "neutralized" under the Phoenix Program between 1968 and 1972. See U.S. Congress, House, Committee on Government Operations, *U.S. Assistance Programs in Vietnam*, Hearings, 92nd Cong., 1st Sess. (Washington, D.C.: U.S. Government Printing Office, 1971).

26. In early 1973 the Senate Foreign Relations Committee Subcommittee on Multinational Corporations held hearings on the ITT Corporation's offer to assist any U.S. Government program to block Allende's election. The hearings focused on ITT's role, however, and not the CIA's. *Congressional Quarterly Almanac 1973*, pp. 845–51; *1974*, p. 538; and *1975*, p. 388.

27. In the House, the committee was chaired by Representative Lucien Nedzi (D-Mich.) and later by Representative Otis Pike (D-N.Y.); in the Senate, by Senator Frank Church (D-Idaho). Nedzi resigned over a dispute with liberal Democrats, who learned that as chairman of the Armed Services Special Subcommittee on Intelligence he had received briefings in 1974 about illegal CIA activities. Nedzi did not inform the newly formed Select Committee of these briefings.

28. Harkin, a member of the "Watergate baby" class of 1974, served on none of the committees dealing with foreign affairs. The Harkin amendment defined "gross violations" of human rights as including "torture or cruel, inhuman, or degrading treatment or punishment, prolonged detention without charges, or other flagrant denial of the right to life, liberty, and the security of the person." The text was drafted principally by two church human rights activists.

29. Donald M. Fraser, "Congress's Role in the Making of International Human Rights Policy," in Donald P. Kommers and Gilburt D. Loescher, eds., *Human Rights and American Foreign Policy* (Notre Dame, Ind.: University of Notre Dame Press, 1979), p. 248.

30. Schoultz, *National Security and U.S. Policy*, pp. 20–21.

31. Gary Schmitt, "Oversight—What For and How Effective?" in Roy Godson, ed., *Intelligence Requirements for the 1980s* (Lexington, Mass.: Lexington Books, 1985), p. 127.

32. See U.S. Congress, Senate, Select Committee to Study Governmental Operations with Respect to Intelligence Activities, *Final Report*, Books I–VI, 94th Cong., 2nd Sess. (Washington, D.C.: U.S. Government Printing Office, 1976); and *Congressional Quarterly Almanac 1975*, p. 387; and *1976*, p. 303.

33. *Congressional Quarterly Almanac 1976*, p. 296.

34. Carter's CIA director, Stansfield Turner, said that Inouye "had the liberal credentials necessary to assure critics that the committee would be inquiring and investigative. His war record, patriotism, and proven support for national security reassured others that the committee would be constructive." See Stansfield Turner, *Secrecy and Democracy: The CIA in Transition* (Boston: Houghton Mifflin, 1985), p. 146.

35. Ibid., p. 146; Annie Karalekas, "Intelligence Oversight: Has Anything Changed?" *Washington Quarterly*, Summer 1983, p. 25.

36. Formally known as Title V of the National Security Act of 1947 (Accountability for Intelligence Activities). See U.S. Congress, House, Permanent Select Committee on Intelligence, *Compilation of Intelligence Laws and Related Laws and Executive Orders of Interest to the National Intelligence Community*, July 1985, 99th Cong., 1st Sess. (Washington, D.C.: U.S. Government Printing Office, 1985), pp. 211–12.

37. Stansfield Turner, CIA director at the time the new law was passed, testified that requiring prior notice without exception would be "an excessive intrusion" on the executive branch. In his memoirs, Turner reiterated his opposition to prior notice and admitted that the requirement was not always observed. Some "fine lines had to be drawn," he said, "and tolerance, understanding, and trust were needed on both sides." Turner, *Secrecy and Democracy*, p. 148. See also Loch Johnson, "Covert Action and American Foreign Policy: Decision Paths for the 'Quiet Option' " (Manuscript), p. 5; and *Congressional Quarterly Almanac 1980*, pp. 66–67.

38. Quoted in Karalekas, "Intelligence Oversight," p. 26.

39. Ellen C. Collier, "Foreign Policy Roles of the President and Congress," Congressional Research Service, Report No. 86-163 F, Washington, D.C., September 16, 1986, pp. 7–17.

40. Alexander Hamilton, "The Federalist No. 25," in Roy P. Fairfield, ed., *The Federalist Papers* (Garden City, N.Y.: Anchor Books, 1966), p. 68.

41. U.S. Congress, House, Committee on Appropriations Subcommittee on Foreign Operations, *Foreign Assistance and Related Programs Appropriations for 1988*, Hearings, Part 4, 100th Cong., 1st Sess. (Washington, D.C.: U.S. Government Printing Office, 1987), p. 529.

42. Jeffrey T. Bergner, "Organizing the Congress for National Security," *Comparative Strategy*, vol. 6, no. 3 (1987), p. 294.

43. Lee H. Hamilton and Michael H. Van Dusen, "Making the Separation of Powers Work," *Foreign Affairs*, vol. 57 (Fall 1978), p. 32. Several years later, Hamilton noted that "presidents don't lose national security issues. If the president goes to bat on any specific issue, he'll win it." Quoted in Murrey Marder, "Hill Fights Reagan for Soul of Foreign Policy," *Washington Post*, September 2, 1984.

44. Quoted in James L. Sundquist, *The Decline and Resurgence of Congress* (Washington, D.C.: Brookings Institution, 1981), p. 293.

45. Michael D. Barnes, "The Constitution and Foreign Policy: The Role of Congress," in Ralph S. Pollock, ed., *Renewing the Dream: National Archives Bicentennial '87 Lectures on Contemporary Constitutional Issues* (Lanham, Md.: University Press of America, 1986), pp. 68, 72.

46. Quoted in Steven V. Roberts, "Foreign Policy: Lot of Table Thumping Going On," *New York Times*, May 29, 1985.

47. Since 1957, *Congressional Quarterly* has compiled statistics on the number of votes in which conservative Democrats joined with blocs of Republicans against a non-southern Democratic majority. In 1971 the conservative coalition emerged on 30 percent of congressional votes. In 1986 the figure was 16 percent; by the first half of 1987, 7.5 percent. Alan Ehrenhalt, "Changing South Perils Conservative Coalition," *Congressional Quarterly*, August 1, 1987, pp. 1699–1705.

48. Southern interest in Latin America is also deeply rooted in U.S. history. Southerners led a mid-nineteenth century expansionist drive aimed at "regenerating" the non-white peoples of Mexico and Central America. Southern support for "filibuster" expeditions (including that of William Walker into Nicaragua) to annex neighboring republics grew out of a desire to redress the sectional balance in favor of slave states. See Cynthia Arnson, "The Reagan Administration, Congress, and Central America," in Nora Hamilton et al., eds., *Crisis in Central America: Regional Dynamics and U.S. Policy in the 1980s* (Boulder, Colo.: Westview Press, 1988); and Robert May, *The Southern Dream of a Caribbean Empire* (Baton Rouge: Louisiana State University Press, 1973).

49. Louis Harris, Press Release, May 17, 1984, p. 1.

50. Shortly before a House vote in June 1985 to provide nonlethal contra aid, a Harris poll found 73 percent of Americans opposed to military aid and 81 percent concerned that the United States would end up sending troops to Nicaragua. Louis Harris, "Almost Three-Fourths of Public Opposes Military Aid to Nicaragua," Press Release, May 23, 1985, p. 1; Barry Sussman, "In Poll, Public Approves Denial of Contra Aid," *Washington Post*, March 26, 1986.

51. Adam Clymer, "Poll Finds Americans Don't Know U.S. Positions on Central America," *New York Times*, July 1, 1983; David K. Shipler, "Poll Shows Confusion on Aid to Contras," *New York Times*, April 15, 1986.

52. Two political scientists have noted: "When confronted by a choice between supporting a popular president and the clear interests of his constituents, the president's public prestige is a poor match for his or her constituents' interests. But on many issues constituency interests are not easily perceived or irrelevant. When constituency opinion . . . is unformed or the constituent interest is not apparent, congressmen are more likely to defer to a popular president or to go along with the party leadership." See Douglas Rivers and Nancy L. Rose, "Passing the President's Program: Public Opinion and Presidential Influence in Congress," *American Journal of Political Science*, vol. 29 (May 1985), p. 187.

53. Robert Tucker, "Their Wars, Our Choices," *New Republic*, October 24, 1983, p. 22.

54. *Congressional Record*, April 9, 1984, p. S 4142.

55. Quoted in David Fromkin and James Chace, "What Are the Lessons of Vietnam?" *Foreign Affairs*, vol. 63 (Spring 1985), p. 730.

Chapter Two. 1976–1980: Congress Discovers Central America

1. See May 11, 1976, memorandum from the Washington Office on Latin America in U.S. Congress, House, Committee on International Relations Subcommittee on International Organizations, *Human Rights in Nicaragua, Guatemala, and El Salvador: Implications for U.S. Policy*, Hearings, June 8 and 9, 1976, 94th Cong., 2nd Sess. (Washington, D.C.: U.S. Government Printing Office, 1976), pp. 155–58.

2. *Public Papers of the Presidents: Jimmy Carter 1977*, vol. 1 (Washington, D.C.: U.S. Government Printing Office, 1977), p. 957.

3. Edward Koch, "How a Foreign Government Won over the U.S. Congress," *Village*

Voice, August 8, 1977, cited in *Congressional Record*, August 4, 1977, pp. 27124–26.

4. 1976 Hearings, *Human Rights in Nicaragua, Guatemala, and El Salvador*, p. 112. Ryan's denials were repeated in subsequent correspondence between the State Department and the subcommittee.

5. Chamorro wrote Fraser that his and Cardenal's testimony were "different but not contradictory" and that he had no "doubts concerning [Cardenal's] good faith or the truthfulness of what he said. . . . My testimony and Father Cardenal's are completely coincident when demonstrating that the Somoza regime systematically violates human rights in Nicaragua."

6. Signers of the pastoral letter included Archbishop Miguel Obando y Bravo, Prelate Pablo Vega, and Bishop Salvador Schlaefer, all harsh critics of General Somoza and later bitter opponents of the Sandinista government. See U.S. Congress, House, Committee on Appropriations Subcommittee on Foreign Operations, *Foreign Assistance and Related Agencies Appropriations for 1978*, Hearings, Part 3, 95th Cong., 1st Sess., 1977, pp. 513–15.

7. U.S. Congress, House, Committee on Appropriations Subcommittee on Foreign Operations, *Foreign Assistance and Related Agencies Appropriations for 1978*, Hearings, Part 1, 95th Cong., 1st Sess., 1977, pp. 724, 746–47.

8. Ibid., p. 749. Asked why the United States was aiding Somoza, Benson replied, "I think we are doing it because we have always done it."

9. Debate excerpts are from the *Congressional Record*, June 23, 1977, pp. 20579, 20583–84.

10. For a detailed account of Somoza government lobbying and public relations outreach, see "A Report on the Nicaragua Lobby," *Congressional Record*, June 21, 1977, pp. 20180–82. See also Lars Schoultz, *Human Rights and United States Policy Toward Latin America* (Princeton: Princeton University Press, 1981), pp. 62–63.

11. *Congressional Record*, June 23, 1977, p. 20587.

12. Telephone interview, December 4, 1986.

13. In early 1977, for example, Deputy Assistant Secretary of State Charles Bray told the Congress that "the United States has no strategic interests in El Salvador." When asked whether there was a revolutionary movement in El Salvador, Bray replied, "It does not seem to be a potent force." U.S. Congress, House, Committee on International Relations Subcommittee on International Organizations, *The Recent Presidential Elections in El Salvador: Implications for U.S. Foreign Policy*, Hearings, March 9 and 17, 1977, 95th Cong., 1st Sess. (Washington, D.C.: U.S. Government Printing Office, 1977), pp. 15, 4.

14. Ibid., p. 54. Only two aides showed up at a congressional staff briefing arranged by the Washington Office on Latin America. See Raymond Bonner, *Weakness and Deceit: U.S. Policy and El Salvador* (New York: Times Books, 1984), p. 34.

15. U.S. Congress, House, Committee on International Relations Subcommittee on International Organizations, *Religious Persecution in El Salvador*, Hearings, July 21 and 29, 1977, 95th Cong., 1st Sess. (Washington, D.C.: U.S. Government Printing Office, 1977).

16. Interview, November 20, 1986, Washington, D.C.

17. U.S. Department of Defense, *Congressional Presentation, Security Assistance Program*, Fiscal Year 1979, Washington, D.C., p. 343.
18. According to a former State Department official, the letter was drafted by an aide on the National Security Council, apparently under orders from President Carter. Carter insisted on sending the letter over the objections of the State Department. Somoza opponents saw the letter as a reaffirmation of U.S. support for the dynasty at a time when public opposition to the regime was on the rise. The full text of the letter appears in Shirley Christian, *Nicaragua: Revolution in the Family* (New York: Random House, 1985), p. 57.
19. Alan Riding, "National Mutiny in Nicaragua," *New York Times Magazine*, July 30, 1978, pp. 12–13, 15, 34, 39, 42, 46–47.
20. Wilson's fellow Texan, Majority Leader Jim Wright, co-signed the letter, as did Deputy Majority Whip William Alexander (D-Ark.). Both Wright and Alexander later became leading supporters of the Carter administration's efforts to provide aid to the Sandinista government. They were also opponents of the Reagan administration's covert operations against Nicaragua.
21. Letter to Jimmy Carter, September 22, 1978.
22. *Congressional Record*, September 22, 1978, p. S 30874.
23. According to a senior State Department official, President Carter himself "was not in favor of our telling Somoza he had to go." If Somoza was to leave, it should be through an internationally sponsored mediation aimed at elections, not through U.S. "intervention." (Telephone interview, November 16, 1987.)
24. Karen DeYoung, "Congressman Denounces U.S. Nicaraguan Efforts," *Washington Post*, December 7, 1978; Graham Hovey, "Breakdown in Nicaragua Talks Creates New Problems for Carter," *New York Times*, January 24, 1979.
25. Interview, November 20, 1986, Washington, D.C.
26. Interview, November 4, 1986, Washington, D.C.
27. Interview, November 20, 1986, Washington, D.C.
28. *Congressional Record*, June 25, 1979, p. S 8405.
29. In May 1979 Senator Kennedy called for a suspension of Nicaragua's meat and sugar quotas and the ending of trade credits.
30. Although the House has no constitutional role in approving treaties, it did have jurisdiction over the "implementing legislation" necessary for the functioning of the joint U.S.-Panamanian Canal Commission. The Senate ratified the treaties on April 18, 1978, 68–32, only one vote more than the needed two-thirds majority.
31. See Jim McGee and Bob Woodward, "Noriega Arms Indictment Stalled in '80," *Washington Post*, March 20, 1988.
32. Administration witnesses J. Brian Atwood and Commander-in-Chief of the U.S. Southern Command General Dennis McAuliffe stated, respectively, that there was "no evidence" of Panamanian gun-running to the Sandinistas and that Panamanian President Aristides Royo had promised an investigation into whether Panamanians in their private capacities were helping the Sandinistas. Mary Russell, "Panama Accused of Running Guns to Rebels," *Washington Post*, June 7, 1979, and "White House Seeks Showdown on Implementing Canal Pacts," *Washington Post*, June 8, 1979; Jeremiah O'Leary, "Panamanian Role in Upheaval Charged on Hill," *Washington Star*, June 7, 1979.

33. Interview, November 6, 1986, Washington, D.C.
34. Zorinsky was then chairman of the Foreign Relations Subcommittee on Western Hemisphere Affairs, and Richard Lugar (R-Ind.) was its ranking minority member. See *Congressional Record*, June 25, 1979. The letter referred to five Andean nations that had called for the Sandinistas to be recognized as belligerents under international law.
35. Vance also called for "an OAS peacekeeping presence to help establish a climate of peace and security," a proposal rejected by the OAS. See U.S. Department of State, Press Release, Statement by the Honorable Cyrus Vance, Secretary of State, Before the Organization of American States, June 21, 1979, pp. 4, 7.
36. John M. Goshko, "OAS Votes for Ouster of Somoza," *Washington Post*, June 24, 1979.
37. Steven R. Weisman, "Congressman Murphy Still Somoza Friend," *New York Times*, July 18, 1979.
38. Press Release, Office of Senator Edward Zorinsky, June 28, 1979.
39. U.S. Congress, House, Committee on Foreign Affairs, Subcommittee on Inter-American Affairs, *Central America at the Crossroads*, Hearings, September 11 and 12, 1979, 96th Cong., 1st Sess. (Washington, D.C.: U.S. Government Printing Office, 1979), pp. 2–3.
40. Interview, November 20, 1986, Washington, D.C.
41. Interview, August 4, 1979, Managua, Nicaragua.
42. Statement by Deputy Secretary of State Warren Christopher before the Subcommittee on Foreign Operations, House Appropriations Committee, September 11, 1979, p. 5.
43. Statement by the Honorable Cyrus Vance, Secretary of State, before the Foreign Policy Association, New York, New York, September 27, 1979, Department of State Press Release No. 238, p. 12.
44. Message from the president, "Special Central American and Caribbean Security Assistance Act of 1979," PM 133, printed in *Congressional Record*, November 9, 1979, p. S 16453.
45. *Congressional Record*, November 28, 1979, p. H 11312.
46. John M. Goshko, "Three From Nicaraguan Junta Get Red-Carpet Welcome Here," *Washington Post*, September 25, 1979.
47. Senator Frank Church, facing a tough reelection fight in Idaho, revealed on August 30, 1979, that 2,300 to 3,000 Soviet combat troops were stationed in Cuba, and maintained that "the buildup of Soviet ground troops to brigade strength has not been reported until recently." He called on President Carter to demand the "immediate withdrawal of all Russian combat troops from Cuba." High-ranking administration officials admitted that it was possible that a Soviet combat unit had been in Cuba since the 1962 missile crisis and had escaped U.S. detection. See Associated Press, "2,300-Man Soviet Unit Now in Cuba," *Washington Post*, August 31, 1979; and Don Oberdorfer, "The 'Brigada': An Unwelcome Sighting in Cuba," *Washington Post*, September 9, 1979.
48. Karen Elliott House and Beth Nissen, "U.S. Tries to Influence Central America Unrest but Finds Task Tricky," *Wall Street Journal*, April 29, 1980.
49. *Congressional Record*, February 22, 1980, pp. H 1163, H 1175.

50. The previous occasion also involved Nicaragua. During consideration of the Panama Canal legislation in June 1979, the House went into secret session to explore charges of Panamanian gun-running to the Sandinista rebels.
51. *Congressional Record*, February 26, 1980, p. H 1284.
52. See *Congressional Record*, February 22–27, 1979, debate on Special Central American Assistance Act of 1979.
53. *Congressional Record*, May 19, 1980, p. 11646.
54. Dreyfus's comments were made during an October 17, 1979, meeting with church and human rights activists lobbying for the aid package.
55. In late February, House and Senate conferees had agreed to incorporate the Nicaragua aid authorization into the Fiscal Year 1980 foreign aid appropriations bill. The Budget Committee action undercut this agreement.
56. Radio Sandino, "Reportage on Reaction to U.S. Loan Freeze Continues," *Foreign Broadcast Information Service* (hereafter cited as *FBIS*), March 7, 1980, p. P12; ACAN-EFE, "Groups React to Freezing of $75 Million U.S. Loan," *FBIS*, March 6, 1980, p. P11.
57. Confidential telegram, Robert White, AmEmbassy San Salvador to SecState WashDC, March 15, 1980, p. 2; declassified February 11, 1985.
58. *Congressional Record*, March 25, 1980, p. 6623.
59. The request was for permission to transfer, or "reprogram," money already approved by Congress. Congress must be informed of reprogramming but has no formal legislative power to block them.
60. Karen DeYoung, "U.S. Weighs a Military Role in El Salvador," *Washington Post*, February 14, 1980.
61. The text of Romero's letter was quoted in *Congressional Record*, March 25, 1980, pp. 6558–59. In November 1979 the Carter administration sold $205,541 of tear gas, gas masks, and protective vests to El Salvador and sent a six-man U.S. Mobile Training Team to train the security forces in riot control. In December 1979 the administration reprogrammed an additional $300,000 for military training of the Salvadoran army and an equal amount for Nicaragua. The House Subcommittee on Foreign Operations claimed that it was not informed of the reprogramming. (Documents received by the author under the Freedom of Information Act; telephone interview, U.S. Department of State, March 4, 1980; letter, Lt. Gen. Ernest Graves to Hon. Daniel K. Inouye, December 14, 1979.)
62. Testimonies of Dr. Jorge Lara-Braud, National Council of Churches; Heather Foote, Washington Office on Latin America; Fr. Simon Smith, S.J., in U.S. Congress, House, Committee on Appropriations Subcommittee on Foreign Operations, *Foreign Assistance on Related Programs Appropriations for 1981*, Hearings, Part 1, 96th Cong., 2nd Sess. (Washington, D.C.: U.S. Government Printing Office, 1980), pp. 373, 380, 396–97.
63. Testimonies of Deputy Assistant Secretary of State for Inter-American Affairs John A. Bushnell and Deputy Assistant Secretary of Defense Franklin Kramer, ibid., pp. 331, 339–40.
64. Ibid., p. 427.
65. U.S. Department of State, Unclassified Incoming Telegram, "Ambassador's Statement on Military Assistance," March 1980, p. 1.

66. *Foreign Assistance and Related Programs Appropriations for 1981*, pp. 345–46.
67. Secret Briefing Memorandum, "Situation in El Salvador and MTT's," Department of State, John A. Bushnell to the Secretary, March 13, 1980, p. 1. Declassified (date illegible on photocopy).
68. U.S. Congress, House, Permanent Select Committee on Intelligence, Subcommittee on Oversight and Evaluation, Staff Report, U.S. *Intelligence Performance on Central America: Achievements and Selected Instances of Concern*, September 22, 1982, 97th Cong., 2nd Sess. (Washington, D.C.: U.S. Government Printing Office, 1982), p. 10.
69. *Foreign Assistance and Related Programs Appropriations for 1981*, pp. 379–80, 434, 428.
70. "Dear Colleague" letter from Representatives Cheney, Beard, and Evans to the House membership, April 29, 1980.
71. Richard L. Lyons, "On Capitol Hill," *Washington Post*, May 13, 1980; John Felton, "House Version of Nicaragua Aid Bill Accepted by Senate," *Congressional Quarterly*, May 24, 1980, p. 1395. Mounting resistance in the House to final passage of the aid authorization led the Senate on May 19, 1980, to accept the House-passed version of the bill. This obviated the need for a House-Senate conference on the differing versions of the legislation, as passed by both bodies.
72. Interview, Kirk O'Donnell, November 6, 1986, Washington, D.C.
73. *Congressional Record*, June 5, 1980, pp. H 4564, H 4572.
74. The Senate approved aid to Nicaragua on June 28, rejecting a Helms amendment to cut economic aid funds from the Fiscal Year 1981 bill.
75. Accompanying Wright were Representatives Bill Alexander (D-Ark.), Steven Neal (D-N.C.), and Kent Hance (D-Texas). According to one House aide on the trip, Alexander was particularly interested in seeing whether the Nicaraguans could intervene with Fidel Castro to convince the Cuban leader to repatriate refugees leaving Cuba during the 1980 Mariel boatlifts.
76. Text, letter to President Jimmy Carter, June 10, 1980, p. 1; Office of Representative Jim Wright, "The Wright Slant on Washington: A Report from Jim," June 30, 1980, p. 1; *Congressional Record*, June 13, 1980, p. H 4947.
77. The column appeared in the *Washington Post* on August 1, 1980, and was quoted in John Felton, "New Dispute Delays Aid to Nicaragua," *Congressional Quarterly*, August 30, 1980, pp. 2607–8.
78. John M. Goshko, "Aid for Nicaragua the Focus of Fierce Internal Policy Dispute," *Washington Post*, August 8, 1980.
79. Juan de Onis, "U.S. Aid to Nicaragua Now Facing Election Year Hurdle," *New York Times*, September 5, 1980.
80. U.S. Congress, House, Permanent Select Committee on Intelligence, Subcommittee on Oversight and Evaluation, U.S. *Intelligence Performance on Central America*, pp. 6–7.
81. See Robert A. Pastor, *Condemned to Repetition: The United States and Nicaragua* (Princeton: Princeton University Press, 1987), pp. 216–21.
82. Ibid.; and Christopher Dickey, *With the Contras* (New York: Simon and Schuster, 1985), p. 75.
83. Ronald Reagan, "Peace and Security in the 1980s," Speech to the Chicago Council on Foreign Relations, March 17, 1980, p. 4.

84. Republican National Convention Platform, July 15, 1980, Detroit, Michigan, in *Congressional Quarterly Almanac 1980*, p. 82-B.
85. See Dickey, *With the Contras*, pp. 72–75; and Arturo Cruz Sequeira, "The Origins of Sandinista Foreign Policy," in Robert Leiken, ed., *Central America: Anatomy of Conflict* (New York: Pergamon Press, 1984), pp. 104–5.
86. U.S. Department of State, Press Statement, January 17, 1981, p. 1.
87. Interview, Lawrence Pezzullo, November 7, 1986, New York, New York.
88. Quoted in Christopher Dickey, "100 Guerrillas Land on Beach in El Salvador," *Washington Post*, January 15, 1981.

Chapter Three. 1981: The Reagan Offensive

1. See Roger D. Hansen, "The Reagan Doctrine and Global Containment: Revival or Recessional," *SAIS Review*, vol. 7 (Winter–Spring 1987), p. 42; and William Schneider, "Conservatism, Not Interventionism: Trends in Foreign Policy Opinion, 1974–1982," in Kenneth A. Oye and Robert J. Lieber, *Eagle Defiant: United States Foreign Policy in the 1980s* (Boston: Little, Brown, 1983), pp. 33–64.
2. Interview, January 14, 1987, Washington, D.C.
3. Secretary Haig, News Conference, January 28, 1981, U.S. Department of State, Bureau of Public Affairs, Current Policy No. 258, p. 5.
4. Juan de Onis, "Soviet Bloc Nations Said to Pledge Aid to Salvador Rebels," *New York Times*, February 6, 1981; Juan de Onis, "U.S. Says Salvador Is 'Textbook Case' of Communist Plot," *New York Times*, February 20, 1981; "Text of Excerpts of Haig Briefing about El Salvador," *New York Times*, February 21, 1981.
5. Department of State, Bureau of Public Affairs, "Communist Interference in El Salvador," Special Report No. 80, February 23, 1981.
6. Don Oberdorfer and John M. Goshko, "U.S. Gives Warning on Cuba-Salvador Arms Flow," *Washington Post*, February 22, 1981; Juan de Onis, "Cuba Warned Direct U.S. Action Against It on Salvador Is Possible," *New York Times*, February 23, 1981; Alexander M. Haig Jr., *Caveat: Realism, Reagan, and Foreign Policy* (New York: Macmillan, 1984), p. 122.
7. Richard Whittle, "Congressional Leaders See Threat to El Salvador and Back Military Aid Pledge," *Congressional Quarterly*, February 21, 1981, p. 359.
8. Interview, January 8, 1986.
9. Hedrick Smith, "House Democrats Seeking to Limit Involvement by U.S. in El Salvador," *New York Times*, March 1, 1981.
10. The attack on "social reformers" was led by conservatives on Reagan's transition team. See Pedro A. Sanjuan, "Interim Report on the Bureau on Inter-American Affairs and Policy Areas," State Department Transition Team, Office of the President-Elect, p. 1.
11. Don Oberdorfer, "Salvador Is 'The Place to Draw the Line' on Communism, Percy Says," *Washington Post*, February 20, 1981.
12. Interview, Winslow Wheeler, aide to Senator Nancy Kassebaum, January 8, 1987, Washington, D.C.
13. Testimony of Robert White, U.S. Congress, House, Committee on Appropriations Subcommittee on Foreign Operations, *Foreign Assistance and Related Programs*

Appropriations for 1982, Hearings, Part 1, 97th Cong., 1st Sess. (Washington, D.C.: U.S. Government Printing Office, 1981), pp. 3, 17.

14. Ibid., pp. 28, 235. On January 29, 1981, Studds and nineteen co-sponsors introduced legislation to cut off all military aid to El Salvador. By November 1981, ninety-one House members were co-sponsors of the bill.

15. Ibid., p. 270.

16. Interview, Deane Hinton, August 25, 1987, Washington, D.C.

17. *Foreign Assistance and Related Programs Appropriations for 1982*, pp. 261–62.

18. Cynthia Arnson, *El Salvador: A Revolution Confronts the United States* (Washington, D.C.: Institute for Policy Studies, 1982), p. 73.

19. Jeane Kirkpatrick, "Dictatorships and Double Standards," *Commentary*, November 1979, pp. 34–45.

20. Charles Mohr, "Human Rights Choice Abhors Scolding as U.S. Tool," *New York Times*, February 13, 1981.

21. U.S. Congress, House, Committee on Foreign Affairs Subcommittee on Inter-American Affairs, *U.S. Policy Toward El Salvador*, Hearings, March 5 and 11, 1981, 97th Cong., 1st Sess. (Washington, D.C.: U.S. Government Printing Office, 1981), p. 9; and U.S. Congress, House, Committee on Appropriations Subcommittee on Foreign Operations, *Foreign Assistance and Related Programs Appropriations for 1982*, Hearings, Part 2, 97th Cong., 1st Sess. (Washington, D.C.: U.S. Government Printing Office, 1981), p. 113.

22. Richard Whittle, "Lefever Withdraws After Committee Vote," *Congressional Quarterly*, June 6, 1981, p. 985.

23. Interview, December 15, 1986, Washington, D.C.

24. Interview, Michael Posner, November 9, 1986, New York, New York.

25. U.S. Congress, House, Committee on Foreign Affairs Subcommittee on Inter-American Affairs, *U.S. Policy Toward El Salvador*, p. 52; *Congressional Record*, September 23, 1981, p. S 10316.

26. U.S. Congress, House, Committee on Foreign Affairs, *Foreign Assistance Legislation for Fiscal Year 1982, Part I*, Hearings, March 13, 18, 19, and 23, 97th Cong., 1st Sess. (Washington, D.C.: U.S. Government Printing Office, 1981), p. 163; and Bernard Gwertzman, "Haig Cites 'Hit List' for Soviet Control of Central America," *New York Times*, March 19, 1981.

27. U.S. Congress, Senate, Committee on Foreign Relations, *Foreign Assistance Authorization for Fiscal Year 1982*, Hearings, March 19, 24, 26, April 3, 10, 22, May 4, 1981, 97th Cong., 1st Sess. (Washington, D.C.: U.S. Government Printing Office, 1981), pp. 36, 40.

28. Jim Castelli, "State Department Says Murdered Nuns Did Not Engage in Political Acts," *Washington Star*, April 24, 1981.

29. U.S. Congress, House, Committee on Foreign Affairs Subcommittee on Inter-American Affairs, *U.S. Policy Toward El Salvador*, p. 134. *Time* magazine, for example, reported that, despite the existence of "an impressive amount of hard evidence about what took place" the day of the murders, "Salvadoran authorities are stonewalling, stubbornly refusing to press the inquiry to the point where security forces might become implicated." See "Stonewalling," *Time*, February 23, 1981.

30. Interview, January 6, 1987, Washington, D.C.

31. The letter, dated March 6, 1981, was printed in the *Congressional Record*, April 7, 1981, pp. S 3428–29.
32. U.S. Department of State, Press Briefing, March 2, 1981, p. 1.
33. Quoted in Ellen Collier, "El Salvador and the War Powers Resolution," Congressional Research Service, *Review*, June 1981, p. 2.
34. Richard Halloran, "Military Aspects of Crisis Are Underlined by Haig and a Pentagon Study," *New York Times*, February 21, 1981. Halloran's article quoted U.S. officials as saying that with a combat ratio of 4 to 1, it would be "impossible" for the government to put down the insurgency. The Salvadoran army was described as "not organized to fight a counterinsurgency" battle and "more like a 19th century constabulary than a 20th century army."
35. Interview, Bill Woodward, aide to Representative Gerry Studds, January 12, 1987, Washington, D.C.
36. U.S. Congress, Senate, Committee on Foreign Relations, *Foreign Assistance Authorization for Fiscal Year 1982*, p. 31.
37. Cited in George Gallup, "2 of 3 in U.S. See El Salvador Becoming 'Another Vietnam,' " *Washington Post*, March 26, 1981.
38. Transcript, Senator John Glenn radio interview with WDIF, Marion, Ohio, March 6, 1981, p. 4.
39. Haig, *Caveat* (note 6 above), pp. 129–32.
40. Section 4(a) of the War Powers Resolution requires the president to submit a written report whenever U.S. armed forces are introduced, without a declaration of war: "1) into hostilities or into situations where imminent involvement in hostilities is clearly indicated by the circumstances; 2) into the territory, airspace or waters of a foreign nation, while equipped for combat, except for deployments which relate solely to supply, replacement, repair, or training of such forces; 3) in numbers which substantially enlarge United States Armed Forces equipped for combat already located in a foreign nation."

    Section 21(c) of the Arms Export Control Act prohibits personnel carrying out defense services from performing "any duties of a combatant nature, including any duties relating to training and advising that may engage United States personnel in combat activities, outside the United States in connection with the performance of those defense services." The section also requires the president to report to Congress "within 48 hours after the outbreak of significant hostilities involving a country in which United States personnel are performing defense services." Quoted in Collier, "El Salvador and the War Powers Resolution," pp. 3–4.
41. Comptroller General of the United States, Report to Senator Zorinsky, *Applicability of Certain U.S. Laws That Pertain to U.S. Military Involvement in El Salvador*, GAO/ID-82-53, General Accounting Office, Washington, D.C., July 27, 1982, p. 4, and letter to Senator Zorinsky, p. 2.
42. See Senator Mark Hatfield, Representative George Miller, and Representative Jim Leach, *U.S. Aid to El Salvador: An Evaluation of the Past, A Proposal for the Future*, Report to the Arms Control and Foreign Policy Caucus, Washington, D.C. (February 1985), pp. 23–24.
43. *Congressional Record*, April 7, 1981, pp. S 3427–28.
44. U.S. Congress, House, Committee on Appropriations Subcommittee on Foreign

Operations, *Foreign Assistance and Related Programs Appropriations for 1982,* Part 1 (note 13 above), p. 299.

45. Ibid., p. 301.

46. *Congressional Record,* April 8, 1981, pp. H 1408–9.

47. "30 Salvadorans Reported Shot Down," *Washington Post,* April 8, 1981.

48. Richard Whittle, "Congress to Monitor Arms for El Salvador, Argentina; Angola Issue Still in Dispute," *Congressional Quarterly,* May 16, 1981, p. 849.

49. Ibid.

50. The sole dissenting vote was cast by Senator Richard Lugar (R-Ind.), who succeeded Percy in 1984 as chairman of the committee.

51. Interview, Luigi Einaudi, January 14, 1987, Washington, D.C.

52. Ibid.

53. Remarks by the Honorable Thomas O. Enders, Assistant Secretary of State for Inter- American Affairs, "El Salvador: The Search for Peace," World Affairs Council, Washington, D.C., July 16, 1981, pp. 1–9.

54. The House had adopted the Fiscal Year 1982 foreign aid authorization bill in December 1981 without debating the certification conditions. This was in response to Haig's plea to House Republicans to pass the legislation with as little controversy as possible.

55. *Congressional Record,* September 23, 1981, p. S 10321.

56. A letter from Duarte was read during the Senate debate by Senator Percy. See ibid., pp. S 10320–21.

57. Ibid., pp. S 10296 and S 10313.

58. The senators, all Republicans, were Andrews (N.D.), Baker (Tenn.), D'Amato (N.Y.), Gorton (Wash.), Grassley (Iowa), Murkowski (Alaska), Rudman (N.H.), and Stafford (Vt.). Senators Durenberger (R-Minn.), Nunn (D-Ga.), and Lugar (R-Ind.), all of whom took leading roles in ensuing Central America debates, voted against the certification and for the "sense of the Congress" language.

59. International Security and Development Cooperation Act of 1981, PL 97-113.

60. Interview, Senate Republican staff aid, December 15, 1986, Washington, D.C.

61. The charge was made during a meeting with editors and reporters at the *Washington Post.* See John M. Goshko, "Nicaragua Helping Arm El Salvador Leftists, Muskie Says," *Washington Post,* January 30, 1981.

62. U.S. Department of State, Press Release, April 1, 1981, pp. 1–2; and Wayne S. Smith, *The Closest of Enemies* (New York: Norton, 1987), p. 243. Haig stated that "the flow of arms into Nicaragua and thence into El Salvador slackened, a signal from Havana and Moscow that they had received and understood the American message" (*Caveat,* p. 131).

63. Oswaldo Bonilla, "Protesta el MDN por Suspensión de la Ayuda de E.U. a Nicaragua," *Diario Las Americas,* April 7, 1981.

64. Richard Halloran, "Proof of Soviet-Aided Terror Is Scarce," *New York Times,* February 9, 1981.

65. John M. Goshko, "Haig Charges on New El Salvador Arms Flow Called Exagger- ated," *Washington Post,* May 16, 1981.

66. See John Dinges, "White Paper or Blank Paper," *Los Angeles Times,* March 17, 1981.

67. Jonathan Kwitny, "Apparent Errors Cloud U.S. 'White Paper' on Reds in El Salvador," *Wall Street Journal*, June 8, 1981. See also Robert G. Kaiser, "White Paper on El Salvador Is Faulty," *Washington Post*, June 9, 1981; and Juan de Onis, "U.S. Officials Concede Flaws in Salvador White Paper but Defend Its Conclusions," *New York Times*, June 10, 1981.

68. U.S. Congress, Senate, Committee on Foreign Relations, *The Situation in El Salvador*, Hearings, March 18 and April 9, 1981, 97th Cong., 1st Sess. (Washington, D.C.: U.S. Government Printing Office, 1981), p. 101.

69. U.S. Congress, Senate, *Foreign Assistance Authorization for Fiscal Year 1982* (note 27 above), p. 452.

70. Elizabeth Farnsworth and Stephen Talbot, "Dispatches," *Nation*, May 30, 1981, p. 657; Barricada, "Ortega Advises U.S. Not to Defend Unjust Causes," in *Foreign Broadcast Information Service*, April 29, 1981, pp. P 15–16.

71. U.S. Congress, House, Committee on Foreign Affairs, Subcommittee on Inter-American Affairs, *Foreign Assistance Legislation for Fiscal Year 1982*, Part 7, Hearings and Markup, March 23, 26, 30, and April 8, 1981, 97th Cong., 1st Sess. (Washington, D.C.: U.S. Government Printing Office, 1981), pp. 39–58.

72. Interview, November 23, 1986, Washington, D.C.

73. Terri Shaw, "Sandinistas Send Envoy to Soothe Capitol Hill," *Washington Post*, October 29, 1981.

74. Arturo Cruz, "Nicaragua Needs U.S. Tolerance," *New York Times*, op-ed, December 9, 1981.

75. See Don Oberdorfer, "U.S., in Secret Dialogue, Sought Rapprochement with Nicaragua," *Washington Post*, December 10, 1981. See also Dickey, *With the Contras*, pp. 109–12.

76. For an account of the negotiations, see Roy Gutman, *Banana Diplomacy: The Making of American Policy in Nicaragua 1981–1987* (New York: Simon and Schuster, 1988), pp. 66–78.

77. John M. Goshko, "Haig Won't Rule Out Anti-Nicaragua Action," *Washington Post*, November 13, 1981.

78. Quotes from the NSC document first appeared in Patrick Tyler and Bob Woodward, "U.S. Approves Covert Plan in Nicaragua," *Washington Post*, March 10, 1982. See also Don Oberdorfer and Patrick Tyler, "U.S.-Backed Nicaraguan Rebel Army Swells to 7,000 Men," *Washington Post*, May 8, 1983. Within days of the NSC meeting, the *Boston Globe* reported that the Reagan administration had decided to "press covert action in Nicaragua." See William Beecher, "U.S. Rejects Military Options in Cuba, Nicaragua, for Now," *Boston Globe*, December 4, 1981.

79. Representative Lee Hamilton, "Nicaragua," *Congressional Record*, June 24, 1986, p. E 2236.

80. U.S. Congress, House, Permanent Select Committee on Intelligence, *Report* [to accompany H.R. 2760], *Amendment to the Intelligence Authorization Act for Fiscal Year 1983*, Part 1, May 13, 1983, 98th Cong., 1st Sess., pp. 7–8; Leslie H. Gelb, "Reagan Backing Covert Actions, Officials Assert," *New York Times*, March 14, 1982; Oberdorfer and Tyler, "U.S. Backed Nicaraguan Rebel Army," May 8, 1983.

Chapter Four. 1982: Standoffs and Half Measures—Congress Responds

1. The aid portion of the CBI envisioned $350 million in economic support funds (ESF) distributed in the following way: $128 million for El Salvador; $70 million for Costa Rica; $35 million for Honduras; $50 million for Jamaica; $40 million for the Dominican Republic; $10 million for the eastern Caribbean states; $10 million for Belize; $5 million for Haiti; $2 million for the American Institute for Free Labor Development (AIFLD). The CBI trade benefits and tax incentives to U.S. investors were never enacted, due to resistance from U.S. labor.

2. I. M. Destler, "The Elusive Consensus: Congress and Central America," in Robert Leiken, ed., *Central America: Anatomy of Conflict* (New York: Pergamon Press, 1984), p. 319; K. Larry Storrs, "Congress and U.S. Policy Toward Central America and the Caribbean," in U.S. Congress, House, Committee on Foreign Affairs, *Congress and Foreign Policy 1982* (Washington, D.C.: U.S. Government Printing Office, 1983), p. 67.

3. Karen DeYoung, "Salvador Land Reform Imperiled, Report Says," *Washington Post*, January 25, 1982.

4. Text of letter quoted in Representative Gerry Studds, "Statement . . . on Introduction of Resolution to Suspend Military Aid to El Salvador," February 2, 1982, p. 9.

5. Amnesty International, "Current Assessment of the Human Rights Situation in El Salvador," January 1982, p. 1, circulated with cover letter to members of Congress from Patricia Rengel, Director, Washington Office of Amnesty International, January 25, 1982.

6. Americas Watch Committee and American Civil Liberties Union, "Human Rights in El Salvador," Press Release, January 26, 1982, p. 2. The ACLU and Americas Watch report was subsequently published as the *Report on Human Rights in El Salvador* (New York: Vintage Books, 1982).

7. Alma Guillermoprieto, "Salvadoran Peasant Describes Mass Killing," *Washington Post*, January 27, 1982; "Massacre of Hundreds Is Reported in El Salvador," *New York Times*, January 27, 1982.

8. The White House, Presidential Determination No. 82-4, Memorandum for the Secretary of State, Subject: Determination to Authorize Continued Assistance for El Salvador," January 28, 1982, pp. 1–2, and accompanying Justification, pp. 1–6.

9. Destler, "The Elusive Consensus," p. 326.

10. Opening Statement, Honorable Don Bonker, "Human Rights in El Salvador," February 2, 1982, p. 2.

11. U.S. Congress, Senate, Committee on Foreign Relations, *Certification Concerning Military Aid to El Salvador*, Hearings, February 8 and March 11, 1982, 97th Cong., 2nd Sess. (Washington, D.C.: U.S. Government Printing Office, 1982), p. 2. The incident Percy referred to occurred in San Antonio Abad, where government troops dragged close to twenty people from their homes in the middle of the night and shot them.

12. Quoted in Raymond Bonner, *Weakness and Deceit: U.S. Policy and El Salvador* (New York: Times Books, 1984), p. 61.

13. American Embassy, San Salvador, to Department of State, "A Statistical Framework for Understanding Violence in El Salvador," January 15, 1982, pp. 5–6.

14. U.S. Congress, House, Committee on Foreign Affairs, Subcommittee on Inter-American Affairs, *Presidential Certification on El Salvador (Volume 1)*, February 2, 23, 25, and March 2, 1982, 97th Cong., 2nd Sess. (Washington, D.C.: U.S. Government Printing Office, 1982), p. 11.

15. Ibid., pp. 44–45 and 53–54.

16. Interview, January 16, 1987, Washington, D.C.

17. The administration assertions concerned the number of Salvadoran soldiers disciplined for certain crimes. See U.S. Congress, House, Permanent Select Committee on Intelligence, Subcommittee on Oversight and Evaluation, *U.S. Intelligence Performance on Central America: Achievements and Selected Instances of Concern*, Staff Report, September 22, 1982, 97th Cong., 2nd Sess. (Washington, D.C.: U.S. Government Printing Office, 1982), p. 17.

18. U.S. Congress, Senate, Committee on Foreign Relations, *Certification Concerning Military Aid to El Salvador*, p. 13.

19. U.S. Congress, House, Permanent Select Committee on Intelligence, Subcommittee on Oversight and Evaluation, *U.S. Intelligence Performance on Central America*, pp. 18–19. The El Mozote episode is also discussed in Cynthia Brown, "U.S. Reporting on Human Rights in El Salvador: Methodology at Odds with Knowledge," Americas Watch Committee, New York, June 1982, p. 21; and Bonner, *Weakness and Deceit*, p. 342.

20. La Comisión de la Verdad para El Salvador, *De la Locura a la Esperanza* (New York: United Nations, 1993), pp. 121–23.

21. Transcript, CBS "60 Minutes," aired March 14, 1993, interview with Todd Greentree, p. 14.

22. Americas Watch, "The Massacre at El Mozote: The Need to Remember," March 4, 1992, pp. 7–9.

23. U.S. Congress, Senate, Committee on Foreign Relations, *Certification Concerning Military Aid to El Salvador*, p. 29.

24. U.S. Congress, House, Committee on Foreign Affairs, *International Security and Development Cooperation Act of 1982*, Report No. 97-547, May 17, 1982, 97th Cong., 2nd Sess. (Washington, D.C.: U.S. Government Printing Office, 1982), p. 16.

25. George Russell, "The Death of a Thousand Cuts," *Time*, September 7, 1981, p. 15.

26. Bernard Gwertzman, "Haig Pledges U.S. Will Act to Block Salvador Rebels," *New York Times*, February 3, 1982. On February 24, President Reagan modified the phrase, saying that the United States would do "whatever is prudent and necessary to ensure the peace and security of the Caribbean area." Quoted in James McCartney, "Salvador, Vietnam—The Similarities," *San Francisco Chronicle*, March 7, 1982.

27. Bernard Gwertzman, "Haig, Rejecting Vietnam Parallel, Refuses to Bar Force in Caribbean," *New York Times*, February 8, 1982; U.S. Congress, House, Committee on Foreign Affairs, *East-West Relations—U.S. Security Assistance*, Hearing, March 2, 1982, 97th Cong., 2nd Sess. (Washington, D.C.: U.S. Government Printing Office, 1982), p. 19.

28. U.S. Congress, House, Committee on Foreign Affairs, *The Role of International Security Assistance in U.S. Defense Policy*, Hearing, March 10, 1982, 97th Cong., 2nd Sess. (Washington, D.C.: U.S. Government Printing Office, 1982), p. 44.

29. Interview, December 3, 1986, Washington, D.C.
30. Public Law 97-113, Sec. 728 (d)(4).
31. See Storrs, "Congress and U.S. Policy . . ." (note 2 above), p. 69.
32. *Congressional Record*, March 2, 1982, pp. H 548, H 551, H 549.
33. "U.S. Interests and Objectives in Central America and Caribbean," April 13, 1982, p. 8.
34. "U.S. Policy in Central America and Cuba Through F.Y. '84, Summary Paper," April 1982. The text of the document appeared in the *New York Times*, April 7, 1983.
35. U.S. Congress, House, Committee on Appropriations Subcommittee on Foreign Operations, *Foreign Assistance and Related Programs Appropriations for 1982*, Hearings, Part 1, 97th Cong., 1st Sess. (Washington, D.C.: U.S. Government Printing Office, 1981), p. 16; and U.S. Congress, Senate, Committee on Foreign Relations, *The Situation in El Salvador*, Hearings, March 18 and April 9, 1981, 97th Cong., 1st Sess. (Washington, D.C.: U.S. Government Printing Office, 1981), p. 117.
36. "D'Aubuisson Blamed for Gun Attack," *El Salvador News Gazette*, San Salvador, March 8–14, 1981, p. 1; Testimony of Robert E. White, in U.S. Congress, House, Committee on Foreign Affairs Subcommittees on Human Rights and International Organizations and Western Hemisphere Affairs, *The Situation in El Salvador*, January 26 and February 6, 1984, 98th Cong., 2nd Sess. (Washington, D.C.: U.S. Government Printing Office, 1984), p. 41; John Brecher et al., "The Darkening Landscape," *Newsweek*, March 29, 1982, pp. 30–32.
37. Barbara Crossette, "Congressman Asserts Salvador Does Not Want U.S. Troops," *New York Times*, February 20, 1982.
38. Interview, January 12, 1987, Washington, D.C.
39. Statement by the U.S. Official Observer Delegation, in U.S. Congress, Senate, Committee on Foreign Relations, Senator Nancy L. Kassebaum, *Report of the U.S. Official Observer Mission to the El Salvador Constituent Assembly Elections of March 28, 1982*, November 1982 (Washington, D.C.: U.S. Government Printing Office, 1982), pp. 5–6. Members of the official U.S. observer team included Senator Nancy L. Kassebaum (R-Kans.), Representative John Murtha (D-Pa.), Representative Robert Livingston (R-La.), Father Theodore Hesburgh, Dr. Clark Kerr, Dr. Howard Penniman, Dr. Richard Scammon, and Deputy Assistant Secretary of State for Inter-American Affairs Everett E. Briggs.
40. John M. Goshko, "Administration Hails Large Voter Turnout," *Washington Post*, March 30, 1982.
41. Undersecretary of State for Political Affairs Lawrence Eagleburger, as quoted in John M. Goshko, "U.S. Prepares to Work with Salvadoran Right," *Washington Post*, March 31, 1982.
42. Interview, Deane Hinton, August 25, 1987, Washington, D.C.; Raymond Bonner, "Heavy Vote in Salvador Can Be Read in Many Ways," *New York Times*, April 4, 1982; and Joanne Omang, "Gen. Walters to Meet with Salvador Politicians," *Washington Post*, April 21, 1982. Hinton denied that the certification was attached to the invitation letter, as originally reported in the press.
43. Confidential Hinton cable to SecState WashDC, "Subject: Post-Election Update, CODEL Wright's Dinner with Salvadoran Leaders," April 1982, pp. 4–6.

44. Joanne Omang, "Coalition Rule, U.S. Aid Linked in El Salvador," *Washington Post*, April 10, 1982.
45. Joanne Omang, "Salvadorans Pick Key Officials," *Washington Post*, April 23, 1982.
46. F. Marian Chambers, staff consultant, "Summary of CODEL Wright Central America Trip," Memorandum to Honorable Clement J. Zablocki, Chairman, April 19, 1982, p. 3.
47. "El Salvador Suspends 'Land to Tiller' Agrarian Reform Program," *Washington Post*, May 20, 1982.
48. John M. Goshko and William Chapman, "Bid to Curb Land Reform in Salvador Stirs Critics," *Washington Post*, May 21, 1982.
49. The levels were $26 million in military assistance and $40 million in economic aid.
50. U.S. Congress, Senate, Committee on Foreign Relations, *U.S. Policy in the Western Hemisphere*, Hearings, April 20, 27, 28, May 4 and 26, 1982, 97th Cong., 2nd Sess. (Washington, D.C.: U.S. Government Printing Office, 1982), pp. 215, 211–12.
51. William Chapman, "U.S. Ambassador Asserts El Salvador Did Not Kill Land Reform Program," *Washington Post*, June 8, 1982.
52. William Chapman, "Plea to Restore Aid to Salvador Does Not Persuade Congress," *Washington Post*, June 12, 1982.
53. Assistant Secretary Abrams to the Secretary, "Trip Report—Thinking About El Salvador," July 1982, pp. 1, 2.
54. Secretary of State Haig to American Embassy, San Salvador, "Program for Political Progress in El Salvador," May 1982, pp. 1–2.
55. This latter interpretation of the cable was made by Morton Halperin of the ACLU during a July press conference calling on the administration not to certify.
56. Department of State, "Report on the Situation in El Salvador with Respect to the Subjects Covered in Section 728(d) of the International Security and Development Act of 1981, P.L. 97-113, July 27, 1982, pp. 1, 2, 8.
57. Text, confidential cable partially released under the Freedom of Information Act, from Am Embassy San Salvador to Sec State Wash DC, Subject: Presidential Certification, July 1982; and Cynthia Arnson and Aryeh Neier, "Report on Human Rights in El Salvador, Second Supplement," Americas Watch and American Civil Liberties Union, January 20, 1983, pp. 67–71.
58. For the opinion of Salvadoran Acting Archbishop Arturo Rivera y Damas, see "Una entrevista Con Mons. Rivera y El Socorro Jurídico," Orientación, San Salvador, June 6, 1982.
59. Don Oberdorfer, "Torture Reported in El Salvador," *Washington Post*, July 26, 1982; and Christopher Dickey, "Torture Case Poses Problems for U.S. Officials," *Washington Post*, August 2, 1982.
60. U.S. Congress, House, Committee on Foreign Affairs, *Presidential Certification on El Salvador (Volume 2)*, Hearings and Mark-Up, June 2, 22; July 29; August 3, 10, and 17, 1982, 97th Cong., 2nd Sess. (Washington, D.C.: U.S. Government Printing Office, 1982), p. 88.
61. U.S. Congress, Senate, Committee on Foreign Relations, *Presidential Certifications on Conditions in El Salvador*, Hearing, August 3, 1982, 97th Cong., 2nd Sess. (Washington, D.C.: U.S. Government Printing Office, 1982), p. 1.
62. Remarks of Representative Howard Wolpe (D-Mich.) and Representative Gerry

Studds (D-Mass.) in House Committee on Foreign Affairs, *Presidential Certification on El Salvador (Volume 2)*, pp. 80 and 75.

63. Ibid., p. 336.
64. Interview, Deane Hinton, August 25, 1987, Washington, D.C.; American Institute for Free Labor Development, "Summary Report—Sheraton Hotel Murder Inquiry," October 7, 1982, pp. 1–5, and "Briefs," October 19, 1982, pp. 1–2; Associated Press, "Labor Institute Says Salvadoran Officer Ordered 3 Killings," *Washington Post*, October 8, 1982.
65. Quoted in Bonner, *Weakness and Deceit*, front cover.
66. "Some Reflections on El Salvador," as prepared for delivery by U.S. Ambassador Deane R. Hinton at the American Chamber of Commerce Luncheon, San Salvador, October 29, 1982, pp. 2–4.
67. Bernard Weinraub, "U.S. Envoy Warns Salvador of Cut in Military Aid," *New York Times*, November 3, 1982.
68. Interview, August 25, 1987, Washington, D.C.
69. Bernard Weinraub, "U.S. Envoy to Salvador Ordered to Stop Criticizing Rights Abuses," *New York Times*, November 10, 1982. Clark's identity was confirmed by Deane Hinton and another senior State Department official in separate interviews.
70. See "Text of Speech by Amb. Deane R. Hinton as prepared for delivery to the American Chamber of Commerce in San Salvador, El Salvador, October 29, 1982," p. 3 (State Department version).
71. Of the $128 million requested under the Caribbean Basin Initiative for economic aid for El Salvador, Congress approved only $75 million. It refused to fund all but $1 million of the administration's requested $35 million in supplemental military assistance.
72. U.S. Congress, Senate, Committee on Foreign Relations, Subcommittee on Western Hemisphere Affairs, *Human Rights in Nicaragua*, Hearings, February 25 and March 1, 1982, 97th Cong., 2nd Sess. (Washington, D.C.: U.S. Government Printing Office, 1982), pp. 72, 66; and U.S. Congress, House, Committee on Appropriations Subcommittee on Foreign Operations, *Foreign Assistance and Related Programs Appropriations for 1983*, Hearings, 97th Cong., 2nd Sess. (Washington, D.C.: U.S. Government Printing Office, 1982), p. 115.
73. House Committee on Appropriations, *Foreign Assistance and Related Programs Appropriations for 1983*, p. 92.
74. Statement by Senate and House Select Intelligence Committee Chairmen, March 4, 1982, pp. 1–2.
75. On February 14, Don Oberdorfer and Patrick Tyler of the *Washington Post* reported that "President Reagan has authorized a broad program of U.S. planning and action . . . in Central America, including the encouragement of political and paramilitary operations." A *Post* story on March 10, 1982, by Patrick Tyler and Bob Woodward quoted from the internal documents proposing the creation of the paramilitary force to fight the Sandinistas. The issue of deliberate leaks is discussed in Cord Meyer, "The Politicizing of Intelligence," *Washington Times*, May 27, 1983.
76. Christopher Dodd and Paul Tsongas, "Dear Colleague," March 18, 1982.
77. *Congressional Record*, March 15, 1982, pp. H 864–65.
78. Text of H. Con. Res. 293.

79. Interview, April 1, 1987, Washington, D.C.
80. *Congressional Record*, March 15, 1982, p. H 864.
81. Christopher Dickey, "Nicaraguan Moderates Assail U.S. for Alleged 'Destabilization' Plan," *Washington Post*, March 18, 1982.
82. Alvaro Jerez, "The Nicaraguan Democratic Movement's Position on Covert Operations in the Region of Central America," Statement to Covert Action Conference, May 27, 1982, pp. 1–4.
83. Interview, senior administration official, April 16, 1987.
84. F. Marian Chambers, Memorandum to Honorable Clement J. Zablocki, Chairman, April 19, 1982, pp. 6–7.
85. Christopher Dickey, "Exiles Battling Sandinistas Say U.S. Undercuts Effort," *Washington Post*, August 8, 1982; Stephen Kinzer, "Sandinista Foe Assails U.S. for Aiding Rightists," *Boston Globe*, November 5, 1982; Glenn Garvin, "Embittered 'Commander Zero' Blames CIA for His Misfortune," *Washington Times*, October 18, 1988.
86. In late August, head of Honduran military intelligence Colonel Leónidas Torres Arias accused armed forces chief General Gustavo Alvarez of "abandoning the policy of neutrality of Honduras" and embarking on a "bloody and criminal campaign" against a "neighboring country." See Cynthia Arnson, "An Uneasy Peace," *Nation*, October 30, 1982, pp. 420–21; Washington Office on Latin America, excerpts, "To the People and the Armed Forces of Honduras," September 1, 1982.
87. *Congressional Record*, June 30, 1982, p. S 7684.
88. *Congressional Record*, August 11, 1982, pp. H 5724, H 5730.
89. See John Brecher et al., "A Secret War for Nicaragua," *Newsweek*, November 8, 1982, pp. 42–55 (cover story); James Kelly, "Fears of War Along the Border," *Time*, December 6, 1982; Philip Taubman, "CIA Is Making a Special Target of Latin Region," *New York Times*, December 4, 1982.
90. Interview, Edgar Chamorro, September 6, 1985. See also Edgar Chamorro with Jefferson Morley, "Confessions of a 'Contra,' " *New Republic*, August 5, 1985, p. 20, and affidavit of Edgar Chamorro, September 5, 1985, Washington, D.C., p. 11.
91. Philip Taubman, "In Exiles' War Against Sandinistas, Florida is H.Q.," *New York Times*, December 7, 1982.
92. *Congressional Record*, December 8, 1982, p. H 9149.
93. Ibid., pp. H 9156–57. The term "Boland amendment" subsequently became a generic one for describing a total ban on aid to the contras. The only true "Boland amendment" bearing Boland's name, however, was the more limited measure adopted in December 1982.
94. U.S. Congress, Senate, Select Committee on Intelligence, *Report, January 1, 1983, to December 31, 1984*, October 10, 1984, 98th Cong., 2nd Sess. (Washington, D.C.: U.S. Government Printing Office, 1985), p. 5.

Chapter Five. 1983: The President Steps In

1. Interview, June 12, 1987, Washington, D.C.
2. *Congressional Quarterly Almanac 1983*, p. 112.

3. Department of State, Briefing Paper, "Central America," June 26, 1982; Alan Riding, "Mexican Officials Obtain U.S. Plan for Region," *New York Times*, August 16, 1982. In another confidential June briefing paper, the State Department said that "without the $128 million emergency funding, El Salvador may conclude it has no alternative but to come to terms with the insurgents." Congress approved only $75 million of the requested $128 million.

4. Interview, Luigi Einaudi, January 14, 1987, Washington, D.C.

5. Interviews, administration officials, April, June, and August 1987; John Goshko and Lou Cannon, "More Aid Urged for El Salvador," *Washington Post*, March 1, 1983; Bernard Weinraub, "The Question About El Salvador: Why a Crisis Now?" *New York Times*, March 4, 1983; Russell Watson et al., "Reagan Sounds the Alarm," *Newsweek*, March 14, 1983, pp. 16–24.

6. See Ron Cordray, "Salvador Option: Coalition or Marines," *Washington Times*, February 9, 1983; Lou Cannon and John M. Goshko, "U.S. Weighs Plan for Two-Track Policy on El Salvador," *Washington Post*, February 10, 1983. Neither of the two newspapers appears to have actually obtained a copy of the Enders proposal.

7. Interview, White House official, June 12, 1987, Washington, D.C.

8. Interview, June 12, 1987, Washington, D.C.

9. Tom Enders to the Secretary, Subject: Certifying El Salvador, January 8, 1983, p. 1.

10. U.S. Department of State, "Report on the Situation in El Salvador with Respect to the Subjects Covered in Section 728(d) of the International Security and Development Cooperation Act of 1981," January 21, 1983, pp. 1–67.

11. U.S. Congress, Senate, Committee on Foreign Relations, *Presidential Certification on Progress in El Salvador*, Hearing, February 2, 1983, 98th Cong., 1st Sess. (Washington, D.C.: U.S. Government Printing Office, 1983), pp. 20, 93, 545–46.

12. U.S. Congress, House, Committee on Foreign Affairs, Subcommittees on Human Rights and International Organizations and Western Hemisphere Affairs, *U.S. Policy in El Salvador*, Hearings, February 4, 28; March 7, 17, 1983, 98th Cong., 1st Sess. (Washington, D.C.: U.S. Government Printing Office, 1983), p. 14.

13. Washington Office on Latin America, "El Salvador Furniture Sale: Marking It Up to Mark It Down," *Update*, vol. 8 (March–April 1983), p. 1.

14. The day after Shultz spoke, Vice President Bush told a private meeting of the Inter-American Dialogue that he was unable to understand how priests reconciled their faith with Marxist ideas and tactics. See U.S. Congress, Senate, Committee on Appropriations Subcommittee on Foreign Operations, *Foreign Assistance and Related Programs Appropriations, Fiscal Year 1984*, Hearings, Part 1, 98th Cong., 1st Sess. (Washington, D.C.: U.S. Government Printing Office, 1983), pp. 1–82; John M. Goshko, "Catholic Aid to Marxists Puzzles Bush," *Washington Post*, March 3, 1983; Don Oberdorfer and John M. Goshko, "Shultz Calls for Move by Hussein," *Washington Post*, March 13, 1983.

15. Senate Committee on Appropriations, *Foreign Assistance and Related Programs Appropriations 1984* (note 14 above), pp. 38, 45; U.S. Congress, Senate, Committee on Foreign Relations, *Presidential Certification on Progress in El Salvador*, Hearings, February 2, 1983, 98th Cong., 1st Sess. (Washington, D.C.: U.S. Government Printing Office, 1983), p. 118.

16. U.S. Congress, House, Committee on Foreign Affairs, *Foreign Assistance Legislation*

for Fiscal Years 1984–1985, Part 1, Hearings, February 8, 15, 16, 22, 23, 24; March 24, 1983, 98th Cong., 1st Sess. (Washington, D.C.: U.S. Government Printing Office, 1984), p. 222.

17. *Public Papers of the Presidents, Ronald Reagan* (Washington, D.C.: U.S. Government Printing Office, 1983), p. 377.
18. *Congressional Record,* March 14, 1983, p. S 2742.
19. Senator Nancy L. Kassebaum, Dear Colleague, March 18, 1983, p. 1.
20. See U.S. Congress, House, Committee on Foreign Affairs, Subcommittee on Western Hemisphere Affairs, *Foreign Assistance Legislation for Fiscal Years 1984–85,* Part 7 (note 16 above), p. xi.
21. John Hughes, "Majority of American Public Opposes Increased Military Aid to El Salvador," Department of State, Information Memorandum to the Secretary, April 6, 1983, pp. 1–2. The memorandum was based on Gallup and Roper polls.
22. Jeane J. Kirkpatrick, "This Time We Know What's Happening," *Washington Post,* April 17, 1983; "Congressmen Attacked Over El Salvador Stand," *New York Times,* May 5, 1983.
23. Transcript, CBS News Interview with José Benito Bravo Centeno, March 31 and April 1, 1983, p. 2.
24. Dickey was one of the first reporters to travel with the contras, and his dispatches provided an independent source of information to members of Congress. House Intelligence Committee Chairman Edward Boland has cited the *Post* articles as formative in his decision to sponsor legislation ending U.S. support for covert operations in Nicaragua. See Christopher Dickey, "Well-Armed Units Show Strongholds," *Washington Post,* April 3, 1983; and "Rebel Odyssey: Foes of Sandinistas Seek to Purge Somoza Stigma," *Washington Post,* April 4, 1983.
25. Honorable Edward P. Boland, statement to the Democratic Caucus, July 14, 1983, p. 5; Don Oberdorfer and Patrick Tyler, "U.S.-Backed Rebel Army Swells to 7,000 Men," *Washington Post,* May 8, 1983; interview, House Democratic aide, May 18, 1987, Washington, D.C.
26. Text, letter to President Reagan, March 24, 1983.
27. Don Oberdorfer, "U.S. Support Bolsters Rebels' Confidence Inside Nicaragua," *Washington Post,* April 3, 1983.
28. *Congressional Record,* April 5, 1983, pp. S 4109–10.
29. Oberdorfer, "U.S. Support Bolsters Rebels' Confidence," April 3, 1983. On April 14, 1983, President Reagan said that his administration was "complying fully" with the Boland prohibition and that "anything we're doing in that area is simply trying to interdict the supply lines which are supplying the guerrillas in El Salvador. . . . We are not doing anything to try and overthrow the Nicaraguan government." (Lou Cannon and Patrick Tyler, "President Admits Aiding Guerrillas Against Nicaragua," *Washington Post,* April 15, 1983.)
30. Statement of Representative Wyche Fowler Jr. (D-Ga.), April 7, 1983, pp. 1–4.
31. Text, letter to Boland, April 22, 1983, pp. 1–2.
32. Honorable Edward P. Boland, statement to the Democratic Caucus, July 14, 1983, pp. 1–11.
33. Interview, former House Intelligence Committee aide, May 11, 1987, Washington, D.C.

34. Interview, June 23, 1987, Washington, D.C.
35. Sidney Blumenthal, "The Boland Achievement," *Washington Post*, June 15, 1987.
36. Text, H.R. 2760, p. 1.
37. White House, Office of the Press Secretary, "Text of the Address by the President to a Joint Session of the Congress," Washington, D.C., April 27, 1983, pp. 1–8. Former Florida Senator Richard Stone was named special negotiator on April 28, 1983. Over the course of the next year, he pursued contacts with the Salvadoran guerrilla opposition and their civilian allies for the purpose of bringing them into an electoral process in El Salvador.
38. Interview with William Clark, "Reagan's Foreign Policy—His No. 1 Aide Speaks Out," *U.S. News & World Report*, May 9, 1983, p. 35.
39. Ellen Hume, "Congress Mood Shifts on Latin Aid," *Los Angeles Times*, May 16, 1983.
40. Whereas the House Western Hemisphere Subcommittee had refused to give any portion of the $50 million supplemental request for El Salvador, the full committee approved $8.7 million of it. The administration also persuaded Senator Kassebaum to increase her proposed limit on Fiscal Years 1983 and 1984 aid by $20 million. See U.S. Congress, Senate, Committee on Foreign Relations, Report, *International Security and Development Cooperation Act of 1983*, May 23, 1983, 98th Cong., 1st Sess. (Washington, D.C.: U.S. Government Printing Office, 1983); and U.S. Congress, House, Committee on Foreign Affairs, Report, *International Security and Development Cooperation Act of 1983*, 98th Cong., 1st Sess. (Washington, D.C.: U.S. Government Printing Office, 1983), pp. 32–36.
41. Interview, December 15, 1986, Washington, D.C.
42. See *Congressional Record*, November 3, 1983, p. S 15292.
43. See "Casey Asks Panel: Who Said 'The CIA Lies'?" *New York Times*, May 27, 1983. According to aides involved in the discussions, most of the proposals involved some form of "symmetry"—an agreement that the United States would end covert operations against Nicaragua if the Nicaraguans stopped supporting the Salvadoran insurgents. Because the determination about Nicaraguan behavior would be left in the hands of the administration, opponents of covert operations concluded that a vote for the compromise would be a vote for the administration.
44. See text, letter to Daniel Ortega, June 2, 1983, signed by Democrats Barnes, Zablocki, Hamilton, Solarz, Fascell, Torricelli, Mikulski, Stark, Alexander, Wright, and Yatron, and Republican Jim Leach.
45. Additional Views of Honorable Dave McCurdy, in U.S. Congress, House, Permanent Select Committee on Intelligence, Report, *Amendment to the Intelligence Authorization Act for Fiscal Year 1983*, Part 1, May 13, 1983, 98th Cong., 1st Sess., p. 21.
46. Ibid., pp. 2, 11, 12.
47. U.S. Congress, House, Committee on Foreign Affairs, *Concerning U.S. Military and Paramilitary Operations in Nicaragua*, Markup, May 18, June 6 and 7, 1983, 98th Cong., 1st Sess. (Washington, D.C.: U.S. Government Printing Office, 1983), pp. 14, 21, 71, 77.
48. *Congressional Record*, July 28, 1983, p. H 5845.
49. Representative Mica (D-Fla.) consulted with a group of fifty-two mostly southern

Democrats on an alternative to the Boland-Zablocki legislation, which he offered as a substitute amendment during floor debate. Only seventeen of the fifty-two Democrats with whom Mica consulted voted to end covert operations. Several of these seventeen—including McCurdy, MacKay, Anthony, English, Watkins, Whitley, Hefner, J. Jones, Bennett, and Andrews—were among those who later supported contra aid in June 1985. See *Congressional Record*, July 28, 1983, pp. H 5020, H 5881–82; and *Congressional Record*, June 12, 1985, pp. H 4169–70.

50. *Congressional Record*, July 27, 1983, pp. H 5727, H 5757; Lou Cannon, "Reagan Sees a Latin 'Axis,' " *Washington Post*, June 21, 1983.

51. *Congressional Record*, July 28, 1983, p. H 5830.

52. *Congressional Record*, July 27, 1983, p. H 5742; and July 28, 1983, p. H 5857.

53. *Congressional Record*, July 27, 1983, p. H 5722.

54. Ibid.

55. Text, Dear Colleague letter from Dave McCurdy, July 26, 1983.

56. Christopher Madison, "Votes on Covert Aid Seen as Critical to Reagan's Central America Policy," *National Journal*, September 17, 1983, pp. 1893–98.

57. Don Oberdorfer, "CIA Planning to Back More Nicaragua Rebels," *Washington Post*, July 14, 1983; Philip Taubman, "U.S. Said to Weigh 40% Increase in Military Funds for Latin Allies," *New York Times*, July 17, 1983.

58. Lou Cannon, "President's Strong Man Stretches South," *Washington Post*, August 3, 1983; Don Oberdorfer, "Shultz's Roar on Policy-Making Got Results," *Washington Post*, October 23, 1983; Steven Weisman, "Reagan Denies Aim Is Bigger Presence in Latin Countries," *New York Times*, July 27, 1983; John Felton, "Congress Irresolute on Central America Plans," *Congressional Quarterly*, August 6, 1983, p. 1596.

59. The Central America Working Group, a mid-level interagency body, was formed following Kirkpatrick's February visit to Central America. It met in the State Department's seventh-floor operations center, reserved for crisis situations, until displaced by the October 1983 bombing of a U.S. Marines barracks in Lebanon.

60. Taubman, "U.S. Said to Weigh . . ." (note 57 above).

61. Interview, January 9, 1986.

62. Members of what came to be called the "Kissinger Commission" for its chairman, Henry Kissinger, were former New Jersey Senator Nicholas Brady; San Antonio Mayor Henry Cisneros; former Texas Governor William Clements Jr.; Yale economist Carlos Díaz-Alejandro; San Mateo businessman Wilson Johnson; AFL-CIO President Lane Kirkland; Washington political scientist Richard Scammon; Boston University President John Silber; former Supreme Court Justice Potter Stewart; former Democratic National Committee Chairman Robert Strauss; and William Walsh of Project Hope. The commission's eight congressional counselors were Senators Jackson, Bentsen, Mathias, and Domenici; and Representatives Wright, Barnes, Kemp, and Broomfield.

63. Quoted in Taubman, "U.S. Said to Weigh. . . ."

64. Philip Taubman, "Pentagon Gets Tough on Latin Policy," *New York Times*, September 12, 1983.

65. Office of the Assistant Secretary of Defense for Public Affairs, "Remarks Prepared for Delivery by the Hon. Fred C. Ikle, Under Secretary of Defense for Policy, to

Baltimore Council on Foreign Affairs, Baltimore, Maryland, September 12, 1983, pp. 4, 6.

66. Taubman, "U.S. Said to Weigh. . . ."

67. U.S. Department of State, "Report on the Situation in El Salvador with Respect to the Subjects Covered in Sections 728(d) and (e) of the International Security and Development Cooperation Act of 1981," July 20, 1983, pp. 4–7.

68. Interview, Luigi Einaudi, January 14, 1987, Washington, D.C. Representative Barnes recalled that "Tony Motley came in very determined to work very closely with the Congress. He was just all over us in the first few months. He wanted to meet us for breakfast, meet us for tea. . . . Gradually that faded." (Interview, January 29, 1987, Washington, D.C.)

69. Interview, January 8, 1987, Washington, D.C.

70. Interview, Paul Michel, December 16, 1986, Washington, D.C.

71. In response to his inquiries, the State Department appointed its own emissary, retired Judge Harold Tyler, to report on progress in the case.

72. Text, P.L. 98-151, Further Continuing Appropriations for Fiscal Year 1984. A House proposal that the 30 percent set-aside also apply to the case of the murdered U.S. agrarian advisers was defeated in a House-Senate conference.

73. Interviews, January 9, 1986, and June 12, 1987.

74. Joanne Omang, "U.S. Seeks to Oust Salvador Officials Tied to Death Squads," *Washington Post*, November 5, 1983; Lydia Chavez, "U.S. Presses Salvador to Act on Men Tied to Death Squads," *New York Times*, November 5, 1983. These articles followed a Reuters report two days earlier that the United States had detailed information on the command structure and leadership of the death squads but was unable to stop them for fear of implicating senior government and military leaders. See Robert Block, "U.S. Knows Death Squad Chiefs but Cannot Stop Killings," Reuters, San Salvador, November 3, 1983.

75. See U.S. Congress, House, Committee on Foreign Affairs, Subcommittees on Human Rights and International Organizations and Western Hemisphere Affairs, *U.S. Policy in El Salvador* (note 12 above), p. 16.

76. Text, U.S. Ambassador to El Salvador Thomas R. Pickering's Address before the American Chamber of Commerce in San Salvador, November 25, 1983, pp. 9, 10.

77. The original certification law, contained in a two-year foreign aid authorization, was due to expire on October 1, 1983. The House (on September 30) and the Senate (on November 17) extended the certification into 1984. The bill was so uncontroversial that it was approved in both houses by voice vote, without debate.

78. See Chris Hedges, "Rumors of Salvador Coup Fly as Army Loses Ground to Rebels," *Christian Science Monitor*, November 10, 1983; Lydia Chavez, "Salvador Rebels Make Gains and U.S. Advisers Are Glum," *New York Times*, November 4, 1983; Sam Dillon, "U.S.-Backed Salvadoran Soldiers Giving Up in Increasing Numbers," *Philadelphia Inquirer*, November 23, 1983; James Kelly et al., "Trouble on Two Fronts," *Time*, December 12, 1983, pp. 32–35.

79. Interview, January 8, 1987, Washington, D.C.

80. In January 1984, *Newsweek* reported that Pickering's trip was prompted by leaks from Pickering's staff opposed to his tough approach on the question of political violence. See Russell Watson et al., "Attacking the Death Squads," *Newsweek*, January 16, 1984, pp. 24–35 (cover story).

81. Interview, Margaret Daly Hayes, senior staff person for the Western Hemisphere, Senate Foreign Relations Committee, January 12, 1986. A House Republican aide maintained that "Republicans did behind the scenes make clear that this human rights stuff had to stop. Republicans were caught between the position of supporting U.S. policy and saying, 'Christ, there is a large problem here.' " (Interview, December 2, 1986, Washington, D.C.)

82. Toast of Vice President Bush at a dinner hosted by Salvadoran President Alvaro Magaña in San Salvador, El Salvador, U.S. Department of State, Bureau of Public Affairs, Current Policy No. 533, December 11, 1983, pp. 1–2.

83. Interview, January 6, 1988, San Salvador. One senior Reagan administration official disputed reports that Bush handed Salvadoran military leaders a list of names of death squad leaders. "Do not be mesmerized about who handed whom what," said this senior policymaker. (Interview, January 9, 1986.) See also "U.S. Bids Salvador Expel the Leaders of Murder Squads," New York Times, December 15, 1983.

84. Patrick Tyler, "U.S.-Backed Rebels Can't Defeat Nicaraguan Regime, CIA Finds," Washington Post, November 25, 1983.

85. U.S. Congress, Senate, Select Committee on Intelligence, Report, January 1, 1983 to December 31, 1984, Report No. 98-665, October 10, 1984 (Washington, D.C.: U.S. Government Printing Office, 1985), p. 6.

86. Text, September 19, 1983, finding, p. 1.

87. Patrick Tyler, "Challenges Rise to CIA Support for Latin Rebels," Washington Post, October 23, 1983; Doyle McManus, "Administration Anti-Nicaragua Push Toughens," Los Angeles Times, September 18, 1983; Philip Taubman, "U.S. Officials Say CIA Helped Nicaraguan Rebels Plan Attacks," New York Times, October 16, 1983; Associated Press, "Oct. 10 Assault on Nicaraguans Is Laid to CIA," New York Times, April 18, 1984; affidavit of Edgar Chamorro, September 5, 1985, Washington, D.C., pp. 16–17.

88. Congressional Record, November 17, 1983, pp. H 10342–45. In January 1983, Mexico, Venezuela, Colombia, and Panama met on the island of Contadora and drafted a peace proposal for Central America.

89. Congressional Record, November 3, 1983, p. S 15282.

90. Susan Benda, "Covert War: Legislative History," in Coalition for a New Foreign and Military Policy and Commission on U.S.-Central America Relations, Central America 1985: Basic Information and Legislative History on U.S.-Central American Relations (Washington, D.C.: Coalition, 1985).

91. Interview, May 18, 1987, Washington, D.C.

Chapter Six. 1984: Driving Policies to Conclusion

1. For a critique of the Kissinger Commission report, see William Leogrande, "Through the Looking Glass: The Kissinger Report on Central America," World Policy Journal, Winter 1984, pp. 251–84.

2. See National Bipartisan Commission on Central America, Report, January 1984, pp. 102, 104.

3. Ibid., p. 116.

4. Stephen Solarz, "A Plan for Curbing the Death Squads," *Washington Post*, February 22, 1984.
5. U.S. Department of State, "Report on the Situation in El Salvador," Washington, D.C., January 16, 1984, p. ii.
6. Fenton Communications, Press Release, "Former Top Salvadoran Military Colonel and Intelligence Chief Reveals Inner Workings of Death Squads," March 21, 1985, Washington, D.C., pp. 1–6, and transcript, "Short Circuit: Inside the Death Squads," March 21, 1985, pp. 1–14.
7. Interview, November 19, 1986, Washington, D.C.
8. The president's $8 billion plan called for $178.7 million in military assistance to El Salvador as part of a Fiscal Year 1984 supplemental appropriation, and $132.5 million for Fiscal Year 1985. Congress had approved $64.8 million for Fiscal Year 1984.
9. U.S. Congress, Senate, Committee on the Budget, *First Concurrent Resolution on the Budget–Fiscal Year 1985*, Hearings, Vol. 4, 98th Cong., 2nd Sess. (Washington, D.C.: U.S. Government Printing Office, 1984), p. 211.
10. *Congressional Record*, February 29, 1984, p. S 1920.
11. Foreign Affairs Committee Chairman Dante Fascell (D-Fla.), who had taken over the chairmanship of the committee following the late 1983 death of Clement J. Zablocki (D-Wisc.), did not want controversy over El Salvador to jeopardize the entire foreign aid request in his first year as chairman.
12. U.S. Congress, House, Committee on Appropriations Subcommittee on Foreign Operations, *Foreign Assistance and Related Programs Appropriations for 1985*, Part 3, Hearings, 98th Cong., 2nd Sess. (Washington, D.C.: U.S. Government Printing Office, 1984), p. 117.
13. Remarks at a White House Luncheon for Elected Republican Women Officials, *Public Papers of the Presidents, Ronald Reagan, 1984*, Book 1 (Washington, D.C.: U.S. Government Printing Office, 1986), p. 329.
14. Department of Defense, Fact Sheet, "Urgent Military Assistance Requirements for El Salvador," March 13, 1984, p. 2.
15. Fred Hiatt, "Hill to Be Accountable, Ikle Says," *Washington Post*, March 9, 1984; Francis X. Clines, "Reagan Calls Salvador Aid Foes Naive," *New York Times*, March 20, 1984.
16. A detailed discussion of the "emergency"—supported by the Pentagon's own documents—is found in Senator Mark Hatfield, Representative Jim Leach, and Representative George Miller, "Aid to El Salvador: An Evaluation of the Past, A Proposal for the Future," report to the Arms Control and Foreign Policy Caucus, February 1985, Washington, D.C., pp. 4–5.
17. See, for example, Robert J. McCartney, "Disorganization, Rebel Raids Disrupt Vote in El Salvador," *Washington Post*, March 26, 1984.
18. John Felton, "Hill Seeks New Strings on Central America Aid," *Congressional Quarterly*, March 31, 1984, p. 705; Hedrick Smith, "Better Prospects Seen for Raising Aid to El Salvador," *New York Times*, March 27, 1984.
19. Of a dozen or so amendments, the only ones to pass ended aid to El Salvador if the Salvadoran president were prevented from taking office or deposed in a military coup; provided $500,000 for the protection of witnesses and jurors involved in the

churchwomen's murder trial; and provided an additional $7 million for refugee assistance.

20. *Public Papers of the Presidents, Ronald Reagan, 1984*, Book 1, pp. 484, 481.
21. Lou Cannon, "Reagan Says Hill Undercuts Foreign Policy," *Washington Post*, April 7, 1984; Steven R. Weisman, "Reagan Attack on Policy Critics Puts New Edge on Campaign," *New York Times*, April 8, 1984; John Felton, "Hill Presses Reagan on Central America Policy," *Congressional Quarterly*, April 14, 1984, p. 832.
22. Joanne Omang, "Reagan to Bypass Congress to Fund El Salvador Fight," *Washington Post*, April 14, 1984; "Reagan Assailed as Untrustworthy," *Washington Post*, April 22, 1984.
23. Interview, January 8, 1987, Washington, D.C.
24. Interview, September 20, 1987, Washington, D.C.
25. Ibid.; *Congressional Record*, May 8, 1984, p. S 5406. The AID project was funded through a reprogramming approved by Congress in the summer of 1983.
26. Lydia Chavez, "U.S. Role in Salvador," *New York Times*, May 5, 1984.
27. *Congressional Record*, May 8, 1984, pp. S 5406–7. Helms said that the Senate Intelligence Committee was briefed on the covert involvement in the Salvadoran elections on May 3. He did not say where he got his information but reportedly was rebuked by the leadership of the Senate Intelligence Committee for publicly divulging intelligence secrets.
28. *Los Angeles Times* wire service, "U.S. Envoy Reportedly Target of Salvadoran Rightists," *Washington Post*, June 23, 1984; James LeMoyne, "Salvadoran Right Reportedly Plotted to Assassinate U.S. Ambassador," *New York Times*, June 23, 1984; Joanne Omang, "U.S. Feared Slaying of Envoy Here," *Washington Post*, June 27, 1984.
29. Interview, January 8, 1987, Washington, D.C.
30. Statement of the Official U.S. Observer Delegation to the May 6, 1984, El Salvador Presidential Election, in Representative Gillespie V. (Sonny) Montgomery, Dear Colleague letter, May 8, 1984, pp. 1–2.
31. *Congressional Record*, May 10, 1984, pp. H 3687, H 3715–16.
32. Ibid., pp. H 3725, H 3711.
33. Statement of Minority Leader Robert Michel, in ibid., p. H 3714.
34. Statement of Representative John Murtha (D-Pa.), ibid., p. H 3711.
35. Ibid., p. H 3740.
36. Text, Telegram from José Napoleón Duarte to Representative Matthew McHugh, May 8, 1984, p. 1.
37. Interview, George Ingram, Washington, D.C., December 3, 1986.
38. Interview, Michael Barnes, January 29, 1987, Washington, D.C.
39. Interview, Representative John Spratt, February 2, 1987, Washington, D.C.
40. Interview, December 2, 1986, Washington, D.C.
41. Interview, Vic Johnson, January 6, 1987, Washington, D.C.
42. Of the total Fiscal Year 1984 request for military aid of $265 million, Congress approved $196.55 million. The Continuing Resolution for Fiscal Year 1985 provided $128.25 million in military aid, out of the $132 million requested.
43. Interview, Salvadoran academic, August 26, 1984, San Salvador.
44. Telephone interview, September 21, 1984.

45. Edgar Chamorro, affidavit to the World Court, September 5, 1985, Washington, D.C., pp. 18–19.

46. Oliver L. North and Constantine Menges, Memorandum to [National Security Adviser] Robert C. McFarlane, "Subject: Special Activities in Nicaragua," March 2, 1984 (Iran-contra committees Exhibit OLN-177). "In accord with prior arrangements," according to North and Menges's memo, a rebel faction led by former Sandinista guerrilla leader Edén Pastora also claimed credit for the mining. Pastora said on March 6, "We are mining the ports . . . and Nicaragua is at war. . . . We have warned the world that the port of Bluefields and the port of Corinto are mined." Voice of Sandino, "Pastora on Mining of Harbors, FSLN Government," *Foreign Broadcast Information Service*, March 7, 1984, p. P15.

47. Doyle McManus, "Nicaragua Fuel Supplies Hurt by Rebel Mines," *Los Angeles Times*, March 23, 1984.

48. David Rogers, "U.S. Role in Mining Nicaraguan Harbors Reportedly Larger Than First Thought," *Wall Street Journal*, April 6, 1984; *Congressional Record*, April 12, 1984, p. H 2918.

49. *Congressional Record*, April 12, 1984, p. H 2918. Questions about the mining arose in the first place because of reports from Nicaraguan and contra sources in the publicly available *Foreign Broadcast Information Service* (hereafter cited as *FBIS*).

50. Interview, September 28, 1987, Washington, D.C.

51. U.S. Congress, Senate, Select Committee on Intelligence, *Report, January 1, 1983, to December 31, 1984*, October 10, 1984, 98th Cong., 2nd Sess. (Washington, D.C.: U.S. Government Printing Office, 1985), p. 7. The administration request for $21 million for the contras was made simultaneously with the request for $93 million in additional military aid for El Salvador. After Casey apologized to the Senate Intelligence Committee for the circumvention, it approved the $21 million by a vote of 14–0, with one abstention.

52. Bernard Gwertzman, "CIA Now Asserts It Sought Delays in Senate Briefing," *New York Times*, April 17, 1984; Don Oberdorfer and Bob Woodward, "Mining Halt Leaves Hill Unmollified," *Washington Post*, April 12, 1984. Columnist William Safire reported in mid-April that the CIA had informed the Senate Committee "on March 8 and March 13, in single, identical sentences amid secret testimony that ran 54 pages and 84 pages." William Safire, "Firestorm in a Teacup," *New York Times*, April 13, 1984.

53. Senate Select Committee on Intelligence, *Report* (note 51 above), p. 9.

54. Quoted in Martin Tolchin, "Of CIA Games and Disputed Rules," *New York Times*, May 14, 1984.

55. Comments of Senator Joseph R. Biden, Transcript of Proceedings, "The Constitution and U.S. Foreign Policy," Fund for New Priorities in America, Washington, D.C., April 12, 1984, pp. 120–27.

56. "Nicaraguan Leader Charges CIA Mined Two Key Ports," *Washington Post*, March 4, 1984; Associated Press, "Ship Said to Hit Mine in Nicaragua," *Washington Post*, March 9, 1984; Stephen Kinzer, "Nicaraguan Port Thought to Be Mined," *New York Times*, March 16, 1984; Alma Guillermoprieto, "Mine Placed by U.S.-Backed Rebels Damages Soviet Tanker, Managua Says," *Washington Post*, March 21, 1984;

Alma Guillermoprieto, "Nicaragua Seeks Soviet Aid After Ships Hit Mines," *Washington Post*, March 30, 1984; AFP and ACAN-EFE, "Reportage on Mines, Other Naval Activity," *FBIS*, April 2, 1984, pp. P25–27; ACAN-EFE, "Boats, Ships Hit by Mine, 'Piranha Boats,' " *FBIS*, March 30, 1984, p. P16.

57. Gwertzman, "CIA Now Asserts"; Philip Taubman, "How Congress Was Informed on Mining of Nicaragua Ports," *New York Times*, April 16, 1984.

58. Intelligence Committee member Senator Leahy had missed Casey's earlier briefing to the committee and requested a separate briefing. It appears that he was told of the CIA's hand in the mining.

59. *Public Papers of the Presidents, Ronald Reagan, 1984*, Book 1 p. 434.

60. Text, Letter, Ronald Reagan to Majority Leader Baker, April 4, 1984, p. 1.

61. *Congressional Record*, April 4, 1984, pp. S 3384–85, S 3764, S 3775.

62. Cohen added, "The administration has not been paying enough attention to the very strict restrictions we have placed upon the type of activity that could be performed [by the contras]. . . . If we are going to hold the bipartisan consensus we have had to date, . . . then we are going to have to insist that the administration strictly follow those guidelines." Ibid., pp. S 3782–83.

63. *Congressional Record*, March 29, 1984, p. S 3384. The one-page State Department memo on the "Use of Naval Mines in the Exercise of Self-Defense" stated that "naval mines [are] one legitimate means of exercising this right of individual and collective self defense in appropriate circumstances. For example, the proportionate use of naval mines can be a legitimate means of interrupting a flow of arms destined for infiltration into the territory of the victim, or to disrupt the flow of military and other materials essential to the attack's overall aggressive effort." Quoted in John Felton, "Administration Defends Mining of Harbors," *Congressional Quarterly*, April 14, 1984, p. 835.

64. *Congressional Record*, April 4, 1984, p. S 3765; "The Mining: Chronology of a Controversy," *Congressional Quarterly*, April 21, 1984, p. 905. In a letter to CIA Director Casey dated April 9, 1984, Goldwater complained that a member of the Intelligence Committee had stated during debate that President Reagan had approved the mining. "I strongly denied that," Goldwater said, "because I had never heard of it." Text in *Congressional Quarterly*, April 14, 1984, p. 833.

65. David Rogers, "U.S. Role in Mining Nicaraguan Harbors Reportedly Larger Than First Thought," *Wall Street Journal*, April 6, 1984; Fred Hiatt and Joanne Omang, "CIA Helped to Mine Ports in Nicaragua," *Washington Post*, April 7, 1984; Philip Taubman, "Americans on Ship Said to Supervise Nicaragua Mining," *New York Times*, April 8, 1984.

66. Interview, September 28, 1987, Washington, D.C.

67. Taubman, "Americans on Ship."

68. Senate Select Committee on Intelligence, *Report* (note 51 above), p. 9.

69. Text, Barry Goldwater to William Casey (note 64 above). Goldwater stated bluntly, "I am pissed off. . . . This is an act violating international law. . . . It is an act of war. For the life of me, I don't see how we are going to explain it." The text of the letter was printed in the *New York Times* on April 11, 1984, with profanities deleted.

70. *Congressional Record*, April 10, 1984, p. S 4198; Senate Select Committee on Intelligence, *Report*, p. 8.

71. Both resolutions were "sense of the Congress" statements that no U.S. funds were to be used for the purpose of mining the ports or territorial waters of Nicaragua. *Congressional Record*, April 10, 1984, p. S 4205, and April 12, 1984, p. H 2878.
72. Interview, Kirk O'Donnell, November 6, 1986, Washington, D.C.
73. Senate Select Committee on Intelligence, *Report*, p. 8.
74. Barnard L. Collier, "McFarlane Says Hill Knew About Mining," *Washington Times*, April 13, 1984.
75. Senate Select Committee on Intelligence, *Report*, p. 9.
76. Interview, White House official, June 23, 1987, Washington, D.C.
77. U.S. Congress, House, Permanent Select Committee on Intelligence Subcommittee on Legislation, *H.R. 1013, H.R. 1371, and Other Proposals Which Address the Issue of Affording Prior Notice of Covert Actions to the Congress*, Hearings, April 1, 8 and June 10, 1987, 100th Cong., 1st Sess. (Washington, D.C.: U.S. Government Printing Office, 1987), p. 36.
78. Ibid., pp. 38–39.
79. As early as July 1983 the press reported that the Israeli government was supplying weapons to the contras. Contra commander Enrique Bermúdez told NBC that the contras had received Israeli weapons taken from the PLO in Lebanon. See Philip Taubman, "Israel Said to Aid Latin Aims of U.S.," *New York Times*, July 21, 1983; and Fred Francis, "NBC Nightly News," April 23, 1984.
80. Iran-contra committees Exhibit DRC #19-3 and #19-4. The warning from CIA Deputy Director John McMahon appears in DRC #19-14. Clarridge traveled to South Africa in April 1984. In testimony to the Iran-contra committee, he insisted that he did not solicit contra aid. The documents released by the committee delete any mention of South Africa as well as the names of U.S. officials mentioned in some of the cables. The country and officials were identified by name in Stephen Engleberg, "U.S. Planned in '84 for South Africa to Help Contras," *New York Times*, August 20, 1987.
81. William J. Casey to Robert C. McFarlane, March 27, 1984, in U.S. Congress, House Select Committee to Investigate Covert Arms Transactions with Iran and Senate Select Committee on Secret Military Assistance to Iran and the Nicaraguan Opposition, *Testimony of Robert C. McFarlane, Gaston J. Sigur Jr., and Robert W. Owen*, Hearings, May 11, 12, 13, 14, and 19, 1987, 100th Cong., 1st Sess. (Washington, D.C.: U.S. Government Printing Office, 1987), pp. 456–57 (hereafter cited as McFarlane Hearings).
82. President's Special Review Board, *The Tower Commission Report* (New York: Bantam Books and Times Books, 1987), pp. 458–59, and McFarlane Hearings, pp. 17, 22–23. According to a Saudi version of events, the money was not "offered" but rather solicited by McFarlane. See David Hoffman and Bob Woodward, "McFarlane Said to Solicit Contra Aid from Saudis, *Washington Post*, May 14, 1987.
83. Constantine C. Menges, Memorandum for Robert C. McFarlane, Subject: NSPG Minutes, July 11, 1984, pp. 9–14; Affidavit, *United States of America v. Oliver L. North*, Criminal No. 88-0080-02-GAG, U.S. District Court, District of Columbia, undated, pp. 1–4 (hereafter cited as Defense Affidavit).
84. Defense Affidavit, pp. 16, 19–23.
85. Memorandum from Oliver L. North to John M. Poindexter, "Press Guidance re Costa Rican Airstrip," September 30, 1986, p. 2.

86. *Congressional Record*, June 18, 1984, p. S 7502.
87. John Felton, "Vote Belies Eroding Support on Nicaragua," *Congressional Quarterly*, June 23, 1984, pp. 1484–85.
88. Senate Select Committee on Intelligence, *Report*, p. 10. Of the Intelligence Committee's seven Democrats, only Sam Nunn voted to continue the program.
89. Don Gregg, Memorandum for the Vice President, Subject: Funding for the Contras, September 18, 1984, Iran-contra committees Exhibit DRC #26; Memorandum from Oliver L. North to Robert C. McFarlane, Subject: FDN Military Operations, April 11, 1985, in McFarlane Hearings, p. 520.
90. Draft, U.S. Department of State and Department of Defense, "Background Paper: Nicaragua's Military Build-up and Support for Central American Subversion," p. 18, delivered to congressional offices on June 27, 1984; and report of same title issued July 18, 1984, p. 18.
91. Associated Press, "Defector Says Sandinistas Smuggle Drugs to U.S.," *New York Times*, August 3, 1984. In January 1986 the DEA said that although one investigation resulted in the indictment of a Nicaraguan aide to the Minister of the Interior, "no evidence was developed to implicate the Minister of the Interior or other Nicaraguan officials."
92. R. Spencer Oliver and Bert Hammond, Letter to Foreign Affairs Committee Chairman Dante B. Fascell, September 7, 1988, p. 2, and accompanying report, "State Department and Intelligence Community Involvement in Domestic Activities Related to the Iran/Contra Affair," p. 30. See also Robert Parry and Peter Kornbluh, "Iran-Contra's Untold Story," *Foreign Policy*, no. 72 (Fall 1988), pp. 3–30.
93. *Congressional Record*, October 3, 1984, p. S 12857; the Senate bill included $28 million for the contra program, slightly more than had been approved the previous year.
94. John Felton, "On Foreign Aid, More Stumbling Blocks," *Congressional Quarterly*, October 6, 1984, p. 2418.
95. The wording of the law said that "the prohibition concerning Nicaragua . . . shall cease to apply if, after February 28, 1985, (1) the President submits to Congress a report . . . and (2) a joint resolution approving assistance for military or paramilitary operations in Nicaragua is enacted." Text, Section 8066, H.J. Res. 648, P.L. 98-618; See also Victor C. Johnson, "Congress and Contra Aid 1986–1987," in Abraham F. Lowenthal, ed., *Latin America and Caribbean Contemporary Record*, vol. 6 (1986–87) (New York: Holmes and Meier, 1989).
96. *Congressional Record*, October 10, 1984, pp. H 11980, H 11884.
97. Ibid., p. H 11980.
98. Telephone interview, Mike O'Neil, House Intelligence Committee, September 10, 1987.
99. Thomas S. Foley, "We Made Ourselves Quite Clear," *Washington Post*, July 7, 1987.
100. Text, Executive Order 12333—United States Intelligence Activities, December 4, 1981, in *Public Papers of the Presidents, Ronald Reagan, 1981* (Washington, D.C.: U.S. Government Printing Office, 1982), p. 1129.
101. Testimony at trial of John M. Poindexter, cited in David Johnston, "Poindexter's

Reassurance on Aid Ban Is Recalled," *New York Times*, March 20, 1990; Joe Pichirallo, "Poindexter Withheld Arms-Deal Details, Trial Told," *Washington Post*, March 20, 1990.

102. Testimony of Alan D. Fiers Jr., in U.S. Congress, Senate, Select Committee on Intelligence, *Nomination of Robert M. Gates*, Hearings, Vol. I, September 16, 17, 19, 20, 1991, 102nd Cong., 1st Sess. (Washington, D.C.: U.S. Government Printing Office, 1992), pp. 655–56.

Chapter Seven. 1985–1986: The Triumph of Presidential Power

1. U.S. Congress, House Select Committee to Investigate Covert Arms Transactions with Iran and Senate Select Committee on Secret Military Assistance to Iran and the Nicaraguan Opposition, *Iran-Contra Affair*, November 13, 1987, 100th Cong., 1st Sess. (Washington, D.C.: U.S. Government Printing Office, 1987), p. 4 (hereafter cited as Report of the Congressional Committees); Memorandum for W. Robert Pearson from J. R. Scharfen, Subject: The 1984 Boland Amendment, August 23, 1985, p. 1.

2. Report of the Congressional Committees, pp. 4–5.

3. In a detailed account of the 1984 elections, *Newsday* reporter Roy Gutman argued that hardliners in both the Nicaraguan opposition and the Reagan administration maneuvered to keep Cruz from participating in the elections in order to discredit them. See *Banana Diplomacy: The Making of American Policy in Nicaragua 1981–1987* (New York: Simon and Schuster, 1988), pp. 232–55.

4. "Democrats Have Net Gain of Two Senate Seats," *Congressional Quarterly Almanac 1984*, pp. 3B–5B; William Schneider, "The November 6 Vote for President: What Did It Mean?" in Austin Ranney, ed., *The American Elections of 1984* (Washington, D.C.: American Enterprise Institute, 1985), p. 232.

5. "GOP Disappointed with Gains in House," *Congressional Quarterly Almanac 1984*, pp. 13B–15B; Margaret Shapiro, "Contra Aid Vote Presages Renewed U.S. Role," *Washington Post*, June 14, 1985.

6. Austin Ranney, "Reagan's First Term," in Ranney, ed., *American Elections of 1984*, p. 33; *Gallup Report*, January 1985, pp. 7, 9; and January 1986, pp. 22, 26.

7. Interview, December 15, 1986, Washington, D.C.; Interview, Representative Bill Richardson (D-N.M.), December 2, 1986, Washington, D.C.

8. Quoted in Raymond E. Wolfinger, "Dealignment, Realignment and Mandates," in Ranney, ed., *American Elections of 1984*, p. 292.

9. Report of the Congressional Committees (see note 1 above), pp. 46, 50.

10. Text, State of the Union Address, February 6, 1985, in *Congressional Quarterly Almanac 1985*, pp. 8D–11D.

11. Charles Krauthammer, "Support the Contras," *Washington Post*, January 11, 1985.

12. Joshua Muravchik, "Topple the Sandinistas," *New York Times*, March 3, 1985.

13. Krauthammer's article originally appeared in *Time*, April 1, 1985. It is reprinted in Robert W. Tucker, "Intervention and the Reagan Doctrine," Ethics and Foreign Policy Lecture Series, Council on Religion and International Affairs, New York, New York, 1985, pp. 19–24.

14. George Shultz, "Shaping American Foreign Policy: New Realities and New Ways of Thinking," *Foreign Affairs*, vol. 63 (Spring 1985), p. 713.

15. Quoted in Joanne Omang and David Ottaway, "U.S. Seems More Willing to Support Insurgencies," *Washington Post*, May 26, 1985.

16. Helen Dewar, "Lugar Says Congress Is Likely to Deny Further 'Contra' Aid," *Washington Post*, January 24, 1984.

17. Remarks of Senator Dave Durenberger Before the National Press Club, March 26, 1985, pp. 1, 5.

18. John M. Goshko, "Shultz Campaigns for 'Contra' Aid," *Washington Post*, February 23, 1985; Lee H. Hamilton, "Nicaragua: We Can't Remake It in Our Image," *Washington Post*, March 24, 1985.

19. Interview, Democratic House member who requested anonymity, Washington, D.C.

20. Interview, former Nicaraguan official, January 30, 1985, Washington, D.C.

21. Joanne Omang, "Sandinista Foe Backs 'Contra' Aid," *Washington Post*, January 4, 1985; Memorandum from Oliver L. North to Robert C. McFarlane, "Subject: Using the March 1 San José Declaration to Support the Vote on the Funding for the Nicaraguan Resistance," April 1, 1985, Iran-contra committees Exhibit OLN-260, p. 2; Document on National Dialogue of the Nicaraguan Resistance, March 2, 1985, San José, Costa Rica, p. 2; Report of the Congressional Committees, p. 48.

22. Interviews, February 2, 1987, and January 28, 1987, Washington, D.C.

23. Agence France Presse, "FDN Leader Predicts Sandinist Defeat in 1985," *Foreign Broadcast Information Service*, January 9, 1985, p. P18.

24. *Weekly Compilation of Presidential Documents*, vol. 21, no. 8 (February 25, 1985), pp. 186–87, 212–13; *Weekly Compilation of Presidential Documents*, vol. 21, no. 10 (March 11, 1985), p. 245.

25. See, for example, Robert K. Goldman et al., *Violations of the Laws of War by Both Sides in Nicaragua 1981–1985*, Americas Watch Committee, New York, New York, March 1985; Arms Control and Foreign Policy Caucus, "Who Are the Contras: An Analysis of the Makeup of the Military Leadership of the Rebel Forces, and of the Nature of Private American Groups Providing them Financial and Material Support," Washington, D.C., April 18, 1985, and subsequent updates.

26. David Johnston with Michael Wines, "Intelligence Material on Sandinistas Is Said to Have Involved Lawmakers," *New York Times*, September 15, 1991.

27. Following press revelations in 1991 of the wiretaps, the House and Senate intelligence committees looked into allegations that transcripts of NSA-monitored telephone calls were distributed improperly within the executive branch. Senate Intelligence Committee chair David L. Boren (D-Okla.) said that the review found one case where "essentially harmless" information had been improperly distributed but that the inquiry uncovered no "improper, illegal, inappropriate or embarrassing" revelations of information by members of Congress or their aides to the Sandinistas. Hoping to make political hay out of the investigation, Republicans called on President George Bush in late 1991 to release transcripts of the telephone calls that might reveal "possibly illegal activities" by House members or their staff. "Intelligence Panels Probe Taps on Sandinista Calls," *Congressional Quarterly*,

October 12, 1991, p. 2968; Karen Schneider, "GOP Seeks Release of Sandinista Tapes," *Miami Herald*, October 6, 1991.

28. Shultz's remarks were substantially toned down in the printed hearing record. Compare Norman Kempster, "Shultz Assails Opponents of Aid to the Contras," *Los Angeles Times*, February 20, 1985; and U.S. Congress, House, Committee on Foreign Affairs, *Foreign Assistance Legislation for Fiscal Years 1986–87*, Part 1, Hearings, February 19, 20, 21, 26, and March 7, 1985, 99th Cong., 1st Sess. (Washington, D.C.: U.S. Government Printing Office, 1985), pp. 51–52; Bernard Gwertzman, "Shultz Sees Peril in Refusing to Aid Nicaragua Rebels," *New York Times*, February 23, 1985; and Aryeh Neier, "The Politics of Paranoia," *New York Times*, April 29, 1985.

29. Report of the Congressional Committees, p. 34.

30. Interview, January 8, 1987, Washington, D.C.; Text, Letter from Comptroller General of the United States Harry R. Van Cleve to Honorable Jack Brooks, Chairman, Committee on Government Operations, September 30, 1987, p. 7.

31. Van Cleve to Brooks (note 30 above), appendix 1 and p. 5. The article on the Soviet military buildup in Nicaragua, by John F. Guilmartin Jr., appeared in the *Wall Street Journal* on March 11, 1985. On April 7, 1985, the *Washington Post* published an op-ed article by FDN leader Adolfo Calero; on December 13, 1985, rebel leaders Calero, Arturo Cruz, and Alfonso Robelo signed an op-ed article in the *New York Times* claiming that the rebel leadership was "united in its goals—peaceful solutions and national reconciliation" and that "we are not, and will never be, the instrument of a foreign power." The GAO did not identify which op-ed articles were produced by the administration. See Adolfo Calero, Arturo José Cruz, and Alfonso Robelo Callejas, " 'Contras' Are on the Right Track," *New York Times*, December 13, 1985.

32. "Chronological Event Checklist," March 7, 1985, pp. 1–9, agency and author unspecified.

33. Interview, November 12, 1986, Washington, D.C.

34. Interview, Winslow Wheeler, January 8, 1986, Washington, D.C.

35. U.S. Congress, House Select Committee to Investigate Covert Arms Transactions with Iran and Senate Select Committee on Secret Military Assistance to Iran and the Nicaraguan Opposition, *Testimony of Robert C. McFarlane, Gaston J. Sigur Jr., and Robert W. Owen*, Joint Hearings, May 11, 12, 13, 14, and 19, 1987, 100th Cong., 1st Sess. (Washington, D.C.: U.S. Government Printing Office, 1987), p. 782 (hereafter cited as Joint Hearings, McFarlane et al.).

36. Oliver L. North and Raymond F. Burghardt, Memorandum for Robert C. McFarlane, Subject: Approach to the Hondurans regarding the Nicaraguan Resistance, February 11, 1985, pp. 1–2; Robert C. McFarlane, Memorandum for George P. Shultz, Caspar W. Weinberger, William J. Casey, General John W. Vessey Jr., Subject: Approach to the Hondurans regarding Nicaraguan Military Build-up, February 12, 1985, p. 1; Robert C. McFarlane, Memorandum for the President, Subject: Approach to the Hondurans regarding the Nicaraguan Resistance, February 19, 1985, pp. 1–2; Oliver L. North and Raymond F. Burghardt, Memorandum for Robert C. McFarlane, Subject: Presidential Letter to President Suazo of Honduras, February 20, 1985, p. 1; Defense Affidavit, pp. 20–23.

37. Memorandum to Robert C. McFarlane from Oliver L. North, "Subject: Fallback Plan for the Nicaraguan Resistance," March 16, 1985, p. 2, in Joint Hearings, McFarlane et al., p. 512.

38. U.S. Congress, Senate, Committee on Foreign Relations, *Security and Development Assistance*, Hearings, March 15, 20, 21, 22, and 26, 1985, 99th Cong., 1st Sess. (Washington, D.C.: U.S. Government Printing Office, 1985), pp. 909–10.

39. Interview with Senator David Durenberger, "Inquiry," *USA Today*, February 26, 1985.

40. Text, Senator Sam Nunn, Speech to the Coalition for a Democratic Majority, April 17, 1985, in *Congressional Record*, April 23, 1985, p. S 4595.

41. Gerald M. Boyd, "Reagan Told House Won't Back Assistance to Nicaraguan Rebels," *New York Times*, April 4, 1985.

42. Gerald M. Boyd, "Reagan Pleased by Replies on Nicaragua," *New York Times*, April 7, 1985; David Hoffman, "Reagan Sets Out 'Contra' Aid Plan," *Washington Post*, April 5, 1985.

43. See memorandums, Oliver L. North to Robert C. McFarlane, March 16, 1985, and April 11, 1985, in Joint Hearings, McFarlane et al., pp. 512, 520–21.

44. White House, Office of the Press Secretary, Text, Remarks of the President on Central America Peace Proposal, April 4, 1985, pp. 2–3.

45. "U.S. Support for the Democratic Resistance Movement in Nicaragua," in Hedrick Smith, "A Larger Force of Latin Rebels Sought by U.S.," *New York Times*, April 17, 1985.

46. Interview, November 5, 1986, Washington, D.C.

47. Interview, Kirk O'Donnell, November 6, 1986, Washington, D.C.

48. The co-sponsors of the bipartisan alternative were Representatives Barnes (D-Md.), Hamilton (D-Ind.), Jones (D-Okla.), Leach (R-Iowa), Fish (R-N.Y.), and Zschau (R-Calif.). For a discussion of the impact of the Contadora negotiations on congressional action, see Cynthia Arnson, "Contadora and the U.S. Congress," in Bruce Bagley, ed., *Contadora and the Diplomacy of Peace in Central America*, vol. 1 (Boulder, Colo.: Westview Press, 1987), pp. 123–41.

49. *Weekly Compilation of Presidential Documents*, vol. 21, no. 17 (April 29, 1985), p. 490.

50. Text, Letter of President Ronald Reagan to Robert Dole, *Congressional Record*, April 23, 1985, pp. S 4622–23.

51. *Congressional Record*, April 23, 1985, pp. S 4593, S 4586–87; and Joanne Omang and Margaret Shapiro, "Senate Approves, House Defeats, 'Contra' Aid," *Washington Post*, April 24, 1985.

52. *Congressional Record*, April 23, 1985, p. H 2378.

53. Ibid., pp. H 2334–35.

54. Joanne Omang, "Reagan Rallied for Aid Til the Hill Surrendered," *Washington Post*, January 2, 1987.

55. Interview, January 28, 1987, Washington, D.C. McCurdy's reference to the $27 million was to the package of humanitarian aid he took the lead in drafting, which later passed the House.

56. Dan Balz and Margaret Shapiro, "Congress Expected to Back Some Form of Aid to 'Contras,' " *Washington Post*, April 26, 1985; Russell Watson, "Retreating on Rebel Aid," *Time*, April 29, 1985, pp. 40–43.

57. Radio Sandino, Managua, "Ortega's Trip to Soviet Union Officially Announced," *Foreign Broadcast Information Service*, April 26, 1985, p. P4; Associated Press, "Nicaraguan Plans Visit to Moscow," *Washington Post*, April 25, 1985.
58. Shirley Christian, "Senator Objects to Trip," *New York Times*, April 25, 1985.
59. Margaret Shapiro and Joanne Omang, "Speaker Says House May Aid 'Contras,' " *Washington Post*, May 7, 1985; Margaret Sharpiro, "Contra Aid Vote Presages Renewed U.S. Role," *Washington Post*, June 14, 1985; Interview, Kirk O'Donnell, November 6, 1986, Washington, D.C.
60. Interview, January 13, 1987, Washington, D.C.
61. Transcript, "Towards a New Policy for Nicaragua," a conversation with Senator Sam Nunn and Representative Dave McCurdy, Coalition for a Democratic Majority, June 3, 1985, p. 3.
62. Interview, November 12, 1986, Washington, D.C.
63. The quotation is from Representative Bill Alexander (D-Ark.), in Stephen V. Roberts, "Anti-Managua Aid Is Seen As Likely," *New York Times*, May 5, 1985.
64. See Bernard Aronson, "Another Choice in Nicaragua," *New Republic*, May 27, 1985, pp. 698–99.
65. Interviews, February 2, 1987, and January 28, 1987, Washington, D.C.
66. Interview, February 2, 1987, Washington, D.C.
67. Interview, November 12, 1986, Washington, D.C.
68. For a different view, see Philip Brenner and William M. Leogrande, "Congress and the Not-So-Secret War Against Nicaragua: A Preliminary Analysis," Paper prepared for delivery at the annual meeting of the American Political Science Association, New Orleans, Louisiana, August 29–September 1, 1985, p. 13.
69. Interview, November 12, 1986, Washington, D.C.
70. "Towards a New Policy for Nicaragua" (note 61 above), p. 2; "Nicaragua: A New Democratic Family Feud," *Congressional Quarterly*, April 27, 1985, p. 809.
71. Interview, December 2, 1986, Washington, D.C.
72. *Congressional Record*, June 12, 1985, p. H 4148.
73. *Weekly Compilation of Presidential Documents*, vol. 21, no. 18 (May 6, 1985), p. 537.
74. *Weekly Compilation of Presidential Documents*, vol. 21, no. 23 (June 10, 1985), p. 754.
75. Interviews, February 2, 1987 and January 13, 1987, Washington, D.C. "Folks tend to believe the President's threat that the Sandinistas will be in Harligen, Texas, by next Tuesday," Cooper added.
76. *Congressional Record*, June 12, 1985, pp. H 4162, H 4191, H 4113–14; Steven V. Roberts, "House Reverses Ban on Aid to Nicaragua Rebels," *New York Times*, June 13, 1985.
77. Roberts, "House Reverses Ban"; *Congressional Record*, June 12, 1985, p. H 4165.
78. Margaret Shapiro, "Contra Aid Vote Presages Renewed U.S. Role," *Washington Post*, June 14, 1985.
79. Report of the Congressional Committees, p. 64.
80. Ibid.; Robert W. Merry, "Congress Shifts Toward Reagan on Aid for Contras in Nicaragua," *Wall Street Journal*, January 13, 1986.
81. Report of the Congressional Committees, pp. 59, 72. According to the report,

North coordinated the operation, which he dubbed "Project Democracy." Retired Air Force General Richard Secord and his business partner Albert Hakim called the organization "the Enterprise."

82. Interview, House Democratic leadership aide, November 5, 1986, Washington, D.C.

83. See, for example, Joel Brinkley, "Nicaragua Rebels Getting Advice from White House on Operations," *New York Times*, August 8, 1985; Jeremiah O'Leary, "U.S. Officer Advises Contra Chiefs," *Washington Times*, August 9, 1985; Joanne Omang, "McFarlane Aide Facilitates Policy," *Washington Post*, August 11, 1985.

84. U.S. Congress, Senate Select Committee on Secret Military Assistance to Iran and the Nicaraguan Opposition and House Select Committee to Investigate Covert Arms Transactions with Iran, *Iran-Contra Investigation*, 100-5, Hearings, June 2, 3, 4, 5, 8, and 9, 1987, 100th Cong., 1st Sess. (Washington, D.C.: U.S. Government Printing Office, 1988), pp. 395–409.

85. Text, Robert C. McFarlane to Honorable Lee H. Hamilton, September 5, 1985, pp. 1, 2.

86. Interviews, Michael Barnes, January 29, 1987, Washington, D.C., and Vic Johnson, January 6, 1987, Washington, D.C.

87. Jeremiah O'Leary and Mary Belcher, "Reagan Opens Campaign for Aid to Contras," *Washington Times*, February 19, 1986; *Weekly Compilation of Presidential Documents*, vol. 22, no. 10 (March 10, 1986), pp. 311–12.

88. *Weekly Compilation of Presidential Documents*, March 10, 1986, p. 301; and White House, Office of the Press Secretary, "Address by the President to the Nation," March 16, 1986, pp. 1–6.

89. Patrick J. Buchanan, "The Contras Need Our Help," *Washington Post*, March 5, 1986.

90. Dave Doubrava and Warren Strobel, "Key Districts Are Targeted in the Blitz," *Washington Times*, March 19, 1986; *Congressional Quarterly Almanac 1986*, p. 400.

91. *Congressional Quarterly Almanac 1986*, p. 400; Interview, January 28, 1987, Washington, D.C.

92. Bob Woodward and Lou Cannon, "CIA Document Based on Lobby Techniques," *Washington Post*, March 1, 1986; *Congressional Record*, March 6, 1986, p. S 2125.

93. Text, Floor Remarks of Speaker Thomas P. O'Neill Jr., March 20, 1986, p. 2.

94. "The Caraballeda Message Towards Central America's Peace, Security, and Democracy," unofficial translation, January 12, 1986, p. 4.

95. Letter to Ronald Reagan, February 3, 1986, pp. 1–3; Communiqué Issued by Members of the Contadora Group and the Group of Support, unofficial translation, February 10, 1986, Washington, D.C., p. 2.

96. *Weekly Compilation of Presidential Documents*, vol. 22, no. 12 (March 24, 1986), p. 396.

97. Victor C. Johnson, "Congress and Contra Aid 1986–1987," in Abraham F. Lowenthal, ed., *Latin America and the Caribbean Contemporary Record*, vol. 6 (New York: Holmes and Meier, 1989), p. 13.

98. Quoted in *Congressional Quarterly Almanac 1986*, p. 402.

99. Joanne Omang, "GAO Probing Origin of Honduran Bid for Aid," *Washington Post*, January 8, 1987; Report of the Congressional Committees, pp. 382–83.

100. In mid-June, for example, the GAO told a House subcommittee that contra aid funds were being funneled to offshore accounts in the Cayman Islands and the Bahamas and to the armed forces of Honduras, rather than to contra suppliers in Central America. U.S. Congress, House, Committee on Foreign Affairs Subcommittee on Western Hemisphere Affairs, *Investigation of United States Assistance to the Nicaraguan Contras*, vol. 2, Hearings and Markup, April 9, May 1, 8, June 11, 1986, 99th Cong., 2nd Sess. (Washington, D.C.: U.S. Government Printing Office, 1986), p. 56.

101. Telephone interview, June 26, 1986.

102. Johnson, "Congress and Contra Aid," p. 13.

103. The three, Representatives Barnes, Slattery, and Richardson, made their comments at a press conference on April 8, 1986, Washington, D.C.

104. Quoted in Jim Morrell and William Goodfellow, "Contadora: Under the Gun," Center for International Policy, Washington, D.C., May 1986, p. 1.

105. Representative Jack Kemp (R-N.Y.) circulated the letter calling for Habib's recall. See Bernard Gwertzman, "Habib Finds Himself in a Hot Seat," *New York Times*, July 17, 1986.

106. John M. Poindexter, Memorandum, "Meeting with the National Security Planning Group," May 15, 1986 (Iran-contra committees Exhibit JMP-50), p. 1.

107. Kagan credited Bruce Cameron, Bernard Aronson, Robert Leiken, and Penn Kemble with serving in that capacity. See Michael Massing, "The Rise and Fall of 'Ollie's Liberals,' " *Washington Post*, June 28, 1987.

108. Edward Walsh, "Reagan Allies in Contra Vote Were Compromise [and] Fatigue," *Washington Post*, June 27, 1986.

109. Interview, House Republican aide, March 4, 1987, Washington, D.C.

110. David Sellers, "Coalition Targets Foes of Contra Aid," *Washington Times*, April 15, 1986. Fahrenkopf declined the request.

111. Interview with Daniel Schorr, "Weekend Edition," National Public Radio, June 28, 1986, Washington, D.C.

112. Omang, "Reagan Rallied for Aid . . ."

113. Jeremiah O'Leary and Christopher Simpson, "Margin Narrowing on Contra Aid," *Washington Times*, March 12, 1986.

114. The aid was finally appropriated under the Fiscal Year 1987 Continuing Resolution (P.L. 99-591), signed by the president on October 24, 1986.

115. Report of the Congressional Committees, pp. 70–71, 148–49.

116. North met with the House Intelligence Committee on August 6. He told the committee, in the words of a colleague present, that he "gave no military advice, knew of no specific military operations" of the FDN or UNO. Joint Hearings, McFarlane et al., p. 751; Report of the Congressional Committees, p. 141.

117. Report of the Congressional Committees, p. 144.

118. See, for example, Alfonso Chardy, "How U.S. Officials Created a Network for Contra Funding," *Miami Herald*, October 28, 1986; Wayne King, "Retired U.S. General Is Called Key to Contra Weapons," *New York Times*, October 24, 1986.

119. Excerpts from the guilty plea in the *United States of America v. Alan D. Fiers Jr.*, U.S. District Court for the District of Columbia, in "Excerpts from Statement on Guilty Plea by Ex-C.I.A. Official," *New York Times*, July 10, 1991.

120. Ibid.
121. Statement of Clair George, Deputy Director for Operations, Central Intelligence Agency, Transcript, U.S. Senate, Committee on Foreign Relations, "The Situation in Nicaragua," October 10, 1986; and transcript, U.S. House of Representatives, Permanent Select Committee on Intelligence, "Briefing on Downed Airplane," October 14, 1986.
122. George statement, "The Situation in Nicaragua."
123. "Excerpts from Iran-Contra Indictment of Former C.I.A. Official," New York Times, September 7, 1991; George Lardner Jr. and Walter Pincus, "Ex-Spy Chief Convicted of Lying to Hill," Washington Post, December 10, 1992.
124. U.S. Congress, House, Committee on Foreign Affairs, Subcommittee on Western Hemisphere Affairs, The Downing of a United States Plane in Nicaragua and United States Involvement in the Contra War, Hearing, October 15, 1986, 99th Cong., 2nd Sess. (Washington, D.C.: U.S. Government Printing Office, 1987), p. 6.
125. Abrams pleaded guilty to having testified untruthfully to the Senate Foreign Relations Committee on October 10, 1986, that "[we] stay away from" people involved in the private support network. He also pleaded guilty to "unlawfully with[holding] material information" for having described as "false" reports that other governments were providing money to the contras. Abrams was asked about the matter by the House Intelligence Committee on October 14, 1986. Abrams had earlier solicited a $10 million contribution for the contras from the sultan of Brunei. George Lardner Jr., "Abrams Pleads Guilty in Iran-Contra Affair," Washington Post, October 8, 1991; U.S. Congress, House Select Committee to Investigate Covert Arms Transactions with Iran and Senate Select Committee on Secret Military Assistance to Iran and the Nicaraguan Opposition, Iran-Contra Affair, November 13, 1987, 100th Cong., 1st Sess. (Washington, D.C.: U.S. Government Printing Office, 1987), pp. 148–49.
126. Text, memorandum from North to Poindexter, in Dan Morgan and Walter Pincus, "Are Deeper Secrets Still Being Hidden?" Washington Post, September 6, 1987.
127. "Excerpts From Iran-Contra Indictment of Former C.I.A. Official, New York Times, September 7, 1991; Lardner and Pincus, "Ex-Spy Chief Convicted."
128. U.S. Congress, Senate, Select Committee on Intelligence, Nomination of Robert M. Gates, Hearings, Vol. I, September 16, 17, 19, 20, 1991, 102nd Cong., 1st Sess. (Washington, D.C.: U.S. Government Printing Office, 1992), p. 662.

Chapter Eight. 1987–1988: The Policy Collapses

1. Tom Blanton, "Where George Was," Washington Post, June 10, 1990.
2. U.S. Congress, House Select Committee to Investigate Covert Arms Transactions with Iran and Senate Select Committee on Secret Military Assistance to Iran and the Nicaraguan Opposition, Iran-Contra Investigation, Testimony of John M. Poindexter, Hearings, July 15, 16, 17, 20, and 21, 1987, 100th Cong., 1st Sess. (Washington, D.C.: U.S. Government Printing Office, 1987), p. 38.
3. Taking the Stand: The Testimony of Lieutenant Colonel Oliver North (New York: Pocket Books, 1987), introduction by Daniel Schorr, pp. v–xiv.

4. U.S. Congress, House Select Committee to Investigate Covert Arms Transactions with Iran and Senate Select Committee on Secret Military Assistance to Iran and the Nicaraguan Opposition, *Iran-Contra Affair*, November 13, 1987, 100th Cong., 1st Sess. (Washington, D.C.: U.S. Government Printing Office, 1987), pp. 437–38. (Hereafter cited as Report of the Congressional Committees, sec. 2, The Minority Report.)

5. Richard J. Meislin, "President Invites Inquiry Counsel; Poll Rating Dives," *New York Times*, December 2, 1986; Gerald M. Boyd, "Many in Poll Say Reagan Is Lying on Diversion of Funds from Iran," *New York Times*, December 10, 1986; Linda Greenhouse, "With a Shift of Gravity, Congress Begins Era," *New York Times*, January 4, 1987.

6. President's Special Review Board, John Tower, Chairman, *The Tower Commission Report* (New York: Bantam Books and Times Books, 1987), pp. 79–83.

7. Report of the Congressional Committees, pp. 11–13, 21–22.

8. Interview, Honorable Jim Wright, November 22, 1988, Washington, D.C.

9. The Arias plan called for dialogues within each country with "all unarmed political groups of internal opposition"; for "free pluralistic and honest elections" and "an authentic pluralistic and participatory democratic process"; for an end to all outside military and logistical support for "irregular forces or insurgent movements"; and for international verification by the United Nations and the Organization of American States. State Department, "Central American Peace Agreement," unofficial translation, pp. 1–8 (undated).

10. John M. Goshko, "Reagan Hits Wright on Peace Talks," *Washington Post*, November 17, 1987; *Congressional Quarterly Almanac 1987*, p. 130.

11. Interview, Honorable Jim Wright, November 22, 1988, Washington, D.C.

12. The White House, Office of the Press Secretary, Address by the President to the Organization of American States, Washington, D.C., October 7, 1987, pp. 5, 6.

13. Democratic critics pointed out that the request included additional hidden costs, such as $23 million for insurance and electronic defense equipment for the planes carrying supplies to the contras. John Felton, "Contra Vote May Not Be Clear Test After All," *Congressional Quarterly*, January 30, 1988, p. 199.

14. Peter LaBarbera, "Reagan's Concession Wins Several GOP 'Swing' Votes," *Washington Times*, February 4, 1988.

15. Karen DeYoung, "Arias Seeks Halt of All Contra Aid," *Washington Post*, December 10, 1987.

16. "Text of Nicaraguan Agreement on a Cease-fire," *New York Times*, March 25, 1988.

17. Roy Gutman, "Contra Peace-Talks Ploy Disclosed," *Newsday*, July 5, 1988.

18. Baker's comments were made on the Evans and Novak television talk show. John Felton, "Foreign Policy Notes: Hill Moving on Iraq Sanctions," *Congressional Quarterly*, October 15, 1988, p. 2983.

19. Statement of Gen. Paul F. Gorman, Commander in Chief, U.S. Southern Command, in U.S. Congress, House, Committee on Foreign Affairs, Subcommittee on Western Hemisphere Affairs, *The Role of the U.S. Southern Command in Central America*, Hearing, August 1, 1984, 98th Cong., 2nd Sess. (Washington, D.C.: U.S. Government Printing Office, 1985), p. 23.

20. In its 1993 report, the U.N. Truth Commission for El Salvador confirmed that

D'Aubuisson gave the order to kill Archbishop Romero and instructed members of his security detail to organize and supervise the assassination.

21. From Duarte's 1988 State of the Union address, cited in Americas Watch, *Nightmare Revisited 1987–1988* (New York: Americas Watch, September 1988), p. 1.

22. Hatfield, along with Representatives Jim Leach (R-Iowa) and George Miller (D-Calif.), had released a November 1987 report on El Salvador documenting the skewing of U.S. assistance toward war-related programs; corruption and mismanagement involving U.S.-administered funds; and lack of progress in defeating the guerrillas. See *Bankrolling Failure: United States Policy in El Salvador and the Urgent Need for Reform*, A Report to the Arms Control and Foreign Policy Caucus, November 1987, pp. 1–36.

23. John Felton, "Salvador-Aid Issue Re-Emerges in Senate Panel," *Congressional Quarterly*, June 25, 1988, p. 1740.

24. Ibid., p. 1741.

Chapter Nine. 1989–1992: The Bush Years

1. The Bush administration made the question of Soviet military aid to Nicaragua an issue in U.S.-Soviet relations. Within days of a U.S. bipartisan accord over contra aid, for example, Bush wrote Gorbachev asking for a cutback in Soviet aid to the Sandinistas. One of the first concrete signs of U.S.-Soviet cooperation in Central America occurred in December 1989, following the downing of an aircraft traveling from Nicaragua to El Salvador laden with arms for the FMLN. The Soviets helped trace the serial numbers of antiaircraft missiles on board the plane to stocks they had provided to the Sandinistas. Don Oberdorfer, "U.S.-Soviet Talks Produce Progress on Regional Issues," *Washington Post*, May 11, 1989; interview, senior U.S. official, September 16, 1992.

2. Congressional Research Service, "U.S. Aid to El Salvador, FY 1980–1992," pp. 1–2. The actual aid figure, including covert intelligence budgets, was much higher. The approximate cost of U.S. involvement over the decade was $6 billion, including approximately $850 million in covert funds. See Benjamin C. Schwarz, *American Counterinsurgency Doctrine and El Salvador* (Santa Monica: RAND Corporation, 1991), p. v; interview, March 30, 1993.

3. David Hoffman and Helen Dewar, "Baker Rules out Early Bid to Aid Contras Militarily," *Washington Post*, December 21, 1988.

4. Jim Wright, "Streams of Hope, Rivers of Blood: A Personal Narrative About Central America and the United States" (Manuscript, 1990), chap. 10, pp. 2–5, cited in Robert Pastor, "The Bush Administration and Latin America: The Pragmatic Style and the Regionalist Option," *Journal of Interamerican Studies and World Affairs*, vol. 33 (Fall 1991), p. 9.

5. Interview, September 17, 1992.

6. U.S. Department of State, Bureau of Public Affairs, "Statement at Senate Confirmation Hearings," January 17, 1989, pp. 1–6, Current Policy No. 1146. Baker made only the briefest mention of El Salvador, stating, "We must insist on protection of human rights."

7. "Text of Accord by Central American Presidents," *New York Times*, February 16, 1989.
8. "We weren't at the meeting," said State Department spokesman Charles Redman when asked about the plan. "We'd like to find out more about it." Robert Pear, "Latin Agreement Raises Eyebrows at White House," *New York Times*, February 16, 1989.
9. John Felton, "Baker, Capitol Hill Near a Deal on New Dose of Contra Aid," *Congressional Quarterly*, March 18, 1989, p. 596.
10. Interview, Republican Hill staffer involved in the negotiations, September 17, 1992. White House counsel C. Boyden Gray publicly criticized the veto power given to the four congressional committees, saying that it violated presidential prerogatives. He was rebuked by President Bush, whose spokesman, Marlin Fitzwater, said the presidential powers were "enhanced" by the agreement. Bernard Weinraub, "While House Rebukes Counsel on Pact," *New York Times*, March 28, 1992. The commitment to honor Congress's role in a November 30 cutoff was made in a letter from Baker to congressional leaders, not in the actual legislation implementing the bipartisan agreement.
11. "Text of Accord on Central America," *New York Times*, March 25, 1989. Echoing the language of the Central American peace accord, the agreement stipulated that the funds could be used for the "voluntary reintegration or voluntary regional relocation" of the contras.
12. U.S. Department of State, Bureau of Public Affairs, "U.S. Support for Democracy and Peace in Central America," Selected Documents, undated, No. 36, p. 2.
13. Interview, October 9, 1990.
14. Interview, senior State Department official, October 9, 1990.
15. Robert Pear, "Bush Pressing Congress to Permit C.I.A. role in Nicaragua Election," *New York Times*, June 11, 1989.
16. *Congressional Record*, August 4, 1989, p. S 10325.
17. Asked directly by Senator Tom Harkin during an April 12, 1989, hearing, for example, Kozak stated, "I do not want to answer and it is not because I am hiding something. It is just not the appropriate forum to be talking about whether the [Central Intelligence] Agency is involved in anything or not involved in anything, or would be." Transcript, Senate Subcommittee on Foreign Operations, April 12, 1989, p. 63.
18. Text, S. 1574, in *Congressional Record*, August 4, 1989, p. S 10325.
19. Text, letter from Representative Joe Moakley to Anthony Beilenson, April 24, 1989. Other letters were written by Representatives Moody, Morrison, and Kostmayer and by members of the House Subcommittee on Western Hemisphere Affairs.
20. National Endowment for Democracy, "Statement of Principles and Objectives," p. 1.
21. National Endowment for Democracy, *Annual Reports*, 1984, 1985, 1986, 1987, 1988, cited in Cynthia Arnson and Johanna Mendelson Forman "Projecting Democracy in Central America: Old Wine, New Bottles?" in Louis W. Goodman, William M. Leogrande, and Johanna Mendelson Forman, eds., *Political Parties and Democracy in Central America* (Boulder, Colo.: Westview Press, 1992), p. 253.
22. In 1987, contra aid supporter Senator Lloyd Bentsen (D-Texas) earmarked $250,000

for opposition political activity in Nicaragua. In October 1988, Congress designated another $2 million for NED activities in Nicaragua as part of the foreign aid appropriations bill; an additional $1.5 million for the "promotion of democracy" was earmarked in a supplemental appropriation that passed in April 1989. Joe Pichirallo, "How the U.S. Supports Nicaraguan Opposition," *Washington Post*, September 29, 1988; Arnson and Mendelson, "Projecting Democracy in Central America," p. 254.

23. Section 505(a)(1) of the NED charter states: "Funds may not be expended, either by the Endowment or by any of its grantees, to finance the campaigns of candidates for public office." See *Congressional Record*, October 4, 1989, p. H 6629.

24. NED Board member Sally Shelton-Colby, for example, stated: "We should support the democratic process, rather than a specific political party." Robert Pear, "U.S. Seeking $3 Million More for Sandinista Foes," *New York Times*, September 10, 1989.

25. Interview, National Democratic Institute Program Officer, July 25, 1990.

26. Letter, James A. Baker III to the Honorable Thomas S. Foley, September 20, 1989, p. 1.

27. U.S. Department of State, "Fact Sheet on Funding for Nicaraguan Internal Opposition," undated, p. 1.

28. John Felton, "Hill May Force a Scaling Back of Bush Election Aid Plan," *Congressional Quarterly*, September 30, 1989, p. 2581; "Out of the Game: The CIA," *Congressional Quarterly*, October 7, 1989, p. 2655.

29. *Congressional Record*, October 12, 1989, p. H 7009.

30. Transcript of colloquy between Chairman Beilenson and House Rules Committee Chairman Joe Moakley, October 3, 1989. Moakley also asked whether the bill had any impact on covert programs already in progress. Beilenson responded, "This bill will not permit covert assistance to the opposition, agreement or not, without the approval [of four congressional committees]." During floor debate on the intelligence bill, Beilenson further assured colleagues that the legislation "authorizes no funds whatsoever for covert support to opposition parties or candidates in that election." *Congressional Record*, October 12, 1989, p. H 7009.

31. Telephone interview, Robert Pastor, Carter Center, October 20, 1992.

32. Tom Post et al., "The CIA on the Stump," *Newsweek*, October 21, 1991, pp. 46–47.

33. In late March, contra leader Alfredo César complained that the Bush administration had eliminated financing for contra political operations and had cut monthly stipends to individual leaders in half. The contras' Miami office was forced to close in late September when the United States cut its funds. A U.S. official told the *Washington Times*, "The issue is not Miami. It's getting the technical and political structure closer to where the troops are." George Volsky, "U.S. Is Said to Cut Payments to the Contras' Political Arm," *New York Times*, March 29, 1989; Peter LaBarbera, "U.S. Halts Funds for Contras in Miami," *Washington Times*, September 29, 1989.

34. Interview, December 18, 1992.

35. Christopher Marquis and Alfonso Chardy, "2 Ex-Contras Now Battle Chamorro," *Miami Herald*, October 14, 1992.

36. *Congressional Record*, October 17, 1989, p. S 13532.

37. Ibid., pp. S 13523–24.

38. Remarks of Representative George Crockett, Chair, House Subcommittee on Western Hemisphere Affairs, *Congressional Record*, October 4, 1989, p. H 6629.

39. The House voted, 263–156, to approve the aid on October 4, 1989; the Senate followed suit on October 17, voting 64–35. In practice, the line between supporting the Chamorro campaign and supporting a free election was a fine one. The entire board of directors of one group that was slated to receive $1.3 million for voter education, poll-watching, and registration verification, for example, were members of the UNO and several were also prominent campaign officials. See George Vickers, "U.S. Funding of the Nicaraguan Opposition: A Preliminary Assessment" (manuscript), pp. 8–9; Jacqueline Sharkey, "Nicaragua: Anatomy of an Election," *Common Cause Magazine*, May–June 1990, pp. 20–29; and Arnson and Mendelson, "Projecting Democracy in Central America" (note 21 above), p. 255.

40. See Carlos M. Vilas, "What Went Wrong," *NACLA Report on the Americas*, vol. 24 (June 1990), pp. 10–18.

41. *Congressional Quarterly Almanac 1990*, p. 771.

42. John Felton, "Power of the Ballot Box Gives U.S. Policy a Fresh Start," *Congressional Quarterly*, March 3, 1990, p. 677.

43. Robert Pear, "Bush Seeks Soviet Help in Nicaragua Transition," *New York Times*, March 1, 1990.

44. Americas Watch, *Fitful Peace: Human Rights and Reconciliation in Nicaragua Under the Chamorro Government* (New York: Human Rights Watch, July 1991), p. 1.

45. John Felton, "Panama-Nicaragua Money Bill Tangled in Other Issues," *Congressional Quarterly*, March 24, 1990, p. 928.

46. Phil Kuntz, "A Pork-Heavy Supplemental Is Belatedly Sent to Bush," *Congressional Quarterly*, May 26, 1990, p. 1630.

47. *Fitful Peace*, p. 51. Before Chamorro's Washington visit, $189 million out of a total pledge of $541 million in economic aid had been disbursed.

48. Interview, State Department official, June 20, 1991; Lee Hockstader, "U.S. Aid Funds, Urgent Last Spring, Delayed in Delivery to Nicaragua," *Washington Post*, December 13, 1990.

49. Interview, State Department official, September 17, 1992; Christopher Marquis, "Envoys' Posting Held Up in Probe," *Miami Herald*, June 26, 1992. Kozak had been acting Assistant Secretary of State for Inter-American Affairs; Sullivan was Director of the Office of Central American Affairs.

50. Interviews, senior Senate aides, March 12, 1992 and October 21, 1992; Al Kamen, "Contra Aid Allegations Block Confirmation of Envoy Choices," *Washington Post*, June 26, 1992; Christopher Marquis, "Nominees for Central America Posts Blocked," *Miami Herald*, September 29, 1992.

51. Kamen, "Contra Aid Allegations." The text of the State Department Inspector General's report remains classified.

52. Obligations of foreign aid funds to countries designated by Congress are treated as "reprogrammings"—that is, four congressional committees are notified of a planned disbursement of money and can choose to delay it, usually pending the provision of further information.

53. Joel Gutierrez, "Chamorro to U.S.: Stay Out of Our Affairs," *Miami Herald*, July 11, 1992.
54. In late July, Secretary of State Baker promised to release approximately half the withheld aid if Nicaragua removed the Sandinista commander of the police, named a civilian to head the police, and sought the State Department's approval in choosing the new police officials. Christopher Marquis, "Nicaragua to Replace Police to Get Aid," *Miami Herald*, August 28, 1992; John M. Goshko, "Nicaraguan Government Criticized," *Washington Post*, September 1, 1992; U.S. Department of State, Office of the Assistant Secretary/Spokesman, "Statement by Richard A. Boucher," September 1, 1992.
55. "Aides: Helms Tells Bush 'No' on Nicaragua Funds," *Miami Herald*, October 3, 1992.
56. Interview, December 18, 1992. State Department spokesman Richard Boucher announced the release of $54 million in aid on December 3, 1992. The State Department reportedly had wanted to release the aid shortly after the U.S. election, but Bush, angered by a statement by Army chief Humberto Ortega that he intended to stay in his post until 1997, initially refused. The remainder of the aid was released by the Clinton administration in April 1993. See Christopher Marquis, "Bush Blocks Aid to Nicaragua After Defiance of Army Chief," *Miami Herald*, November 19, 1992.
57. Lindsey Gruson, "Besieged San Salvador Feels Realities of War," *New York Times*, January 23, 1989; Robert Pear, "Extremist Gains Seen in Salvador," *New York Times*, January 29, 1989.
58. Duarte had said the proposal "lacked all validity" and was "plagued by unconstitu-tionality." By contrast, State Department spokesman Charles E. Redman called it "worthy of serious and substantive consideration," and other officials urged Duarte to reconsider. Douglas Farah, "Left, Diplomats Fear Step-up of Salvadoran Fight-ing," *Washington Post*, January 27, 1989.
59. Reagan's former U.N. Ambassador Jeane Kirkpatrick, meanwhile, echoed the words of El Salvador's Defense Minister and denounced the FMLN's proposal as a "trap." Jeane Kirkpatrick, "Setting a Trap in El Salvador," *Washington Post*, February 27, 1989.
60. Douglas Farah, "El Salvador Acts Against Army Officers," *Washington Post*, March 9, 1989.
61. John Felton, "Peace Prospects, New Elections Cloud U.S. Policy Options," *Con-gressional Quarterly*, March 4, 1989, pp. 470–71.
62. John Felton, "Cristiani Asks U.S. Officialdom for Benefit of the Doubt," *Congres-sional Quarterly*, April 15, 1989, pp. 387–88.
63. The full committee watered down the provision, stipulating instead that both houses of Congress could stop aid only if they passed separate legislation, virtually ensuring a presidential veto. See John Felton, "Restrictions on El Salvador Snarl Authoriza-tion Bill," *Congressional Quarterly*, June 10, 1989, p. 1419.
64. One year after a similar amendment had been defeated in the Appropriations Committee, the amendment passed by one vote, 15–14. Three new liberals (Brock Adams of Washington, Wyche Fowler of Georgia, and Bob Kerrey of Nebraska) had joined the committee in 1989 and provided votes that tipped the balance. See John

Felton, "Foreign Aid Enjoys Boomlet of Support in Hill Panel," *Congressional Quarterly*, September 16, 1989, pp. 2402–3.

65. *Congressional Record*, September 20, 1989, p. S 11449.

66. Ibid., pp. S 11468, 11474.

67. Ibid., p. S 11471.

68. For an analysis of the competing visions within the FMLN, see Tom Gibb and Frank Smyth, *El Salvador: Is Peace Possible?* (Washington, D.C.: Washington Office on Latin America, 1990), pp. 5–12.

69. Robert Pear, "Rebel Drive Long Planned, U.S. Says," *New York Times*, November 14, 1989; Robert Pear, "U.S. Sees 'No Threat' to Salvador Government," *New York Times*, November 15, 1989.

70. John M. Goshko, "Baker Accuses Soviets of Abetting Salvadoran Strife," *Washington Post*, November 14, 1989.

71. Extrajudicial confession of José Ricardo Espinoza Guerra, reporting on a conversation with Colonel Guillermo Benavides, in "Interim Report of the Speaker's Task Force on El Salvador," April 30, 1990, Appendix B, p. 10.

72. Author's interviews, San Salvador, February 1990; Lawyers Committee for Human Rights, "The Jesuit Case a Year Later: An Interim Report," November 15, 1990, pp. 17–18; Centro Universitario de Documentación e Información, "Cronología del caso jesuitas," *Proceso*, November 14, 1990, p. 4.

73. United Nations, La Comisión de la Verdad para El Salvador, *De la Locura a la Esperanza* (San Salvador and New York: United Nations, 1993), p. 44.

74. For a comprehensive and moving portrayal of the Jesuits and their role in Salvadoran society, see Teresa Whitfield, *Paying the Price: The Life and Death of the Jesuits of El Salvador* (manuscript), especially chaps. 2 and 7; Lawyers Committee for Human Rights, "The Jesuit Case," pp. 5–10.

75. The accounts of the killings come from San Salvador's Fourth Criminal Court, based on extrajudicial confessions of several of the soldiers later indicted for the crime. See "Interim Report of the Speaker's Task Force on El Salvador," pp. 16–20 and Appendix B, pp. 1–17.

76. Interview, October 21, 1992.

77. Robert Pear, "U.S. Official Links Salvadoran Right to Priests' Deaths," *New York Times*, November 18, 1989.

78. Testimony of Bernard W. Aronson, Assistant Secretary of State for Inter-American Affairs, before the Senate Foreign Relations Committee, November 17, 1989, p. 4.

79. Robert Pear, "House Rejects Curb on Salvador Aid," *New York Times*, November 21, 1989.

80. *Congressional Record*, November 20, 1989, p. H 9055.

81. Remarks of Senator Charles Robb (D-Va.), in ibid., p. 16345.

82. Ibid., pp. H 9186, S 16491.

83. Remarks of Senator Patrick Leahy, in ibid., p. S 16270.

84. Lee Hockstader, "Central America Back in U.S. Foreign Policy Spotlight," *Washington Post*, November 19, 1989. Following a firestorm of protest from U.S. religious and human rights organizations, Baker wrote Cristiani asking him to safeguard the rights and security of religious and humanitarian workers. U.S. Department of State, Office of the Assistant Secretary/Spokesman, "Secretary's Letter to President Cristiani," December 11, 1989, p. 1.

85. Lee Hockstader, "Our Man in El Salvador, Upbeat Amid the Crisis," *Washington Post*, December 19, 1989; Mark Uhlig, "Lesson from San Salvador: Rebels Come and Go at Will," *New York Times*, November 24, 1989.

86. Uhlig, "Lesson from San Salvador." President Bush dispatched the Delta Force to prepare to free the U.S. advisers and then erroneously claimed that the "hotel was liberated" by U.S. troops. David Hoffman and Patrick E. Tyler, "Bush Contradicted on Rescue Report," *Washington Post*, November 23, 1989.

87. Elaine Sciolino, "Witnesses in Jesuit Slayings Charge Harassment in U.S.," *New York Times*, December 18, 1989.

88. Interview, October 31, 1990.

89. AmEmbassy San Salvador to SecState, WashDC, "Jesuit Murders—Progress Report No. 7," December 27, 1989, p. 2.

90. Robert Pear, "Salvador Evidence Escaped U.S. Envoy," *New York Times*, January 16, 1992.

91. Telephone interview, Jim McGovern, November 16, 1992.

92. Robert Pear, "Aid Fight Is Likely as Salvador Links Army to Slayings," *New York Times*, January 9, 1990.

93. Affidavit, Major Eric Warren Buckland, Washington, D.C., January 10, 1990, p. 6; and Addenda to Affidavit of Major Eric Warren Buckland, Washington, D.C., January 11, 1990, pp. 2–3 (a handwritten addenda to affidavit given the U.S. Federal Bureau of Investigation on January 10, 1990). One week later, Buckland retracted the statements made to the FBI. Although news sources suggested that he had been pressured to recant, a more plausible version is that Army lawyers suggested that he retract his statements in order to protect himself against any possible criminal charges involving the Jesuit case.

94. Interview, Washington, D.C., September 24, 1992.

95. Calling it an "unbelievable and inexcusable error in judgment," Moakley denounced U.S. officials in mid-October 1990 for withholding from Salvadoran authorities the statement Buckland gave to the FBI ten months before. In January 1990, the FBI gave summaries of Buckland's statements to both the Embassy and the State Department. The Embassy showed portions of a videotape of Buckland's declaration to President Cristiani in late January or early February 1990. Cristiani did not turn the tape over to the investigating judge. Statement of Representative Joe Moakley, Chairman, Speaker's Special Task Force on El Salvador, October 18, 1990; Jim McGovern and Bill Woodward, Memorandum to Honorable Joe Moakley, "Staff Trip to El Salvador," January 7, 1991, pp. 11–12.

96. Transcript of the video declaration of Major Eric Warren Buckland, January 12, 1990, Washington, D.C., pp. 7, 11–14.

97. "A Scandalous Record," *Time*, December 4, 1989.

98. Major Garrett, "Cristiani to Arrive Here Amid Debate Over Role," *Washington Times*, February 1, 1990.

99. Text, S. 2125, pp. 1–9; "Senate Proposes Curbs on Aid to El Salvador," *New York Times*, February 9, 1990.

100. U.S. Congress, House, Committee on Foreign Affairs Subcommittee on Human Rights and International Organizations, and on Western Hemisphere Affairs, *El Salvador at the Crossroads: Peace or Another Decade of War*, Hearings, January 24,

31, and February 6, 1990 (Washington, D.C.: U.S. Government Printing Office, 1990), p. 17.

101. Ibid., pp. 14, 32.

102. Maureen Dowd, "Bush Seeks a Rise in Aid to Salvador," *New York Times*, February 2, 1990.

103. John Felton, "Fascell Panel Votes to Slash Salvador Arms Assistance," *Congressional Quarterly*, April 28, 1990, p. 1280; John Felton, "Politics, Salvador Issue Delay Panama-Nicaragua Funds," *Congressional Quarterly*, April 7, 1990, p. 1086.

104. The report noted that "not one member of the Salvadoran armed forces has voluntarily provided information of real value." Senior military officials had described the murders as " 'stupid,' 'self-defeating,' and 'dumb,' " but "no senior military official with whom we talked said it was wrong." "Interim Report of the Speaker's Task Force on El Salvador," April 30, 1990, pp. 6–7, 9–10.

105. John Felton, "Hill Group Paints Dark Picture of Rights in El Salvador," *Congressional Quarterly*, May 5, 1990, p. 1370.

106. United Nations, Press Release, "General Agenda and Schedule for Comprehensive Negotiation Process Between Government of El Salvador and FMLN," May 21, 1990, p. 1.

107. Interviews, U.S. officials, September 16, 1992, and January 7, 1993.

108. *Congressional Record*, May 22, 1990, p. H 2712.

109. John Felton, "House Fires a Warning Shot Over El Salvador Policy," *Congressional Quarterly*, May 26, 1990, p. 1670.

110. See Chapter 7.

111. The administration wanted, for example, to withhold 15 percent, with another 15 percent to be withheld if the FMLN, not the military, engaged in good-faith negotiations to end the war. Telephone interview, senior Senate aide, July 17, 1990.

112. Frank Smyth, "The Truth Will Out," *Village Voice*, July 31, 1990. According to a House aide, Aronson was unsuccessful in impressing on Salvadoran officers the importance of resolving the case.

113. Congressman Joe Moakley, "Statement on the Jesuits' Case and the Salvadoran Negotiations," August 15, 1990, p. 1.

114. Alfredo Cristiani, "On Eve of Congressional Debate, an Appeal for Aid to Salvador," reprinted in the *Philadelphia Inquirer*, October 4, 1990.

115. Bernard Aronson, "Peace in El Salvador," *Washington Post*, October 12, 1990.

116. Carroll J. Doherty, "Aid to El Salvador Slashed," *Congressional Quarterly*, October 27, 1990, p. 3628.

117. The administration was required to terminate all aid, for example, if the Salvadoran government failed to negotiate in good faith or refused a U.N. mediation role; failed to conduct a thorough and professional investigation and prosecution of the Jesuit case; or directed violence at civilian targets. The administration could restore aid in full if the FMLN refused to negotiate in good faith; mounted an offensive which threatened the survival of the Salvadoran government; directed violence at civilian targets; or obtained significant amounts of lethal weapons from abroad. Text, Section 531(d) of P.L. 101-513, November 5, 1990.

118. A White House statement said the "decision was based on the FMLN's violation of

the conditions against 'engaging in acts of violence directed at civilian targets' and acquiring or receiving 'significant shipments of lethal military assistance from outside El Salvador.' " The White House, Office of the Press Secretary, "Statement by the Press Secretary," January 15, 1991, p. 1.

119. Statement of Representative Joe Moakley, Chairman of the Speaker's Task Force on El Salvador, January 16, 1991, p. 1.

120. Chris Dodd, "Dodd Terms Administration Decision to Release Salvador Funding Unwarranted and Dangerous," January 16, 1991, p. 1.

121. Interview, House Democratic aides, January 15, 1991 and December 18, 1992.

122. Text, letters to President George Bush, March 6, 1991, and March 8, 1991.

123. Interview, September 16, 1992.

124. Interview, State Department official, December 18, 1992.

125. Ibid.

126. Clifford Krauss, "U.N. Aide Assailed in Salvadoran Talks," New York Times, February 1, 1991.

127. In condemning the murders of the servicemen, the Jesuit order in El Salvador flatly rejected the comparison. "The massacre at the UCA was a deliberate and premeditated action for which the highest levels of the Salvadoran army are responsible," said UCA Rector Miguel Francisco Estrada. "The victims were unarmed civilians, taken out of their residence during the night. On the other hand, the U.S. officers were flying military aircraft over conflictive territory, they themselves were armed and they were providing logistical support to one of the parties in the current conflict." Miguel Francisco Estrada, S.J., "The Rector of the Central American University in San Salvador (UCA) Condemns the Killing of the Two U.S. Military Officers and Opposes the Release of U.S. Military Aid," January 15, 1991, p. 2.

128. Interview, Jim McGovern, aide to Representative Joe Moakley, December 18, 1992.

129. Carroll J. Doherty, "Panel Unanimously Approves Authorization Measure," Congressional Quarterly, June 8, 1991, p. 1524.

130. Congressional Record, July 25, 1991, p. S 10874.

131. Interview, December 18, 1992.

132. Text, reprinted in CIDAI (Center for Information, Documentation and Research Support of the UCA), Proceso, No. 480, July 3, 1991, p. 7.

133. Interview, December 18, 1992. The town to which Moakley and Walker traveled, Santa Marta, was under the control of the FMLN faction that the Embassy viewed as being the most flexible in the peace talks, the Resistencia Nacional.

134. Interview, November 24, 1992.

135. Interview, September 24, 1992.

136. Ibid.

137. On August 1, 1991, the United States and the Soviet Union issued a joint statement calling on the United Nations and other countries to "intensify their efforts to resolve the remaining political issues, secure a cease-fire and final peace settlement in El Salvador." The communiqué urged the U.N. Secretary General to involve himself more directly in the peace talks, something which eventually occurred. "U.S.-Soviet Cooperation in Central America," Joint statement issued in Washington, D.C., August 1, 1991, in U.S. Department of State, "Dispatch," August 12, 1991, p. 595.

138. Interview, source close to the negotiations, July 5, 1992.

139. United Nations, Press Statement, "Secretary-General Announces 'Break in Deadlock' in El Salvador Talks," SG/SM/4624, CA/51, September 25, 1991.

140. Joe Moakley, "Justice Disserved in the Jesuit Murders," *Washington Post*, October 14, 1991.

141. Statement of Representative Joe Moakley, Chairman of the Speaker's Task Force on El Salvador," November 18, 1991, pp. 1–6.

142. Transcript, State Department Regular Briefing, Richard Boucher, November 18, 1991.

143. Letter, Acting Secretary Lawrence Eagleburger to Representative David Obey, October 23, 1991, p. 1.

144. Representative Joe Moakley, News Release, "Congressional Leaders Introduce New El Salvador Legislation; Bill Subjects All New Military Aid to Congressional Reprogramming," November 14, 1991, pp. 1–2.

145. Interview, December 18, 1992.

146. Tim Golden, "The Salvadorans Make Peace in a 'Negotiated Revolution,' " *New York Times*, January 5, 1992.

Conclusion

1. The peace accord provided for a civilian "Ad Hoc" Commission to review the records of the military officer corps with an eye toward weeding out corrupt and brutal officers. The commission's confidential report was delivered to President Cristiani and the Secretary General of the United Nations in September 1992. It recommended the removal or transfer of 103 officers, including the Minister and Vice-Minister of Defense.

2. United Nations, "Letter Dated 7 January 1993 from the Secretary General Addressed to the President of the Security Council," S/25078, January 9, 1993, p. 2.

3. "Acuerdos de Mexico" (interim agreement between the Salvadoran government and the FMLN), Mexico City, April 27, 1991, p. 5.

4. Comisión de la Verdad para El Salvador, *De la Locura a la Esperanza: La guerra de 12 años en El Salvador* (San Salvador and New York: United Nations, 1993), pp. 1–211.

5. Ibid., p. 41.

6. On March 24, 1993, the thirteenth anniversary of the murder of Archbishop Romero, Secretary of State Warren Christopher named a small commission to look into the allegations that State Department and Embassy human rights reporting on El Salvador might have been, in Christopher's words, "stifled by political considerations." Transcript, hearing of the House Appropriations Committee Subcommittee on Foreign Operations, March 25, 1992.

7. After Duarte's election in 1984, Congress's willingness to provide unrestricted aid no doubt expanded the army's tolerance for civilian rule. Even if the army still disdained civilians, its dominant sector came at least to recognize them as useful and necessary in the process of governing.

8. One notorious case involves Colonel Mauricio Staben, a U.S.-trained officer implicated in the planning of the Romero assassination and in a kidnapping-for-

profit ring that operated against wealthy Salvadoran businessmen in the mid-1980s. When the ring was broken up in 1986, a *New York Times* report described Staben as "a favorite of the Central Intelligence Agency and American military advisers who have seen him as a successful commander." Another case involves Air Force chief Juan Rafael Bustillo, implicated in the Jesuit murder plot and in a host of disappearances, who permitted the U.S. contra support network to operate out of Ilopango air base. See Jefferson Morley, "The Secret of the Skeletons," *Washington Post*, November 15, 1992; and Charles Lane, "The Pilot Shark of El Salvador," *New Republic*, September 24, 1990.

9. Guy Gugliotta and Douglas Farah, "12 Years of Tortured Truth on El Salvador," *Washington Post*, March 12, 1993.

10. See Chapter 5.

11. "The U.S. was involved because of its own geopolitical interests, to demonstrate that it was a world power," said Salvadoran General Mauricio Vargas. "It was not because we were the poor little ones and you the good ones." Interview, May 31, 1992. See also Benjamin C. Schwarz, *American Counterinsurgency Doctrine and El Salvador: The Frustrations of Reform and the Illusions of Nation Building* (Santa Monica: RAND Corporation, 1991), pp. 82–83.

12. "U.S. Goal with Contras Should Be Limited," Interview with Senator Richard Lugar, *Washington Times*, February 11, 1985.

13. Tad Szulc, "Contras," *Los Angeles Times*, March 15, 1987, Part 4, p. 1.

14. Interview, senior Western diplomat, May 4, 1985, Managua.

15. See Henry Kissinger, "America's Contra Muddle," *Washington Post*, July 28, 1987; and John B. Oakes, "Reagan Keeps Gearing Up to Overthrow the Sandinistas," *New York Times*, August 6, 1985.

16. Roger D. Hansen, "The Reagan Doctrine and Global Containment: Revival or Recessional," *SAIS Review*, vol. 7 (Winter–Spring 1987), p. 63.

17. In March 1987, for example, Arturo Cruz withdrew from the contra leadership, only to be pilloried by some of the same champions of the contra policy who had earlier cited him as proof of the democratic nature of the resistance. See Jeane Kirkpatrick, "Cruz and Congress Bruise the Contras," *Los Angeles Times*, March 15, 1987. See also Charles Lane, "Pack It In," *New Republic*, April 6, 1987.

18. Robert W. Tucker, "Intervention and the Reagan Doctrine," Ethics and Public Policy Lecture Series, Council on Religious and International Affairs, New York, New York, 1985, p. 4.

19. Representative Lee Hamilton, remarks, SAIS Forum, "Congress and Foreign Policy, Johns Hopkins University School of Advanced International Studies, April 18, 1988, Washington, D.C.

20. Cynthia J. Arnson and Johanna Mendelson Forman, "Projecting Democracy in Central America: Old Wine, New Bottles?" in Louis W. Goodman, William M. Leogrande, and Johanna Mendelson Forman, *Political Parties and Democracy in Central America* (Boulder, Colo.: Westview Press, 1992), p. 251.

21. See, for example, George F. Will, "End of the 'Progressive' Pilgrimage," *Washington Post*, March 1, 1990; Charles Krauthammer, "Stiffling the Neocons—Again," *Washington Post*, January 15, 1993; Robert Pastor, letter to the editor, "Nicaragua Election Wasn't Contra Policy's Goal," *New York Times*, September 30, 1991.

22. Mark A. Uhlig, "Latin America: The Frustrations of Success," *Foreign Affairs*, vol. 70, no. 1 (1991) pp. 103–19.
23. Robert Pastor, "The Bush Administration and Latin America: The Pragmatic Style and the Regionalist Option," *Journal of Inter-American Studies*, vol. 33 (Fall 1991), p. 11.
24. *Public Papers of the Presidents, Ronald Reagan, 1988*, Book 1 (Washington, D.C.: U.S. Government Printing Office, 1990), pp. 360–61.
25. Elliott Abrams, "Ortega's Empty Concessions," *New York Times*, March 2, 1989.
26. For a critique of U.S. involvement in the elections, see William I. Robinson, *A Faustian Bargain: U.S. Intervention in the Nicaraguan Elections and American Foreign Policy in the Post–Cold War Era* (Boulder, Colo.: Westview Press, 1992).
27. Bush made this remark in a speech to the 1992 Republican convention. Christopher Marquis and Tim Johnson, "Sandinistas Retain Power, Report Says," *Miami Herald*, August 30, 1992.
28. Joe Eldridge and Alex Wilde, "Nicaragua Votes for End to Washington's Siege," letter to the editor, *New York Times*, March 9, 1990.
29. "Text of President Bush's Statement on the Pardon of Weinberger and Others," *New York Times*, December 25, 1992.
30. "Independent Counsel's Statement on the Pardons," *New York Times*, December 25, 1992.
31. In a subsequent report to Congress, Walsh said Bush and Reagan knew that a statement by then–Attorney General Edwin Meese regarding presidential knowledge of a key aspect of the Iranian arms sales was false and that they made no effort to correct it. Carroll J. Doherty, "Walsh Says Pardon Thwarted New Evidence on Arms Deal," *Congressional Quarterly*, February 13, 1993, p. 325.
32. Walter Pincus, "White House Consulted Foley, Aspin in Advance of Weinberger Pardon," *Washington Post*, December 29, 1992.
33. See, for example, the Minority Report of the Iran-contra committees.
34. Richard G. Lugar, *Letters to the Next President* (New York: Simon and Schuster, 1988), p. 63.
35. Pamela Fessler, "Senate Clears Retooled Measure Strengthening Hill Oversight," *Congressional Quarterly*, August 3, 1991, pp. 2187–88.
36. U.S. Congress, House, Committee on Foreign Affairs Subcommittee on Inter-American Affairs, *Central America at the Crossroads*, Hearings, September 11 and 12, 1979, 96th Cong., 1st Sess. (Washington, D.C.: U.S. Government Printing Office, 1979), p. 3.
37. See Aryeh Neier, "Watching Rights," *The Nation*, April 12, 1993, p. 475.
38. See Michael Kinsley, "So Why Aren't the Sandinistas in San Diego?" *Washington Post*, March 1, 1990.
39. "Forgotten Central America," *New York Times*, May 26, 1992.

Epilogue

1. Transcript, Testimony of Secretary of State Warren Christopher Before the Senate Appropriations Committee Subcommittee on Foreign Operations, Federal News Service, March 30, 1993, p. 1; Office of the Assistant Secretary/Spokesman,

"Statement by Secretary Christopher," March 24, 1993, in U.S. Department of State, *Dispatch*, vol. 4, no. 13, March 29, 1993, p. 188.

2. Transcript, Testimony of Secretary of State Warren Christopher Before the House Appropriations Subcommittee on Foreign Operations, Federal News Service, March 25, 1993, p. 2.

3. Text, letter to the Honorable John Joseph Moakley, The White House, June 7, 1993, pp. 1–2. The congressional request to declassify documents was made by seventeen members of the House and Senate, including Senator Claiborne Pell and Representative Lee Hamilton (chairs, respectively, of the Senate Foreign Relations Committee and the House Foreign Affairs Committee), on March 26, 1993.

4. Transcript, Testimony of Secretary of State Warren Christopher Before the House Appropriations Committee Subcommittee on Foreign Operations, Federal News Service, March 30, 1993, p. 1.

5. U.S. Department of State, "Report of the Secretary of State's Panel on El Salvador," July 1993 (hereafter cited as Report of the Panel on El Salvador), pp. 41, 34, 1–3, 24, 10. The lines of policy, according to the report, were set by the Carter administration but followed by the Reagan administration, with some modifications.

6. Ibid., pp. 1–2.

7. Ibid., p. 9.

8. Ibid., pp. 29, 34.

9. Ibid., pp. 7, 24.

10. In its section on the State Department's annual human rights reports to Congress, the report did note that "during the early eighties, human rights reports shied away from assigning responsibility for human rights abuses to the military as an institution. . . . Annual reports at the end of the period stated more directly that the military committed human rights abuses. Such directness should have been employed in the earlier reports as well, when such abuses were more frequent." Ibid., p. 29.

11. Ibid., pp. 38–39, 24.

12. Ibid., p. 36.

13. John M. Goshko, "Mistakes Cited in El Salvador," *Washington Post*, July 16, 1993; Clifford Krauss, "Testimony in '82 on Salvador Criticized," *New York Times*, July 16, 1993.

14. Report of the Panel on El Salvador, p. 41.

15. Ibid.

Index

About the Author

Cynthia J. Arnson served as a foreign policy legislative assistant during the first year of the Carter administration and was a senior foreign policy aide for five years for Representative George Miller (D-Calif.) during the Reagan years. She holds a Ph.D. in international relations from the Johns Hopkins University School of Advanced International Studies in Washington, D.C., and has taught at the School of International Service of the American University. She is currently Associate Director of Americas Watch, a division of Human Rights Watch.